ON Y VA!

PREMIER * NIVEAU

Le français par étapes

Teacher's Annotated Edition

Jeannette Bragger & Donald Rice
The Pennsylvania State University
Hamline University

ON Y VA!

PREMIER * NIVEAU

Le français par étapes

Teacher's Annotated Edition

HH HEINLE & HEINLE PUBLISHERS, INC.
Boston, Massachusetts 02116 USA

Publisher: Stanley J. Galek
Editorial Director: Janet L. Dracksdorf
Assistant Editor: Julianna Nielsen
Production Coordinator: Patricia Jalbert
Project Management: Spectrum Publisher Services
Production Editor: Barbara Russiello
Manufacturing Director: Erek Smith
Art Direction and Design: Marsha Cohen/Parallelogram
Photographer: Stuart Cohen
Illustrator: Jane O'Connor
Illustration Coordinator: Len Shalansky

Manufactured in the United States of America.

ISBN 0-8384-1617-9

10 9 8 7 6 5 4 3 2 1

Printed in the United States of America.

To the student

You are about to begin an exciting and valuable experience. Learning a new language is a first step to increasing the size of your world. It will open up cultures other than your own: different ways of living, thinking, and seeing. Many of you will one day, sooner or later, have the opportunity to visit France or a French-speaking country. Your experience will be all the richer if you can enter into that culture and interact with its members. Some of you may never get the chance to spend time in France. Nevertheless, you too can profit from learning French because, if nothing else, you will become more aware of your own language and culture. The *ON Y VA!* program is designed to give all of you the linguistic skills (listening, speaking, reading, writing) and cultural knowledge needed to meet these goals.

Once you begin to use the French language in class (and you will do so very early on), you will discover that you can interact with French speakers or your classmates right away. It might help to persuade you of this to know that of the 80,000 words found in the French language, the average French person uses only about 800 on a daily basis. *Therefore, the most important task ahead of you is NOT to accumulate a large quantity of knowledge about French grammar and vocabulary, but rather to USE what you do know as effectively and creatively as you can.*

Communication in a foreign language means *understanding* what others say and *transmitting* your own messages in ways that avoid misunderstandings. As you learn to do this, you will make the kinds of errors that are necessary to language learning. DO NOT BE AFRAID TO MAKE MISTAKES! Instead, try to see errors as positive steps toward effective communication. They don't hold you back; they advance you in your efforts.

ON Y VA! has been written with your needs in mind. It places you in situations that you (as a young person) might really encounter in a French-speaking environment. Whether you are working with vocabulary or grammar, it leads you from controlled exercises (that show you just how a word or structure is used) to bridging exercises (that allow you to introduce your own personal context into what you are saying or writing) to open-ended exercises (in which you are asked to handle a situation much as you might in actual experience). These situations are intended to give you the freedom to be creative and express yourself without anxiety. They are the real test of what you can DO with the French you have learned.

Learning a language is hard work, but it can also be lots of fun. We hope that you find your experience with *ON Y VA!* both rewarding and enjoyable.

Table des matières

Unité six On fait les courses / 325

Chapitre seize: Qu'est-ce qu'on va manger?

Première étape /327 Point de départ: À la boulangerie-pâtisserie Note culturelle Structure: The interrogative expression quel Débrouillons-nous! Pourquoi?

Deuxième étape /333 Point de départ: À la charcuterie Note culturelle Prononciation: The vowel é Reprise Structure: The partitive Note grammaticale Débrouillons-nous!

Troisième étape /340 Point de départ: À la boucherie Note culturelle Reprise Structure: Demonstrative adjectives Note grammaticale Débrouillons-nous! Lexique

Chapitre dix-sept: Achetons des fruits et des légumes!

Première étape /349	Deuxième étape /356
Point de depart: Au marché Note culturelle	Point de départ: Au supermarché Note culturelle
Reprise	Prononciation: The vowels $\hat{\mathbf{e}}$ and $\hat{\mathbf{e}}$
Structure: Expressions of general	Reprise
quantity	Structure: Expressions of comparison
Note grammaticale: Expressions of	Note grammaticale: Expressions of
specific quantity	sufficiency
Débrouillons-nous!	Débrouillons-nous!
	Lexique

Chapitre dix-huit: Moi, j'ai des courses à faire

comparison

Première étape /367		
Point de départ: A la Fnac		
Note culturelle		
Prononciation: The vowel \mathbf{e}		
Reprise		
Structure: Numbers from 70 to 100		
Note grammaticale: 101 to 1 000 000		
Débrouillons-nous!		

Deuxième étape /374 Point de départ: Au centre commercial Note culturelle Reprise Structure: The irregular verb devoir Débrouillons-nous! Lexique

Mise au point навинания на 381

Lecture: Les grands noms du rock-The Who Reprise Révision Point d'arrivée

Dernière étape / 394 Glossary of Functions / 399 Glossary / 403

Acknowledgments

Creating a secondary language program is a long, complicated, and difficult process. We must express our great thanks first of all to our editor, Janet Dracksdorf—who patiently, sometimes nervously but always very supportively guided the project from its inception through to its realization. She and our assistant editor, Julianna Nielsen, probably know *ON Y VA!* as well as we do. We would also like to thank our production manager, Pat Jalbert; our copy editor, Cynthia Fostle; our native readers Sylvaine Egron-Sparrow and Sylvie Romanowski, as well as our designer, Marsha Cohen; our photographer, Stuart Cohen; and our illustrator, Jane O'Connor. All of these people worked very closely and very ably with the actual book that you are now holding in your hands. We would be remiss, however, if we did not also point out the help of those behind the scenes—in particular, José Wehnes Q., Roger Hooper and Jeanne Fryar (in Sales and Marketing), and, of course, the publisher, Stan Galek.

We also wish to express our appreciation to Bernard Petit for creating the *ON Y VA!* video program; to André and Roby Ariew for the *ON Y VA!* software program, to Rebecca Kline for her excellent work on the Testing Program, to the students who helped with the training video, and to Carlyle Carter and Colleen Campion, who provided additional editorial help.

Finally, as always, our special thanks go to Baiba and Mary, who once again have cheerfully (for the most part) supported and encouraged us throughout another endeavor. As for Alexander (age 5) and his baby sister (whose arrival on the scene preceded that of this book by only a few months), we hope that they both will have the chance to learn French from *ON Y VA!* when they get to high school!

J.D.B.
D.B.R.

The Publisher and authors wish to thank the following teachers who pilot tested the *ON Y VA!* program. Their valuable feedback on teaching with these materials has greatly improved the final product. We are grateful to each one of them for their dedication and commitment to teaching with the program in a prepublication format.

David Hamilton
Lynn Nahabetian
Ada Cosgrove Junior High School
Spencerport, NY

Beth Harris
Alief ISD
Houston, TX

Beryl Hogshead
Elsik High School
Houston, TX

Sandy Parker
Michele Adams
Hastings High School
Houston, TX

Donna Watkins
Holub Middle School
Houston, TX

Janet Southard
Olle Middle School
Houston, TX

Floy Miller
Boston Archdiocese Choir School
Cambridge, MA

Geraldine Oehlschlager
Central Catholic High School
Modesto, CA

Mary Lee Black
Sacred Heart
Danville, VA

Joyce Goodhue
Verna Lofaro
Cherry Creek High School
Englewood, CO

Renée Rollin
Valentine Petoukhoff
Cherry Hill East High School
Cherry Hill, NJ

Linda Dodulik
Beck Middle School
Cherry Hill, NJ

Judith Speiller
Marta De Gisi
Mary D. Potts
Andrea Niessner
Cherry Hill West High School
Cherry Hill, NJ

Ann Wells
Carusi Junior High School
Cherry Hill, NJ

Yvonne Steffen
Hogan High School
Vallejo, CA

Cynthia DeMaagd
Holland Junior High School
Holland, MI

Galen Boehme
Kinsley High School
Kinsley, KS

Mary Harris
LSU Laboratory School
Baton Rouge, LA

Shirley Beauchamp
Pittsfield High School
Pittsfield, MA

Paul Connors
Lynn Harding
Randolph High School
Randolph, MA

Nicole Merritt
San Mateo High School
San Mateo, CA

Jane Flood
Marge Hildebrandt
Somers High School
Lincolndale, NY

Joseph Martin
St. Ignatius High School
Cleveland, OH

Analissa Magnelia
Turlock High School
Turlock, CA

Peter Haggerty
Sylvia Malzacher
Wellesley High School
Wellesley, MA

Lynn Moore-Benson
Linda Zug
Wellesley Middle School
Wellesley, MA

The publisher and authors would also like to thank the following people who reviewed the *ON Y VA!* program at various stages of its development. Their comments and suggestions have also been invaluable to us.

Virginia Duffey (Riverside Sr High School, Riverdale, GA); Charlotte Cole (Walpole High School, Walpole, MA); Mary Hayes (Wellesley High School, Wellesley, MA); Claire Jackson (Newton High School South, Newton Center, MA); Janet Wohlers (Weston High School, Weston, MA); Gail Connell (Enloe High School, Raleigh, NC); Pam Cross (Cary High School, Cary, NC); Bettye Myer (Miami University, Oxford, OH); Mary Troxel (Hamilton High School, Oxford, OH); Nancy Gabel (Strath Haven High School, Wallingford, PA); Diana Regan (John Bartram High School, Philadelphia, PA); Mary Flynn (H. B. Woodlawn Program, Arlington, VA); Kathy Hardenbergh (Millard South High School, Omaha, NE); Beth Llewellyn (Southwest High School, Ft. Worth, TX); Karen Neal (J. J. Pearce High School, Richardson, TX); Theresa Curry (Berkner High School, Richardson, TX); Linda Robertson (Bolton High School, Alexandria, LA); Pamela Raitz (Louisville Collegiate School, Louisville, KY); Jane Baskerville (Chesterfield Public Schools, Chesterfield, VA); Fran Maples (Richardson School District, Richardson, TX); Annette Lowry (Ft. Worth ISD, Ft. Worth, TX); Kathleen Riordan (Springfield Public Schools, Springfield, MA); Joan Feindler (The Wheatley School, Old Westbury, NY); Marilyn Bente (San Diego City Schools, San Diego, CA); Robert Decker (Long Beach Unified School District, Long Beach, CA); Kaye Nyffeler (Millard Sr. High School, Omaha, NE); Carmine Zinn (Pinellas County School District, Largo, FL); Michelle Shockey (Henry M. Gunn High School, Palo Alto, CA); Mary de Lopez (La Cueva High School, Albuquerque, NM); Al Turner (Glenbrook South High School, Glenview, IL); Doris Kays (Northeast ISD, San Antonio, TX); Mary Francis Crabtree (Glenbrook South High School, Glenview, IL); Marilyn Lowenstein (Hamilton High School, Los Angeles, CA); Kathleen Cook (Cheyenne Mt. High School, Colorado Springs, CO)

To the teacher

PRINCIPLES OF THE PROGRAM

ON Y VA! Le français par étapes is an integrated learning system designed to provide beginning-level secondary-school students with immediately useful language skills in French. Because the authors believe that creative use of the language is possible from the outset, the texts have been written to allow maximum interaction among students and between students and teachers, beginning with the preliminary lessons. Such interaction is based on tasks to be accomplished and on effective linguistic functioning in real situations. Class time is seen as an opportunity for students to practice the French they will hear and speak when visiting a French-speaking country or when interacting with speakers of French. Furthermore, it is seen as a time when trial and error are a necessary part of the language-acquisition process and when free expression must be encouraged.

Just as everyday spoken French does not include every grammar structure and every vocabulary item available in the French language, the authors have limited the text to the elements most frequently used by native speakers in daily life. Grammar is not presented for its own sake, but as a means of transmitting a spoken or written message as accurately as possible. Each unit contains the necessary grammar and vocabulary related to the central theme to give students the freedom to be as creative as possible in expressing their ideas.

The contexts presented in *ON Y VA!* have been selected according to the frequency with which they occur in the real-life experience of someone interested in discovering French-speaking countries and in maximizing such an experience through interaction with their peoples. These contexts are designed to build students' confidence and to enable them not only to survive in the language but to do so with enjoyment. It is through active participation in simulations that students will assure themselves of their ability to interact with others in French.

The authors' proficiency-oriented, integrative approach to teaching assumes that the four skills and culture reinforce one another in an ever-widening spiral, that enough time be allowed for assimilation of material, that teaching techniques be student-centered and, perhaps most importantly, that the goal of teaching be to make students independent users of French. The degree to which this program is successful will, of course, depend largely on your use of the materials. Your success will be greatly enhanced if you accept the premises that trial and error are necessary parts of language acquisition and that the objective of any language class is effective communication through creative use of the language. With a proficiency-based curriculum becoming a reality in many states, we have kept in mind the principles set forth in the *ACTFL Proficiency Guidelines* so that we may help students to function as accurately as possible in the situations they are most likely to encounter.

ON Y VA! is realistic and positive in its expectations. The material presented in the texts is accessible to and learnable by all students, and enough time has been reserved to allow instructors the flexibility necessary for effective teaching.

Perhaps the most important feature of *ON Y VA!* is the authors' belief that the essential goal of language teaching is to inspire in students the confidence and therefore the willingness to use whatever elements of language they have at their disposal. In other words, *ON Y VA!* aims at dispelling the notion that students must wait until they enter advanced French courses to participate in real communication.

WHY WAS *ON Y VA!* WRITTEN?

The *ON Y VA!* program is designed to answer a number of concerns voiced by teachers throughout the country. It is becoming increasingly clear that materials that have the teacher in mind, not just the students, will go a long way in facilitating teachers' tasks. In writing *ON Y VA!*, we have very specifically addressed the following teacher concerns:

1. Teachers are assigned many duties in addition to their teaching. This raises the question of time—for preparation, for correction, and for testing, and for being innovative and creative in the teaching process.
   Our solution: To organize our books in such a way that no time needs to be spent on reorganizing or rewriting. Furthermore, the organization of the texts greatly reduces preparation time.
2. Classes are often very large and heterogeneous.
   Our solution: To provide many opportunities for stu-

dents to interact in small groups. Research increasingly shows that students will develop their communicative competence as well when they interact with each other as when they work as a class with the teacher.

3. Teachers should be able to express their own personalities and teaching styles and should not be constrained by the textbook or a particular method.
   Our solution: No single teaching method is espoused in *ON Y VA!* In an integrative approach such as ours, teachers are given a variety of options for working with the material. Furthermore, it is assumed that teachers will enhance the texts by infusing them with their own personalities, their own preferences, their own teaching styles.
4. Teacher effectiveness can be reduced by stress and fatigue factors.
   Our solution: ON Y VA! uses small group work to place more responsibility on students and thus give teachers regular breathers in each class period. Our student-centered approach does not, of course, remove the teacher from the learning process. But it does encourage students to look to each other and the materials as resources rather than just to the teacher.
5. Teachers are accountable for the success rates of their students in terms of both their effectiveness at communicating and their performance on a variety of standardized tests.
   Our solution: The scope and sequence of grammar, vocabulary, and linguistic functions over the three-year program provides students ample time and opportunity to assimilate the material. Grammar is presented incrementally, in understandable language, and is always linked to communicative functions. Structures and vocabulary are recycled regularly and in a variety of contexts so that students will become comfortable using them.

When textbooks keep in mind both teacher and student concerns, we believe that more effective learning can take place and that teaching and learning will be more enjoyable.

TEACHER AND STUDENT CONTRIBUTIONS TO THE *ON Y VA!* PROGRAM

We, the authors, owe a great deal to the many teachers who have contributed to the project. Before we began writing, we met with teachers from all over the country who explained their needs and concerns. Their initial input helped to shape our ideas.

The teachers who piloted the materials made invaluable suggestions as our work progressed. They examined the texts from every point of view and suggested modifications that will benefit all who use the texts in the future.

The teachers who served as reviewers at every stage of the project brought invaluable insights to the presentation of the content.

Finally, we gained a great deal from sitting in on some of the classes where *ON Y VA!* was being piloted, including the opportunity to talk to students and get their feedback. Throughout our conversations, a number of recurring themes reinforced our conviction that our program is very effective in realizing our goals. For example, students observed that they learned more in a few months with *ON Y VA!* than they had learned in more time in other languages. Some indicated that they looked forward to coming to class and enjoyed learning French, and they particularly noted that grammar seemed easy to learn. Many stated that they liked working in small groups and that they especially liked communicating about things they are interested in. Overall, their feeling was that they could do a great deal with French, even during the early phases of the learning process.

COMPONENTS OF THE *ON Y VA!* PROGRAM

Student Texts

As you become acquainted with the *ON Y VA!* program, it is important to remember that it is an integrated learning system, not simply textbooks with a series of unconnected ancillaries. All components are tightly interwoven to integrate skills and culture, the American students' lives with the people of the target cultures. Furthermore, all components support each other to allow for maximum articulation, both horizontal and vertical.

The three student texts are designed for years 1, 2, and 3 of French study. They have been written in such a way that the material *can be covered* in the projected amount of time and still leave sufficient time for testing, school activities, and the administrative details that reduce the typical number of teaching hours. A more detailed examination of the student texts can be found in a later section of this text.

Teacher's Annotated Edition

The Teacher's Edition for each text consists of the following:

1. Front matter that includes an introduction to the program
2. A list of program components and explanations
3. Instructions for how to use the teacher training video
4. A key to the symbols used in the margin annotations
5. A guide to the basic organization of the text
6. Sample lesson plans for the year
7. A very detailed table of contents
8. Text-wide margin annotations with suggestions for presentation of grammatical structures, implementation of exercises and activities, exercise variations and follow-up, pre- and post-reading exercises, supplementary vocabulary, audio and videotape indications, workbook (homework) cross-references, answers to listening and reading comprehension exercises and cultural questions, and additional explanations for grammatical structures when necessary

    The following symbols are used in the margin annotations for suggested group work:
    ⇄ pairs
    △ groups of three
    □ groups of four
    O number of students per group to be decided by instructor.

Teaching Guides

Each level of *ON Y VA!* is accompanied by a Teaching Guide intended to expand the Teacher's Annotated Edition on a unit-by-unit basis. These guides are best used for lesson planning and class preparation. They include:

1. Suggestions for using the Planning Strategy in the workbook
2. Suggestions for using the Teacher's Audio Tape
3. The script and comprehension questions of the Teacher's tape
4. Alternative suggestions for the various sections of each unit (classroom techniques, integration of book and Resource Kit materials, methods of presentation, exercise variations, information to expand the cultural content of the unit, additional **Débrouillons-nous** situations, reading strategies, etc.)

Teacher's Methods Manual

This manual is best used in conjunction with the Teacher Training Video. The manual acquaints you with the philosophy and organizational details of the entire *ON Y VA!* program. It offers a good orientation for both new and experienced teachers.

Teacher Training Video: "Teaching with *ON Y VA!*"

Filmed with a class of high school students, ages 15 to 17, this video demonstrates teaching techniques for each segment of a unit. For experienced teachers, the tape will serve primarily as an orientation to the *ON Y VA!* program. For novice teachers, the video may also offer some new pedagogical insights. In either case, the viewer's attention should focus more on teaching techniques than on student performance. Although students did quite well, they were not coached and had studied very little French before the videotaping began.

As you watch the video, you should also keep in mind the following:

- Students had been given French names.
- Students were working with manuscript pages of the textbook.
- All exercises were taken directly from the text.
- Many of the presentations were shortened due to time limitations. It is assumed, for example, that each aspect of a presentation needs to be practiced more extensively than demonstrated on the videotape.
- The material presented comes from various parts of all six units of Level 1. This means, for example, that only the words that we explicitly present are new to students.
- Although students appear to be reading when they do a particular activity, they are in fact only consulting the cues provided by the exercise and displayed for you on the screen. None of the activities were written out for them before they performed them.

It is hoped that teachers who use *ON Y VA!* will share the video with other teachers in their region, either at local or regional conferences or by lending the tape to other schools.

The videotape includes the following sections:

1. Beginning a unit
2. Beginning an **étape:** Introducing vocabulary
3. Presenting grammatical structures
4. Working with grammatical structures
5. Ending an **étape:** Integrating vocabulary and structures
6. Developing reading skills
7. Cumulative activities
8. Ending a unit
9. The workbook
10. Pedagogical considerations

Student Workbook

The workbook units correspond to the textbook units. Each chapter within the unit begins with the **Lexique** from the book for student reference. This is followed by review of each structure and corresponding written exercises. Students can therefore use the workbook at home without having the textbook with them.

For each structure, the exercise sequence moves from mechanical practice to more real-life writing (lists, notes, postcards, parts of letters, etc.).

Each **étape** contains a **Lisons!** section using an authentic text or document to further develop the reading skills.

Each workbook unit ends with a cumulative **Mise au point** in which students are given another reading text, a series of real-life writing tasks, and a game that focuses on material they have learned.

Because the workbook gives students the opportunity to develop their writing and listening skills in particular, it is important that the teacher give them the necessary corrective feedback on the work they have done. The materials in the workbook are comprehensive and should provide the necessary practice students will need to support the skills they are developing in class.

Listening Masters

These black-line masters accompany the exercises on the Laboratory Tapes. Students may do some writing, but often they will fill in blanks, answer true/false questions, work with multiple-choice items, and so forth.

Answer Key and Tapescript for the Laboratory Tape Program

These materials serve primarily to make correction easier for you, the teacher. Although corrective feedback is important if students are to understand the errors they're making, the task of correction should not be so time-consuming that you have little time for creative teaching. The answer key and tapescript should greatly reduce the time spent on correction.

Laboratory Tapes

These tapes have a dual role. First, they provide speaking practice in controlled exercises that reinforce the grammar, vocabulary, and functions presented in the textbook. Second, they offer extensive practice in listening comprehension through dictations, simulated conversations, interviews, and a variety of exchanges in many different contexts.

The use of these lab tapes will vary according to the facilities in the school. Students may go to a lab as a class on a regular basis, they may have tapes duplicated to take home, or they may hear the tapes during class time. Whatever mode of delivery is used, it is important that teachers correct the work students do on the Listening Masters.

Teacher Tape

The Teacher Tape contains simulated, nonscripted conversations for each unit. (The tapescripts are in the Teaching Guides.) These conversations are intended to be used in introducing and closing the unit. The first time students hear a conversation, they are asked to answer only very general comprehension questions that require no grasp of detail (such as, How many people are speaking? Where do you think the conversation is taking place?). Once students have studied the unit, the conversation can be played again and followed by detailed comprehension questions.

The use of the tape at the beginning and end of a unit gives students tangible evidence of how much they have learned. The first time they listen to the conversation, they may understand very little of what is said. But the second time (at the end of the unit), they will have the satisfaction of understanding most of it. Such regular confidence-builders in the *ON Y VA!* program help to maintain a high level of motivation and sense of accomplishment.

Video Programs

These book-specific videos are designed to be used much like the Teacher Tape. The unit segments may serve to introduce the context and to end the unit. If you have easy access to a VCR, you may, of course, wish to show the video more frequently. The first time students see a segment, they will probably answer only very general comprehension questions. Due to the visual support, they will also note some cultural differences and similarities between France (or the Francophone country) and the United States. The second time they see the segment (at the end of the unit), they will be able to answer more specific questions based on the language they hear. They may also notice more subtle cultural features that escaped them the first time.

Because video more accurately represents the listening we do in real life (i.e., usually with visual support), it is essential that it be fully integrated into the language learning process. It is therefore advisable to use the *ON Y VA!* video as frequently as possible.

Video Activity Masters

These black-line masters contain comprehension exercises and conversation activities based on each segment of the video. They include both exercises for understanding the gist and exercises that require students to pay close attention to details of language, culture, and information.

Software Program

Intended to be used with the Apple IIe, the various segments of the software correspond to the material in the textbooks. Students may work with the program independently to reinforce the grammatical structures and lexical items they have learned.

Testing Program

The Testing Program consists of the following components:

1. Tests and quizzes for all units and chapters. This includes cumulative exams to be given at the end of marking periods. All tests include grammar, writing, listening, reading, and suggestions for speaking parts.
2. Tests for the **Chapitres préliminaires** for Levels 2 and 3. These tests could be used to diagnose areas where students still have some difficulty and where more review may be needed.
3. A Testing Manual that provides ideas for correction and grading, as well as formats for speaking tests, again accompanied by correction and grading strategies.

The Testing Tapes are designed to be used for the listening comprehension portions of a test, or as separate quizzes. All of the tape segments are accompanied by comprehension exercises.

Transparencies

A set of full-color transparencies accompanies each unit of each book. Cues for the use of transparencies are presented in the margin notes of the Teacher's Annotated Edition. Many of the illustrations for the **Points de départ** have been reproduced so that students can keep their books closed and focus on the teacher while learning vocabulary. An index is provided with the transparency package.

Teacher's Resource Kit

The Resource Kit contains essential supplementary materials to be integrated with the textbook lessons.

TEXT ORGANIZATION (LEVELS 1, 2, 3)

ON Y VA!, Premier niveau

Organization of the typical unit

The units in Level 1 are all organized in the same way. A unit is divided into three chapters, and each chapter is divided into **étapes.** The **étapes** contribute to the theme of the chapter, while the chapters contribute to the overall theme of the unit.

The photos, illustrations, and realia have all been carefully selected to illustrate the unit topic and functions. Included for more than aesthetic purposes, they are to be used in class to further students' understanding of the linguistic functions and the various aspects of French and francophone culture.

UNIT ORGANIZATION

1. Each unit consists of three chapters.
2. The unit opens with a photograph that illustrates the theme of the unit.
3. It is followed by a unit title page that includes:
   a. The title
   b. The unit objectives (for receptive and productive skills)
   c. Chapter and **étape** titles
   d. A photograph of a young person from France or a Francophone country
4. This is followed by the three chapters, each divided into **étapes.**
5. The end of the unit includes:
   a. The **Mise au point** (reading section and review of the unit)
   b. The **Point d'arrivée** (cumulative activities)
   c. A photo of the young person featured in the unit opener. This time, the young person provides details about him- or herself.

CHAPTER ORGANIZATION

The three chapters in a unit each deal with one aspect of the general unit theme.

1. Each chapter begins with a photo and a short conversational exchange.
2. The first chapter consists of three **étapes,** the second chapter has two **étapes,** and the third has two **étapes.**
3. Each chapter ends with the **Lexique,** which includes the expressions and vocabulary presented in the chapter.

ORGANIZATION OF AN ÉTAPE

The most important aspect of *ON Y VA!* is the self-contained **étapes,** which serve as the basic lesson plans for class. Each **étape** has a clear beginning and end, and includes the presentation of new materials, a review of the previous **étape,** and a review of the **étape** under consideration.

All photos, illustrations, and realia contribute to the **étape** subtheme, which contributes to the theme of the chapter, which, in turn, leads to the general theme of the unit.

Each **étape** contains the vocabulary, functions, and grammar necessary for the subtheme of the **étape.** These in turn contribute to the functions and contexts of the chapter, which, in turn, illustrate the larger context of the unit.

Articulation within units and between units has thus been assured through the interplay and integration of functions, contexts, and accuracy features. As the teacher, you may therefore choose to proceed through the units linearly, without having to reorganize the material or worry about such questions as the recycling of material, variety, or pacing. However, you also have the flexibility to reserve some parts of the **étape** for a later date, and you may, of course, move the review activities according to your own preferences and time constraints.

Each **étape** follows this pattern:

Point de départ
À vous!
Note culturelle (placement may vary)
Prononciation (in one **étape** per chapter) / **Pratique**
Reprise (in all **étapes** except the first one in each unit)
Structure
Application
Note grammaticale (when needed) / Continuation of **Application**
Débrouillons-nous!

Point de départ

This first section of the **étape** introduces the vocabulary that is central to the theme of the **étape.** Because the **Point de départ** takes various forms, the vocabulary may be introduced through a variety of teaching strategies.

1. Sometimes vocabulary is presented explicitly, that is, linked to illustrations. In this case, you may either present it using real objects (classroom objects, student clothing, foods you bring to class, etc.), or you may use the transparencies. The margin notes in the Teacher's Annotation Edition signal the availability of transparencies.

2. In other **étapes,** the vocabulary is presented through a short narration. The first time the narration is presented, students should have their books closed. As you slowly go through the narration with the class, you may illustrate new vocabulary with real objects or visuals. Then read the narration again without interruption, and, finally, have students open their books while you read the narration again.
3. A third variation is vocabulary presented through a dialogue. In this case you may present the main ideas with explanations in narrative form (illustrating new vocabulary) and then act out the dialogue. Note that the dialogue is also recorded on the Teacher Tape, so you don't have to act it out yourself. Students should have their books closed. Once students have heard the dialogue and understand the main ideas, you may have them open their books and repeat the dialogue after you, one sentence at a time. Finally, they can role-play the conversation.

À vous!

Whatever the format and method of presentation, each **Point de départ** is followed by a section called **À vous!** that allows students to practice the new vocabulary. The sequence of these exercises eventually leads students to controlled conversations in which the vocabulary is contextualized in a real-life situation.

All of the **étapes** begin in this same way, with a vocabulary presentation followed by a set of exercises. The goal is to have students use all new words in a context as quickly as possible.

Note culturelle

The placement of the **Note culturelle** may vary, but it is usually found somewhere near the beginning of the **étape.** It contains cultural information that expands the theme of the **étape.** Because it is written in English, the information is readily accessible to students even at the beginning of their language learning. Once students have read it, you may ask them some questions and have them draw comparisons between the target culture and the culture of the United States.

Prononciation / Pratique

In this section, students learn the most common French graphemes (letters or letter combinations) along with their phonemes (the sounds that the letters represent). The presentations always move from symbol to sound so that students are given the tools to pronounce the sounds in new words as they proceed through the program.

Before doing the **Pratique** exercises with the class, you may wish to write several examples on the board as a way of quickly and efficiently underlining the main point or problem.

When you first do the **Pratique** exercises, students should have their books open so that they continue to associate symbol and sound. Then you may wish to have them repeat the words or sentences with books closed so that they can focus purely on pronunciation.

It is assumed, of course, that you will correct student pronunciation from the outset, even before the sounds are formally presented in the book. It is also assumed that this correction will continue with regularity after the sound has been formally presented.

Reprise

These exercises, found in all **étapes** except the first of the initial chapter of a unit, provide consistent review of the structures, vocabulary, and functions of the previous **étape.** They may be done as warm-ups at the start of the class period or as breaks in the middle of the session.

Structure

Each **étape** contains the presentation of a new grammatical structure. In *ON Y VA!,* grammar is dealt with communicatively—that is, grammar is tied logically to the context of the **étape,** chapter, and unit and to the tasks that students are expected to carry out linguistically.

A **Structure** section offers one of three types of presentations:

1. The introduction of a new verb
2. The introduction of a more complex grammatical structure
3. The introduction of a set of lexical items that has grammatical implications

In general, all structures can be presented either inductively or deductively, although it is recommended that, whenever possible, an inductive technique be used. In either case, students should have their books closed so that they can pay close attention to your examples and explanations.

The *inductive approach* proceeds from example to rule. For instance, if you are presenting the **passé**

composé, you may wish to put a drawing on the board or a transparency that first shows things that someone does typically (using the present tense of verbs that students have already learned). Next you may show what the person did yesterday (using the **passé composé**). Then you may give a quick explanation in English or French about the formation of the tense. Next you may have students put themselves in the place of the person in the drawing and use **je** to repeat the sequence of actions. And finally, you may do the exercises following the **Structure** section.

The *deductive approach* moves from rule to example. Although this is not the most recommended technique, some grammar points may be presented most efficiently in this way. For instance, it is preferable to present demonstrative adjectives deductively with quick translations. This avoids possible misunderstandings and saves time. When the agreement rules and meaning have been established, you may then proceed to the exercises.

Specific techniques for presenting the **Structures** are suggested in the Teacher's Annotated Edition and in the Teaching Guides.

Application

Following each **Structure** section is a series of exercises that move from controlled or mechanical drills to bridging exercises to open-ended activities.

1. *Controlled or mechanical exercises.* These exercises, usually some kind of pattern drill, (such as, replace the italicized word) provide both structure and meaning. Because their goal is to familiarize students with the structure itself, these exercises are often not contextualized. To maximize practice, you may do several items with the entire class and then have students work in pairs.
2. *Bridging or meaningful exercises.* These exercises provide structure but ask students to provide personalized meaning (such as, answer these questions about yourself and your family). After giving the model, have students work in pairs or small groups. Then go over the exercise with the entire class in order to verify accuracy. If time is short, you may, of course, simply do the exercise with the whole class.
3. *Open-ended or communicative exercises.* In these exercises, students provide both structure and meaning (for example, go to an imaginary **épicerie** and buy supplies for a party). Traditionally neglected by many textbooks, these exercises may be done by having one pair or group of students model the exercise in front of the class. Students may then work in groups, with several groups then asked to report back to the entire class (that is, act out the scene, present results, etc.).

It is important to remember that, in *ON Y VA!*, grammar is a means rather than an end in itself. It is therefore essential that exercise sequences be carried through completely if students are to reach the communication stage of language development.

Note grammaticale / Application

In some instances, the grammar point presented in a **Structure** may have additional refinements (negative, past, etc.). To avoid presenting too many rules at the same time, we often put such information in the section called **Note grammaticale.** This is often placed right after the mechanical exercise for the **Structure,** with the meaningful and communicative exercises following the **Note grammaticale.**

Suggestions for presenting the content of the **Notes grammaticales** can be found both in the Teacher's Annotated Edition and in the Teaching Guides.

Débrouillons-nous!

These exercises are designed to review the vocabulary, functions, and structures of the **étape.** In some **étapes,** this section consists of two exercises: an **Échange,** which consists of short personal questions that two students ask each other, and a mini-situation in which students are given a task to accomplish. In other **étapes,** only the latter exercise is found.

The mini-situations are designed to prepare students for the cumulative **Point d'arrivée** activities found at the end of the unit. They usually follow one of two basic formats:

1. A step-by-step outline of what students are expected to do—for example:
   Le dessert. You have been put in charge of buying desserts for a party your class is having. You're at the **boulangerie-pâtisserie.**
   a. Greet the salesperson.
   b. Say that you want some pastries (name them).
   c. Ask the price of the chocolate cake, the apple pies, and the lemon tarts.
   d. Decide what and how much you're going to buy.
   e. Pay, thank the salesperson, and say good-bye.

2. A general direction line with one or two suggestions—for example:
   Tu viens chez moi? You have invited a classmate to come to your house. Give him/her directions on how to get from his/her house to yours. If necessary, begin by asking your classmate where he/she lives.

In doing the first form of activity (step-by-step outline), it is important to stress that these are *not* translation exercises and that there are often several ways of getting the meaning across. In doing the second form of activity (general direction line with suggestions), it is often useful to help students brainstorm appropriate vocabulary items and expressions before they break into groups. In both cases, it is recommended that one group (or pair) of students model the activity for the rest of the class, that students then work in small groups or pairs, and that, finally, one or two groups redo their conversation for the entire class.

Mise au point

Coming at the end of each three-chapter sequence, the **Mise au point** serves as a cumulative review of the entire unit. It consists of four components:

1. **Lecture**—a section-opening reading usually taken from authentic documents (newspapers, magazines, brochures, advertisements, etc.), including literature. The **Lecture** is always an expansion or illustration of the unit theme and is followed by the **Compréhension** section, which serves as a check on understanding.
2. **Reprise**—a review of the previous **étape.**
3. **Révision**—a systematic, capsule review of the unit's vocabulary and grammatical structures. Each section is followed by one or several exercises.
4. **Point d'arrivée (Activités orales et écrites)**—communicative activities that are the culminating point of the unit. They tie together the vocabulary, functions, structures, and cultural information presented in the unit. Everything in the unit leads up to this performance point, when students can demonstrate their independence in using the French language.

   For the most part, these activities involve pairs or groups of students. The instructions are always in English to avoid giving away structures and vocabulary, and to encourage students to use a variety of ways to express themselves. Using English in the direction lines also approximates the "real" situations in which students might find themselves (for example, if they were to enter a French store, their reason for being there would exist in their minds in English).

   You should feel free to do some or all of the activities. Depending on the amount of time you have, you may wish to do one activity on one day, assign a second to be prepared in advance as homework, and work on one or two others on the second day.

   The most important thing to remember is that the **Point d'arrivée** activities demonstrate what language learning is all about. They show the tasks that students can accomplish with the language they know and in which contexts and with what degree of accuracy they can function. To sacrifice these activities to time constraints or to treat them as optional would be to subvert both the goals of the *ON Y VA!* program and the goals of proficiency-oriented language instruction and learning. It is therefore imperative that the process be carried out fully and that students have the opportunity to demonstrate their accomplishments.

Developing reading skills

It is important to note that reading skills are developed throughout the *ON Y VA!* program. Because reading and listening are the most durable skills (least easily forgotten), and because they do not develop accidentally or haphazardly, systematic inclusion of reading is essential in a foreign language program.

In *ON Y VA!* reading texts are placed in the following sections:

1. In the **Mise au point** at the end of each unit. This text can take a variety of forms and be read for a variety of purposes. It is always followed by a comprehension check that deals with both the gist of the text and its details.
2. In each **étape** of the workbook, corresponding to the **étapes** in the textbook. Each workbook unit therefore contains an additional seven readings related to the unit topic. Again, comprehension checks accompany the texts.
3. In the Resource Kit, where a series of supplementary readings and comprehension checks are designed to accompany each unit.
4. And finally, in the reading unit (one in each level), which focuses on aspects of the French and francophone world.

In many instances, the reading text is preceded by a reading strategy that students are asked to use when going through the text. For instance, they may be asked to isolate cognates, they may be required to guess unknown words from the surrounding context, they may be told to isolate main or subordinate ideas, etc. In every case, however, students should be encouraged to read first for the gist of the passage. They should be told that they need not understand every word, and they should be given a time limit so that they learn to read in meaningful segments rather than word-for-word.

In-class, timed reading is perhaps the best strategy for teaching students to read smoothly and fluently. At first, they may not complete a text in the allotted time. But as they gain practice and realize that comprehension depends on key words, they will increase their reading speed. To develop their reading skills effectively, students should be asked to read silently rather than aloud. This corresponds to the way we read most frequently in real life and represents our true rate of reading.

To arrive at the approximate silent reading time for a given text, read the passage twice out loud. The amount of time it takes you to do this will equal a realistic amount of time for students to read the same text silently in class.

Organization of the reading unit *(Unité 5: On visite Paris)*

In each level of the *ON Y VA!* program, one unit focuses on reading and culture. In Level 1, Unit 5 deals primarily with Paris and serves, by extension, as a model for describing any city or town. The goal of the reading unit is to have students learn some of the information known by the average French person.

In general, the reading unit is organized in the same way as the other units—that is, the formats of the unit, the chapter, and the **étape** stay essentially the same. However, a few differences should be noted:

1. Instead of a **Point de départ,** the reading unit begins with a **Lecture** centering on various aspects of the unit topic (in this case, Paris). Because reading in *ON Y VA!* means reading for comprehension, the texts at the beginning of each **étape** should be read silently (for homework or in class) for comprehension of information only.
2. The unit contains many more illustrative photographs.
3. The **Structure** sections tend to focus on a major grammar point that is carried throughout most of the unit. In Unit 5, the focus is on the **passé composé.**
4. The speaking skill continues to be developed through the exercises and activities. In addition, students are asked to integrate some of the factual cultural information they have learned in the **étape.**

You have several options in presenting the context of the reading unit:

1. You may have students read the material ahead of time, review it quickly during class, and do the exercises.
2. You may present the information in the readings through your own short narratives, then have students read the texts, and finally do the exercises.
3. You may have students read the texts as in-class timed readings to find out what general information they can glean from them. This would be followed by the exercises.

Whatever your approach, it's important that students not translate the texts and that they read first for the gist and then for supporting detail.

ON Y VA!, Deuxième niveau

Organization of the typical unit

Although the principles and philosophy of Level 2 remain consistent with those of the entire *ON Y VA!* program, the format of Level 2 has been changed slightly to give students a greater variety of materials. The idea of the unit, the chapter, and the **étape** remains essentially the same, and many of the earlier teaching suggestions apply here as well. But the focus of Level 2 is on the receptive skills (in particular, reading) as students work with a variety of texts as catalysts to their speaking and writing.

The role of culture in *ON Y VA!, Premier niveau* and *Deuxième niveau*

It is important to note the various ways in which culture is integrated throughout the Level 1 and 2 texts. The role of culture in Level 3 will be discussed separately.

A variety of techniques are used to immerse students in the French and francophone cultures as they learn French. Rather than isolating cultural phenomena from the language students are learning, they are tightly integrated into every aspect of the textbooks.

1. Culture is ever-present in that it is inseparable from language. As students learn to express themselves in various situations, the language they use and the behaviors that accompany this language are culturally authentic. This means that language in *ON Y VA!* has *not* been doctored or modified for the sake of grammar rules. For example, sentence fragments are acceptable because they are natural in speech, communicative functions are taught from the outset, and certain adverbs are presented when they are needed.
2. The vocabulary reflects the preoccupations of young people in France and various francophone regions of the world, as well as the interests of our students.
3. **Le savez-vous?,** short multiple-choice items placed in the margins at regular intervals throughout the units, focus on interesting facts that are related to **étape** topics.
4. **Notes culturelles** further student understanding of a particular topic.
5. **Pourquoi?,** short culture assimilators, present students with problems that come about due to cultural misunderstanding. Some time should be spent discussing the solution to each problem with students.
6. The visual components of the program—the photos and video—contain a wealth of cultural material, both factual and behavioral. They should be fully integrated into classroom time to the greatest extent possible. Depending on facilities, the video may also be made available to students in a library or laboratory.
7. Reading units focus on one major cultural topic and provide students with a great deal of factual information about modern life and historical events.
8. Readings in the **Mise au point** and workbook expose students to a variety of passages for a variety of purposes. They include ads, poems, magazine and newspaper articles, brochures, various types of guidebooks, recipes, classified ads, and literary sketches.
9. Supplementary readings in the Resource Kit, all authentic, provide additional insights into French and francophone cultures.

ON Y VA!, Troisième niveau

Organization of the typical unit

The units in Level 3 have culture as their focal point. This means that, once again, the format has been adjusted slightly to give the book a different look as well as to add sections that involve students in culturally driven activities.

In addition to the new format features discussed later, the **Structure** titles and exercise direction lines in *ON Y VA!, Level 3* are written entirely in French. The same is true of most of the reading and listening comprehension checks, unless a discussion involves very complex issues that are beyond the students' production skills.

All of the elements of the communicative/interactive approach that make the *ON Y VA!* program unique have been preserved in this third level. Whereas in Level 1 listening and speaking are highlighted to give students a sense of accomplishment from the outset, in Level 2 the receptive skills receive additional emphasis. Finally, in Level 3 culture becomes the centerpiece, and all the skills are practiced through the concepts presented in the various culture sections.

Regardless of their specific emphasis, all three levels of *ON Y VA!* integrate skills and culture in meaningful communication. The slight shifts in emphasis from one text to another should maintain student motivation while assuring smooth articulation from one year to the next.

YEARLY SYLLABI

The following are three suggested yearly syllabi, one for each level of *ON Y VA!,* based on 180 class days.

The goal of our program is for you to be able to complete the material for each level in one year. We have not, however, included specific time requirements for the completion of each **étape** because we believe that you need to retain as much flexibility as possible in designing your yearly plan. Some **étapes** will take longer than others, depending on the general ability of the students and the complexity of the material. For example, **Structure** sections that are essentially lexical will probably require less time than those that involve primarily grammatical structures.

ON Y VA!, Premier niveau

Text content: Étapes préliminaires, 6 units, Dernière étape
Total number of class days: 180

- 15–20 days reserved for administrative details, review, testing, and class cancellations due to extra-curricular activities
- 2–6 days for the **Étapes préliminaires**
- 25–30 days for each of the 6 units
- 1–4 days for the **Dernière étape**

The number of days for each category can be modified according to your particular school calendar and your own preferences. For example, you may prefer to allow fewer or more days for the **Étapes préliminaires,** the **Dernière étape,** testing, and other activities.

If you use the suggested maximum number of class days for the units, you will need to adjust the number of class days for the other components accordingly.

ON Y VA!, Deuxième niveau

Text content: 3 Chapitres préliminaires, 5 units, Dernière étape
Total number of class days: 180

- 15–20 days reserved for administrative details, review, testing, and class cancellations due to extracurricular activities
- 12–15 days for **Chapitres préliminaires A, B, and C**
- 25–30 days for each of the 5 units
- 1–4 days for the **Dernière étape**

If you use the suggested maximum number of class days for the units, you will need to adjust the number of class days for the other components accordingly.

ON Y VA!, Troisième niveau

Text content: 2 Chapitres préliminaires, 4 units, Dernière étape
Total number of class days: 180

- 15–20 days reserved for administrative details, review, testing, and class cancellations due to extracurricular activities
- 12–16 days for the **Chapitres préliminaires**
- 25–30 days for each of the 4 units
- 1–4 days for the **Dernière étape**

If you use the suggested maximum number of days for each component, you will use exactly 160 days. This will leave 20 days that may be used in a variety of ways: (1) to increase the number of days for each unit, (2) to add reading materials to the course (supplementary readings from the Resource Kit or readings of your own choosing), (3) to build in additional review periods, or (4) take more time for the **Chapitres préliminaires** and the **Dernière étape.**

THE *ON Y VA!* PROGRAM
Premier niveau

	FUNCTIONS	CONTEXTS	ACCURACY
UNITÉ 1	Ordering a beverage at a café Greeting, introducing, leave-taking Ordering something to eat Finding out about other people	Café, briocherie, fast food establishments Meeting new friends and people	Indefinite articles **un, une** Present tense of regular **–er** verbs Asking and answering yes/no questions Conjugated verbs followed by an infinitive Present tense of the irregular verb **être** Adjectives of nationality/nouns of profession
UNITÉ 2	Identifying personal possessions Talking about preferences Talking about my family Getting information about other people	School, home, various settings	Present tense of the irregular verb **avoir** Indefinite article **des** Numbers from 0 to 10 Definite articles **le, la, l', les** Possessive adjectives (1st, 2nd persons) Questions with **où, combien de, que, pourquoi** Present tense of the irregular verb **faire**/expressions using **faire**
UNITÉ 3	Identifying places in a city Identifying public buildings Asking for directions Giving directions Talking about leisure-time activities Making plans to meet Giving the time Telling people to do something	City or town, festival	Present tense of the irregular verb **aller** Preposition **à** and the definite article Numbers from 11 to 29 Preposition **de** and the definite article/prepositions of place The imperative Telling time Possessive adjectives (3rd person)
UNITÉ 4	Making plans to go into town Identifying what to do in town Talking about when and how to go to town Talking about taking the Paris subway Buying subway tickets Taking a taxi Expressing wishes and desires	Town, subway station	The immediate future The days of the week Present tense of the irregular verb **prendre** Adverbs used for present and future Present tense of the irregular verb **vouloir** Numbers from 30 to 69 Expressions for discussing plans
UNITÉ 5	Talking about events in the past Situating events in the past Talking about things to see and do in Paris Talking about actions in past, present, and future time	Paris, any city	**Passé composé** with **avoir** Adverbs and prepositions used for the past **Passé composé** with **être** **Passé composé** with **avoir** and **être** Past, present, and future time
UNITÉ 6	Making purchases/choices Expressing quantity Asking for prices Expressing obligation Getting and giving information Making comparisons	Boulangerie/pâtisserie, charcuterie, boucherie, marché, supermarché, Fnac, centre commercial	Interrogative expression **quel** The partitive Demonstrative adjectives Expressions of general quantity/comparison/sufficiency Numbers up to 1 000 000 The irregular verb **devoir**

Deuxième niveau

	FUNCTIONS	CONTEXTS	ACCURACY
	Chapitres préliminaires A, B, and **C** are a review of all major functions, structures, and vocabulary items covered in *ON Y VA!* **Premier niveau**. Consult the *ON Y VA!* Methods Manual for a listing of specific items.		
UNITÉ 1	Describing weather/climate Identifying months and seasons Giving the date Describing things Describing people	Vacations, a variety of situations in which descriptions occur	Months, dates, and seasons Regular **–ir** verbs Inversion with interrogatives Agreement/position of adjectives Definite and indefinite articles with parts of the body
UNITÉ 2	Using hotel guide books Getting a hotel room Paying the hotel bill Writing a thank you letter Understanding classified ads Talking about furniture arrangement Understanding official time	Hotel, a stay with a family in France, an apartment	Ordinal numbers The irregular verb **dormir** Irregular verbs **sortir/partir** Time expressions The 24-hour clock The irregular verb **dire** The irregular verb **mettre**
UNITÉ 3	Talking about daily routine Making weekend plans Understanding entertainment guides Talking about films Preparing for a party Making plans for vacation	Morning, afternoon, evening at home or at school At the movies, at a party, a family vacation, a camping trip	Present tense of pronominal verbs Negation of pronominal verbs The imperative of pronominal verbs Direct object pronouns **le, la, les** The immediate future of pronominal verbs Pronominal vs. nonpronominal verbs Object pronouns with the imperative
UNITÉ 4	Talking about health/fitness Describing the past Making purchases (pharmacy) Identifying medicines Identifying healthy foods Finding out about specific past events Expressing one's abilities Expressing what one knows how to do	Pharmacy, school, various places where conversations about health might occur	The imperfect tense **Passé composé** of pronominal verbs The irregular verb **savoir** The irregular verb **pouvoir** The irregular verb **connaître** The expressions **depuis quand, depuis combien de temps, depuis**
UNITÉ 5	Talking about geography Expressing past time Identifying things/places one has seen Understanding texts about France Talking about the recent past Planning a trip to France	Travel, various parts of France	The imperfect and the **passé composé** The irregular verb **voir** The object pronouns **me, te, nous, vous** The irregular verb **venir** The expression **venir de**

Troisième niveau

	FUNCTIONS	CONTEXTS	ACCURACY
	Chapitres préliminaires A and **B** are a comprehensive review of the materials presented in *ON Y VA!* **Deuxiéme niveau.** Consult the Methods Manual for a listing of specific items.		
UNITÉ 1	Purchasing clothing/shoes Asking for information Giving clothing sizes Asking to try on clothing Commenting on clothing Expressing one's needs	Clothing stores, department stores, shoe stores	L'emploi de subjonctif pour exprimer la nécessité Les pronoms d'objets indirects **lui** et **leur** L'infinitif avec les verbes **dire, demander, proposer, permettre, promettre**
UNITÉ 2	Organizing a trip Talking about means of transportation Buying train tickets and making reservations Understanding a road map Making arrangements (car/plane) Expressing doubt/certainty	Train station, airport, on the road	Les noms géographiques et les prépositions Le pronom **y** L'emploi du subjonctif pour exprimer le doute et l'incertitude L'emploi de l'indicatif pour exprimer la certitude Les pronoms interrogatifs
UNITÉ 3	Understanding a variety of texts about the French-speaking world Making comparisons Expressing emotion	Travel in various French-speaking regions	Les pronoms relatifs **qui/que** Le comparatif Les verbes réguliers en **–re** Les expressions négatives **ne. . .rien/ne. . .personne** Le subjonctif et l'infinitif (l'émotion) Le superlatif
UNITÉ 4	Understanding a menu Making restaurant plans Ordering food Paying in a restaurant Inviting someone to dinner Discussing dinner preparations Understanding a written invitation Writing an invitation Expressing thanks/social amenities Understanding a recipe Expressing wishes/preferences	The restaurant, dinner at home, on the telephone, at the post office	Le pronom **en** Le subjonctif et l'infinitif (le désir) Les pronoms accentués Le verbe irrégulier **devoir** Les expressions **avant de/après** Les verbes irréguliers **envoyer/recevoir** Le verbe irrégulier **écrire**

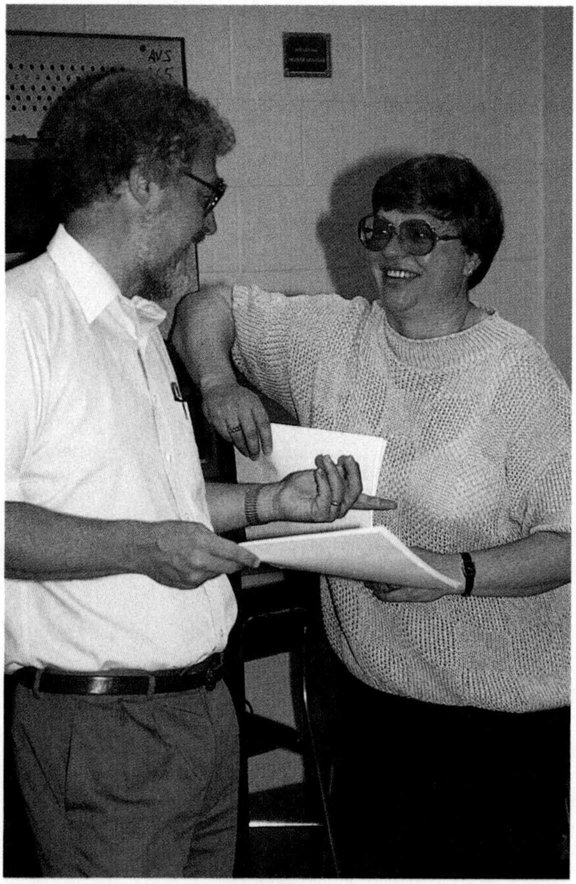

We wish you much success with the *ON Y VA!* program. We hope that you find teaching with it rewarding and enjoyable. We are always interested in your comments and suggestions. Please contact us through our publisher at this address:

HEINLE & HEINLE PUBLISHERS, INC.
20 Park Plaza
Boston, Massachusetts 02116

J. D. B.
D. B. R.

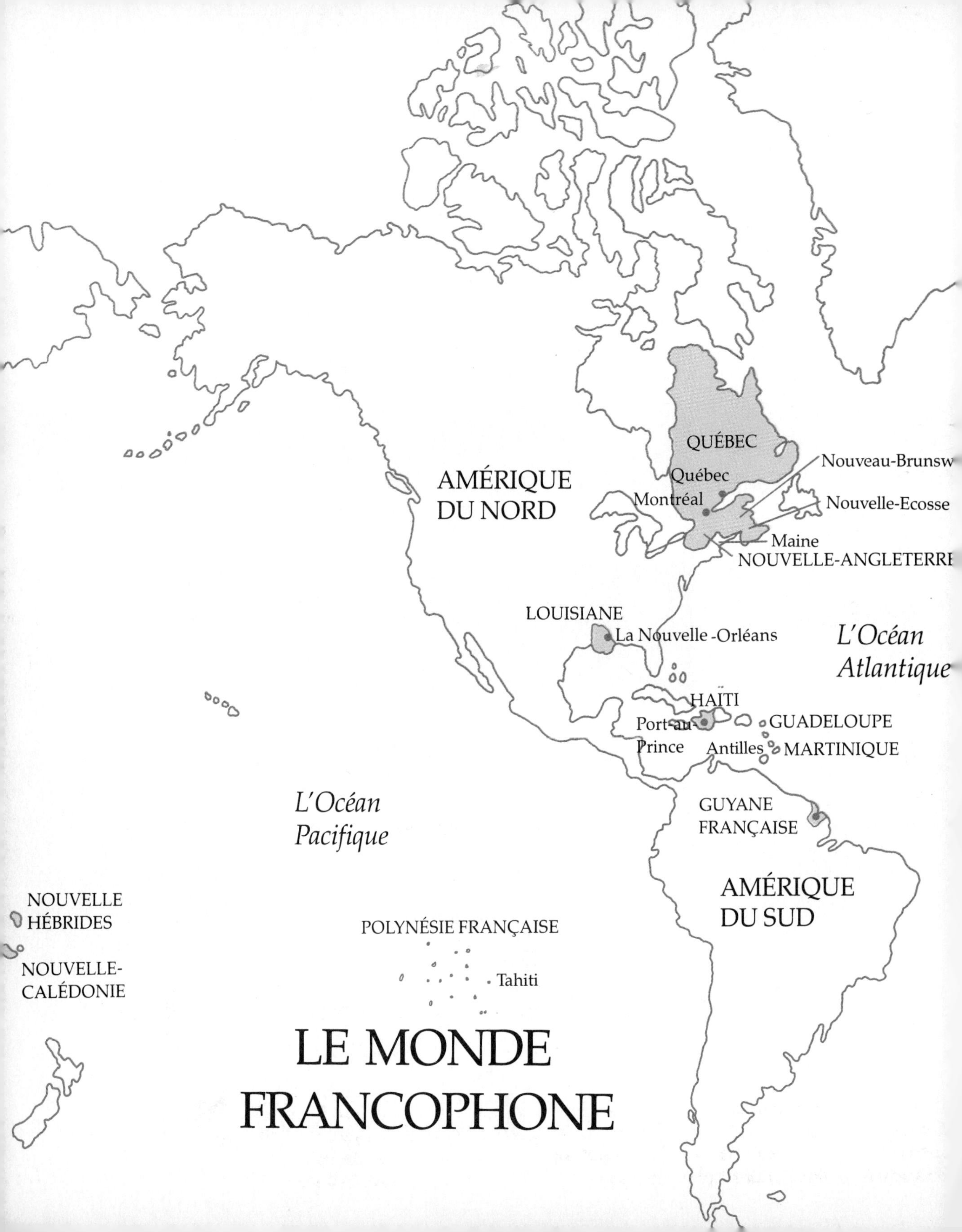

LE MONDE FRANCOPHONE

. Mali
. Niger
. Tchad
. Sénégal
5. Mauritanie
6. Guinée
7. Côte-D'Ivoire
8. Burkina-Fasso
9. Bénin
10. République Centrafricaine
11. Cameroun
12. Gabon
13. Congo
14. Zaïre
15. Djibouti
16. Rwanda
17. Burundi
18. Togo

Mer du Nord
ANGLETERRE
PAYS-BAS
ALLEMAGNE
BELGIQUE
Rhin
Lille
Valenciennes
LUXEMBOURG
La Manche
Le Havre
Rouen
Seine
Reims
Meuse
PARIS
Nancy
Strasbourg
Brest
VOSGES
Fougères
Rennes
Orléans
Loire
Mulhouse
Tours
Dijon
LIECHTENSTEIN
Nantes
AUTRI
JURA
SUISSE
Saône
Lyon
OCÉAN
Limoges
Clermont-Ferrand
Saint-Etienne
Grenoble
ATLANTIQUE
ITALIE
Bordeaux
Rhône
ALPES
MASSIF CENTRAL
Garonne
Nice
Tarascon
Grasse
Toulouse
Montpellier
Aix-en-Provence
Cannes
Antibes
Marseille
Toulon
PYRÉNÉES
ANDORRE
ESPAGNE
Aj
Mer Méditerranée
SARD

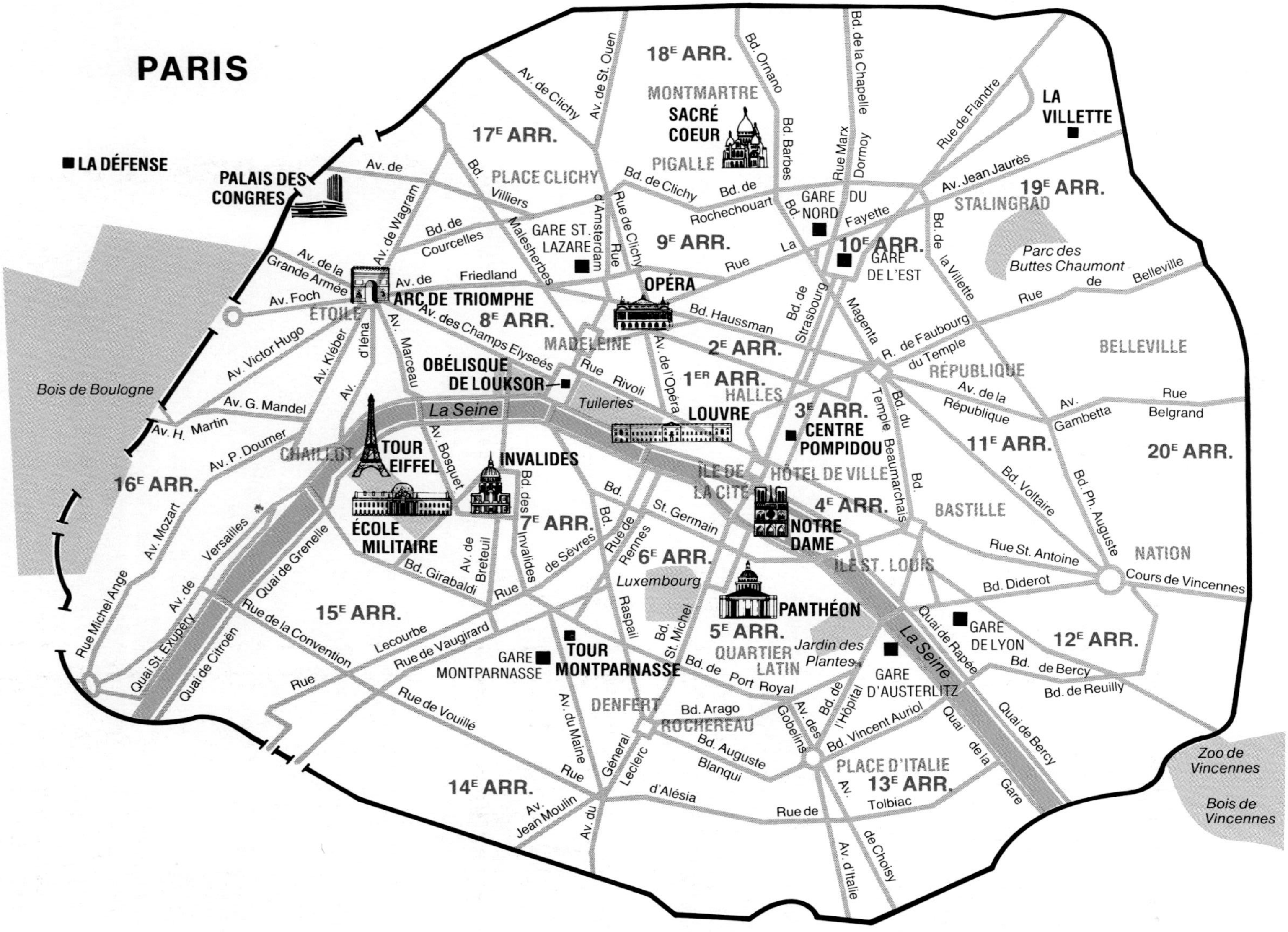
PARIS
LA DÉFENSE
PALAIS DES CONGRES
Bois de Boulogne
18E ARR.
17E ARR.
19E ARR.
9E ARR.
10E ARR.
8E ARR.
2E ARR.
1ER ARR.
3E ARR.
11E ARR.
20E ARR.
16E ARR.
7E ARR.
4E ARR.
6E ARR.
5E ARR.
15E ARR.
12E ARR.
14E ARR.
13E ARR.
MONTMARTRE
SACRÉ COEUR
PIGALLE
PLACE CLICHY
LA VILLETTE
STALINGRAD
Parc des Buttes Chaumont
GARE DU NORD
GARE DE L'EST
GARE ST. LAZARE
OPÉRA
ARC DE TRIOMPHE
ÉTOILE
MADELEINE
OBÉLISQUE DE LOUKSOR
Tuileries
LOUVRE
HALLES
RÉPUBLIQUE
BELLEVILLE
CENTRE POMPIDOU
HÔTEL DE VILLE
ÎLE DE LA CITÉ
NOTRE DAME
BASTILLE
ÎLE ST. LOUIS
NATION
La Seine
CHAILLOT
TOUR EIFFEL
INVALIDES
ÉCOLE MILITAIRE
Luxembourg
PANTHÉON
QUARTIER LATIN
Jardin des Plantes
GARE DE LYON
GARE D'AUSTERLITZ
GARE MONTPARNASSE
TOUR MONTPARNASSE
DENFERT ROCHEREAU
PLACE D'ITALIE
Zoo de Vincennes
Bois de Vincennes
Av. de Clichy
Av. de St. Ouen
Bd. Ornano
Bd. de la Chapelle
Rue Marx Dormoy
Bd. Barbes
Rue de Flandre
Av. Jean Jaurès
Bd. de la Villette
Rue de Belleville
Av. de Wagram
Bd. de Courcelles
Bd. Villiers
Malesherbes
Rue d'Amsterdam
Rue de Clichy
Bd. de Clichy
Bd. de Rochechouart
Rue La Fayette
Bd. de Strasbourg
Magenta
R. de Faubourg du Temple
Av. de la Grande Armée
Av. de Friedland
Av. Foch
Av. des Champs Elysées
Bd. Haussman
Av. Victor Hugo
Av. Kléber
Av. d'Iéna
Av. Marceau
Rue Rivoli
Av. de l'Opéra
Av. de la République
Av. Gambetta
Rue Belgrand
Av. G. Mandel
Av. H. Martin
Av. P. Doumer
Av. Bosquet
Bd. du Temple
Bd. Beaumarchais
Bd. Voltaire
Bd. Ph. Auguste
Bd. des Invalides
Bd. St. Germain
Bd. Raspail
Rue de Rennes
Rue de Sèvres
Av. de Breteuil
Bd. Girabaldi
Rue St. Antoine
Cours de Vincennes
Av. Mozart
Av. de Versailles
Quai de Grenelle
Rue Michel Ange
Quai St. Exupery
Quai de Citroën
Rue de la Convention
Rue Lecourbe
Rue de Vaugirard
Bd. St. Michel
Bd. de Port Royal
Bd. Diderot
Quai de Rapée
Bd. de Bercy
Bd. de Reuilly
Rue de Vouillé
Av. du Maine
Bd. Arago
Bd. de l'Hôpital
Av. des Gobelins
Bd. Vincent Auriol
Quai de la Gare
Quai de Bercy
Bd. Auguste Blanqui
Général Leclerc
Av. Jean Moulin
Av. du
Rue d'Alésia
Rue de Tolbiac
Av. de Choisy
Av. d'Italie

Chauds
FRANCFORT/FRITES
ENTRECÔTE
ESCALOPE/FRITES
HAMBURGER
STEAK
ROSBEEF/FRITES
CHOUCROUTE GARNIE
MAISON
Le CLUB
SANDWICHE
RAPIDE
OMELETTES VARIEES
ŒUFS AU PLAT
CROQUE PROVENCAL
PIZZA . QUICHE
SANDWICHES
ROSBEEF SALADE
SALADES COMPOSÉES

Unité première

On prend quelque chose

Planning Strategy: See Workbook.

Audio Tape and/or Video: See Teaching Guide.

On prend quelque chose: We are having something (to eat or drink)

Objectives:

In this unit, you will learn:

- to meet and greet people;
- to get something to eat and drink;
- to ask for and give information about basic activities;
- to read a café menu;
- to understand a simple conversation upon meeting someone for the first time.

Chapitre premier:	**Allons au café!**
Première étape:	Un Coca, s'il vous plaît
Deuxième étape:	Salut! . . . Au revoir!
Troisième étape:	Mangeons!
Chapitre deux:	**On va à la briocherie**
Première étape:	À la briocherie
Deuxième étape:	Bonjour! . . . Au revoir!
Chapitre trois:	**Tu aimes les fast-food?**
Première étape:	Quick? Macdo?
Deuxième étape:	On va au Quick?

Mireille Loiseau
Paris, France

Chapitre premier

Allons au café!

— *Je voudrais un Coca!*
— *Moi aussi.*
Allons au café!

Première étape

Point de départ:

Un Coca, s'il vous plaît!

Allons au café!: Let's go to the café!

— ***S'il vous plaît,*** *Monsieur.*
— *Un moment, Mademoiselle. . .*
Oui, Mademoiselle, vous désirez?
— *Un Coca, s'il vous plaît.*

— *Voilà. . . Un Coca pour Mademoiselle.*
— *Merci, Monsieur.*
— ***Je vous en prie,*** *Mademoiselle.*

please

you're welcome

Suggestion, Point de départ: Dramatize the mini-dialogue; have students repeat, books closed; have students repeat, looking at text; have students read, then recreate the dialogue. Present beverage alternatives, using the transparency of hot and cold drinks.

Des boissons chaudes — hot drinks

un café-crème

un café (un express) un café au lait

un thé nature

un thé citron un thé au lait

Transparency, Point de départ: hot and cold drinks

Reminder: Point out to students the difference between **un café-crème** (a cup of coffee with cream) and **un café au lait** (equal parts of coffee and steamed milk, usually served at breakfast).

Des boissons froides — cold drinks

un Coca un Orangina une limonade un lait fraise un diabolo citron

Supplementary Vocabulary, Mineral waters: **un Perrier** (carbonated), **un Vittel** (noncarbonated)
Alcoholic beverages: **un demi** (draught beer), **un verre de rouge, un verre de blanc**

citron: with lemon

au lait: with milk

un Orangina: carbonated orange-flavored soft drink

une limonade: very sweet, carbonated soft drink

un lait fraise: milk with strawberry syrup

une menthe à l'eau: water with mint syrup; can also be made with other flavors—**une fraise à l'eau**

un citron pressé: lemonade

une orange pressée: orangeade

un diabolo citron: limonade (see below) mixed with lemon-flavored syrup; can also be made with other flavors—**un diabolo menthe** (mint), **un diabolo fraise** (strawberry)

Note Culturelle

In France, people of all ages and from all walks of life frequent **cafés.** They go there for breakfast or a light lunch, to chat with friends after school or work, or simply to spend an hour or two reading the newspaper or a book and watching people walk by. In the summertime, the tables on the sidewalk in front of the café **(la terrasse)** are full. In the winter, most of the activity moves inside.

Service is almost always provided by men, **garçons,** who have been trained to work as waiters; there are, however, cafés where women, **serveuses,** wait on tables. Waiters and waitresses work very quickly and efficiently and thus deserve the service charge (15 percent) that is automatically added to the price of your food and drink. In addition to this charge, a tip **(le pourboire)** is often expected.

There are different kinds of cafés. On exclusive avenues such as the Champs-Élysées, you will find elegant cafés that cater primarily to tourists. There you can eat exotic ice cream dishes or pay 14F ($2.30) for a Coke as you watch a constant parade of passersby. In the business centers of French cities, the cafés attract primarily workers and shoppers, who stop by for lunch or to relax for a moment on their way home. Near every school and university, you are sure to find cafés filled with students discussing their classes and arguing about politics. Finally, every town and city has its **cafés du coin** (neighborhood cafés). There you will find, seated at little tables or standing at the counter, a mixture of customers—factory workers discussing politics, retirees playing cards, teenagers trying their luck at pinball or electronic games.

Look at the pictures of cafés on p. 7 and try to distinguish among the various types of cafés.

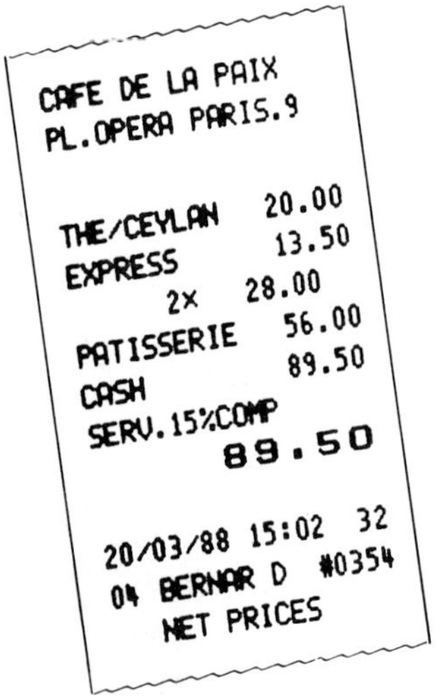
CAFE DE LA PAIX
PL.OPERA PARIS.9

THE/CEYLAN	20.00
EXPRESS	13.50
2x	28.00
PATISSERIE	56.00
CASH	89.50
SERV.15%COMP	
	89.50

20/03/88 15:02 32
04 BERNAR D #0354
NET PRICES

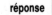

À vous! (Exercices de vocabulaire)

A. Order the suggested beverages.

MODÈLE: un café-crème
— *Vous désirez, Mademoiselle (Monsieur)?*
— *Un café-crème, s'il vous plaît.*

1. un Coca
2. un thé citron
3. une limonade
4. une menthe à l'eau
5. un Orangina
6. un café
7. un diabolo citron
8. un thé au lait
9. un citron pressé
10. un express
11. une orange pressée
12. un lait fraise
13. un thé nature
14. une fraise à l'eau

Le savez-vous?

Approximately how many cafés are there in the city of Paris?
a) 1,000
b) 6,000
c) 12,000

réponse

Variation, Ex. A: Books closed; use the transparency of hot and cold drinks with overlay; point to choices

Suggestion, Ex. B: You play the role of waiter; each student must get waiter's attention and order a drink. Students are not allowed to repeat an order until all drinks are mentioned.

Follow-up, Ex. B: If your students have already learned numbers (**Étape préliminaire**—Option D), allow them to order whatever they wish. Ask them all to keep track of orders; do a summary at the end—e.g., **trois limonades, cinq diabolos citron,** etc.

Follow-up, Ex. C: Students do the exercise in pairs, alternating roles.

B. Get the waiter's attention and order a drink of your choice.

MODÈLE: — *S'il vous plaît, Monsieur (Madame).*
— *Oui, Monsieur (Mademoiselle). Vous désirez?*
— *Un Orangina, s'il vous plaît.*

C. Play the role of waiter or student in the following situation. The student orders what he or she wishes to drink, but the waiter brings the wrong beverage.

MODÈLE:

GARÇON:	*Vous désirez?*
ÉLÈVE:	*Un diabolo menthe, s'il vous plaît.*
GARÇON:	*Voilà, Mademoiselle (Monsieur)... un diabolo citron.*
ÉLÈVE:	*Non, Monsieur... un diabolo menthe.*
GARÇON:	*Ah, pardon, Mademoiselle (Monsieur), un diabolo menthe.*
ÉLÈVE:	*Merci, Monsieur.*
GARÇON:	*Je vous en prie, Mademoiselle (Monsieur).*

c

Suggestion, Indefinite article: Draw on board a Coke bottle, a **limonade** bottle, a cup of expresso. Distinguish between **un** [ɛ̃], **une** [yn], **un** [ɛ̃n]. Have students repeat in chorus, then drill individually until every student clearly distinguishes between masculine and feminine.

Alternative Presentation: Use **c'est** with people or things in the class **(C'est un élève. C'est une élève. C'est un crayon. C'est une chaise.)** Especially useful if you have used **Étape préliminaire**—Option D.

STRUCTURE

The indefinite article ***un, une***

un garçon *(boy)* — **une** jeune fille *(girl)*
un café — **une** limonade
un citron pressé — **une** orange pressée

The English equivalents of the above nouns would be preceded by the indefinite article *a* (or *an*). In French, however, one must distinguish between the *masculine* indefinite article **un** and the *feminine* indefinite article **une.**

For an English speaker, there is nothing surprising about the fact that a boy **(un garçon)** is masculine and a girl **(une jeune fille)** is feminine. But it is much more startling to learn that a cup of coffee **(un café)** is masculine and a bottle of soda **(une limonade)** is feminine, or that a lemon **(un citron)** is masculine while an orange **(une orange)** is feminine. All nouns in French have gender, even those that do not refer to people. Since there are no infallible rules for determining gender, it is best to associate each noun with the appropriate article from the very beginning. For example, remember **un café,** not just **café.**

Ordinarily, the **n** of **un** is not pronounced. However, when the word that follows **un** begins with a vowel or a silent **h**, the **n** is pronounced: **un‿Orangina, un‿homme,** but **u~~n~~ thé.** The **n** of **une** is always pronounced.

Application

D. Replace the words in italics.

Suggestion, Ex. D: For structural exercises of this sort, either (1) do with the whole class or (2) model with the whole class (group or individual response), then have students work in pairs.

1. *Un café,* s'il vous plaît. (un thé au lait / un Orangina / un café-crème / une limonade / un diabolo citron / un lait fraise / une menthe à l'eau)
2. Voilà, Mademoiselle... *un diabolo menthe.* (un express / une orange pressée / un thé nature / un citron pressé / un Coca / une fraise à l'eau)

E. **Moi, je voudrais... Et toi?** *(I would like... And you?)* Indicate that you would like one of the following items. Then ask another student about his/her choice.

Variation, Exs. D and/or E: Books closed; use the transparency of hot and cold drinks without overlay for cues.

MODÈLE: café
Moi, je voudrais un café. Et toi, (Peter)?

1. thé citron
2. Orangina
3. limonade
4. diabolo fraise
5. orange pressée
6. citron pressé
7. express
8. Coca
9. menthe à l'eau
10. café au lait

DÉBROUILLONS-NOUS!

(Petite révision de l'étape)

F. **Qu'est-ce que tu prends?** *(What are you having?)* You go to a café with two or three friends. Find out what each of them wants to drink. Then get a waiter and order.

Ex. F: △ or □. Choose several students to play the role of waiter. You may wish to do a model for the class before dividing into groups.

MODÈLE: — *Qu'est-ce que tu prends?*
— *Un diabolo citron.*
— *Et toi?*
— *Un Orangina.*
— *S'il vous plaît, Monsieur.*
— *Un moment... Oui, vous désirez?*
— *Un diabolo citron, un Orangina et moi, je voudrais une menthe à l'eau.*

Written Work: See Workbook.

Deuxième étape

Point de départ:

Salut! . . . Au revoir!

Salut!. . . Au revoir! Hi!. . . Good-bye!

— *Salut, Jean-Marc.* ***Comment ça va?***
— *Ça va bien. Et toi, Martine, ça va?*
— *Oh, oui. Ça va.*

— *Jean-Marc Fortier, Suzanne Lecaze.*
— *Bonjour, Suzanne.*
— *Bonjour, Jean-Marc.*

— ***Allez, au revoir,*** *Jean-Marc.*
— *Au revoir, Martine.* ***À bientôt.***
— *Au revoir, Jean-Marc.*
— *Au revoir, Suzanne.*

Comment ça va? How're you doing?
Allez, au revoir: So long.
À bientôt: See you soon.

Suggestion, Point de départ: Act out each mini-dialogue: have students repeat and/or read; then have them practice with original expressions and alternatives (e.g.,—**Comment ça va?—Ça va?—Ça va bien? / —Allez, au revoir.—À bientôt.—À tout à l'heure.** Also, have students practice several introductions.

Les salutations		**Les réponses**	
Bonjour.	→	Bonjour.	
Salut.	→	Salut.	
Comment ça va? / Ça va? / Ça va bien?	→	(Oui,) ça va bien. / (Oui,) ça va. / (Oui,) pas mal.	Et toi?

Les présentations

Yvonne, François.	→	Bonjour, François. (Bonjour, Yvonne.)
Je te présente Thierry.	→	Salut, Thierry.

On prend congé

On prend congé: Saying goodbye.

Au revoir.
Allez, au revoir.
Salut.
À tout à l'heure. — See you in a while.
À bientôt.

Note Culturelle

In France, custom requires that you shake hands when you greet someone and when you take leave of them. This social rule is followed by men and women, young and old. If the two people are related or are very good friends, instead of shaking hands they often kiss each other on both cheeks.

— *Ça va?*
— *Oui, ça va bien!*

Le savez-vous?

French young people often use an expression from a foreign language when they are taking leave of someone. What do they say?
a) Bye-bye!
b) Ciao!
c) ¡Adios!

réponse →

À vous! (Exercices de vocabulaire)

A. **Répondons!** *(Let's respond!)* Respond appropriately to each statement or question.

MODÈLE: — Bonjour, Georges.
— *Bonjour, Martine.*

Follow-up, Ex. A: Redo Ex. A, having students substitute the names of people in the class: e.g., TEACHER: **Mary, numéro 1.** MARY: **Salut, Ralph.** RALPH: **Salut, Mary.**

1. Salut, Martine.
2. Comment ça va, Georges?
3. Ça va, Martine?
4. Salut, Chantal. Comment ça va?
5. Chantal, je te présente Hélène.
6. Vincent, Pierre.
7. Allez, au revoir, Vincent.
8. À bientôt, Anne-Marie.

Ex. B: △. Do one or two model dialogues before breaking into groups.

B. **Salut!** . . . Greet a friend in the class, then introduce your friend to another classmate. Remember to shake hands or kiss when saying hello, when meeting someone, and when saying good-bye.

b

Prononciation: *Unpronounced final consonants*

As a general rule, final consonants in French are silent. Because speakers of English are accustomed to pronouncing most final consonants, you will have to pay close attention to final consonants when speaking French.

English	**French**
par**t**	étudian~~t~~
uncle**s**	George~~s~~
mi**x**	pri~~x~~
cu**p**	cou~~p~~

Pratique

C. Read each word aloud, being careful *not* to pronounce the final consonant.

1. Paris
2. s'il vous plaît
3. garçon
4. à bientôt
5. un moment
6. un thé citron
7. Monsieur
8. un café au lait
9. salut
10. je voudrais

REPRISE

Ex. D: ○. Direct each "waiter" to distribute three or four drinks; then designate a new one.

D. **Pour Éric, un citron pressé.** Your class has organized a party with a French theme. Thus, the only liquid refreshments available are drinks served in a café. You play the role of waiter, giving out drinks to your classmates. If a person likes what you offer, he/she will thank you. If not, he/she will request a different drink. Don't forget to give yourself something to drink!

MODÈLE:	GARÇON:	*Pour Éric, un citron pressé.*
	ÉRIC:	*Merci.*
	GARÇON:	*Pour Christine, un Coca.*
	CHRISTINE:	*Non, je voudrais une limonade.*
	GARÇON:	*Pour. . . , etc. Et pour moi, un diabolo menthe.*

STRUCTURE

The present tense of regular -er *verbs—first and second persons*

Je mange beaucoup. — *I eat* a great deal.
Tu danses bien. — *You dance* well.
Nous parlons anglais. — *We speak* English.
Vous chantez bien. — *You sing* well.

Subject Pronouns	
English	**French**
I	**je**
we	**nous**
you	**tu** (one person you know well)
you	**vous** (one person you do not know well *or* two or more people)

1. Verbs consist of two parts: a *stem*, which carries the meaning, and an *ending*, which indicates the subject.
2. In English, verb endings seldom change (with the exception of the third-person singular in the present tense—*I read*, but *she reads*).
   In French, verb endings are very important, since each verb ending must agree in person (first, second, or third) and number (singular or plural) with the subject.
3. Most French verbs are regular and belong to the first conjugation—that is, their infinitive ends in **-er**.
   The stem is found by dropping the **-er** from the infinitive **(danser → dans-).**
4. To conjugate a regular **-er** verb, add the appropriate endings to the stem:

Structure: The presentation of verbs is initially limited to first- and second-person forms in order to establish the interactions between **vous/tu** ⟷ **je, vous** ⟷ **nous.**

Suggestion, Subject pronouns: Using gestures and yourself as the subject, establish the difference between singular **(je, tu)** and plural **(nous, vous).** Have students perform gestures using themselves as subjects. Then add **tu/vous** distinctions. Have students repeat gestures using **vous** when pointing to you or to a group of students and **tu** when pointing to one other student.

Reminder: Tu is always used when referring to small children and animals; **tu** is also frequently used among colleagues. You may wish to point out the complexities of the **tu/vous** questions with respect to social class, traditions, etc.

Suggestion, Verb conjugation: (1) Establish orally the link between subject and verb ending using several verbs. (2) Introduce orally the sound changes (elision, liaison) for **étudier** and **habiter.** (3) Write on board the four forms of **parler** and **étudier.** (4) Explain the notion of infinitive and the English equivalents of **le présent.**

The exercises have been set up so that you will not need to discuss at this point the spelling changes associated with the **nous** forms of **manger** and **voyager.** These changes will be presented in the written exercises of the Workbook. If you wish to deal with these changes at this time, simply include the written forms of **manger** or **voyager** in step 3 above.

Verb: **danser** *(to dance)*			
Stem	**Subject**	**Ending**	**Conjugated verb form**
(drop **-er** from infinitive) **dans-**	je tu nous vous	**-e** **-es** **-ons** **-ez**	je dans**e** tu dans**es** nous dans**ons** vous dans**ez**

Conjugated verb forms	
parler *(to speak)* **parl-**	**manger** *(to eat)* **mang-**
je parl**e** tu parl**es** nous parl**ons** vous parl**ez**	je mang**e** tu mang**es** nous mange**ons**[1] vous mang**ez**

Although English distinguishes between *I dance, I am dancing,* and *I do dance,* French does not. The equivalent of all three English forms is **je danse.**

Some other **-er** verbs that follow this pattern are **chanter** *(to sing),* **étudier** *(to study),* **voyager** *(to travel)* and **habiter** *(to live).*

When a verb begins with a vowel **(étudier)** or a silent **h (habiter), je** becomes **j'.** This dropping of a sound is called **élision.** Notice that the **tu** form is not elided. In a similar fashion, when a verb begins with a vowel or a silent **h,** the **s** of **nous** and **vous** is pronounced and linked with the following sound. This linking is called **liaison.**

Conjugated verb forms	
étudier *(to study)* **étudi-**	**habiter** *(to live)* **habit-**
j'étudie tu études nous‿**é**tudions vous‿**é**tudiez	**j'h**abite tu habites nous‿**h**abitons vous‿**h**abitez

[1]When writing the **nous** form of **manger,** add an **e** before the **-ons** ending in order to preserve the soft sound of the **g.** This change also occurs in the **nous** form of **voyager** *(to travel):* **nous voyageons.**

Application

E. Replace the subjects in italics and make the necessary changes.

MODÈLE: *Je* danse beaucoup. (vous / tu / nous / je)
Vous dansez beaucoup.
Tu danses beaucoup.
Nous dansons beaucoup.
Je danse beaucoup.

1. *Je* parle anglais. (tu / nous / vous / je)
2. *Nous* chantons bien. (je / vous / tu / nous)
3. *Tu* habites à Paris. (vous / nous / je / tu)
4. *Vous* étudiez le français. (nous / je / tu / vous)
5. *Tu* danses bien. (vous / nous / je / tu)

NOTE GRAMMATICALE

Here are some frequently used French adverbs. An adverb modifies a verb and is usually placed directly *after* the conjugated verb.

bien	well	**souvent**	often	**beaucoup**	a lot
mal	poorly	**rarement**	rarely	**un peu**	a little

Nous étudions **beaucoup.**	We study *a lot.*
Tu chantes **bien.**	You sing *well.*

The adverbs **très** *(very)* and **assez** *(rather, enough)* can be used with all of these adverbs except **beaucoup.** When they are used with **un peu, très** and **assez** take the place of **un: très peu, assez peu.**

Vous dansez **assez bien.**	You dance *fairly well.*
Je voyage **très peu.**	I travel *very little.*
Nous voyageons **souvent.**	We travel *often.*

F. **On pose des questions aux nouveaux élèves.** *(The new students are asked some questions.)* Patrick and Laura are new students in a French secondary school. First, some French students ask Patrick about himself. Play the role of Patrick and answer the questions using the expressions in parentheses.

MODÈLE: Tu parles beaucoup? (non / très peu)
Non, je parle très peu.

1. Tu parles français? (oui, mais *(but)*/très peu)
2. Tu étudies beaucoup? (non, mais/assez)
3. Tu chantes bien? (non, mais/assez bien)
4. Tu danses souvent? (non/rarement)
5. Tu manges beaucoup? (non, mais/assez)
6. Tu voyages beaucoup? (non/très peu)

Then they ask Laura about her and her friends. Play the role of Laura and answer the questions using the expressions in parentheses.

MODÈLE: Vous chantez bien? (non/très mal)
Non, nous chantons très mal.

7. Vous chantez bien? (oui/assez bien)
8. Vous voyagez beaucoup? (oui)
9. Vous parlez anglais? (oui)
10. Vous dansez rarement? (non/souvent)
11. Vous étudiez beaucoup? (oui)
12. Vous mangez beaucoup? (non, mais/assez)

G. **On vous pose des questions.** Imagine that you are at the same school as Patrick and Laura. Answer the questions the French students ask on the basis of your own situation.

1. Tu habites à Paris?
2. Tu parles français?
3. Tu voyages souvent?
4. Tu manges beaucoup?
5. Tu étudies beaucoup?
6. Tu chantes bien?
7. Tu danses souvent?

DÉBROUILLONS-NOUS!

(Petite révision de l'étape)

Ex. H: △

Written Work: See Workbook.

H. **Au café.** You and a friend are seated in a café when another friend arrives to join you. Greet your arriving friend, introduce him/her to your first friend, and order drinks for everyone. Your first friend then finishes his/her drink very quickly and has to leave.

Troisième étape

Point de départ: *Mangeons!*

Transparency, Point de départ: breakfast and lunch food.

Le petit déjeuner

le petit déjeuner: breakfast

un thé au lait

un café au lait

un croissant

un chocolat

Suggestion, Point de départ: Use the transparency of lunch and breakfast food to present new vocabulary. Then act out café scene, having students repeat and/or read it.

Le déjeuner

le déjeuner: lunch

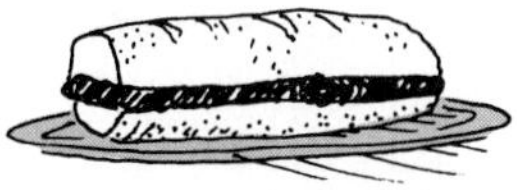

un sandwich **au pâté**

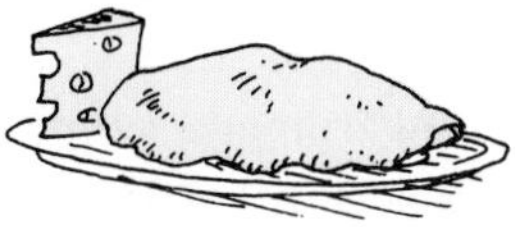

une omelette **au fromage**

un croque-monsieur

with pâté (meat spread)
with cheese
open-faced grilled ham and cheese

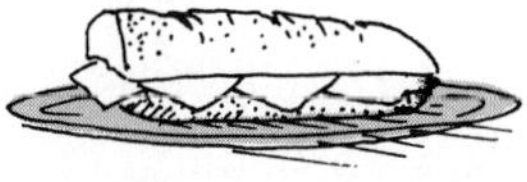

un sandwich **au jambon**

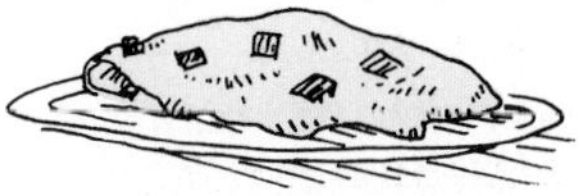

une omelette au jambon

with ham

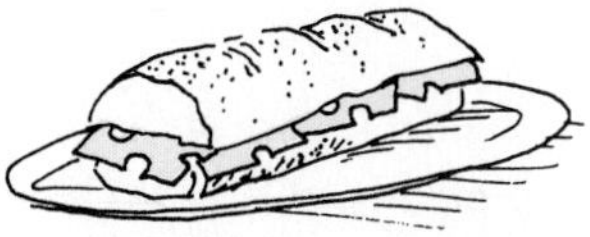

un sandwich au fromage

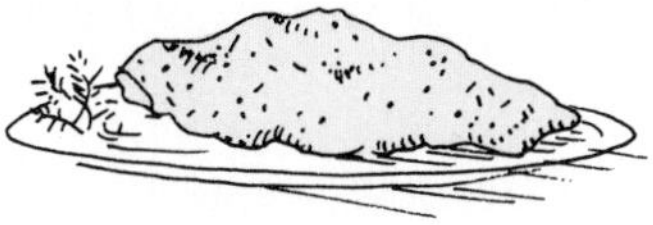

une omelette **aux fines herbes**

un croque-madame

with mixed herbs
open-faced grilled ham and cheese with egg

Une scène au café

ANTOINE: S'il vous plaît, Monsieur.
GARÇON: Oui. Vous désirez?
HÉLÈNE: Je voudrais un sandwich au jambon et un thé citron.
GARÇON: Et pour vous, Monsieur?
ANTOINE: Moi, **je vais prendre** une omelette aux fines herbes et un thé citron **aussi.**
GARÇON: Merci.

je vais prendre: I'll have
aussi: also (too)

Note Culturelle

A **croque-monsieur** is different from what Americans know as a grilled ham and cheese sandwich. To make a **croque-monsieur,** you need two pieces of white bread, a slice of ham, and some grated Swiss cheese. You can also use some **sauce béchamel** (a basic white cream sauce—flour, butter, milk), if you wish. You begin by placing the ham on one slice of bread (spread with the sauce if you are using it). You then place the second slice of bread on top of the ham, sprinkle the grated cheese on top of the sandwich, and grill it in a toaster oven for 5 minutes.

If you wish to put a fried egg on top of the finished sandwich, you then have a **croque-madame.** *Bon appétit!*

À vous! (Exercices de vocabulaire)

Ex. A: ⇄

Variation, Ex. A: After looking at model, students close books and you can give cues from transparency.

A. **Qu'est-ce que tu prends?** You and a friend are in a café. Using the words suggested, discuss what to have for lunch.

MODÈLE: un sandwich au fromage / un sandwich au jambon
— *Qu'est-ce que tu prends?*
— *Je voudrais un sandwich au fromage. Et toi?*
— *Moi, je vais prendre un sandwich au jambon.*

1. un sandwich au jambon / un croque-monsieur
2. une omelette au fromage / un sandwich au fromage
3. un sandwich au pâté / une omelette aux fines herbes
4. un croque-monsieur / une omelette au jambon

Implementation, Exs. B and C: You play the role of **garçon.**

Expansion, Ex. B: Give students the option of saying **Pas de croissants.**

Variation, Ex. C: Students alternate in role of **garcon.**

B. **Le petit déjeuner.** Order the breakfast of your choice in a café.

MODÈLE: — *Vous désirez?*
— *Un café au lait et un croissant, s'il vous plaît.*

C. **Le déjeuner.** With a friend, order the lunch of your choice in a café.

MODÈLE: — *Oui, Mademoiselle (Monsieur). Qu'est-ce que vous désirez?*
— *Un sandwich au jambon et un Coca.*
— *Et pour Monsieur (Mademoiselle)?*
— *Je vais prendre une omelette au fromage et une limonade.*

REPRISE

D. **Salut, . . .** Greet the student whose name is on the piece of paper you receive. Then introduce this person to someone else, who will in turn introduce the two of you to some other people. Continue greeting and introducing until your teacher signals that it is time to say good-bye to the people with whom you are talking.

Ex. D: O

Implementation, Ex. D: Divide class into two equal groups ahead of time. Give half the class small bits of paper, each with the name of one member from the other group.

E. **Qui. . . ?** *(Who. . . ?)* Answer the questions according to your own situation and using expressions from the model.

Suggestion, Ex. E: Do not limit yourself to the model. Continue asking questions so as to involve as many individuals **(vous, je)** and small groups **(vous, nous)** as possible.

MODÈLE: PROFESSEUR: *Qui chante bien?*
ÉLÈVE A: *Moi, je chante bien.*
ÉLÈVE B: *Moi aussi, je chante bien.*
PROFESSEUR: *Ah, vous chantez bien, vous deux. Et vous?*
ÉLÈVE C: *Moi? Non, je chante mal.*

1. Qui habite à. . . ?
2. Qui parle anglais? espagnol *(Spanish)?* allemand *(German)?*
3. Qui voyage beaucoup?
4. Qui étudie beaucoup?
5. Qui chante bien?
6. Qui danse souvent?
7. Qui mange beaucoup?

STRUCTURE

Asking and answering yes/no questions

Tu étudies beaucoup?
Do you study a lot?

Oui, j'étudie beaucoup.
Yes, I study a lot.

Est-ce que vous parlez espagnol?
Do you speak Spanish?

Non, nous ne parlons pas espagnol.
No, we don't speak Spanish.

Tu habites à Lyon, **n'est-ce pas?**
You live in Lyon, *don't you?*

Oui, j'habite à Lyon.
Yes, I live in Lyon.

Structure: Since **est-ce que** and intonation are the most common interrogative forms in conversation and since they present little structural difficulty, they are presented before inversion.

N'est-ce pas, another simple form, has also been included; however, it should be stressed that **n'est-ce pas** is used much less frequently.

Suggestion, Yes/no questions and answers: (1) Write an affirmative statement on board, such as **Tu voyages beaucoup.** Point out intonation (voice falling at end of phrase) and have students repeat the statement. (2) Transform the statement into a question using each of the three question forms and pointing out the change in intonation; have students repeat. (3) Have students answer, affirmatively and negatively (if necessary, go from **très peu** to **ne . . . pas beaucoup).** (4) Repeat step 3 with **Tu habites à Paris?**

A great many questions can be answered *yes* or *no*. There are three basic ways to ask such questions in French:

1. Make your voice rise at the end of a group of words:

   Vous habitez à Bordeaux?

2. Place the expression **est-ce que** before a group of words and make your voice rise at the end:

   Est-ce que tu voyages souvent?

   Note that the phrase **est-ce que** has no meaning other than to signal that a question is coming.

3. Add the phrase **n'est-ce pas** to end a group of words:

   Je chante bien, **n'est-ce pas?**

   The phrase **n'est-ce pas** is the equivalent of *don't you? aren't you? isn't that right?,* and the like at the end of an English sentence. Usually you expect a yes answer.

Vous voyagez beaucoup?

Oui, nous voyageons beaucoup.

Non, nous ne voyageons pas beaucoup.

To answer a yes/no question negatively, place **ne** before and **pas** immediately after the conjugated verb:

NE **PAS**
Je \/ parle \/ espagnol.
Je **ne** chante **pas** très bien.
Nous **ne** mangeons **pas** beaucoup.

If the verb begins with a vowel or a silent **h, ne** becomes **n'**:

Nous **n'**habitons **pas** à Paris.
Je **n'**étudie **pas** assez.

Application

F. Change each statement to a question by making your voice rise at the end of the sentence.

1. Vous désirez.
2. Tu habites à Grenoble.
3. Tu parles français.
4. Vous étudiez beaucoup.
5. Tu chantes bien.

G. Now use **est-ce que** as well as the rise of your voice to change the following statements into questions.

1. Tu manges beaucoup.
2. Vous parlez espagnol.
3. Vous désirez un café.
4. Tu voyages beaucoup.
5. Tu danses souvent.

H. **Posez des questions.** Now it's the turn of the American students (Patrick and Laura) to ask questions of their new French classmates. Using the expressions suggested below, play the roles of Patrick and Laura. Change the infinitive to agree with the subject and vary the question form you use. Begin by asking questions of the whole class.

MODÈLE: vous / parler anglais
Vous parlez anglais? or:
Est-ce que vous parlez anglais?

1. vous / habiter à Paris
2. vous / étudier beaucoup
3. vous / chanter assez bien
4. vous / danser souvent
5. vous / manger beaucoup

Then ask questions of individual students.

MODÈLE: tu / habiter à Paris
Tu habites à Paris? or:
Est-ce que tu habites à Paris?

6. tu / parler anglais
7. tu / étudier souvent
8. tu / danser bien
9. tu / voyager beaucoup
10. tu / chanter souvent

I. **Paul et Françoise.** Because Paul and Françoise are brother and sister, they tend to disagree a lot. Whenever one of them answers a question affirmatively, the other contradicts the answer. Play the roles of Paul and Françoise in answering the following questions.

Ex. I: △

Suggestion, Ex. I: Have one student play the role of Paul, another the role of Françoise, and a third the person who asks the question. Then have students rotate roles.

MODÈLE: Tu chantes bien, n'est-ce pas?
PAUL: *Oui, je chante bien.*
FRANÇOISE: *Mais non, tu ne chantes pas bien!*

1. Tu parles allemand, n'est-ce pas?
2. Tu manges très peu, n'est-ce pas?

Follow-up, Ex. I: Ask similar questions of students in the class; have other students react by agreeing or disagreeing.

3. Tu danses bien, n'est-ce pas?
4. Tu voyages beaucoup, n'est-ce pas?
5. Tu étudies souvent, n'est-ce pas?

Ex. J: ⇄

J. **Toi. . .** Using the expressions given below and asking only yes/no questions, find out as much information as possible about one of your classmates.

MODÈLE: habiter à Chicago
— *Tu habites à Chicago?* or:
Est-ce que tu habites à Chicago?
— *Non, je n'habite pas à Chicago. J'habite à. . .*

1. habiter à New York
2. parler anglais (espagnol, allemand)
3. étudier souvent
4. chanter très bien
5. manger beaucoup
6. voyager beaucoup

DÉBROUILLONS-NOUS!

(Petite révision de l'étape)

Ex. K: ⇄ You can circulate taking lunch orders.

Written Work: See Workbook.

K. **Le déjeuner au café.** You go to a café at lunchtime and run into a classmate, whose name you remember but whom you don't know very well. Greet each other, then order lunch. While waiting for your food, ask each other questions in order to get acquainted. Suggestion: Each of you should find out where the other person lives, what languages he/she speaks, whether he/she is a good singer and dancer, if he/she travels a great deal, etc.

Lexique

Lexique: We have not included English translations in the **Lexique.** This allows students to dintinguish the words they know from those they do not remember. You may wish to review the **Lexique** with the class—either at the end of the chapter or just before you do the Point d'arrivée activities at the end of the unit.

The **Lexique** consists of all new words and expressions presented in the chapter. When reviewing or studying for a test, you can go through the list to see if you know the meaning of each item. In the glossary at the end of the book, you can check the words you do not remember.

Pour se débrouiller

Pour saluer

Bonjour
Salut
Comment ça va?
Ça va (bien)?

Pour répondre à une salutation

Bonjour
Salut
Ça va (bien).
Pas mal.

Pour prendre congé

Au revoir.
Allez, au revoir.
À bientôt.
À tout à l'heure.
Salut.

Pour faire une présentation

Je te présente. . .

Pour commander

Je voudrais. . .
Je vais prendre. . .

Pour être poli (polite)

S'il vous plaît.
Merci (bien).
Je vous en prie.

Thèmes et contextes

Les boissons

un café
un café au lait
un café crème
un chocolat
un citron pressé
un Coca
un diabolo citron (fraise, menthe)
un express
un lait fraise
une limonade
une menthe à l'eau
une orange pressée
un Orangina
un thé citron
un thé au lait
un thé nature

Le déjeuner

un croque-monsieur
un croque-madame
une omelette aux fines herbes
au fromage
au jambon
un sandwich au fromage
au jambon
au pâté

Vocabulaire général

Verbes

chanter
danser
désirer
étudier
habiter
manger
parler
voyager

Adverbes

assez
beaucoup
bien
mal
un peu
rarement
souvent
très peu

Autres expressions

aussi
moi
n'est-ce pas
toi

Chapitre deux

On va à la briocherie

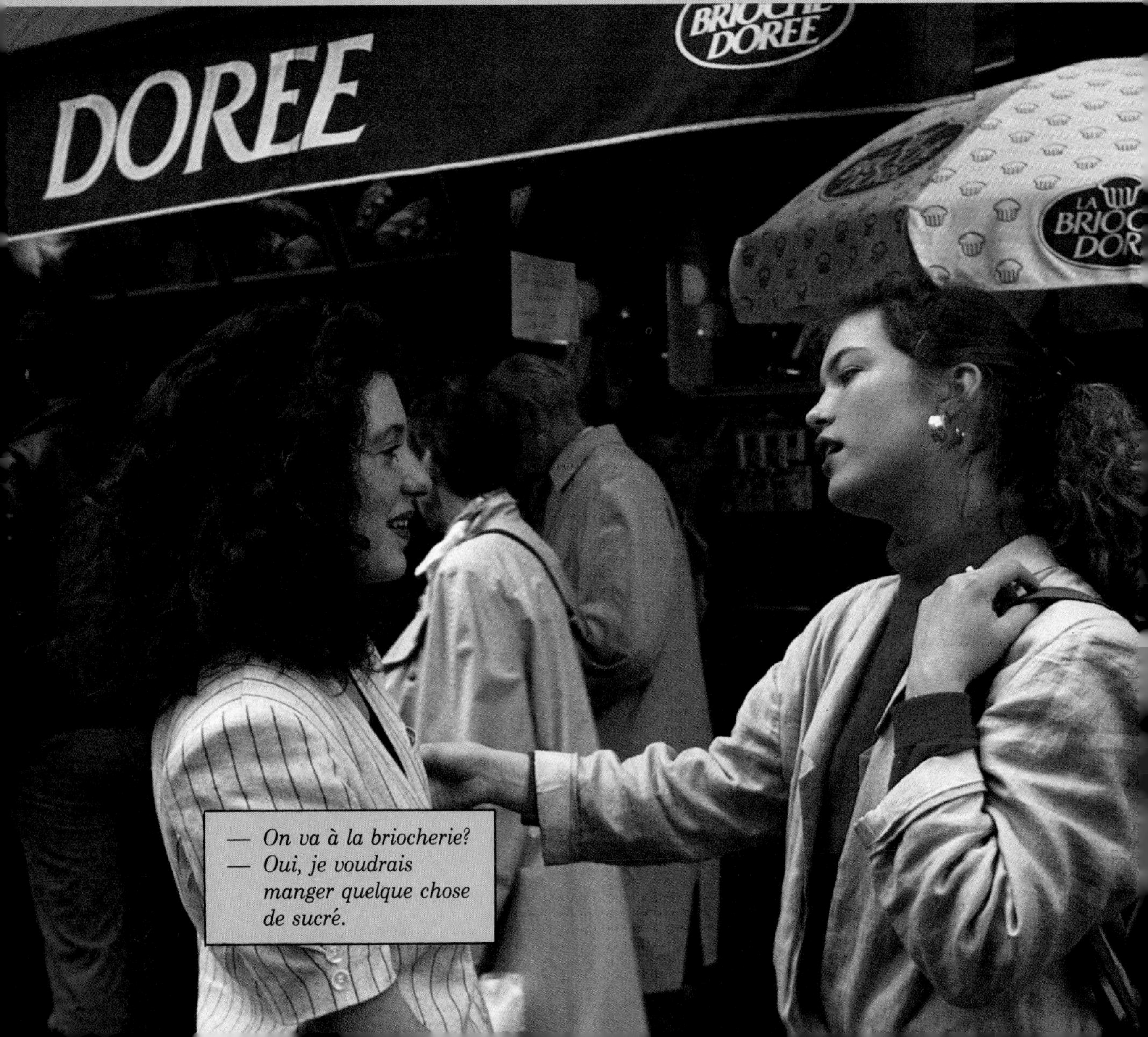

— *On va à la briocherie?*
— *Oui, je voudrais manger quelque chose de sucré.*

Première étape

Point de départ:

À la briocherie

Transparency, Point de départ: briocherie items

Quelque chose de sucré

Quelque chose de sucré: something sweet

un pain au chocolat

une brioche

un pain aux raisins

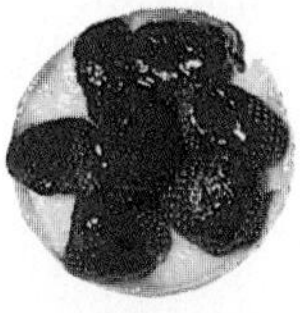

une tartelette aux fraises

un chausson aux pommes

un croissant aux amandes

Suggestion, Point de départ: Begin by doing a mini-planning strategy. Ask students what they do after school if they are hungry, then point out photos of **briocherie** in text. Use the transparency of the briocherie items (or the photos in the book) to present sweet and salty snacks.

Quelque chose de salé

Quelque chose de salé: something salty

une quiche

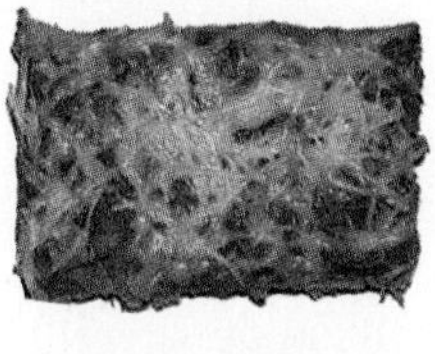

une part de pizza

une tarte à l'oignon

un pain au chocolat: a roll with a piece of chocolate in the middle

une brioche: a light, sweet roll

un pain aux raisins: a roll with raisins

une tartelette: a tart, a small open-faced pie in various flavors—**fraises** (strawberries), **citron** (lemon), plus others

un chausson aux pommes: a puff pastry filled with cooked apple slices

un croissant aux amandes: a croissant with almonds

une quiche: an open-faced pie filled with an egg and cheese mixture

une part de pizza: a slice of pizza

une tarte à l'oignon: a kind of quiche made with onions (a specialty of Alsace)

Note Culturelle

After school, instead of sitting in a café, French high school students will often stop and buy something that they can eat in the street while walking home. A favorite place to go is **une briocherie.** This shop gets its name from **une brioche**—a light, sweet bun raised with yeast and eggs. However, you can buy numerous other treats there, both sweet and salty. Many **briocheries** sell their foods from a counter opening out onto the sidewalk, thus making it a quick and easy way to buy an afternoon snack.

À vous! (Exercices de vocabulaire)

A. **Sucré ou salé?** *(Sweet or salty?)* Answer your friend's question about whether you want something sweet **(sucré)** or salty **(salé)** by specifying the item in parentheses.

MODÈLE: — Tu voudrais quelque chose de sucré? (une brioche)
— *Oui, je voudrais une brioche.*

1. Tu voudrais quelque chose de sucré? (une tartelette aux fraises)
2. Tu voudrais quelque chose de salé? (une tarte à l'oignon)
3. Tu voudrais quelque chose de sucré? (un pain aux raisins)
4. Tu voudrais quelque chose de sucré? (un pain au chocolat)

MODÈLE: — Tu voudrais quelque chose de salé? (une brioche)
— *Non, je voudrais quelque chose de sucré.*
— *Prends* (have) *une brioche.*

5. Tu voudrais quelque chose de sucré? (une part de pizza)
6. Tu voudrais quelque chose de salé? (un croissant aux amandes)
7. Tu voudrais quelque chose de salé? (un chausson aux pommes)
8. Tu voudrais quelque chose de sucré? (une quiche)

B. **Une tartelette aux pommes, s'il vous plaît.** Buy yourself an afternoon snack, choosing each item indicated.

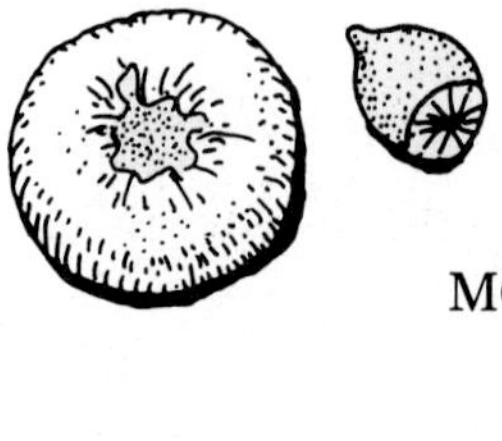

MODÈLE: *Une tartelette au citron, s'il vous plaît.*

1.

2.

3.

Variation, Ex. B: If you have done numbers in the **Étape préliminaire**—Option D, expand the model:—**Une tartelette au citron, s'il vous plaît.—Voilà. C'est quatre francs. —Merci.—Je vous en prie.** Put prices on board: **croissant, pain au chocolat (aux raisins) brioche = 4F; chaussons, tartelettes = 8F; pizza, quiche, tarte à l'oignon = 10F.**

4.

5.

6.

C. **Qu'est-ce que tu voudrais?** *(What would you like?)* Ask some of your classmates what they would like for a snack. They will first indicate whether they want something sweet **(quelque chose de sucré)** or something salty **(quelque chose de salé)**. Suggest an appropriate item to buy. They will agree or choose something else.

Ex. C: ○

MODÈLE: — *Qu'est-ce que tu voudrais?*
— *Moi, je voudrais quelque chose de sucré.*
— *Un pain au chocolat?*
— *Oui, un pain au chocolat.* or:
Non, je voudrais une brioche.

Prononciation: *Pronounced final consonants*

Prononciation: You may wish to point out some words ending in **r** or **c** in which the final consonants *are* pronounced: **Perrier, régulier, premier, blanc, franc, tabac.**

The major exceptions to the rule of unpronounced final consonants are **c, r, f,** and **l.** These four consonants are usually pronounced when they are the last letter of a word. It may be helpful to use the English word **CaReFuL** as a memory aid.

par**c**	bonjou**r**	acti**f**	ma**l**
chi**c**	au revoi**r**	che**f**	espagno**l**

This rule does not apply to the infinitives of **-er** verbs: **parler, chanter, voyager.**

Tu as faim?
Qu'est-ce que tu voudrais?

Pratique

D. Read each word aloud, being careful to pronounce the final consonant unless the word is an infinitive.

1. Marc
2. cher
3. bref
4. mal
5. étudier
6. bonjour
7. sec
8. espagnol
9. amour
10. Montréal
11. manger
12. Jean-Luc
13. fil
14. tarif
15. voyager

REPRISE

E. **Posons des questions.** Use the verbs and the expressions below to ask questions of your classmates. They will answer you according to their situation.

MODÈLE: danser beaucoup
— *Tu danses beaucoup?*
— *Non, je ne danse pas.*

1. habiter à Houston
2. étudier souvent
3. chanter bien
4. voyager beaucoup
5. parler allemand (espagnol, français, anglais)

Now ask the same questions of your teacher.

MODÈLE: — *Vous dansez beaucoup?*
— *Non, . . .*

F. **Une conversation au café.** You and two other students meet in a café at noontime. One of you makes introductions. Then order lunch. While waiting for the waiter to bring your food and beverages, ask each other questions. On a signal from the teacher, the student who arrived last at the café says good-bye to the other two.

Ex. F: You play the role of **garçon.**

STRUCTURE

*The present tense of regular **-er** verbs—third person*

Jacques? ***Il voyage*** *beaucoup.*

Hélène? ***Elle parle*** *espagnol.*

Paul et Philippe? ***Ils chantent*** *bien.*

Marie et Jeanne? ***Elles n'étudient*** *pas beaucoup.*

Claire et Vincent? ***Ils dansent****.*

Suggestion, Verb conjugation: (1) Repeat the gestures which you used previously to explain **je, tu, nous, vous,** then establish references for **il, elle, ils, elles.** (2) Substitute pronouns for proper names: **Francine ⟶ elle.** (3) Establish link between subject and verb ending. Stress sound similarity of **je, tu, il, elle, ils, elles** forms. (4) Point out meaning of **on;** emphasize its plural sense but its singular grammatical status.

Subject pronouns	
English	**French**
he	**il**
she	**elle**
they	**ils** (two or more males or a group of males and females)
they	**elles** (two or more females)

1. **Il, elle, ils,** and **elles** all refer to a particular person or persons. However, when you want to talk about *people in general*, use **on:**

   À Paris on parle français. *In Paris they (people) speak French.*

2. To form the present tense of an **-er** verb in the third person, add the appropriate ending to the stem. Remember, the stem is found by dropping the ending the (**-er**) from the infinitive (**étudier ⟶ étudi-**).

Subject	**Ending**	**Conjugated verb form**		
		danser **dans-**	**parler** **parl-**	**habiter** **habit-**
il	**-e**	il dans**e**	il parl**e**	il habit**e**
elle	**-e**	elle dans**e**	elle parl**e**	elle habit**e**
on	**-e**	on dans**e**	on parl**e**	on habit**e**
ils	**-ent**	ils dans**ent**	ils parl**ent**	ils habit**ent**[1]
elles	**-ent**	elles dans**ent**	elles parl**ent**	elles habit**ent**[1]

Some additional **-er** verbs that fit this model are **travailler** *(to work)* and **gagner** *(to earn).*

[1]Remember to make a liaison between the **s** of **ils** or **elles** and a verb beginning with a vowel or silent **h: ils‿habitent, elles‿étudient.**

Application

G. Replace the subject in italics and make the necessary changes.

MODÈLE: *Je* chante bien. (tu / Monique et moi / elles)
Tu chantes bien.
Monique et moi, nous chantons bien.
Elles chantent bien.

1. *Marie* parle allemand. (Jean et Yvette / Patrick / elles / je / nous)
2. *Il* habite à Montréal. (elle / ils / elles / tu / vous / je)
3. *Hervé* travaille rarement. (ils / on / nous / elles / tu / je)
4. *Elle* ne danse pas. (ils / il / Jeanne et moi / on / tu / je)

H. **Encore des questions.** *(Some more questions.)* Your French classmates are curious to know more about American students in France with you. Answer their questions using the expressions in parentheses.

MODÈLES: Est-ce que John parle espagnol? (non)
Non, il ne parle pas espagnol.

Est-ce que Mary et Dawn voyagent beaucoup? (très peu)
Non, elles voyagent très peu.

1. Est-ce que Robert habite à Chicago? (à Milwaukee)
2. Est-ce qu'on parle français à Boston? (anglais)
3. Est-ce que Nancy et Susan parlent français? (non)
4. Est-ce que Beverly travaille? (oui)
5. Est-ce qu'elle gagne beaucoup? (très peu)
6. Est-ce que George et Bill voyagent souvent? (rarement)
7. Est-ce que Mark chante bien? (mal)
8. Est-ce que Carol mange beaucoup? (oui)

I. **Michèle et Daniel.** One of your French classmates has an older sister **(Michèle)** and an older brother **(Daniel)**. Using the expressions below, first ask your classmates questions about Michèle. Ex. I: ⇄

MODÈLE: habiter à Paris
Est-ce que Michèle habite à Paris?

1. étudier beaucoup   2. parler anglais   3. manger beaucoup

Now ask questions about Daniel.

4. habiter à Paris   5. travailler   6. gagner beaucoup

Finally, ask questions about the two of them.

7. voyager beaucoup
8. étudier souvent
9. chanter bien
10. danser souvent

DÉBROUILLONS-NOUS!

(Petite révision de l'étape)

Ex. J: □ Model the conversation with two pairs of students before having class work in groups of four.

Written Work: See Workbook.

J. **Devant la briocherie.** *(In front of the briocherie.)* You and a friend are standing in line waiting your turn to buy something at the **briocherie.** First, discuss what you would like to eat. Second, greet two other people who are standing in line and introduce them to your friend. Third, after the other two leave, answer your friend's questions about the two people to whom you have just introduced him/her.

Deuxième étape

Point de départ:

Bonjour! . . . Au revoir!

Suggestion, Point de départ: Act out dialogue (books closed). Discuss with students the difference in level of language between this conversation and the one in Chapter I, **Étape 1.** Then have students read and/or repeat the dialogue and expressions.

As they come out of the **briocherie,** Jean-Claude Merrien and his friend Alain Duvalier run into two friends of Jean-Claude's parents, Monsieur et Madame Maire.

M. ET MME MAIRE: Bonjour, Jean-Claude.
JEAN-CLAUDE: Ah, bonjour, Monsieur. Bonjour, Madame. **Comment allez-vous?** (How are you?)
M. MAIRE: Très bien, merci. Et vous?
JEAN-CLAUDE: **Je vais très bien,** (I am very well.) merci. Je voudrais vous présenter **mon ami,** (my friend) Alain Duvalier. Monsieur et Madame Maire.
M. ET MME MAIRE: Bonjour, Alain.
ALAIN: **Enchanté,** (Delighted (to meet you)) Madame, Monsieur.
MME MAIRE: Ah, tu manges une brioche. Et toi, Jean-Claude, un chausson aux pommes. C'est bon?
JEAN-CLAUDE: Oh, oui. C'est délicieux.
M. ET MME MAIRE: Au revoir, Jean-Claude. Au revoir, Alain.
JEAN-CLAUDE ET ALAIN: Au revoir, Madame. Au revoir, Monsieur.

Les salutations

Bonjour.
Comment allez-vous?
(Je vais) très bien, merci. Et vous?

Les présentations

Je voudrais vous présenter. . .
Enchanté(e).
Bonjour.

On prend congé

Au revoir.
À tout à l'heure.
À bientôt.

Note Culturelle

In formal situations, **Monsieur, Madame,** or **Mademoiselle** always accompany **Bonjour** and **Au revoir.** Many of the expressions in *Chapitre premier* can be used both with friends and in more formal situations; others cannot. Expressions such as **Salut, ça va?**, and **Allez, au revoir** are quite informal and would not be appropriate to use with older people whom you do not know very well. On the other hand, expressions such as **Comment allez-vous?, Je voudrais vous présenter,** and **Enchanté** are too formal to use with young people of your own age.

À vous! (Exercices de vocabulaire)

A. **Répondons.** Complete the dialogue with an appropriate expression.

MODÈLE: Bonjour, Madame. (Monsieur)
Bonjour, Monsieur.

1. Bonjour, Henri. (Catherine)
2. Comment allez-vous, Étienne? (Monsieur Dupont)
3. Madame Piquet, je voudrais vous présenter mon amie, Anne Praz.
4. Au revoir, Mademoiselle. (Madame)
5. À bientôt, Dominique. (Thierry)

B. **Bonjour, Madame (Monsieur, Mademoiselle).** Greet and shake hands with your teacher, introduce a classmate to him/her, and then say good-bye.

Salut!

REPRISE

Ex. C. □

C. **Écoutez bien.** *(Listen carefully.)* Play the roles of the following students, and model their conversation. Anne asks Marc a question. After Marc answers, Jacques asks Chantal what he said. If Chantal has been listening, she should be able to answer with no problem.

MODÈLE: parler

ANNE:	*Marc, tu parles anglais?*
MARC:	*Non, je ne parle pas anglais.*
JACQUES:	*Chantal, est-ce que Marc parle anglais?*
CHANTAL:	*Non, il ne parle pas anglais.*

1. habiter à. . .
2. étudier beaucoup
3. manger beaucoup
4. voyager beaucoup
5. chanter souvent
6. chanter bien
7. parler espagnol (allemand, français)
8. travailler / gagner beaucoup

D. **Mon ami(e).** *(My friend.)* Mention the name of one of your friends to some of your classmates. They will ask you questions about this friend, using the following verbs: **habiter, parler, étudier, chanter, danser, manger, voyager, travailler, gagner.**

Ex. D. O

MODÈLE: Mon amie Carole
— *Est-ce qu'elle habite à New York?*
— *Non, elle habite à. . .*

STRUCTURE

Structure: At this point, we only consider sentences where both verbs have the same subject.

The conjugated verb followed by an infinitive

Suggestion, Verb plus infinitive: (1) Ask a student: **Vous dansez? Vous dansez bien? Vous aimez danser? Et vous, vous aimez danser? Vous n'aimez pas danser? Et Georges, il aime danser? (Tu aimes danser?)** (2) Write some of the sentences on board to show sound similarities and spelling differences.

J'aime chanter.	*I like to sing.*
Est-ce que **tu aimes étudier?**	*Do you like to study?*
Elles n'aiment pas travailler.	*They don't like to work.*
Est-ce que **tu voudrais danser?**	*Would you like to dance?*

When there are two verbs in the same sentence or in the same part of a sentence, the first verb is conjugated (that is, made to agree with the subject), but the second verb remains in the infinitive form. This construction occurs frequently with the verb **aimer** *(to like, to love)* and the expressions **je voudrais** and **tu voudrais** (*I would like* and *you would like*).

Moi, j'aime danser!

Moi, je n'aime pas danser!

Application

Ex. E: ⇄

E. **Tu voudrais. . . ?** At a party, you try to impress a boy or a girl whom you like by asking in French if he/she would like to do certain things. Use the suggested expressions to form your questions. He/she can answer either affirmatively or negatively.

MODÈLE: manger
— *Tu voudrais manger?*
— *Oui, je voudrais manger.* or:
Non, je voudrais danser.

1. danser
2. chanter
3. manger quelque chose de sucré
4. manger quelque chose de salé
5. boire *(to drink)* quelque chose
6. parler français
7. habiter à Paris

Ex. F: ⇄

Preparation, Ex. F: Ask class: **Qui aime danser? Qui n'aime pas danser?, Qui aime manger les choses sucrées?** Etc.

F. **Moi, je n'aime pas. . .** Indicate whether or not you like to do the following things. Then check with a classmate to see if he/she has the same likes and dislikes as you. If your classmate gives the same *positive* response as you, he/she will add **aussi** *(also)* to the answer. If your classmate gives the same *negative* response as you, he/she will add **non plus** *(either)*.

MODÈLE: danser
— *J'aime (beaucoup) danser. Et toi?*
— *Moi, j'aime (beaucoup) danser aussi.* or:

— *Je n'aime pas danser. Et toi?*
— *Je n'aime pas danser non plus.*

1. chanter
2. voyager
3. manger les choses *(things)* sucrées
4. manger les choses salées
5. danser
6. étudier
7. travailler

DÉBROUILLONS-NOUS!

(Petite révision de l'étape)

Ex. G: △. Model the conversation with three students before dividing class into groups of three.

G. **Bonjour, Monsieur (Madame).** While walking with a friend, you run into a French colleague of your parents, Monsieur (Madame) Laval. Introduce Monsieur (Madame) Laval to your friend. Tell Monsieur (Madame) Laval about your friend—where he/she lives and one thing he/she likes to do. Monsieur (Madame) Laval will ask the two of you questions about other activities. On a signal from the teacher, Monsieur (Madame) Laval will say good-bye.

POURQUOI?

A few days after her arrival in France, a teenage exchange student from the United States comes home from school rather late in the afternoon. When she arrives at the apartment of her host family, she finds her French "mother" and "father" seated in the living room with several of their friends. The young American says hello to her French parents, nods to the other people, and sits quietly on a chair in the corner. After a few moments, however, she senses that her French parents disapprove of something. What is the problem?

a. In France, when you come home late, you are expected to explain where you've been.
b. When you enter a group in France, it is customary to shake hands with everyone.
c. French young people do not usually sit with their parents' friends.
d. In France, it is impolite to sit in the corner.

Answer, Pourquoi?: b. See your teacher guide for further explanation.

Suggestion, Pourquoi?: Have all students give their answers. If no consensus, discuss the various possibilities. Point out that you also shake hands when *leaving* a group.

Written Work: See Workbook.

Lexique

Pour se débrouiller

Pour saluer
Comment allez-vous?

Pour répondre à une salutation
Je vais (très) bien.

Pour faire une présentation
Je vous présente...
Enchanté(e).

Thèmes et contextes

La briocherie
une brioche
un chausson aux pommes
un croissant aux amandes
un pain au chocolat
un pain aux raisins
une part de pizza
quelque chose de salé
quelque chose de sucré
une quiche
une tarte à l'oignon
une tartelette au citron
une tartelette aux fraises

Vocabulaire général

Noms
une chose

Verbes
gagner
travailler

Autres expressions
non plus

Chapitre trois

Tu aimes les fast-food?

— *Mireille, tu aimes les fast-food?*
— *Pas beaucoup. Et toi?*

Première étape

Point de départ:

Quick? Macdo?

Thierry, Angélique, and Francine are downtown at lunchtime.

FRANCINE:	On mange quelque chose?	
THIERRY:	Oui, **pourquoi pas?** On va au Quick?	Why not?
ANGÉLIQUE:	**D'accord.** J'aime bien les fast-food.	OK

Suggestion, Point de départ: Ask students about French food and French restaurants in the U.S. Then ask them what aspects of American food and American restaurants they would expect to be popular in France.

Explain to students that **le fast-food** refer to a fast food restaurant, while **les fast-food** refers to the food served there. **Les fast-food** is an irregular formation and has no **s** in the plural.

Note Culturelle

Fast-food restaurants are almost as popular in France as they are in the United States. The best known is McDonald's, sometimes called **Macdo** in French. However, there are numerous Burger King restaurants, including two on the famous Champs-Élysées in Paris. The major French fast-food restaurant chain is called **Le Quick,** run by a supermarket corporation called **Casino.** It has restaurants in all the big cities.

À vous! (Exercices de vocabulaire)

A. **Le fast-food en France et aux États-Unis.** *(The fast food restaurant in France and the United States.)* Study the menu and picture below. In what ways are French fast-food restaurants similar to their American counterparts? What differences do you notice?

B. **On mange quelque chose?** When asked this question, the people pictured below all answered **oui,** but each had a different place in mind. Match each statement with the appropriate person on the basis of the clues in the drawings.

1.

2.

3.

4.

Ex. B, Answers: 1. b 2. d 3. a 4. c

a. Je voudrais manger au Quick.
b. J'aime bien les fast-food américains. Allons au Macdo.
c. Je n'aime pas les fast-food. Je voudrais manger dans un café.
d. Moi, je voudrais acheter *(to buy)* quelque chose de sucré à La Brioche Chaude.

C. **On va au Quick?** Suggest to a friend that you go to the following places for a bite to eat. Your friend can either agree or suggest a different place.

Ex. C: ⇄

MODÈLE: au Quick
— *On mange quelque chose?*
— *Oui, pourquoi pas?*
— *On va au Quick?*
— *D'accord.* or:
Non, je n'aime pas Le Quick. Allons au Macdo.

1. au Macdo
2. au Burger King
3. au Café Minet
4. au Quick

Prononciation: *Final consonant +* ***e***

If a word ends in an **e** without an accent mark, the preceding consonant is always pronounced. This **e**, called a mute **e**, remains silent. If there is a double consonant before the **e**, only one consonant sound is heard.

chante	femme	fromage
parle	salade	omelette

Pratique

D. Read each pair of words aloud, being careful not to pronounce the final consonant of the first word and making sure to pronounce the final consonant before the **e** of the second word.

1. français, française
2. américain, américaine
3. allemand, allemande
4. Denis, Denise
5. François, Françoise
6. part, parte

E. Say each word aloud, being careful to pronounce a final consonant before an **e** and not to pronounce a final consonant alone (with the exception of **c, r, f, l**).

1. Madame
2. bien
3. limonade
4. Rome
5. chocolat
6. pour
7. jambon
8. Saint-Denis
9. chose
10. croissant
11. tarte
12. Vittel
13. voudrais
14. danse
15. parc
16. chef

REPRISE

F. **Bonjour!. . . Salut!. . .** Play the roles of the people in each of the following situations. Pay attention to the level of language—formal or informal.

Ex. F: ⇄ and △

Variation, Ex. F: Have students act out the roles, using appropriate greetings.

Henri *Jean-Jacques*

MODÈLE: — *Salut, Jean-Jacques.*
— *Salut, Henri. Ça va?*
— *Oui, ça va. Et toi?*
— *Oh, ça va bien.*

1. M. Ventoux *Chantal*

2. *Sylvie* *Renée*

3. *Claude Angèle Henri*

4. *Martine Annick Mme Leroux*

5. *Mme Didier Gérard*

6. *Ahmed Jean*

G. **Qui aime danser?** Survey several classmates about their attitudes towards the following topics. Be prepared to report your results to the class. Ex. G: O

MODÈLE: danser
— *Tim, tu aimes danser?*
— *Oui, j'aime danser.*
— *Louise, tu aimes danser?*
— *Non, je n'aime pas danser.*
— *Ralph, tu aimes danser?*
— *Non, je n'aime pas danser non plus.*
— *Tim aime danser. Louise et Ralph n'aiment pas danser.*

1. danser
2. étudier
3. parler français
4. manger les choses sucrés
5. manger les choses salés
6. voyager
7. chanter

Suggestion, être:
(1) Have students repeat conjugation of a regular **-er** verb while you write pronouns in two groups: **je, tu, il, elle, on, ils, elles / nous, vous.** (2) Have students repeat conjugation of **être** while you write pronouns in five groups: **je / tu, il, elle / ils, elles / nous / vous.** (3) Have students repeat in negative. (4) Add written verb forms to pronouns.

STRUCTURE

The present tense of the irregular verb ***être***

Sylvie **est** de New York.	Sylvia *is* from New York.
Ils ne **sont** pas ici. Ils **sont** à Montréal.	They *are* not here. They'*re* in Montreal.
—Vous **êtes** américains?	—*Are* you American?
—Non, nous **sommes** canadiens.	—No, we *are* Canadian.

Some French verbs do not follow the pattern of conjugation you have learned for regular **-er** verbs. They are called *irregular verbs* because they do not follow a fixed pattern. One of the most frequently used irregular verbs is **être** *(to be)*. Here are its present-tense forms:

être	
je **suis**	nous **sommes**
tu **es**	vous **êtes**
il, elle, on **est**	ils, elles **sont**

The interrogative and negative forms follow the same patterns as for **-er** verbs.

—**Est-ce que** tu es française? —Non, je **ne** suis **pas** française. Je suis américaine.

Application

H. Replace the subject in italics and make the necessary changes.

1. *Éric* est à Bordeaux. (Je / Hélène et moi / tu / elles)
2. *Monique* est de Paris. (Jean-Jacques / je / vous / ils / nous / tu)
3. Est-ce que *Mathieu* est au Macdo? (Nathalie / Monsieur et Madame Ledoux / vous / tu / on / nous)
4. *Yves et Mathilde* ne sont pas au café. (Jean-Luc / je / Denise / vous / elles / on / tu)

I. **Marielle n'est pas ici. Elle est à Nice.** You notice that the classroom is almost empty just two days before a vacation break. When the teacher calls on certain people, you explain that they are not here and, using the cities given below, you indicate where they are.

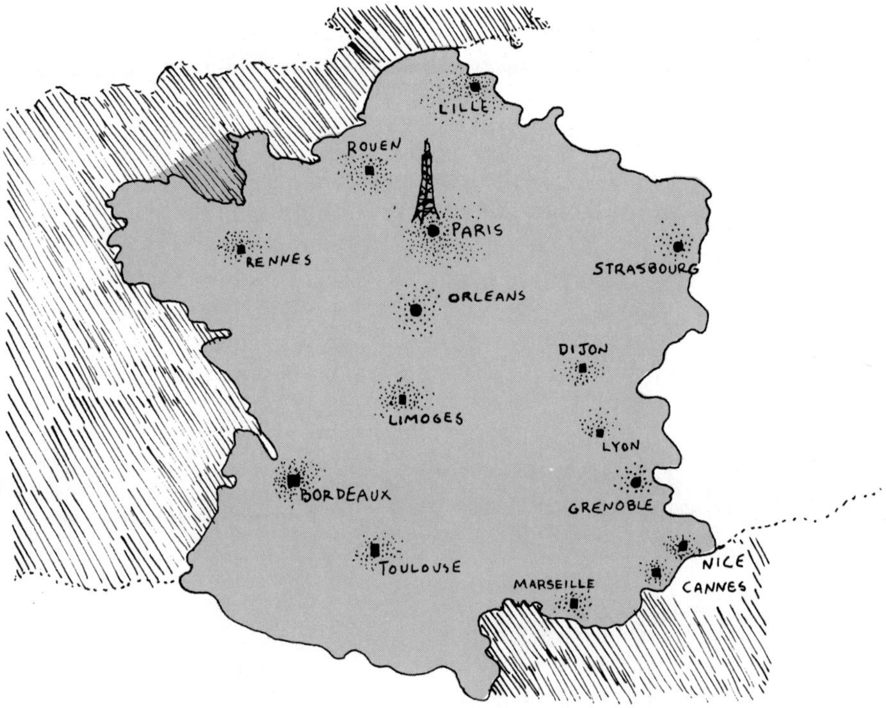

Le savez vous?

Paris is the largest city in France. What is the second largest?
a) Marseille
b) Lyon
c) Bordeaux

réponse

MODÈLE: Renée / Strasbourg
Renée? Elle n'est pas ici. Elle est à Strasbourg.

1. Georges / Toulouse
2. Chantal et Marcel / Grenoble
3. Michèle et Jeanne / Cannes
4. Vincent / Orléans
5. Brigitte / Bordeaux
6. Jean-Pierre et Henri / Rennes

J. **Ils ne sont pas de Paris.** Even though many of your French friends live in Paris, they were not born there. When you ask them if they are from Paris, they tell you where they are from. Using the cities below, ask and answer questions according to the models.

Ex. J: ⇄

MODÈLES: Pierre / Toulouse
— *Est-ce que Pierre est de Paris?*
— *Non, il n'est pas de Paris. Il est de Toulouse.*

vous / Marseille
— *Vous êtes de Paris?*
— *Non, nous ne sommes pas de Paris. Nous sommes de Marseille.*

1. Jacqueline / Lyon
2. tu / Nice
3. Étienne et Dominique / Lille
4. vous / Rouen
5. Édouard / Limoges
6. Yvette et Monique / Dijon

DÉBROUILLONS-NOUS!

a

(Petite révision de l'étape)

K. **Échange.** Ask a classmate the following set of questions. After answering them, he/she will ask you the same set of questions.

Ex. K: ⇄

1. Tu habites à. . . , n'est-ce pas?
2. Tu es de. . . aussi?
3. Tu parles espagnol (allemand)?
4. Tu manges beaucoup?
5. Tu aimes chanter?
6. Tu chantes bien?
7. Tu voyages souvent?
8. Tu voudrais visiter Paris?

Written Work: See Workbook.

Deuxième étape

Point de départ:

On va au Quick!

Transparency, Point de départ: Quick menu board

Reminder, Point de départ: One difference between American and French fast-food restaurants is that in France, beer and wine are served, while in America they are not.

ANGÉLIQUE:	Qu'est-ce que tu manges?	
THIERRY:	Pour moi, un Giant, des **frites,** et un milk-shake au chocolat.	french fries
FRANCINE:	Moi, je voudrais un BigCheese, des frites et un Coca.	
ANGÉLIQUE:	D'accord. Mademoiselle, **deux** Giants, un BigCheese, **trois** frites, un Coca, un milk-shake au chocolat et un milk-shake **à la vanille.**	two / three vanilla
THIERRY:	Tiens! Voilà Jeanne.	
ANGÉLIQUE:	Elle est américaine, n'est-ce pas?	
THIERRY:	Non, non, elle est canadienne. Elle est de Montréal. Elle chante très bien—en français et en anglais.	
FRANCINE:	**C'est chouette, ça.**	That's great (neat).

À vous! (Exercices de vocabulaire)

A. **Un, deux, trois. . . au Quick.** On the basis of the drawings below, order food for you and your friends.

MODÈLE:
Deux cheeseburgers, deux frites, un Coca et un milk-shake à la vanille.

1.

2.

Le savez-vous?

Many older French people complain about the increased presence of *franglais* on television, in the newspaper, and on the streets. What is *franglais*?

a) a slang spoken and understood mainly by high school students.
b) a language spoken on some islands between France and England.
c) the large number of words from American English that have found their way into the French language.

réponse

Follow-up, Ex. A: Have students give their own orders from the Quick menu.

REPRISE

Follow-up, Ex. B: Find out where each of the students in the class is from, either by asking them yourself, or by having students do so and reporting back to the class.

B. **Ils habitent à. . . , mais ils sont de. . .** The French **lycée** *(high school)* students are very interested in the backgrounds of you and your fellow American students. Using the cities given below, explain where the following people live and where they come from.

MODÈLE: Neil / Louisville / Chicago
— *Est-ce que Neil est de Louisville?*
— *Non, il habite à Louisville, mais il est de Chicago.*

→ c

1. Carolyn / Los Angeles / San Francisco
2. tu / Minneapolis / Philadelphia
3. vous / Denver / Nashville
4. Janet et Pat / Dallas / Atlanta
5. Josh / Boston / Indianapolis

STRUCTURE

Adjectives of nationality

Suggestion, Adjectives of nationality: (1) Establish the idea of agreement by having students say **Je suis (je ne suis pas) américain/américaine.** (2) Draw male and female figures on board. Introduce nationalities in two groups—those that have no sound difference between *m/f* and those that have a sound difference. For the second group, begin with the feminine and tell students to drop the final consonant sound. (Point out **espagnol** as an exception.) (3) Write some forms on board to illustrate spelling and pronunciation changes. Begin with the masculine form in this case.

Jacques est **français.** Jacques is *French.*	Bernard et Yves sont **canadiens.** Bernard and Yves are *Canadian.*
Claire est **française.** Claire is *French.*	Yvette et Simone sont **canadiennes.** Yvette and Simone are *Canadian.*

In French, adjectives agree in *gender* (masculine or feminine) and *number* (singular or plural) with the person or thing to which they refer.

1. Some adjectives have identical masculine and feminine forms:

Il est **belge.**	He is *Belgian.*	Elle est **belge.**	She is *Belgian.*
Il est **russe.**	He is *Russian.*	Elle est **russe.**	She is *Russian.*
Il est **suisse.**	He is *Swiss.*	Elle est **suisse.**	She is *Swiss.*

2. Many adjectives have a feminine form that consists of the masculine form + **-e:**

Il est **français.** Elle est **française.**
Il est **anglais.** Elle est **anglaise.**
Il est **américain.** Elle est **américaine.**
Il est **mexicain.** Elle est **mexicaine.**
Il est **allemand** *(German).* Elle est **allemande.**
Il est **espagnol** *(Spanish).* Elle est **espagnole.**
Il est **japonais** *(Japanese).* Elle est **japonaise.**
Il est **chinois** *(Chinese).* Elle est **chinoise.**
Il est **sénégalais** *(Senegalese).* Elle est **sénégalaise.**

Supplementary Vocabulary: algérien(ne), argentin(e), australien(ne), autrichien(ne), danois(e), grec(que), iranien(ne), israélien(ne), libanais(e), marocain(e), norvégien(ne), polonais(e), portugais(e), soudanais(e), suédois(e), tunisien(ne), turc(que), vénézuélien(ne)

3. Finally, some adjectives have a feminine form that consists of the masculine form + **-ne:**

Il est **haïtien.** Elle est **haïtienne.**
Il est **italien.** Elle est **italienne.**
Il est **canadien.** Elle est **canadienne.**
Il est **égyptien.** Elle est **égyptienne.**
Il est **vietnamien.** Elle est **vietnamienne.**

4. To form the plural of all these adjectives, simply add **-s** to the masculine or feminine singular form. If the singular form already ends in **-s,** the singular and the plural are the same:

Ils sont **allemands.** Elles sont **chinoises.**
Ils sont **français.** Elles sont **italiennes.**

Application

C. **Et Roger?** Answer the questions according to the model. In the first six items, the first person is female and the second is male.

MODÈLE: Jacqueline est française. Et Roger?
Il est français aussi.

1. Janet est américaine. Et Tom?
2. Sophia est italienne. Et Vittorio?
3. Olga est russe. Et Boris?
4. Fatima est égyptienne. Et Ahmed?
5. Miko est japonaise. Et Yoshi?
6. Juanita est mexicaine. Et Artemio?

Now the first person is male and the second is female.

MODÈLE: Paul est américain. Et Linda?
Elle est américaine aussi.

7. Harold est anglais. Et Priscilla?
8. Maurice est canadien. Et Jeanne-Marie?
9. Gunther est allemand. Et Helga?
10. Tchen est chinois. Et Sun?
11. Alfred est suisse. Et Jeannette?
12. Yves est français. Et Mireille?

Variation, Ex. D: Teach students the expression **Je suis d'origine** + feminine adjective. Then have students tell you and/or each other about their nationalities and their ethnic backgrounds.

D. **Les nationalités.** You are with a group of young people from all over the world. Find out their nationalities by making the indicated assumption and then correcting your mistake.

MODÈLE: Marguerite — portugais / New York
— *Est-ce que Marguerite est portugaise?*
— *Mais non, elle est de New York.*
— *Ah, bon. Elle est américaine.*
— *C'est ça. Elle est américaine.*

Follow-up, Ex. D: Have each student choose a new identity: i.e., a new nationality and city of origin. Have other students try to find out by asking, **Tu es italienne? Tu es de Berlin?** Etc.

1. Monique — suisse / Paris
2. Lin-Tao *(m.)* — japonais / Pékin
3. Francesca — mexicain / Rome
4. Jean-Pierre — belge / Québec
5. Verity — américain / Londres
6. Fumiko et Junko *(f.)* — égyptien / Tokyo
7. Juan et Pablo — espagnol / Guadalajara
8. Natasha et Svetlana *(f.)* — canadien / Moscou
9. Eberhard *(m.)* et Heidi — suisse / Berlin

STRUCTURE

Nouns of profession

Most nouns that refer to work or occupation follow the same patterns as adjectives of nationality.

1. Some nouns have identical masculine and feminine forms:

Il est **secrétaire.**	Elle est **secrétaire.**
Il est **médecin.**	Elle est **médecin.**
Il est **professeur** *(teacher).*	Elle est **professeur.**
Il est **ingénieur** *(engineer).*	Elle est **ingénieur.**
Il est **élève** *(student).*	Elle est **élève.**

2. Some nouns have a feminine form that consists of the masculine form + **-e:**

Il est **avocat** *(lawyer).*	Elle est **avocate.**
Il est **étudiant** *(college student).*	Elle est **étudiante.**

Suggestion, Nouns of profession: Using the male and female drawings on the board, distinguish between professions with a sound change between French and English and those that don't have a change. Proceed in a manner similar to the one used with the adjectives of nationality.

Reminder: If necessary, point out the difference in article usage between **Je suis avocat** and *I am a lawyer.*

3. Other nouns have a feminine form that consists of the masculine form + **-ne:**

Il est **mécanicien** *(mechanic).*	Elle est **mécanicienne.**
Il est **pharmacien** *(druggist).*	Elle est **pharmacienne.**

4. Nouns of profession, like adjectives of nationality, form the plural by adding **-s** to the masculine or feminine singular:

Ils sont **avocats.**	Elles sont **professeurs.**
Ils sont **mécaniciens.**	Elles sont **étudiantes.**

Application

E. **Voilà Monsieur Chevalier. Il est avocat.** You and a friend are attending a function with your parents. You point out to your friend various acquaintances of your parents and state their professions.

MODÈLES: Monsieur Chevalier / avocat
Voilà Monsieur Chevalier. Il est avocat.

M. et Mme Richard / pharmacien
Voilà Monsieur et Madame Richard. Ils sont pharmaciens.

1. Monsieur et Madame Aubert / médecin
2. Madame Forestier / professeur
3. Madame Longin / avocat
4. Monsieur Cordier / pharmacien
5. Monsieur Dumoulin / avocat
6. Nicole / élève dans un lycée
7. Patrick / élève dans un lycée
8. Georges Denis / secrétaire
9. Madame Beaujour / ingénieur
10. Mademoiselle Jacquier / mécanicien
11. Monsieur Gautier / mécanicien
12. Catherine Raymond et Jeanne Duval / étudiant

F. **Est-ce que tu voudrais être avocat(e)?** From the following list, choose several careers or jobs that you would like and several that you would not like.

MODÈLE: *Je voudrais être médecin, mais je ne voudrais pas être avocat(e).*

1. architecte
2. comptable *(accountant)*
3. dentiste
4. avocat(e)
5. journaliste
6. professeur
7. secrétaire
8. pharmacien(ne)
9. homme (femme) d'affaires *(businessman, businesswoman)*
10. mécanicien(ne)
11. ingénieur
12. musicien(ne)
13. agriculteur (-trice) *(farmer)*
14. acteur (actrice)
15. astronaute

Variation, Ex. F: Have students ask each other: **Tu voudrais être . . . ?** Then ask them about others: **Est-ce que . . . voudrait être dentiste?** or **Qu'est-ce que . . . voudrait être?** or **Qui voudrait être . . . ?** (Answer for yourself and for other people.)

DÉBROUILLONS-NOUS!

(Petite révision de l'étape)

G. **Au Quick.** You and two friends decide to have lunch at a nearby Quick fast-food restaurant. You talk about what you will eat. Then one of you places the order. While eating, each of you notices an acquaintance from another country. You each point this person out to your friends and tell them something about him/her.

Ex. G: △. Model this dialogue with three students before dividing class into groups.

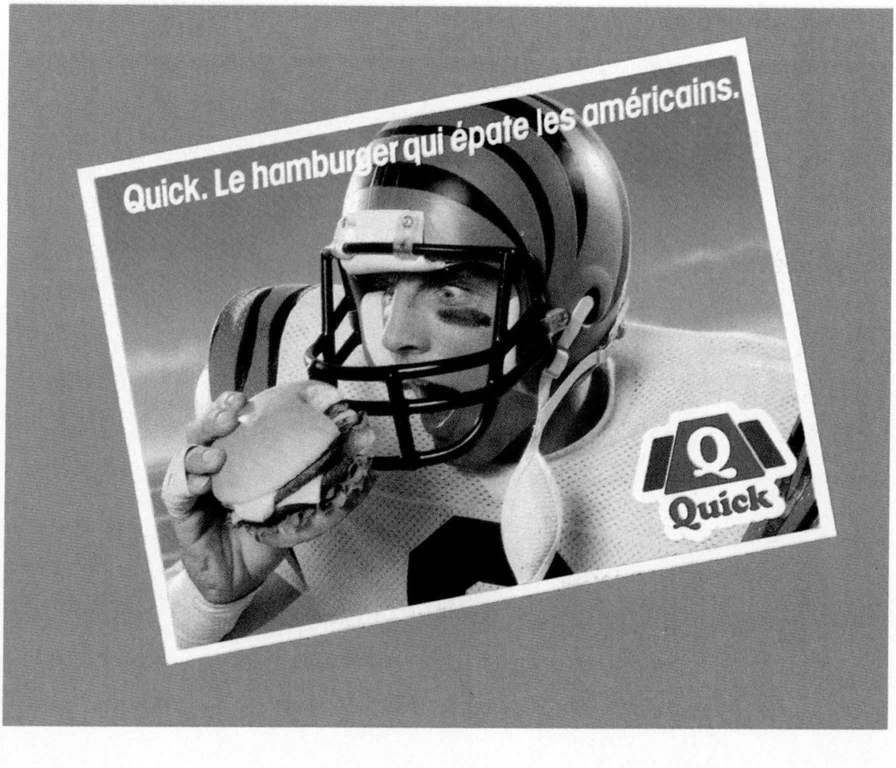

Suggestion, photo: Ask students why they think a French ad would feature an American football player. What is this publicity gimmick? Why might French young people be persuaded by this ad?

Written Work: See Workbook.

Lexique

Thèmes et contextes

Les nationalités

allemand(e)
américain(e)
anglais(e)
belge
canadien(ne)
chinois(e)
égyptien(ne)
espagnol(e)
français(e)
haïtien(ne)
italien(ne)
japonais(e)
mexicain(e)
portugais(e)
russe
sénégalais(e)
suisse
vietnamien(ne)

Les professions

un(e) astronaute
un acteur (-trice)
un(e) architecte
un(e) avocat(e)
un(e) comptable
un(e) dentiste
un(e) élève
un(e) étudiant(e)
un(e) agriculteur (-trice)
un homme (une femme) d'affaires
un ingénieur
un(e) journaliste
un(e) mécanicien(ne)
un médecin
un(e) pharmacien(ne)
un professeur
un(e) secrétaire

Quelque chose à manger

des frites *(f.pl.)*
un milk-shake au chocolat
à la vanille

Vocabulaire général

Noms

un lycée

Verbes

être

Autres expressions

à
Ah, bon.
C'est ça.
C'est chouette, ça!
de
mais
mais non
Pourquoi pas?

Mise au point

Lecture: *La Dauphine vous propose*

Here is a list of items served in a café called **La Dauphine.** Because you would rarely order more than two or three items to eat and drink, it is not really necessary to understand every single item on the list when you try to read the menu. What you *can* do, however, is to use the French you already know as well as your general knowledge to try to recognize or figure out as many items as you can. Study the menu below, then do the exercises that follow.

Prereading: Discuss possible reactions to a café menu: Do you just go ahead and order **un hot dog** and **un Coca?** Do you take a wild guess? What strategies might you use to figure out unfamiliar words (e.g., cognates, grouping of like items)?

La Dauphine Vous Propose

Plats Chauds

CROQUE-MONSIEUR	15F
CROQUE-MADAME	18F
OMELETTE JAMBON OU FROMAGE	18F
OMELETTE MIXTE	22F
HOT DOG	15F
FRANCFORT FRITES	22F

Sandwiches

JAMBON OU GRUYÈRE OU PÂTÉ	8F
AMÉRICAIN: crudités et jambon	22F

Salades

SALADE NATURE	15F
SALADE DE TOMATES	22F
CAROTTES RÂPÉES	16F
SALADE DE CONCOMBRES	22F

Boissons

COCA-COLA	12F
JUS DE FRUITS	12F
JUS PRESSÉS	14F
EAUX MINÉRALES	10F
CAFÉ	5F25
CRÈME	12F
CHOCOLAT	12F
THÉ LAIT OU CITRON	12F
THÉS AROMATISÉS	12F
CAFÉ VIENNOIS	20F
CHOCOLAT VIENNOIS	20F
CAPPUCCINO	18F

Compréhension

A. The members of your family, who are traveling in France with you, do not speak French at all. They tell you what they would like to eat or drink, and you tell them what they should order and how many francs it will cost.

1. I'm not very hungry. All I want is a cup of espresso.
2. I can't eat meat. I want something with cheese.
3. I'm really thirsty. I'd like a nice glass of lemonade.
4. Can I have a ham and cheese omelet?
5. Is it possible to get just a plain lettuce salad?

Answers, Ex. B:
1. sandwich with ham, lettuce, tomato, etc.
2. coffee with cream
3. hot dog and fries
4. cucumber salad
5. grated carrots
6. coffee with whipped cream

B. **Devinez!** *(Guess!)* You are more adventuresome than your relatives, so you decide to try an item whose name you don't recognize. If you were to order each of the following items, what do you think you would get?

1. un sandwich américain
2. un crème
3. un francfort frites
4. une salade de concombres
5. des carottes râpées
6. un chocolat viennois

REPRISE

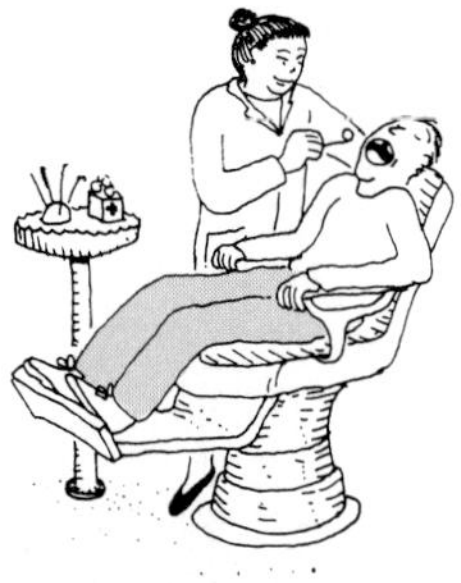

C. **Des photos.** While in France, you met people from several different countries. Upon your return, you are showing photographs of these people to your family. Using the information given below, give each person's profession, tell where he/she lives, and indicate his/her nationality. Remember to make all adjectives agree with the person to whom they refer.

MODÈLE: Monsieur Cordero / professeur / Madrid
Monsieur Cordero est professeur.
Il habite à Madrid. Il est espagnol.

1. Michael Frye / avocat / Londres
2. Madame Sebastiani / médecin / Rome
3. Natasha Fedchenko / mécanicien / Moscou
4. Jean-Yves Péronnet / étudiant / Paris
5. Monsieur Dalbach / ingénieur / Munich
6. Janine Néel / élève dans un lycée / Bordeaux
7. Li Ping *(f.)* / dentiste / Shanghai
8. Susan Yaeger / étudiant / Pittsburgh

D. **Je te présente...** You and your partner decide on new identities—that is, a new name, nationality, and city of origin for each of you. Introduce your partner to several other people in the class, following the model below. Then have your partner introduce you to a different group of people.

Ex. D: ⇄, then ○

Variation, Ex. D: Make up identities on slips of paper and have students pick them.

MODÈLE: ÉLÈVE A: *Barbara, je te présente Henri.*
ÉLÈVE C: *Bonjour, Henri.*
ÉLÈVE B: *Bonjour, Barbara.*
ÉLÈVE C: *Henri, tu es français?*
ÉLÈVE B: *Non, je suis canadien.*
ÉLÈVE A: *Oui, il est de Montréal.*

— *Pierre, tu es français?*
— *Non, je suis suisse!*

RÉVISION

In this **Révision,** you will review:

- food vocabulary;
- regular **-er** verbs;
- questions and responses;
- the irregular verb **être;**
- adjectives of nationality;
- names of professions.

Le café, la briocherie et le fast-food

E. **On prend quelque chose.** For each of the drawings, indicate where the people are and what they are eating and drinking.

1.

2.

3.

Regular *-er* verbs

je travaill**e**	nous travaill**ons**
tu travaill**es**	vous travaill**ez**
il, elle, on travaill**e**	ils, elles travaill**ent**

Questions	**Responses**
Tu voyages beaucoup?	**Oui,** je voyage beaucoup.
Est-ce que tu voyages beaucoup?	**Non,** je **ne** voyage **pas** beaucoup.
Tu voyages beaucoup, **n'est-ce pas?**	

F. **La ronde de questions.** *(The question circle.)* Using one of the suggested cues, each student in the group plays the role of questioner. Ask questions of one person **(tu)** or two people **(vous).** The other members of the group respond according to what they know or hear.

Ex. F: □. This is a very useful exercise for practicing verb forms and will be used at other points in the book. Take time to demonstrate and practice so that students get used to the basic pattern.

Variation, Ex. F: Complicate the exercise by using the subject pronouns **il** and **elle.**

MODÈLE: parler espagnol

JEANNE:	*Éric, tu parles espagnol?*
ÉRIC:	*Oui, je parle espagnol.*
JEANNE:	*Mary et Frank, vous parlez espagnol?*
MARY, FRANK:	*Non, nous ne parlons pas espagnol.*

1. chanter bien
2. manger beaucoup
3. habiter à...
4. aimer danser
5. travailler
6. parler allemand

The irregular verb *être*

je **suis**	nous **sommes**
tu **es**	vous **êtes**
il, elle, on **est**	ils, elles **sont**

Adjectives of nationality

m.	***f.***
suisse	suisse
français	français**e**
italien	italien**ne**

Names of professions

m.	***f.***
élève	élève
avocat	avocat**e**
pharmacien	pharmacien**ne**

Extension, Ex. G: Additional countries and names: **la Russie (Arkady/Natasha/nous), le Mexique (Dorotea et Miranda/José/toi), le Brésil (Marguerita/moi/Silvao et Lucio)**

G. **Un festival international.** At an international meeting of young people, the organizers call the roll of nations to find out who is there. When a country's name is called, various people identify themselves or other people as coming from that country.

MODÈLE: l'Italie (Bruno / Francesca / nous)
Bruno est italien. Francesca est italienne. Nous sommes italiens.

1. la Suisse (Jean-Pierre / Hélène et moi, nous / Gunther)
2. le Canada (Marguerite / moi, je / Vincent et Jean-Yves)
3. les États-Unis *(United States)* (vous / Ralph et John / Kathy et Erin)
4. l'Allemagne (Otto et Helga / toi, tu / Marlene)
5. la Chine (Su Su *[m.]* / Li Yan *[f.]* / nous)
6. l'Angleterre (Jill / Alan et Graham / Marsha et Beverly)

Implementation, Ex. H: Use the cards from your kit with the names and occupations of the people in the drawings.

Suggestion, Ex. H: △ or □. Choose one person in each group to play the role of the people in the drawings.

H. **En attendant à l'aéroport.** *(Waiting at the airport.)* While waiting for a plane at an international airport, you and your friend take turns guessing the nationalities and professions of various people. After making your guesses, one of you goes up to the person(s) and finds out the correct information. Play the role indicated on the card your teacher gives you.

MODÈLE: — *À mon avis* (in my opinion), *elle est italienne et elle est avocate.*
— *Pardon, Madame. Vous êtes italienne?*
— *Non, je suis espagnole. Je suis de Madrid.*
— *Vous travaillez à Madrid?*
— *Oui, je suis avocate à Madrid.*

Ex. I: △

Implementation, Ex. I: You play the role of **garçon,** circulating from table to table.

Variation, Exs. I and J: Can be presented as skits in class. Give students time to work out the details.

Ex. J: △ or □

Implementation, Ex. J; Assign three students to different corners of the room to play the roles of **garçon** (at the café), employees (at the **briocherie** and the fast-food restaurant).

Point d'arrivée

(Activités orales et écrites)

I. **Au café.** You and a friend meet at a café after school. You greet each other and order something to eat and/or drink. Then another friend arrives. Introduce him/her to your first friend. The two people who have just met try to get better acquainted by asking each other questions. Don't forget to have the third person order something also.

J. **On mange quelque chose?** While downtown on a Saturday afternoon, you and a friend run into one or more other classmates. You are hungry. Therefore, you try to get people interested in going somewhere (café, fast-food restaurant, **briocherie**) for something to eat. When you have decided, go to the place and order your food. (If you can't all agree, split into smaller groups, say good-bye, and go off to the place of your choice.)

K. **Une présentation.** Question another student in order to introduce him/her to the class. Find out (1) his/her nationality, (2) where he/she is from, (3) where he/she lives now, (4) what languages he/she speaks, (5) whether he/she likes to sing, dance, travel, etc., and (6) what kinds of snack food he/she eats. Don't try to translate your questions literally from English to French. Instead, use the French you have learned to find a way to get the needed information. When you have finished, present the student to the class.

Implementation, Ex. K: If class is large, have students split into groups of six (three pairs) for the presentations.

MODÈLE: *Je vous présente Anita. Elle est américaine. Elle habite à Providence, mais elle est de Manchester. . .*

L. **Qui suis-je?** Assume the identity of an international celebrity—actor or actress **(acteur, actrice)**, political figure **(homme politique, femme politique)**, or author **(auteur)**. Give a short description of yourself—your nationality, where you are from, where you live, and what you like to do, eat, etc. Your classmates will try to guess your identity. (Limit yourself as much as possible to words and structures you have studied in this first unit.)

Variation, Ex. L: Have students ask questions of the celebrities in an effort to guess their identities.

Mireille Loiseau

Je suis parisienne. Je suis élève au lycée Fénelon. J'aime beaucoup manger, mais pas au fast-food. Je préfère aller au café ou à la briocherie.

Written Work, See Workbook.

Unité deux

On fait connaissance

Planning Strategy: See Workbook.

Audio Tape and/or Video: See Teacher's Guide.

On fait connaissance: People get to know each other

Michel Maillet
Aix-en-Provence
France

Objectives

In this unit, you will learn:

- to talk about your possessions;
- to express your likes and dislikes;
- to describe your family;
- to read a short descriptive text about people;
- to understand people talking about themselves and their families.

Chapitre quatre

C'est à toi, ça?

—C'est à toi, ça, Michel?
—Oui, c'est mon ordinateur.

Première étape

Point de départ:

Ce que j'ai avec moi aujourd'hui

C'est à toi, ça?: Is that yours?

Ce que j'ai avec moi aujourd'hui: What I have with me today

Pour aller en classe, j'ai

(in order) to go to class, I have

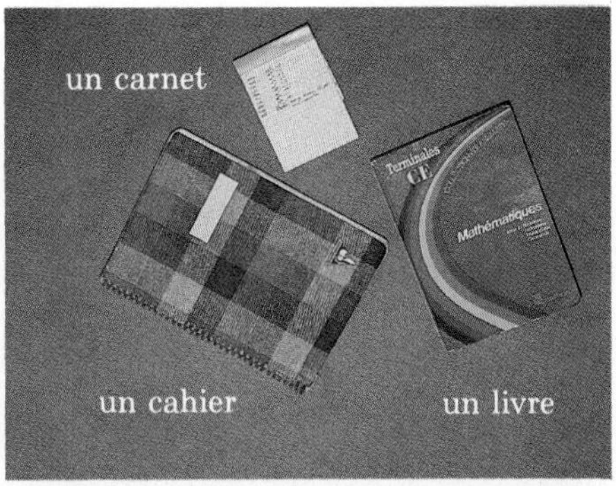

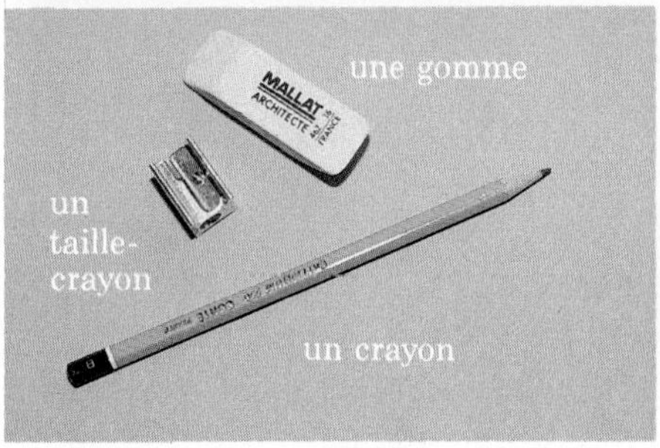

Suggestion, Point de départ: Bring the objects to class. Introduce by saying, **C'est un sac à dos. Qu'est-ce que c'est? C'est un sac à main? Qu'est-ce que c'est? Et ça, c'est un sac à main aussi?** (pointing to backpack). Present in groups and review continually.

Supplementary vocabulary: une trousse, un classeur, un trombone, une feuille de papier, un cartable, une saccoche

Vocabulary activities

Transparency, Ex. A and B: school supplies

À vous!

A. **Qu'est-ce que c'est?** *(What is it?)* Identify each object in the drawing.

MODÈLE: *C'est un crayon.* 

1.

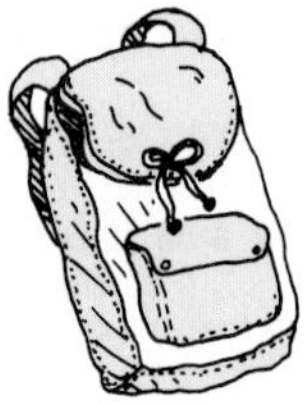

2.

3.

4.

5.

6.

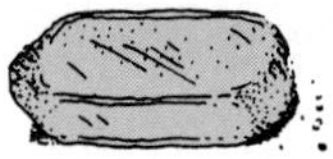

7.

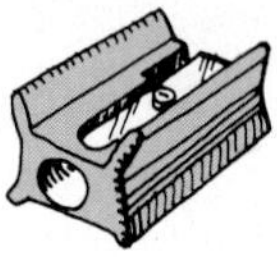

8.

B. **Mais non. . .** Correct the initial assumption on the basis of the drawings.

MODÈLE:
C'est un livre?
Non, ce n'est pas un livre. C'est un cahier.

1. C'est un stylo?

2. C'est un sac à dos?

3. C'est un cahier?

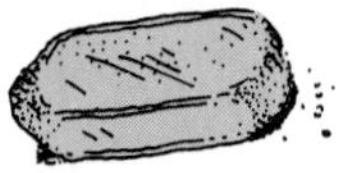

4. C'est un crayon?

5. C'est un taille-crayon?

6. C'est un sac à main?

STRUCTURE

The present tense of the irregular verb ***avoir***

J'ai deux stylos.	*I have* two ballpoint pens.
Est-ce que vous avez un cahier?	*Do you have* a notebook?
Nous n'avons pas de gomme.	*We don't have* an eraser.
Elles n'ont pas d'ordinateur.	*They don't have* a computer.

The verb **avoir** *(to have)* is irregular. Here are its conjugated forms:

avoir	
j'**ai**	nous **avons**
tu **as**	vous **avez**
il, elle, on **a**	ils, elles **ont**

In a negative sentence, the indefinite articles **un** and **une** change to **de** (**d'** before a vowel or a silent **h**). This often occurs with the verb **avoir:**

J'ai **un** portefeuille.	Je **n'**ai **pas de** portefeuille.
Bruno a **une** calculatrice.	Bruno **n'**a **pas de** calculatrice.

Suggestion, avoir: (1) Have students repeat conjugation while you write pronouns on board: **je / tu, il, elle, on / ils, elles / nous, vous.** (2) Repeat in negative. (3) Put written forms on board. (4) Draw male and female figures on board; divide school materials from the **Point de départ** between the two. Ask class, **Est-ce que Pierre a un cahier? Est-ce que Jeanne a une gomme?** Begin with affirmative answers, then introduce **pas de.**

Application

C. Replace the subject in italics and make the necessary changes.

1. *Luc* a deux stylos. (Alex / nous / je / Irène et Claude / tu / ils)
2. Est-ce que *François* a un taille-crayon? (tu / Élisabeth / vous / on / Jean-Luc ou André[1])
3. *Ils* n'ont pas de calculatrice. (elle / tu / nous / je / on / elles / Éric)

D. **Écoute, tu as. . . ?** *(Listen, do you have. . .?)* Each time that you ask whether one of your classmates has something, you learn that he/she does not have it but does have something else.

MODÈLE: Est-ce que Philippe a un crayon?
Non, il n'a pas de crayon, mais il a un feutre.

1. Est-ce que Nathalie a un sac à main? (un sac à dos)
2. Est-ce que Jean-Jacques a un carnet? (un cahier)
3. Est-ce que tu as un feutre? (un stylo)
4. Est-ce que Monique ou Didier ont un taille-crayon? (trois crayons)
5. Est-ce que vous avez une calculatrice? (un crayon)
6. Est-ce que Madeleine a un sac à main? (un portefeuille)

Follow-up, Ex. D: Ask the students **Est-ce que vous avez un(e) . . . ?** using either the objects from the **Point de départ** or the transparencies of school supplies.

[1]In French, two nouns connected by **ou** *(or)* are treated as a plural; therefore, use the **ils, elles** form of the verb—**Marc ou Chantal ont (sont, parlent,** etc.).

Suggestion, Note grammaticale, avoir besoin de: (1) Hold up objects (e.g., dull pencil—**J'ai besoin d'un taille-crayon**). (2) Ask students: **Est-ce que vous avez un(e) . . . ?** When you get a negative answer, ask: **Est-ce que vous avez besoin d'un(e) . . . ?**

NOTE GRAMMATICALE

The idiomatic expression **avoir besoin de**

Many common French idiomatic expressions use the verb **avoir.** Usually, these expressions cannot be translated word for word. Instead, you must learn the meaning and use of the entire expression. For example, the expression **avoir besoin de** is the equivalent of the English verb *to need:*

J'ai besoin d'un taille-crayon.	*I need* a pencil sharpener.
Nous avons besoin d'un carnet?	*Do we need* a notepad?

Note: Remember that **de** changes to **d'** before a vowel sound.

J'ai besoin d'*une calculatrice.*

E. **Pour aller en classe, on a besoin de. . .** On the basis of the drawings, indicate what the students need to go to class.

MODÈLE: Pour aller en classe, Anne-Marie. . .
Pour aller en classe, Anne-Marie a besoin d'un sac à dos et d'un sac à main.

1. Pour aller à la classe de français, Danielle. . .

2. Pour aller à la classe de mathématiques, Serge et Michèle...

3. Pour aller à la classe d'anglais, moi, je...

4. Pour aller à la classe de physique, nous...

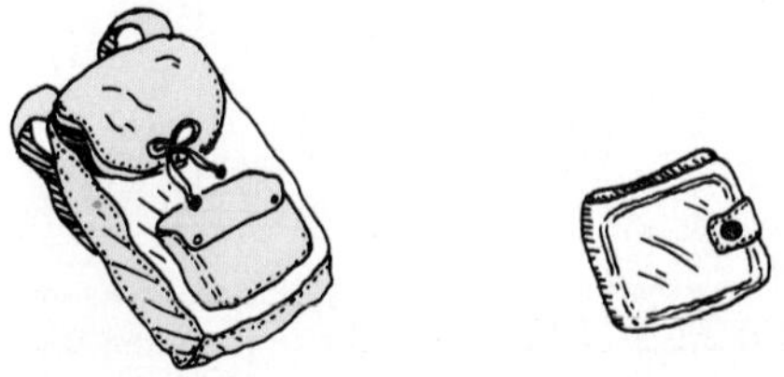

5. Pour aller à la classe de biologie, Jean-François...

Le savez-vous?

In France, students attend the *lycée* from the age of _____ to the age of _____.
a) 5/16
b) 11/19
c) 13/18

réponse ➡

F. **Moi, j'ai besoin d'un(e)...** Indicate that you need one of the following items. Then ask a classmate if he/she has one. Your classmate may answer affirmatively or may refer you to someone else.

Ex. F: ⇄

MODÈLE: crayon
ÉLÈVE A: *J'ai besoin d'un crayon. Joan, est-ce que tu as un crayon?*
ÉLÈVE B: *Oui, j'ai un crayon.* or:
Non, je n'ai pas de crayon, mais Paul a un crayon.

1. un stylo
2. une calculatrice
3. un feutre
4. une gomme
5. un taille-crayon
6. un carnet

DÉBROUILLONS-NOUS !

➡ b Review of **étape** Ex. G: ⇄ or △

G. **Moi, j'ai. . . Et toi?** Compare the items that you brought to school and class today with the items brought by one or two of your classmates.

Written Work: See Workbook.

Deuxième étape

Point de départ:

Ce que j'ai chez moi

Ce que j'ai chez moi: What I have at my house

Transparency, Point de départ: female and male students' rooms

Frédérique Bayard et Jean-Jacques Vidal sont élèves dans un lycée à Amiens.

in my (bed)room

Dans ma chambre, j'ai

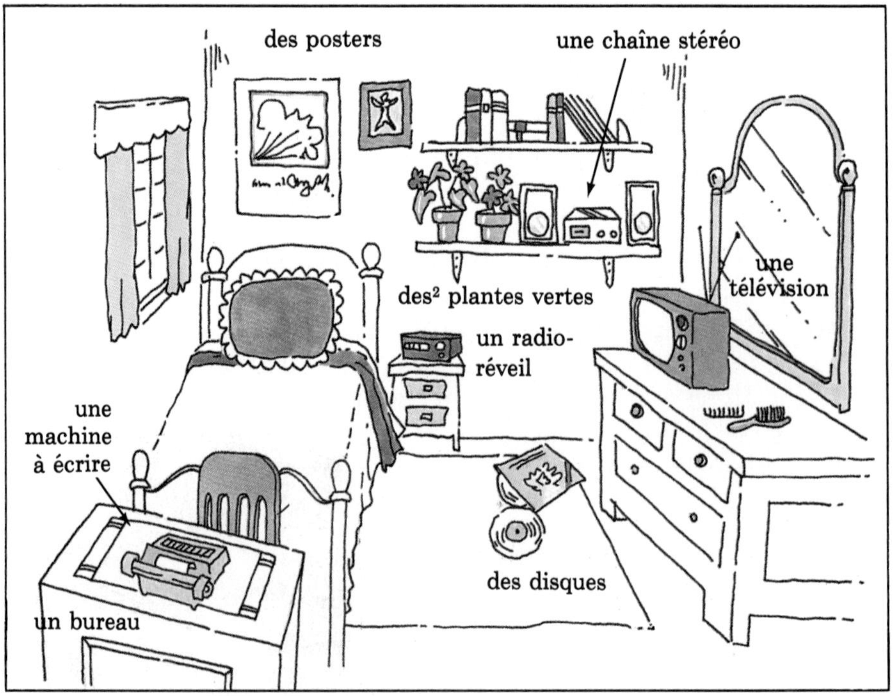

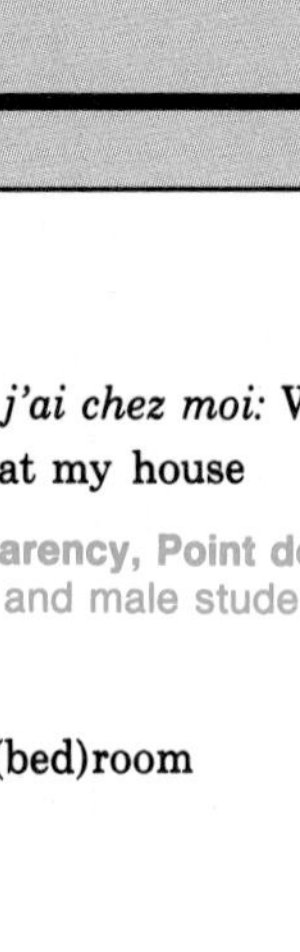

Frédérique Bayard

[2]**Des** *(some)* is the plural form of **un** or **une.** This structure will be explained more fully later in this **étape.**

Dans ma chambre, j'ai

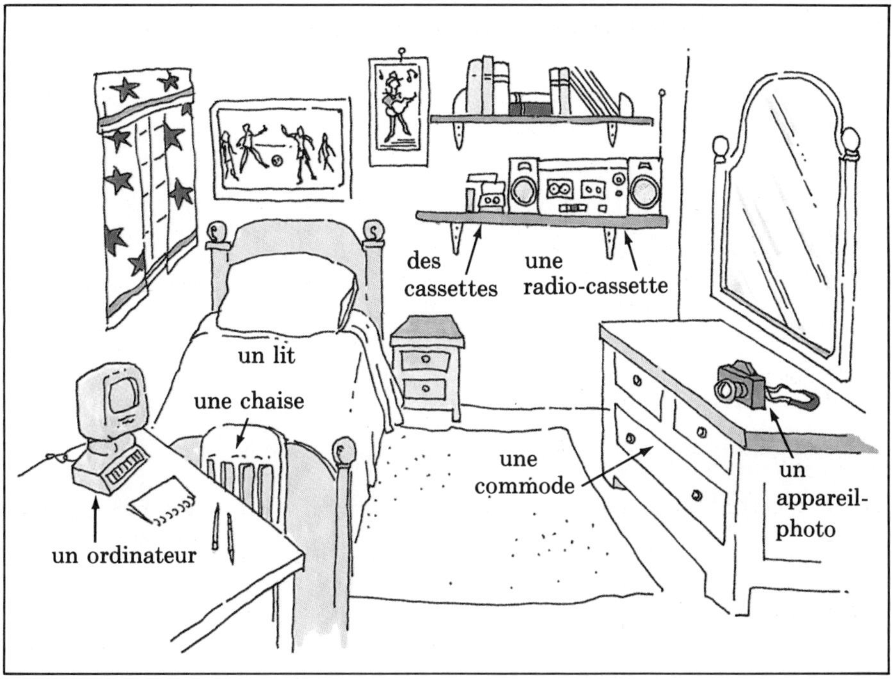

Supplementary vocabulary: des coussins, un animal en peluche, une lampe, une armoire, un miroir

Jean-Jacques Vidal

À vous!

Vocabulary activities

A. **Qui a. . . ?** Based on the pictures, answer the following questions about Frédérique's and Jean-Jacques' rooms.

MODÈLES: Qui a une télévision?
Frédérique a une télévision.

Qui a une chaise?
Frédérique et Jean-Jacques ont une chaise.

1. un ordinateur?
2. une radio-cassette?
3. un radio-réveil?
4. un lit?
5. une chaîne stéréo?
6. des posters?
7. une machine à écrire?
8. un appareil-photo
9. des cassettes?
10. des disques?
11. des plantes vertes?

Suggestion, Point de départ: (1) Begin with the female student's room by introducing items with **C'est . . . , Qu'est-ce que c'est?** Then summarize: **Elle a un lit,** etc. (2) Start with male student's room by reviewing those items that are also in the first room: **Est-ce qu'il a un lit? un bureau?** Etc. Then go to: **Est-ce qu'il a un radio-réveil? (Non) Mais il a un radio-cassettes.** Etc.
The plural form **des** is introduced here as a lexical item; it will be presented more thoroughly in the **Structure** section.

B. **Et vous?** Indicate what you have and do not have in your room at home.

MODÈLE: *Dans ma chambre, j'ai un lit et une chaise, mais je n'ai pas de bureau. J'ai des posters au mur* (on the wall). . .

Prononciation: *The combination* ***qu***

In English, the combination *qu* is usually pronounced **[kw]:** *quote, quick, request.* In French, the combination **qu** is always pronounced **[k],** and the **u** is silent. Notice the difference between:

English	**French**
Quebec	**Qu**ébec
se**qu**ence	sé**qu**ence

Pratique

C. Read each word aloud, being careful to pronounce the **qu** sound combination as **[k].**

1. est-ce que
2. croque-monsieur
3. qu'est-ce que
4. quelque chose
5. Jacqueline
6. Véronique
7. disque
8. critique
9. Québec

REPRISE

Recycling activity

Ex. D: △

Preparation, Ex. D: You may begin by doing a **Demandez à** type exercise as a review of **avoir besoin de: Demandez à . . . s'il a besoin d'un(e) . . .**

D. **Demande à Marie si elle a. . .** *(Ask Marie if she has. . .)* When you indicate that you need something, your friend asks someone else if he/she has it. Follow the model.

MODÈLES: feutre / Marie / oui
ÉLÈVE A: *J'ai besoin d'un feutre.*
ÉLÈVE B: *Marie, tu as un feutre?*
ÉLÈVE C: *Oui, j'ai un feutre.*

cahier / Marc et Pierre / non
ÉLÈVE A: *J'ai besoin d'un cahier.*
ÉLÈVE B: *Marc et Pierre, vous avez un cahier?*
ÉLÈVE C: *Non, nous n'avons pas de cahier.*

1. taille-crayon / Guy / oui
2. calculatrice / Sophie et Mireille / non
3. gomme / Michel et Nicolas / oui
4. stylo / Annie / non
5. livre / Roger / oui
6. crayon / Dominique et Jean-Yves / non

STRUCTURE

The indefinite article **des**

Vous avez **des** amis à Paris?	Do you have friends in Paris?
Oui, j'ai **des** amis à Paris.	Yes, I have *(some)* friends in Paris.
Non, je n'ai pas **d'**amis à Paris.	No, I don't have *(any)* friends in Paris.
Tu as **des** disques?	Do you have *any* records?
Oui, mais j'ai besoin **de** cassettes aussi.	Yes, but I need *some* cassettes, also.

The plural form of the indefinite articles **un** and **une** is **des. Des** is the equivalent of the English words *some* or *any.* French requires the use of **des** in cases where English does not use an article because *some* or *any* is understood:

J'ai **des** posters.	I have *(some)* posters.
Est-ce que tu as **des** plantes vertes dans ta chambre?	Do you have *(any)* plants in your room?

After the verb **avoir** in the negative form, and after the expression **avoir besoin, des** becomes **de** or **d':**

Elles n'ont pas **de** livres.	They don't have *any* books.
Nous avons besoin **de** posters.	We need *some* posters.

Suggestion, Des: Introduce the indefinite nature of **des** by comparing **un livre, deux livres, des livres; une cassette, deux cassettes, des cassettes; un élève, deux élèves, des élèves.**

Reminder: If it becomes a problem, point out to students that **ce n'est pas** and **ce ne sont pas** are followed by **des** (not **de**).

Application

E. Make each expression plural.

MODÈLE: un livre
des livres

1. un cahier
2. un disque
3. une cassette
4. une calculatrice
5. une gomme
6. un lit
7. une plante verte
8. un ami
9. une amie
10. un ordinateur
11. une omelette
12. un sandwich

F. **Oui, et j'ai des . . . aussi.** When you ask whether someone has something, you are told that they do and that they have something else also.

MODÈLE: Est-ce que tu as des crayons? (stylos)
Oui, j'ai des crayons et j'ai des stylos aussi.

1. Est-ce que tu as des disques? (cassettes)
2. Est-ce que Jean-Paul a des livres? (cahiers)
3. Est-ce que vous avez des plantes vertes? (posters)
4. Est-ce que Michèle et Dominique ont des crayons? (feutres)
5. Est-ce que tu as des sandwichs? (boissons)

Follow-up, Ex. F: Ask students if they have **des disques, des cassettes, des livres, des plantes vertes, des affiches,** etc.

G. **Tu as besoin de disques?** Ask a classmate if he/she needs the following items. He/she will answer yes and explain that he/she doesn't have any at the moment.

MODÈLE: disques
— *Tu as besoin de disques?*
— *Oui, parce que je n'ai pas de disques en ce moment* (now).

1. clés
2. cassettes
3. posters
4. plantes vertes
5. cahiers
6. stylos

Suggestion, Note grammaticale, il y a and **voilà:** (1) Using some of the terms for school supplies learned in the **Première Étape,** ask students: **Qu'est-ce qu'il y a (sur le bureau)? Est-ce qu'il y a des livres? un feutre?** Get yes/no answers. (2) Then ask students to point out some objects scattered around the room: **Est-ce qu'il y a un cahier? Voilà un cahier.**

Suggestion: If you wish, introduce **voici** at the same time.

NOTE GRAMMATICALE

The expressions ***il y a*** *and* ***voilà***[3]

The expressions **il y a** and **voilà** both are the equivalent of *there is* or *there are* in English. Both expressions are invariable—that is, they have only one form:

Il y a un livre dans ma chambre.	*There is* a (one) book in my room.
Il y a trois livres dans ma chambre.	*There are* three books in my room.
Voilà un livre.	*There is* a book.
Voilà des livres.	*There are* some books.

Il y a is used to state that a person, place, or thing exists. It does not necessarily mean that the item in question can be seen from where you are

[3]**Voilà** has a companion expression, **voici** *(here is, here are).* **Voici une calculatrice** (near the speaker). **Voilà une maison** (away from the speaker).

standing. **Voilà** is used to point out the location of a person, place or thing. It is usually intended to get someone to look in that direction.

Il y a *une souris dans la chambre!*

Voilà *la souris!*

Dans ma chambre **il y a** un lit, un bureau et une chaise.	In my room, *there is* a bed, a desk, and a chair. (They exist.)
Voilà un bureau et une chaise.	*There are* a desk and a chair. (They are located nearby. Look at them.)

The negative of **il ya un (une, des)** is **il n'y a pas de:**

Il n'y a pas d'ordinateur dans ma chambre.
Il n'y a pas de disques ici. *(here).*

Voilà does not have a negative form.

H. **La chambre d'Hélène.** First, indicate whether each item is or is not found in the room pictured.

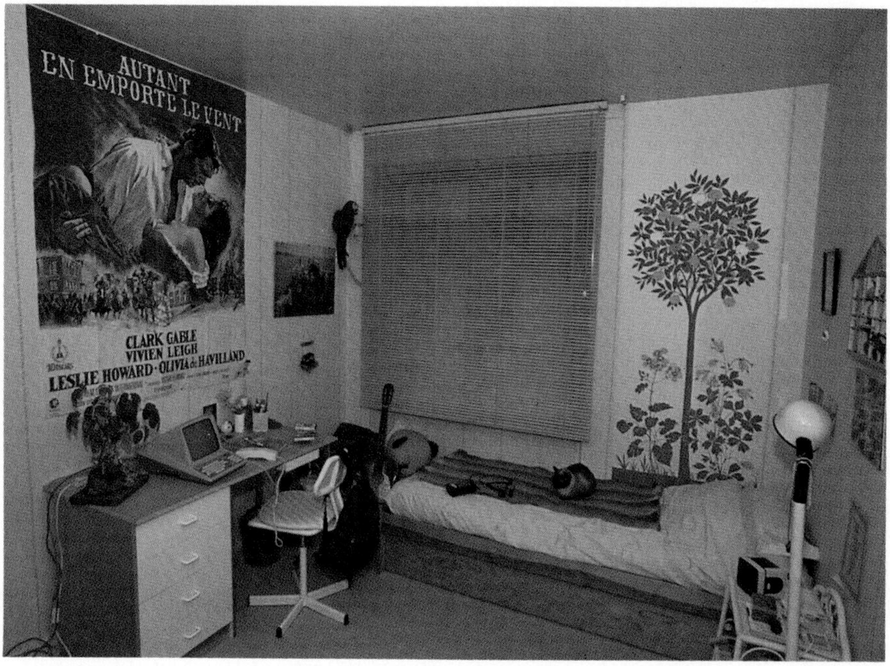

MODÈLE: un sac à dos
Dans la chambre d'Hélène il y a un sac à dos.

des sandwichs
Il n'y a pas de sandwichs.

un lit
des posters
une chaise
des cassettes
un ordinateur
une télévision
une chaîne stéréo

des livres
des crayons et des stylos
un bureau
des plantes vertes
une machine à écrire
un radio-réveil
des cahiers

Now, point out to another student those items that are in the room.

MODÈLE: *Voilà un lit. Voilà des plantes vertes.* Etc.

NOTE GRAMMATICALE

Suggestion, Note grammaticale, avoir faim and avoir soif: Act out being hungry and thirsty. Then ask students: **Vous avez faim? Vous désirez un sandwich?** Etc.

The idiomatic expressions ***avoir faim*** *and* ***avoir soif***

Two expressions that you'll find quite useful are **avoir faim,** *to be hungry,* and **avoir soif,** *to be thirsty.* Note that in these idiomatic expressions, **avoir** translates as *to be* rather than *to have.*

Tu as faim?	*Are you hungry?*
Je n'ai pas faim, mais **j'ai très soif.**	*I'm not hungry,* but *I'm very thirsty.*

J'ai faim.

J'ai soif.

I. **Tu as faim? Tu as soif?** When you see a place to get something to eat or drink, you point it out and ask your friend if he/she is hungry or thirsty. When your friend answers affirmatively, you talk about what you will have. Follow the model.

Ex. I: ⇄

MODÈLE: un café / avoir soif / quelque chose de froid *(cold)*
— *Voilà un café. Tu as soif?*
— *Oui, j'ai soif.*
— *Tu voudrais quelque chose de froid?*
— *Oui, je voudrais un Coca.*
— *Et moi, je vais prendre une menthe à l'eau.*

1. un café / avoir soif / quelque chose de froid
2. un café / avoir faim / un sandwich
3. une briocherie / avoir faim / quelque chose de sucré
4. un café / avoir soif / quelque chose de chaud *(hot)*
5. une briocherie / avoir faim / quelque chose de salé
6. un café / avoir faim / une omelette

DÉBROUILLONS-NOUS !

Review of the **étape**

Ex. J: O

Written Work: See Workbook.

J. **Dans ta chambre est-ce qu'il y a. . . ?** Find out from several classmates what they have and do not have in their rooms at home.

Troisième étape

Transparency, Point de départ: houses and possessions

Point de départ:

Chez nous: At our house

Chez nous

Suggestion, Point de départ: Using the transparency of houses and possessions, begin each vocabulary group by talking about yourself: **Moi, j'habite dans une maison. Et vous? Qui habite dans un appartement? Chez nous, nous avons une télévision couleur et une chaîne stéréo, mais nous n'avons pas de magnétoscope. Et chez vous? Pour aller en ville,** etc.

Supplementary vocabulary: un immeuble, une bicyclette

J'habite dans

une maison

un appartement

Chez nous, nous avons

une chaîne stéréo

un magnétoscope

une télévision couleur

(in order) to go into town (downtown)

Pour aller en ville, nous avons

une voiture (une auto)

une motocyclette (une moto)

un vélomoteur

un vélo

À vous!

A. **Chez vous.** Answer the following questions about where you live.

Vocabulary activities

Follow-up, Ex. A: Have students ask each other the questions. Remind them to change **vous** to **tu.**

1. Est-ce que vous habitez dans une maison ou dans un appartement?
2. Est-ce que vous avez une chaîne stéréo chez vous? une télévision couleur? un magnétoscope? un ordinateur?
3. Qu'est-ce que vous avez pour aller en ville—une voiture? un vélo? un vélomoteur? une motocyclette?

Pour aller en ville, nous avons des vélos.

B. **Christine, Bertrand et Antoinette.** On the basis of the drawings, complete each person's description of where he/she lives.

1. Je m'appelle *(my name is)* Christine Devise. J'habite dans. . . Chez nous il y a. . . et. . . , mais nous n'avons pas de (d'). . . Pour aller en ville, j'ai. . .

2. Je m'appelle Bertrand Perreaux. J'habite dans. . . Nous avons. . . et. . . Pour aller en ville, moi, j'ai. . .

3. Je m'appelle Antoinette Salanches. J'habite dans. . . aussi. Nous n'avons pas de (d'). . . , mais nous avons. . . Pour aller en ville, j'ai. . .

Follow-up, Ex. B: Have students compose a short description of their living situations.

REPRISE

C. **Échange.** Ask the following questions of a classmate, who will answer them.

Recycling activity

Ex. C: ⇄

1. Dans ta chambre est-ce qu'il y a des livres? des plantes vertes? des posters au mur?
2. Est-ce que tu as une chaîne stéréo? des disques? des disques de jazz? de rock? de musique classique?
3. Est-ce que tu as un radio-réveil? une radio-cassette? des cassettes?
4. Est-ce que tu as une machine à écrire? un ordinateur? un appareil-photo?
5. Tu as besoin d'un stylo? d'une calculatrice? d'un taille-crayon?
6. Tu as faim? (Qu'est-ce que tu voudrais?) Tu as soif? (Qu'est-ce que tu voudrais?)

STRUCTURE

Numbers from 0 to 10

Note that **un, une** agree with the noun they are introducing. Zero and the numbers from two through ten always stay the same.

0	**zéro**	3	**trois**	6	**six**	9	**neuf**
1	**un, une**	4	**quatre**	7	**sept**	10	**dix**
2	**deux**	5	**cinq**	8	**huit**		

When a number precedes a noun beginning with a vowel or a silent **h**, liaison occurs and the final consonant is pronounced: **cinq‿élèves, huit‿appareils.** In liaison, **x** and **s** are pronounced as **z**: **deux‿appartements, trois‿amis, six‿ordinateurs, dix‿omelettes.**

Structure, Numbers: For many classes, these numbers will have already been presented in the **Étape préliminaire.** In that case, you may wish to review them quickly and go right to the expressions **avoir raison** and **avoir tort** and Ex. E.

Suggestion, Numbers: Present progressively, students repeating in chorus: 0; 0, 1; 0, 1, 2; etc.

Reminder: The final sounds of **six, huit,** and **dix** are silent before a consonant. For now, you may wish to treat this primarily as a listening problem. In theory, the final sound of **cinq** is also silent before a consonant, but in practice, many speakers pronounce the /k/.

Application

D. Follow the directions in French.

1. Comptez de 0 jusqu'à 10. Comptez de 10 jusqu'à 0.
2. Répétez les nombres pairs *(even)*: 0, 2, 4, 6, 8, 10. Répétez les nombres impairs *(odd)*: 1, 3, 5, 7, 9.

Suggestion, Note grammaticale, avoir raison and **avoir tort:** Do some simple arithmetic on the board; ask class if you are right or wrong.

NOTE GRAMMATICALE

The expressions ***avoir raison*** *and* ***avoir tort***

Two more idiomatic expressions that use **avoir** are **avoir raison** *(to be right)* and **avoir tort** *(to be wrong):*

Tu as raison: un et un font deux.	*You're right:* one and one are two.
Elle a tort: on ne parle pas français à Zurich.	*She's wrong:* they don't speak French in Zurich.

Ex. E: ⇄. You may wish to encourage students to make some errors.

Variation, Ex. E: You do the calculations, making errors from time to time and having students correct you.

E. **Raison ou tort?** One of your classmates will do a simple arithmetic problem. Indicate whether he/she is right or wrong.

MODÈLES: $2 + 2 = ?$
— *Deux et deux font quatre.*
— *Tu as raison.*

$2 + 3 = ?$
— *Deux et trois font six.*
— *Mais non! Tu as tort. Deux et trois font cinq!*

1. $2 + 5 = ?$	2. $4 + 1 = ?$	3. $7 + 3 = ?$	4. $3 + 5 = ?$
5. $6 + 3 = ?$	6. $2 + 4 = ?$	7. $8 + 2 = ?$	8. $1 + 2 = ?$
9. $6 + 0 = ?$	10. $5 + 4 = ?$		

DÉBROUILLONS-NOUS!

Review of the **étape**

Ex. F: ○

Follow-up, Ex. F: Ask students: **Chez qui est-ce que vous voudriez rester? Pourquoi?**

Written Work: see Workbook.

F. **Je voudrais passer le week-end chez un(e) ami(e).** *(I would like to spend the weekend at a friend's house.)* Your parents are going out of town for the weekend and do not want you to stay home alone. They have told you to ask a friend if you can spend the weekend at his/her house. In order to determine where you would like to stay, find out about your classmates' homes. For example, find out whether they live in a house or an apartment, what they have for amusement, etc.

Lexique

Thèmes et contextes

Les habitations
- un appartement
- une chambre
- une maison

Les matériaux scolaires (school supplies)
- un cahier
- une calculatrice
- un carnet
- un crayon
- un feutre
- une gomme
- un livre
- un sac à dos
- un stylo
- un taille-crayon

Les moyens de transport
- une auto
- une moto
- une motocyclette
- un vélo
- un vélomoteur
- une voiture

Les possessions
- un appareil-photo
- un bureau
- une cassette
- une chaîne stéréo
- un chat
- un chien
- une clé
- un disque
- un lit
- une machine à écrire
- un magnétoscope
- un ordinateur
- une plante verte
- un portefeuille
- un poster
- une radio-cassette
- un radio-réveil
- un sac (à main)
- une télévision (couleur)

Vocabulaire général

Verbes
- avoir
- avoir besoin de
- avoir faim
- avoir raison
- avoir soif
- avoir tort

Autres expressions
- dans
- il y a
- pour aller en ville
- voilà

Chapitre cinq

Moi, j'aime beaucoup ça!

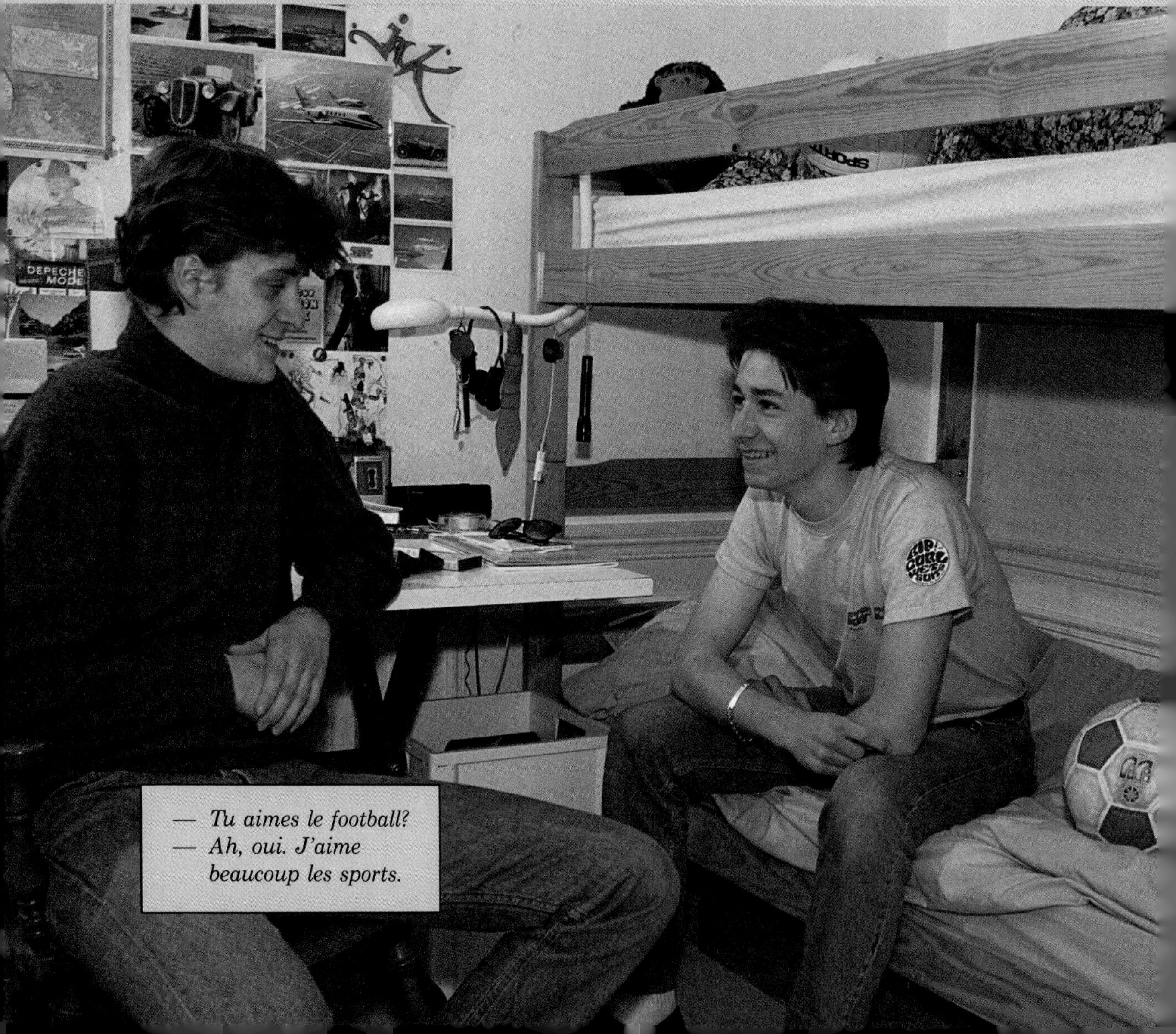

— *Tu aimes le football?*
— *Ah, oui. J'aime beaucoup les sports.*

Première étape

Point de départ:

Mes goûts

Mes goûts: My tastes (likes)

Suggestion, Point de départ: Review the various expressions on a like/dislike continuum: begin with **aimer,** then work up to **adorer** and down to **détester.**

Bonjour. **Je m'appelle** Martine. Voici Jean-Louis. C'est **mon petit ami,** mais nous avons des goûts très différents.

my name is / my boyfriend

Martine	**Jean-Louis**	
J'aime beaucoup la nature.	Moi, je déteste la nature.	
J'aime les animaux.[1]	Moi, je n'aime pas les animaux.	
Je n'aime pas les sports.	Moi, j'adore les sports.	
J'aime l'art et la musique.	Moi, je n'aime pas l'art et je n'aime pas la musique **non plus.**	either (neither)
J'aime bien la politique.	Moi, j'aime la politique un peu, mais pas beaucoup.	
J'étudie les **langues** et les mathématiques.	Moi, j'étudie les sciences et la littérature.	languages
Pourtant, j'aime bien Jean-Louis.	Et moi, j'aime bien Martine.	however (nevertheless)

[1]The singular of **animaux** is **animal: un animal, des animaux.**

À vous!

Je déteste

Je n'aime pas

J'aime assez

J'aime

J'aime bien

J'aime beaucoup

J'adore

A. **Il aime beaucoup la musique.** On the basis of the drawings, indicate how each person feels about the subject or activity shown.

Gérard

MODÈLE: Gérard aime beaucoup la musique.

Sylvie

Daniel

Christophe

Nathalie

Françoise

Chantal

Michel

B. **Et vous?** Indicate how you feel about each activity.

MODÈLE: les sports
J'aime les sports. ou:
Je n'aime pas les sports. ou:
J'aime beaucoup les sports. Etc.

1. la musique
2. la politique
3. les sports
4. les animaux
5. les sciences
6. l'art
7. la littérature
8. la nature
9. les mathématiques
10. les langues

Follow-up, Ex. B: Have students ask you about your likes and dislikes.

Prononciation: *The combination* ***ch***

Reminder: There are a few French words, mainly of Greek origin, in which the **ch** is pronounced /k/: **orchestre, écho, chrétien, Christian(e).**

In English, the combination **ch** is usually pronounced with the hard sounds **[tch]** or **[k]: ch**icken, rea**ch**, **ch**aracter, ar**ch**itect. In French, the combination **ch** usually has a softer sound, much like the **sh** in the English word **sheep.** Notice the differences in the following pairs:

English	**French**
champion	**ch**ampion
tou**ch**	tou**che**
ar**ch**itect	ar**ch**itecte

Pratique

C. Read each word aloud, being careful to pronounce **ch** as **[sh].**

1. chante
2. chose
3. Chantal
4. chinois
5. chambre
6. machine
7. chaîne
8. chef
9. chercher
10. chic

REPRISE

Recycling activities

Follow-up, Ex. D: Do some simple addition problems orally; other students can comment on the results: **Il a raison. Elle a tort.**

Ex. E: ⇄. Encourage partners to ask questions.

D. Read in French: 3, 7, 2, 5, 0, 9, 1, 10, 6, 4, 8.

E. **Ma famille et moi, nous. . .** *(My family and I. . .)* Tell a classmate where you and your family live and what you own.

MODÈLE: *Ma famille et moi, nous sommes de New York, mais nous habitons à Minneapolis. Nous habitons dans une maison. Nous avons une chaîne stéréo, une télévision couleur et un ordinateur. Nous n'avons pas de magnétoscope. Pour aller en ville, nous avons deux voitures et deux vélos.*

Suggestions, Definite articles: Introduce definite articles by contrasting them with indefinite articles: **Monique, vous avez un livre? Voilà le livre de Monique.** Objects: **calculatrice, clés, ordinateur, ami(e).**

STRUCTURE

The definite article ***le, la, l', les***

J'aime **le** camping.	I like camping.
Vous avez **la** clé?	Do you have *the* key?
C'est **l'**ordinateur de Pierre.	It's Pierre's computer (*the* computer belonging to Pierre).
Voici **les** disques.	Here are *the* records.

The French definite article has three singular forms and one plural form:

masculine singular	**le**	**le** livre, **le** camping, **le** professeur
feminine singular	**la**	**la** nature, **la** clé, **la** pharmacienne
masculine or feminine singular before a vowel or a vowel sound	**l'**	**l'**ordinateur, **l'**omelette, **l'**actrice, **l'**avocat
plural (masculine *or* feminine)	**les**	**les** livres, **les** clés, **les** langues

The **s** of **les** is silent. In liaison **s** is pronounced as **z.**

les‿ordinateurs   les‿omelettes   les‿actrices

The definite article has two main uses:

1. It may designate a noun in a general or collective sense:

Anne aime ***les sports.*** *Anne likes* sports (all sports).

Michel n'aime pas ***la musique.*** *Michel doesn't like* music.

2. It may also designate a noun in a specific sense. **J'ai les clés** means that I have *the* specific keys that have already been mentioned. **L'ordinateur de Pierre** refers to the particular computer that belongs to Pierre. Notice in the last example that the definite article can be used along with **de** to indicate possession *(Pierre's computer).*

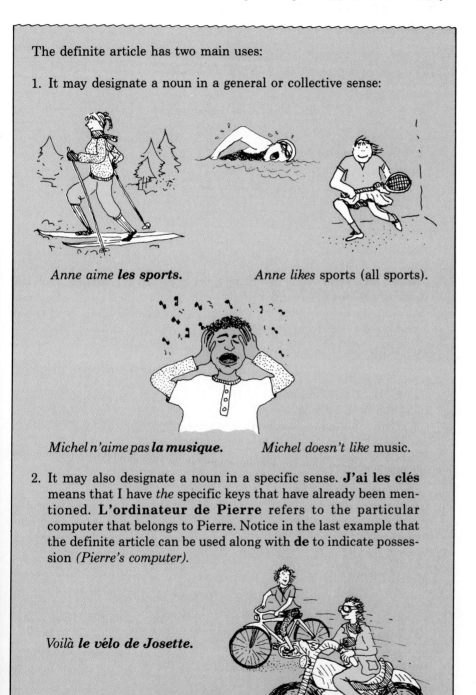

Voilà ***le vélo de Josette.***

Voici ***la motocyclette d'Henri.***

Application

F. Replace the indefinite article with the appropriate definite article **(le, la, l', les).**

MODÈLES: un cahier — *le cahier*
des crayons — *les crayons*

1. un café
2. une maison
3. des sandwiches
4. une omelette
5. un sac à dos
6. des plantes vertes
7. une chambre
8. une télévision
9. des disques
10. un élève
11. une élève
12. des élèves
13. une clé
14. un taille-crayon
15. des animaux

G. **J'aime les sports, mais je n'aime pas beaucoup la politique.** You and your friends are talking about what you like and dislike. In each case, indicate that the person likes the first activity or item but does not like the second one very much.

MODÈLE: je / sports / politique
J'aime les sports, mais je n'aime pas beaucoup la politique.

1. je / nature / camping
2. Jean-Paul / musique / art
3. Henri / animaux / sciences
4. Michel et Nicole / langues / littérature
5. nous / politique / sports
6. vous / sciences / mathématiques

H. **Ça, c'est. . .** *(That's. . .)* When you and a friend stay after class one day, you notice that your other classmates have left behind several of their belongings. You show these objects to your friend, who identifies the owners. With a singular noun, use **c'est.**

MODÈLE: Voici un livre. (Béatrice)
Ça, c'est le livre de Béatrice.

1. Voici un cahier. (Vincent)
2. Voici une calculatrice. (Sylvaine)
3. Voici un feutre. (Bernard)

With a plural noun, use **ce sont.**

MODÈLE: Voici des crayons. (Marc)
Ça, ce sont les crayons de Marc.

4. Voici des cassettes. (Martine)
5. Voici des livres. (Jean-Pierre)
6. Voici des cahiers. (Yvonne)

Now continue, being careful to distinguish between **c'est** and **ce sont.**

7. Voici un stylo. (Michel)
8. Voici des clés. (Gérard)
9. Voici un taille-crayon. (Jean-Paul)
10. Voici une gomme. (Annick)
11. Voici des cahiers. (Pierrette)
12. Voici un sac à dos. (Mireille)
13. Voici des feutres. (Jacques)
14. Voici une cassette. (Claude)

Follow-up, Ex. H: Use possessions of the students. For example, pick up someone's pen: **Qu'est-ce que c'est? C'est un stylo. C'est le stylo de Daniel? Non, c'est le stylo de Janice.**

DÉBROUILLONS-NOUS!

I. **Qui aime. . . ?** Choose two items from the list below and find out how your classmates feel about them.

l'art moderne / la musique classique / le jazz / la politique / les sports / la nature / le camping / les animaux / les sciences / les mathématiques / la littérature / les langues

Review of the **étape**

Ex. I: O. To ensure variety, you may wish to assign or have students draw for items.

Written Work: see Workbook.

Deuxième étape

Point de départ:

Mes préférences

Transparency, Point de départ: people

Suggestion, Point de départ: Point out the pictures on the transparency of people, read the statements about the people, then have several students answer the questions **(Qu'est-ce que vous aimez mieux—le cinéma ou le théâtre?** Etc.).

Christiane aime les films et les **pièces de théâtre.** *Qu'est-ce que vous* **aimez mieux**—*le cinéma ou le théâtre?*

plays
prefer (like better)

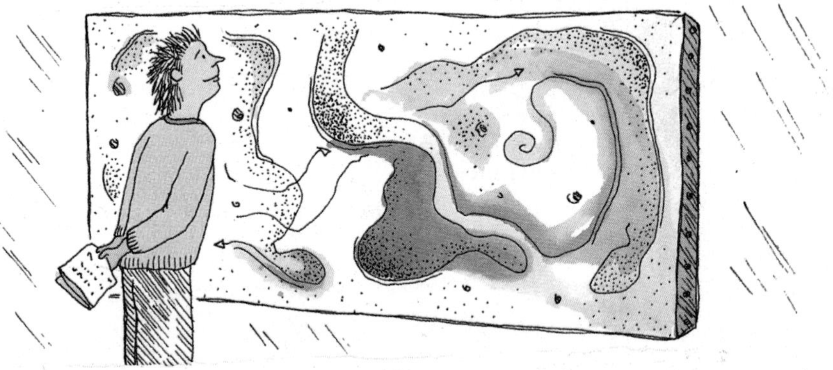

painting

Roger aime beaucoup l'art. Qu'est-ce que vous préférez—la ***peinture*** *ou la sculpture?*

dog / cats

Michèle adore les animaux. Elle a un ***chien*** *et deux* ***chats.*** *Qu'est-ce que vous aimez mieux—les chiens ou les chats?*

to look at
prefer (like the best)

André aime beaucoup les sports. Il aime ***regarder*** *le football à la télévision. Qu'est-ce que vous* ***aimez le mieux****—le football, le football américain, le basket ou le base-ball?*

*Élisabeth et Jean aiment bien la musique. Ils aiment **écouter** des disques de jazz. Qu'est-ce que vous préférez—la musique populaire, le jazz, le rock ou la musique classique?*

to listen to

À vous!

Vocabulary activities

A. **Qu'est-ce que vous aimez mieux?** Indicate your preferences. Use both the expression **aimer mieux** and the verb **préférer** by alternating your answers.

Ex. A: ⇄

MODÈLE: le football ou le basket
— *J'aime mieux le football. Et toi?*
— *Moi aussi, j'aime mieux le football.* ou:
Moi, je préfère le basket.

1. le football américain ou le base-ball
2. les chiens ou les chats
3. la peinture ou la sculpture
4. le cinéma ou le théâtre
5. la musique populaire ou le rock
6. la musique classique ou le jazz
7. les choses sucrées ou les choses salées
8. les sandwiches ou les omelettes

BRUCE SPRINGSTEEN
168 FR
en espèces
exclusivement

Qu'est-ce que vous aimez mieux, la musique populaire ou le rock?

Ex. B: △

Suggestion, Ex. B: Point out to students that when answering a question involving a comparison of more than two items, the article **le** before **mieux** is dropped, as there is no longer a comparison being made.

B. **Qu'est-ce que vous aimez le mieux?** When comparing more than two items, you must add the article **le** to **aimer mieux**—**aimer le mieux.** No change is made in the verb **préférer.** Ask two of your classmates to choose from the following sets of items.

MODÈLE: la musique classique, le jazz ou le rock
— *Qu'est-ce que tu aimes le mieux—la musique classique, le jazz ou le rock?*
— *Moi, j'aime mieux le rock.*
— *Et toi?*
— *Moi, je préfère la musique classique.*

1. le football, le football américain ou le basket
2. la peinture, la sculpture ou l'architecture
3. la musique, la danse ou le cinéma
4. la musique populaire, le funk ou le rock
5. les hamburgers, les cheeseburgers ou les fishburgers
6. les chiens, les chats ou les hamsters
7. les films d'aventure, les films d'horreur ou les films comiques
8. le tennis, le golf ou la natation *(swimming)*

REPRISE

Recycling activity

Ex. C: ⇄ or △

C. **À qui est . . . ?** *(Whose is . . . ?)* Identify each of the items pictured. When someone asks you to whom each belongs, respond with the name of the person indicated.

MODÈLES:

Anne-Marie

— *Voilà une voiture.*
— *À qui est la voiture?*
— *C'est la voiture d'Anne-Marie.*

Philippe

— *Voici des crayons.*
— *À qui sont les crayons?*
— *Ce sont les crayons de Philippe.*

1. Jean

2. Marcelle

3. Jacques

4. Guy

5. *Martine*

6. *Gilles*

7. *Stella*

8. *Françoise*

Follow-up, Ex. C: You walk around the class, picking up various objects and asking **À qui est . . . ? À qui sont . . . ? C'est le . . . de . . . ? Ce sont les . . . de . . . ?** This exercise will lead directly into the presentation of the possessive adjectives. Thus you can move from **C'est le livre de Christine** to **Ah, Christine, c'est votre livre?**

STRUCTURE

Possessive adjectives—first and second persons

— Tu aimes **ton** professeur?	— Do you like *your* teacher?
— Oui, j'aime **mon** professeur.	— Yes, I like *my* teacher.
— Où est **ta** chambre?	— Where is *your* room?
— Voilà **ma** chambre.	— There's *my* room.
— Tu aimes **mes** amis?	— Do you like *my* friends?
— Oui, j'aime beaucoup **tes** amis.	— Yes, I like *your* friends a lot.
— C'est **votre** maison?	— Is that *your* house?
— Non, ce n'est pas **notre** maison.	— No, that's not *our* house.
— Où sont **mes** clés?	— Where are *my* keys?
— Voici **vos** clés.	— Here are *your* keys.

Like articles, possessive adjectives in French agree with the noun they modify. Consequently, French has three forms for both *my* and *your* (familiar) and two forms for *our* and *your* (formal or plural). The following chart summarizes the first- and second-person possessive adjectives:

Subject	Masculine singular	Feminine singular	Masc. and fem. plural	English equivalent
je	**mon**	**ma**	**mes**	*my*
tu	**ton**	**ta**	**tes**	*your*
nous	**notre**	**notre**	**nos**	*our*
vous	**votre**	**votre**	**vos**	*your*

Structure: The presentation of possessive adjectives is divided into two parts in order to establish the notion of double agreement (with modified noun as well as with possessor) before students face the confusing his/her problem. Third-person possessive adjectives appear in Unit Three.

Suggestion, Possessive adjectives: Show objects to students: **Voici un livre. C'est mon livre. Voici un autre livre. C'est votre livre?** Begin with **votre, vos / mon, ma, mes.** Expand to **notre, nos,** then have students ask each other **ton, ta, tes / mon, ma, mes** questions. Objects: **livre, cahier; calculatrice, gomme; clés, livres; ami(e).** Ask questions only of the owner.

C'est mon livre.

C'est ton livre.

Ce sont nos clés.

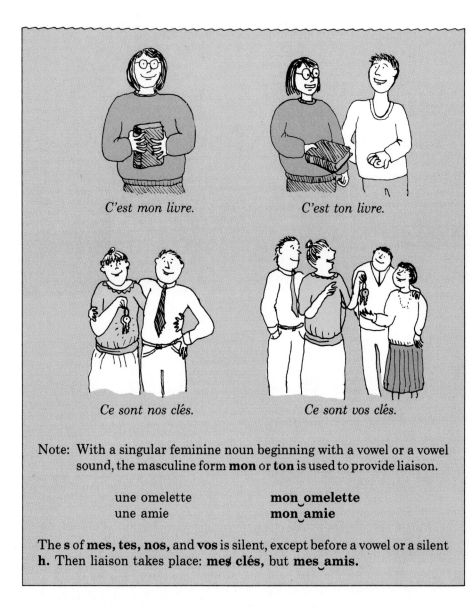

Ce sont vos clés.

Note: With a singular feminine noun beginning with a vowel or a vowel sound, the masculine form **mon** or **ton** is used to provide liaison.

une omelette	**mon‿omelette**
une amie	**mon‿amie**

The **s** of **mes, tes, nos,** and **vos** is silent, except before a vowel or a silent **h.** Then liaison takes place: **me~~s~~ clés,** but **mes‿amis.**

Application

D. Replace the noun in italics and make the necessary changes.

1. Voilà mon *vélo.* (crayon / chien / appartement)
2. Voilà ma *calculatrice.* (maison / chaîne stéréo / gomme)
3. Voilà mes *cassettes.* (disques / clés / amis)
4. Où est ta *serviette?* (maison / chambre / cahier / appareil-photo / portefeuille / calculatrice)

5. Où sont tes *disques?* (cassettes / posters / plantes vertes / animaux / amis)
6. Nous aimons notre *voiture.* (machine à écrire / chat / livres / amis / magnétoscope / disques / professeur)
7. Est-ce que vous avez votre *stylo?* (voiture / calculatrice / cahiers / clés / disques / sac à dos)

E. **Quelle confusion!** All of a sudden everyone seems confused about who certain things belong to. First, a stranger tries to take your school possessions, but you politely set him/her straight. Remember to use **c'est** with a singular noun and **ce sont** with a plural noun.

Le savez-vous?

Radio and TV stations in France are:
a) privately owned
b) publicly owned
c) a mix of public and private ownership

réponse

MODÈLE: Ah, voici mon crayon.
Je m'excuse. Ce n'est pas votre crayon. C'est mon crayon.

1. Ah, voici mon cahier.
2. Et mon stylo.
3. Et ma calculatrice.
4. Et ma gomme.

MODÈLE: Ah, voici mes cassettes.
Je m'excuse. Ce ne sont pas vos cassettes. Ce sont mes cassettes.

5. Ah, voici mes livres.
6. Et mes clés.
7. Et mes cahiers.
8. Et mes disques.

Then your neighbors get confused between what belongs to them and what belongs to your family.

MODÈLE: C'est notre voiture?
Non, non. Ce n'est pas votre voiture. C'est notre voiture.

9. C'est notre télévision?
10. C'est notre radio-réveil?
11. C'est notre appareil-photo?

MODÈLE: Ce sont nos plantes vertes?
Non, non. Ce ne sont pas vos plantes vertes. Ce sont nos plantes vertes.

12. Ce sont nos disques?
13. Ce sont nos vélos?
14. Ce sont nos clés?

Finally, your friend thinks your possessions belong to him/her.

MODÈLE: Eh bien, donne-moi *(give me)* ma clé.
Mais non, ce n'est pas ta clé. C'est ma clé.

15. Donne-moi mon feutre.
16. Donne-moi mon carnet.
17. Donne-moi ma cassette.
18. Donne-moi ma gomme.

MODÈLE: Eh bien, donne-moi mes livres.
Mais non, ce ne sont pas tes livres. Ce sont mes livres.

19. Donne-moi mes posters.
20. Donne-moi mes disques.
21. Donne-moi mes clés.
22. Donne-moi mes cahiers.

➡ c

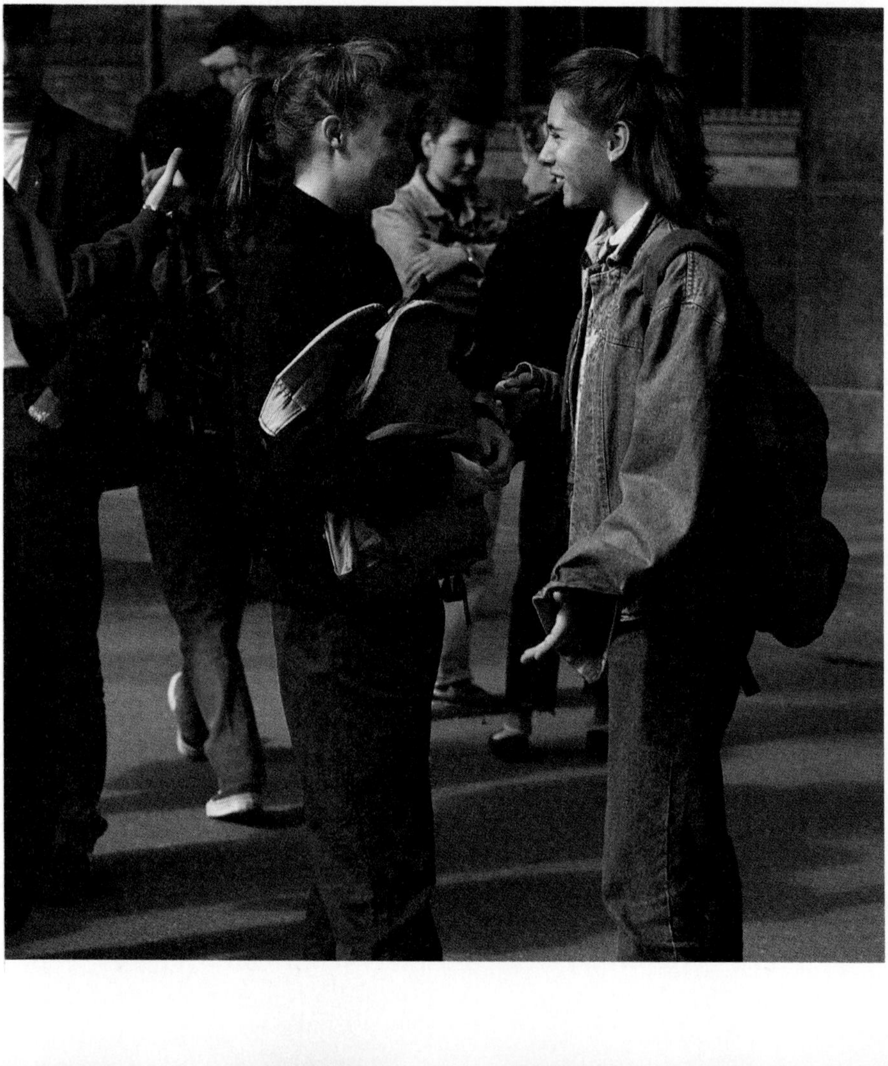

Donne-moi mes cahiers!

F. **Non, non. Ce n'est pas mon Coca!** Your classmates are being particularly difficult today. First, when you point out the foods and beverages pictured below and ask someone if they belong to him/her, that person responds negatively.

Ex. F: △

Variation, Ex. F: After denying ownership, the other students assign it to the questioner. **Non, non, ce n'est pas mon Coca, c'est ton Coca.**

MODÈLES:

— *Voilà un Coca. C'est ton Coca?*
— *Non, non. Ce n'est pas mon Coca.*

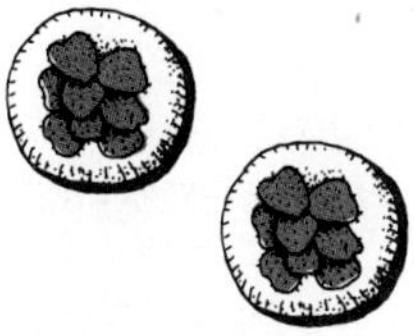

— *Voilà des tartelettes. Ce sont tes tartelettes?*
— *Non, non. Ce ne sont pas mes tartelettes.*

1.

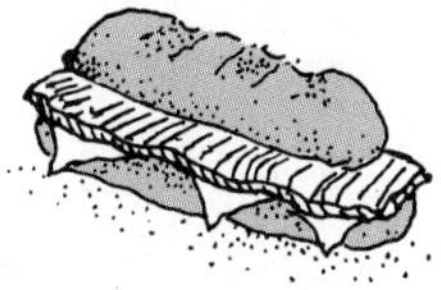

2.

3.

4.

5.

6.

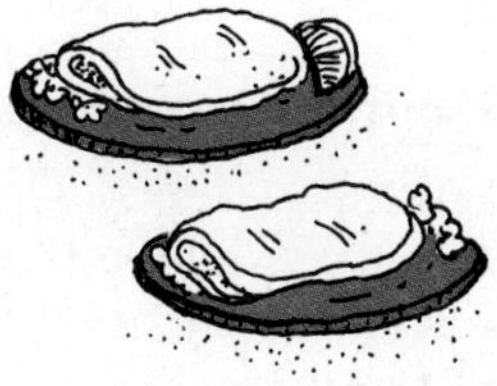

7.

8.

Then, when you ask two people whether the objects pictured below belong to them, they continue to deny ownership.

MODÈLES:

— *Voilà un appareil-photo. C'est votre appareil-photo?*
— *Non, non. Ce n'est pas notre appareil-photo.*

— *Voilà des plantes vertes. Ce sont vos plantes vertes?*
— *Non, non. Ce ne sont pas nos plantes vertes.*

1.

2.

3.

4.

5.

6.

7.

8.

DÉBROUILLONS-NOUS!

Review of the **étape**

Ex. G: ⇄. You may wish to have each student ask a number of questions about the other's likes and dislikes

Written Work: See Workbook.

G. **Moi, je m'appelle. . .** Imagine that it is your first day in an international school where the common language is French. Go up to another student and introduce yourself. Tell where you are from and where you live. Then try to give the other person an idea about what you like and dislike.

Lexique

Pour se débrouiller

Pour indiquer ses goûts et ses préférences

adorer
aimer (assez bien, beaucoup, mieux)
ne pas aimer
détester
préférer

Thèmes et contextes

Les goûts et les préférences

l'art *(m.)*
le camping
le cinéma
les langues *(f.pl.)*
la littérature
les mathématiques *(f.pl.)*
la musique
la nature
la politique
les sciences *(f.pl.)*
la sculpture
les sports *(m.pl.)*
le tennis
le théâtre

Vocabulaire général

Noms
un(e) petit(e) ami(e)
une pièce de théâtre

Adjectifs
classique
populaire

Autres expressions
voici

Chapitre six

Voici ma famille!

Voici ma famille . . . ma mère, ma sœur et mon père!

Première étape

Point de départ:

J'habite avec. . .

Supplementary Vocabulary: un beau-père *(stepfather)*, une belle-mère *(stepmother)*

Bonjour. Je m'appelle Dominique Tavernier. Dominique, c'est mon ***prénom.*** *Tavernier, c'est mon* ***nom de famille.*** *Nous sommes sept dans ma famille. J'ai un* ***père,*** *une* ***mère,*** *un* ***frère*** *et une* ***soeur.*** *Mon frère* ***s'appelle*** *Jean-Pierre et ma soeur s'appelle Sophie. Nous habitons dans une maison à Lille avec mon* ***grand-père*** *et ma* ***grand-mère.***

first name / last name
father / mother / brother / sister
is named
grandfather / grandmother

À vous!

A. **Vous et votre famille.** First, complete the following sentences with information about you and your family.

1. Je m'appelle. . .
2. Mon prénom, c'est. . .
3. Mon nom de famille, c'est. . .
4. Nous sommes . . . dans ma famille.
5. Mon père s'appelle. . .
6. Ma mère s'appelle. . .
7. J'ai . . . frères. (ou: Je n'ai pas de frères.)
   Il s'appelle. . . (ou: Ils s'appellent. . .)
8. J'ai . . . soeurs. (ou: Je n'ai pas de soeurs.)
   Elle s'appelle. . . (ou: Elles s'appellent. . .)
9. J'habite avec mes grands-parents. (ou: Je n'habite pas avec mes grands-parents.)

Ex. B: ⇄. Have students choose a different partner.

B. **La famille de votre camarade.** Now ask one of your classmates the following questions about him/herself and his/her family.

1. Comment est-ce que tu t'appelles? *(Je m'appelle. . .)*
2. Quel *(what)* est ton prénom?
3. Quel est ton nom de famille?
4. Vous êtes combien dans ta famille? *(Nous sommes. . .)*
5. Comment s'appelle ton père?
6. Comment s'appelle ta mère?
7. Combien de *(how many)* frères est-ce que tu as?
8. Comment est-ce qu'il s'appelle? (Comment est-ce qu'ils s'appellent?)
9. Combien de sœurs est-ce que tu as?
10. Comment est-ce qu'elle s'appelle? (Comment est-ce qu'elles s'appellent?)
11. Est-ce que tu as des grands-pères et des grands-mères?
12. Est-ce que tu habites avec tes grands-parents?

Follow-up, Ex. B: Have students ask you questions about your family.

Prononciation: *The consonants* c *and* g

In French, the consonants **c** and **g** may represent either a hard or a soft sound. When followed by a consonant or by the vowels **a, o,** or **u,** they have a hard sound:

[k] (as in *car*): **c**lasse, **c**ouleur, **c**ahier, é**c**u
[g] (as in *gun*): **g**rand, **g**omme, **g**uide

When either is followed by the vowels **e, i,** or **y,** or when **c** is marked with a cedilla **(ç),** they have a soft sound:

[s] (as in *nice*): fa**c**e, **c**inéma, fran**ç**ais
[ʒ] (as in *sabotage*): â**g**e, ri**g**ide, **g**ymnase

Pratique

C. Read each word aloud, being careful to give the appropriate hard or soft sound to the consonants **c** and **g.**

1. café	5. cahier	9. Orangina	13. belge
2. citron	6. pièces	10. goûts	14. langue
3. croissant	7. combien	11. fromage	15. Roger
4. ça	8. Françoise	12. portugais	16. égyptien

REPRISE

D. **C'est votre. . . ?** Your instructor will ask you to identify certain objects and indicate to whom they belong.

MODÈLE: — *Qu'est-ce que c'est?*
— *C'est un livre.*
— *C'est votre livre?*
— *Oui, c'est mon livre.* ou:
Non, c'est le livre de Nancy.

Recycling activities

Implementation, Ex. D: Use objects from the classroom (**stylo, cahier,** etc.) Distribute the items so that some belong to one student and others to two students.

E. **Échange.** Ask these questions to another student, who will answer them.

Ex. E: ⇄

1. Est-ce que tu aimes les sports? Qu'est-ce que tu aimes le mieux—le football, le basket, le baseball ou le football américain?
2. Est-ce que tu aimes mieux la musique ou la peinture?
3. Est-ce que tu préfères les mathématiques ou les langues? les sciences ou la littérature?
4. Est-ce que tu aimes les animaux? Est-ce que tu aimes mieux les chiens ou les chats?
5. Est-ce que tu préfères regarder la télévision ou écouter des disques?
6. Qu'est-ce que tu aimes le mieux—le camping, la politique ou le cinéma?

Moi, j'adore les chats. Est-ce que tu aimes mieux les chats ou les chiens?

Structure, Information questions: Make a statement, then ask students to verify their response. **Jean-Pierre habite à Rouen. (Où est-ce qu'il habite?)** Write form on board. Other models: **Chantal a trois frères. Hélène aime manger les choses sucrées. Georges n'étudie pas parce qu'il n'aime pas les sciences.**

STRUCTURE

Information questions with ***où, combien de, que,*** *and* ***pourquoi***

You have already learned how to ask questions that take *yes* or *no* as an answer. Frequently, however, you ask a question because you seek specific information. In most cases, you can use **est-ce que** after one of the following question words:

To find out *where* something or someone is located, use **où** + **est-ce que (qu'):**

— ***Où est-ce que*** *ton frère habite?*
— *Il habite à Marseille.*

— Where does *your brother live?*
— *He lives in Marseille.*

When a question with **où** contains the verb **être, est-ce que** is not usually used:

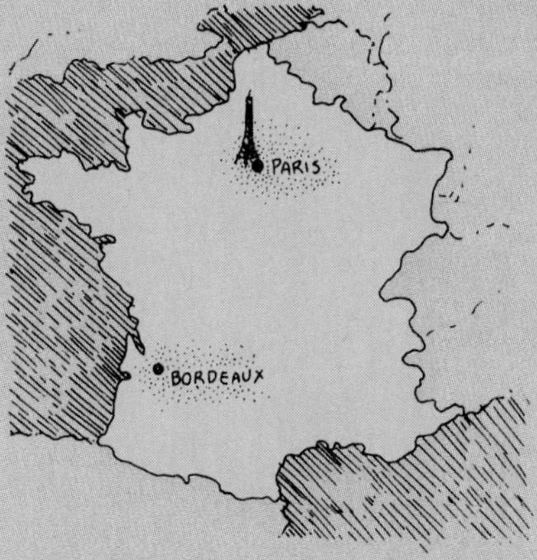

— ***Où est*** *Bordeaux?*
— *Bordeaux est au sud-ouest de Paris.*

— Where is *Bordeaux?*
— *Bordeaux is southwest of Paris.*

To ask about a *quantity*, use **combien de (d') + est-ce que (qu'):**

— ***Combien de*** *sœurs* ***est-ce que*** *vous avez?*	— How many *sisters* do *you have?*
— *J'ai deux sœurs.*	— *I have two sisters.*

To find out *what* someone wants or is seeking, use **que + est-ce que.** Notice the elision: **qu'est-ce que (qu'):**

— ***Qu'est-ce qu'****ils cherchent?*	— What are *they looking for?*
— *Ils cherchent la maison de Chantal.*	— *They are looking for Chantal's house.*

To ask *why*, use **pourquoi + est-ce que (qu').** The answer to this question usually begins with **parce que (qu'):**

— ***Pourquoi*** *est-ce que Claudine n'est pas au match de football?*	— Why *isn't Claudine at the soccer game?*
— ***Parce qu'****elle aime mieux le tennis.*	— Because *she likes tennis better.*

Additional structure: You may also wish to teach the question word **qui,** especially if you limit its use to situations where **qui** is the subject of the sentence: **Qui habite là? Qui a une voiture? Qui aime les croissants?**

Application

F. Replace the subject in italics and make the necessary changes.

1. Où est-ce que *vous* travaillez? (tu / ta mère / Alain / ton père)
2. Où est *Bordeaux?* (Toulouse / ta maison / mes clés / mes livres)
3. Combien de soeurs est-ce que *vous* avez? (tu / ils / Jean-Paul / nous)
4. Qu'est-ce qu'*ils* cherchent? (tu / vous / vos amis / on)
5. Pourquoi est-ce qu'*elle* n'a pas de disques? (tu / ton frère / tes parents / vous)

G. **Faisons connaissance!** *(Let's get to know each other!)* In order to get to know an exchange student from Dijon a little better, you ask her questions about herself, her brother, and her parents. Use the suggested words to form your questions.

tu

MODÈLE: où / habiter
Où est-ce que tu habites?

tu

1. combien de / frères / avoir
2. qu'est-ce que / aimer mieux / musique / sports
3. pourquoi / être ici à *(your town)*

ton frère

4. où / travailler
5. pourquoi / ne pas avoir de livres
6. qu'est-ce que / aimer manger
7. où / être / maintenant

tes parents

8. où / habiter
9. pourquoi / ne pas habiter à Dijon
10. qu'est-ce que / regarder à la télévision
11. où / être / maintenant

H. **Précisons!** *(Let's give more details!)* Conversation depends on the listener's paying attention to the speaker's comments and reacting to them.

You are talking with some of the French exchange students in your school. Ask follow-up questions, using the cues in parentheses.

MODÈLE: **Claude Fournier**
Je n'habite pas à Paris. (où)
Où est-ce que tu habites?

Claude Fournier

1. J'ai des soeurs, mais je n'ai pas de frères. (combien de)
2. Mes soeurs étudient beaucoup. (qu'est-ce que)
3. Elles n'aiment pas les mathématiques. (pourquoi)

Bénédicte Cadet

4. Mon père et ma mère travaillent tous les deux *(both)*. (où)
5. Ma soeur gagne beaucoup d'argent. (combien de)
6. Mon frère gagne très peu. (pourquoi)

Edith Poncet

7. Ma grand-mère habite à Cassis. (où / être)
8. Elle a des chiens et des chats. (qu'est-ce que / aimer mieux)
9. Elle parle beaucoup. (pourquoi)

Follow-up, Ex. H: Make statements about members of your family; have students ask you follow-up questions.

DÉBROUILLONS-NOUS!

I. **Échange.** Ask the following questions to another student, who will answer them.

1. Vous êtes combien dans ta famille?
2. Comment s'appelle ton père? Et ta mère?
3. Est-ce qu'ils travaillent tous les deux? Où?
4. Combien de soeurs est-ce que tu as? Est-ce que tu as des frères aussi?
5. Est-ce qu'ils (elles) sont élèves dans un lycée aussi?
6. Où est-ce que tes grands-parents habitent? Est-ce qu'ils habitent dans une maison ou dans un appartement?

Review of the **étape**

Ex. I: ⇄

Implementation, Ex. I: Pair students with partners other than those with whom they worked in Ex. B.

J. **Ta famille.** Find out as much as you can about another student's family. Begin by getting information about the size and composition of the family. Then choose one member of the family (mother, father, brother, sister, or grandparent) and ask more detailed questions.

Ex. J: ⇄

Implementation, Ex. J: Pair students with partners other than those they had for Exs. B or I.

Written Work: See Workbook.

Deuxième étape

Point de départ:

J'ai une famille nombreuse: I have a big family

Supplementary vocabulary: un beau-frère *(brother-in-law)*, une belle-soeur *(sister-in-law)*, un neveu, une nièce

J'ai une famille nombreuse

La famille de Dominique Tavernier

that

married / his wife / son
big / brown hair /eyes
wears glasses

J'ai aussi de la famille ***qui*** *n'habite pas à Lille. Regardons les photos dans notre album. Voilà mon oncle Jacques. C'est le frère de mon père. Il est* ***marié. Sa femme*** *s'appelle tante Élise. Ils ont un* ***fils***—*c'est mon cousin André. Il est* ***grand.*** *Il a les* ***cheveux bruns*** *et les* ***yeux*** *bruns aussi. Il* ***porte des lunettes.***

her husband / children / daughter
quite small

Et voilà ma tante Béatrice. C'est la sœur de ma mère. Elle est mariée aussi. ***Son mari*** *s'appelle oncle René. Ils ont deux* ***enfants***—*un fils et une* ***fille.*** *Ce sont mon cousin Robert et ma cousine Jacqueline. Jacqueline a les cheveux blonds. Ses yeux sont bleus. Elle est* ***assez petite.***

À vous!

A. **Du côté de votre mère.** *(On your mother's side.)* Answer the following questions about family members on your mother's side of the family.

1. Est-ce que vous avez une petite *(small)* famille ou une famille nombreuse du côté de votre mère?
2. Combien d'oncles est-ce que vous avez? Comment est-ce qu'ils s'appellent?
3. Est-ce qu'ils sont mariés? Est-ce qu'ils ont des enfants? des fils? des filles?
4. Comment s'appellent vos cousins? Où est-ce qu'ils habitent?
5. Est-ce que vous avez des tantes aussi du côté de votre mère?

B. **Du côté de votre père.** *(On your father's side.)* Answer the following questions about family members on your father's side of the family.

Variation, Ex. B: Have students work in pairs; remind them to change **vous** to **tu.**

1. Est-ce que la famille du côté de votre père est nombreuse?
2. Combien de tantes est-ce que vous avez du côté de votre père? Est-ce qu'elles sont mariées? Combien d'enfants est-ce qu'elles ont?
3. Comment s'appellent vos cousins et vos cousines du côté de votre père?
4. Est-ce que votre père a des frères aussi? Où est-ce qu'ils habitent?

NOTE GRAMMATICALE

To describe hair and eyes in French, you can use either the verb **avoir** or the verb **être.** If you use **avoir,** the subject of the sentence is the person you are describing and you need a definite article:

J'ai les cheveux roux.	*I have red hair.*
Mon grand-père a les cheveux gris.	*My grandfather has gray hair.*

If you use **être,** the subject of the sentence is the part of the body being described and you need an expression that indicates possession:

Mes cheveux sont noirs.	*My hair is black.*
Les yeux de ma mère sont bleus.	*My mother's eyes are blue.*

To indicate whether someone is short or tall, use the adjectives **petit** and **grand.** If the person is female, add an **e.** If you are talking about more than one person add an **s:**

Ma sœur est très petite.	*My sister is very short (small).*
Mes frères sont assez grands.	*My brothers are fairly tall (big).*

C. **Ma famille.** Describe each member of your family, indicating whether he/she is short or tall as well as the color of his/her hair and eyes. Mention also whether or not he/she wears glasses. Remember to include yourself!

MODÈLE: *Mon père est très grand. Il n'a pas de cheveux. Il est chauve* (bald). *Il a les yeux bruns et il ne porte pas de lunettes.*

REPRISE

Recycling activity

Ex. D: ⇄. Since this is the first time to do an exercise of this type, you may wish to work through all the items with the class and then break them up into pairs.

D. **Des questions.** Ask a classmate questions in order to get the following information. DO NOT translate word for word. Instead, find a French expression that will get the information for you. Your classmate will answer your questions.

MODÈLES: where he/she lives
— *Où est-ce que tu habites?*
— *J'habite à Walpole.*

where his/her father and mother work
— *Où est-ce que ton père et ta mère travaillent?*
— *Mon père travaille à Central High School et ma mère travaille à City Hospital.*

1. where his/her grandparents live
2. how many brothers and sisters he/she has
3. how many dogs and/or cats he/she has
4. what he/she is studying
5. what he/she prefers (give two choices)
6. what he/she likes to eat
7. why he/she eats a lot (or very little)
8. why he/she is studying French

Suggestions, faire: (1) Have students repeat the conjugation of **faire** while you write pronouns in four groups: **je, tu, il, elle, on / ils, elles / nous / vous.** (2) Repeat in negative. (3) Write verb forms in five groups **(je, tu / il, elle, on / ils, elles / nous / vous).**

STRUCTURE

The present tense of the irregular verb ***faire***

Qu'est-ce que **vous faites?**	What *are you doing?*
Nous faisons les devoirs.	*We are doing* homework.
Je ne fais pas mon lit.	*I don't make* my bed.

Here are the present-tense forms of the irregular verb **faire** *(to do, to make)*:

faire	
je **fais**	nous **faisons**
tu **fais**	vous **faites**
il, elle, on **fait**	ils, elles **font**

The verb **faire** is often used to ask a question. In such cases, the answer frequently involves a verb other than **faire:**

— Qu'est-ce que **tu fais?** — What *are you doing?*
— Je travaille. — I'm working.

— Qu'est-ce que tu aimes **faire?** — What do you like *to do?*
— J'aime danser. — I like to dance.

Le savez-vous?

Mémé **and** ***pépé*** **are terms often used by French children when talking to or about their**
a) mother and father
b) grandmother and grandfather
c) brother and sister

réponse

Application

E. Replace the subject in italics and make the necessary changes.

1. Qu'est-ce que *Pierre* fait? (tu / vous / Jean-Michel et Patrice / on / nous / Chantal)
2. *Marie-Claire* fait des devoirs. (je / vous / mon frère / tu / nous / mes cousins)
3. *Jean* ne fait pas les lits. (Béatrice / nous / les parents de Sylvie / je / vous / tu)

F. **Qu'est-ce qu'on fait ce soir?** You would like to organize a group activity for this evening. However, you can't find anyone to join your group. Every time you mention someone and ask your friend what that person is doing, your friend replies with the activity indicated.

MODÈLE: Martine / travailler
— *Qu'est-ce que Martine fait ce soir* (tonight)?
— *Elle travaille ce soir.*

1. Jean-Pierre / étudier
2. Bernadette / danser
3. ton oncle Paul / chanter
4. ta tante Yvonne / regarder un film
5. tes parents / regarder le football à la télévision
6. tu / écouter des disques de jazz

Suggestion, Note grammaticale, Expressions with **faire:** (1) Act out the various activities while saying **Je fais du ski. Je fais une promenade.** Etc. (2) Ask students: **Qui aime faire du ski? Qui aime faire un tour à vélo?** Etc.

NOTE GRAMMATICALE

Some idiomatic expressions with ***faire***

Similar to the verb **avoir,** the verb **faire** is often used in idiomatic expressions that do not have word-for-word English translations.

Here are a few such expressions. You will encounter others in future chapters:

faire un voyage	to take a trip, to go on a trip
faire une promenade	to take a walk, to go for a walk
faire du sport	to participate in sports
faire du tennis	to play tennis
faire du ski	to go skiing
faire du vélo	to go bike riding
faire de la moto	to go biking (motorcycle)
faire un tour (en voiture / à vélo / à moto)	to go for a ride (in a car / on a bicycle / on a motorcycle)

Nous faisons une promenade.	*We are taking a walk.*
Tu fais du ski?	*Do you go skiing?*

➡ b

Ex. G: △

Preparation, Ex. G: Ask students what each person is doing in the drawings: **Qu'est-ce que Marie fait?** Etc.

G. **Qu'est-ce qu'on fait ce week-end?** You call up your brother or sister to find out what your family and friends are doing this weekend. He/she in turn asks them about their plans. Follow the model, using the pictures to determine what each person is planning to do.

Marie

MODÈLE:	VOUS:	*Qu'est-ce que Marie fait ce week-end?*
	VOTRE FRÈRE:	*Marie, qu'est-ce que tu fais ce week-end?*
	MARIE:	*Je fais un tour en voiture.*
	VOTRE FRÈRE:	*Elle fait un tour en voiture.*

1. Martin

2. M. et Mme Simon

3. Anne et Louis

4. M. et Mme Genisse

5. Annick et Victor

6. Claudine

H. **Qu'est-ce que tu voudrais faire ce soir?** Ask several classmates what they would like to do tonight. They will answer using one of the possibilities listed below. In each case, indicate whether their idea coincides with yours.

Ex. H: O. To allow for variety, you may wish to assign activities or have students pick them from a hat.

MODÈLE: — *Qu'est-ce que tu voudrais faire ce soir?*
— *Je voudrais danser.*
— *Moi aussi, je voudrais danser.* ou:
Non, moi, je voudrais faire une promenade.

faire du tennis / faire une promenade / regarder la télévision / écouter des disques / parler / manger / danser / chanter / faire un tour à vélo / faire mes devoirs / regarder un film / faire de la moto

DÉBROUILLONS-NOUS!

Review of the **étape**

Ex. I: ○

Implementation, Ex. I: Allow students to circulate for a short time. Then ask the four questions, comparing answers from different parts of the classroom (i.e., students will not have had time to talk to everyone).

Written Work: See Workbook.

I. **Qui a le plus grand nombre de. . . ?** *(Who has the most. . . ?)* Go around the class asking other students how many aunts, uncles, male cousins, and female cousins they each have. Based on your findings, your teacher will then try to determine:

1. Qui a le plus grand nombre de tantes?
2. Qui a le plus grand nombre d'oncles?
3. Qui a le plus grand nombre de cousins?
4. Qui a le plus grand nombre de cousines?

J. **Qui est-ce?** *(Who is it?)* Give a short description of someone in your class. The others will try to guess who it is. Include in your description size, color of hair and eyes, and whether or not the person wears glasses. If no one guesses, add another detail (something the person has, something you know about the size of the person's family, what he/she likes to do, etc.).

J'ai une famille très petite. Et toi?

Lexique

Pour se débrouiller

Pour s'identifier
je suis. . .
je m'appelle. . .

Pour se renseigner
combien de
comment s'appelle. . .
où
pourquoi
qu'est-ce que

Thèmes et contextes

Les activités
faire une promenade
faire du ski
faire du sport
faire du tennis
faire un tour
faire un voyage

La famille
un(e) cousin(e)
une femme
une fille
un fils
un frère
une grand-mère
un grand-père
un mari
une mère
un oncle
un père
une sœur
une tante

Vocabulaire général

Noms
un nom de famille
un prénom

Verbes
chercher
écouter
faire
regarder

Adjectifs
marié(e)

Autres expressions
parce que

Mise au point

Prereading: Ask students how to define one's identity (i.e., who you are). Have them look at the four photos in the **Lecture** section and try to make some guesses about the identity of each person.

Suggestion, Lecture: Have students read the four descriptions once, do Ex. A with the entire class, then have students reread the passage in order to do Ex. B.

Lecture: *Mon identité*

The ability to read in French develops more rapidly than the skills of speaking, listening, and writing. One reason is the large number of cognates (similar words) shared by French and English. Use the many cognates in the paragraphs below to help you get the general idea WITHOUT consulting the definitions that follow.

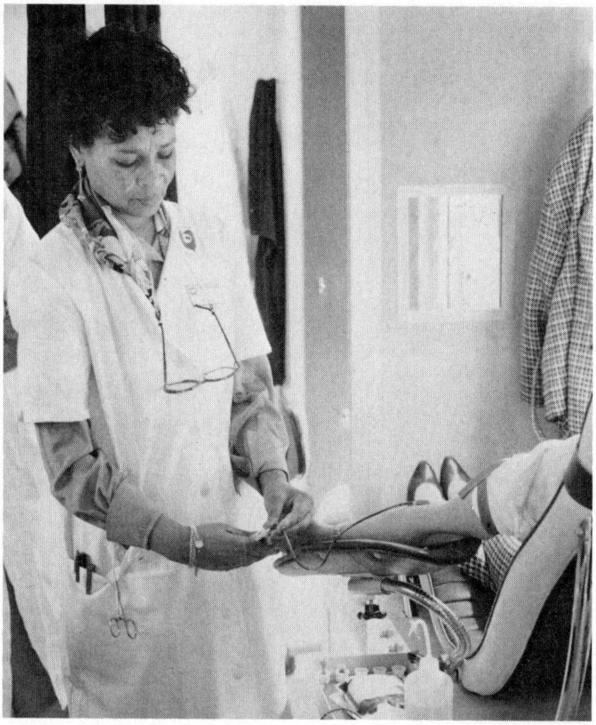

Je suis médecin et mère de famille. Je travaille à l'hôpital Saint-Nicolas à Bordeaux. Mon mari est journaliste. Il est souvent à la maison avec nos enfants. Nous avons un fils et trois filles. Le week-end nous faisons beaucoup de choses avec[1] les enfants. Nous aimons le camping et les sports. Moi, je fais du ski, mais mon mari aime mieux le football. Nous aimons aussi les arts. Mon fils voudrait être architecte et une de mes filles étudie la peinture à l'université.

[1]with

Je suis élève au Lycée Montaigne à Lyon. J'étudie les langues modernes—l'anglais et l'espagnol—parce que j'aime beaucoup la littérature et aussi parce que je voudrais voyager un jour.[2] Mes parents sont divorcés. J'habite avec ma mère, qui travaille dans une banque. Mon père, qui est ingénieur, habite à Grenoble. J'ai un petit frère qui s'appelle Alexandre. Je n'ai pas de sœurs. Nous n'avons pas beaucoup d'argent.

Je suis président d'une grande[3] entreprise. J'ai une grande maison, quatre télévisions couleur et trois voitures dans le garage. Ma femme et moi, nous voyageons beaucoup. Nous avons un chalet en Suisse et un appartement à Paris. Mes enfants sont dans une école[4] privée. Mon fils a une chaîne stéréo, une grande quantité de disques et une voiture. Ma fille a un ordinateur et un magnétoscope. Nous avons une vie[5] très confortable.

[2]one day (someday) [3]large [4]school [5]life

Je suis en retraite[6]. Ma femme est morte[7] en 1985. J'habite avec mon fils Michel à Rennes. Il est marié. Sa femme s'appelle Renée. Ils ont deux filles. Je ne travaille pas. J'aime beaucoup la nature et je fais souvent des promenades. Le soir[8] je mange avec la famille et après le dîner je regarde la télévision. Ma vie est assez agréable.

Compréhension

A. **Les mots apparentés.** *(Cognates)* What do you think each of the following words means?

le président, le garage, privé(e), une quantité, confortable, moderne(s), divorcé(s), une banque, l'hôpital, un journaliste, l'université, le dîner, agréable

Answers, Ex. B:
1. a. faux, b. faux, c. vrai, d. faux
2. a. faux, b. vrai, c. faux, d. faux
3. a. vrai, b. faux, c. vrai, d. faux
4. a. vrai, b. faux, c. faux, d. vrai.

B. **Vrai ou faux?** Reread the **Lecture,** referring to the definitions at the end. Then decide whether the statements made by each person are true or false. Support your answers by pointing out the relevant information in the **Lecture.**

1. Le médecin:
   a. J'ai cinq enfants.
   b. Mon mari travaille le week-end.
   c. J'aime la nature.
   d. Mes enfants sont très petits.

[6]retired [7]died [8]in the evening

2. L'élève:
   a. J'habite avec mon père et ma mère à Lyon.
   b. Je parle trois langues.
   c. J'ai une famille nombreuse.
   d. Je suis riche.

3. Le président d'entreprise:
   a. Je suis matérialiste.
   b. J'ai une grande maison à Paris.
   c. Je suis riche.
   d. Je fais beaucoup de choses avec mes enfants.

4. L'homme en retraite:
   a. J'habite avec la famille de mon fils à Rennes.
   b. Je fais souvent des promenades avec ma femme.
   c. Je prends le déjeuner dans un restaurant fast-food avec mes amis.
   d. Le soir je suis à la maison.

Postreading: Compare the impressions based on the pictures with what the students learned from reading about the four people. Then have students write a description of themselves.

REPRISE

Recycling Activity

C. **Échange.** Ask these questions of a classmate, who will answer you.

Ex. C: ⇄

1. Est-ce que tu as une famille nombreuse?
2. Combien est-ce que tu as de tantes et d'oncles du côté de ta mère? Du côté de ton père?
3. Comment s'appelle ta tante préférée? Où est-ce qu'elle habite? Est-ce qu'elle est mariée? Est-ce qu'elle a des enfants? Comment est-ce qu'ils s'appellent?
4. Est-ce que ta tante travaille? Qu'est-ce qu'elle fait?
5. Comment s'appelle ton oncle préféré? Où est-ce qu'il habite? Est-ce qu'il est marié? Est-ce qu'il a des enfants? Est-ce qu'ils sont au lycée?
6. Est-ce que ton oncle travaille? Qu'est-ce qu'il fait?

D. **Qu'est-ce qu'il fait?** Ask a classmate what the person in each picture is doing. Use the noun or pronoun printed under the picture in your question. Your partner will answer your question on the basis of the drawing.

Ex. D: ⇄

Marc

MODÈLE: — *Qu'est-ce que Marc fait?*
— *Il fait un tour (à vélo.)*

1. Mireille

2. Roger et son frère

3. vous

4. tu

5. on

6. Jeanne et ses sœurs

7. Paul

8. tu

RÉVISION

In this **Révision,** you will review:

- numbers from 0 to 10
- indefinite and definite articles;
- the irregular verbs **avoir** and **faire;**
- information questions;
- expressions with avoir;
- possessive adjectives.

Possessions, tastes and the family

E. **Trois portraits.** On the basis of the drawings, give as much information as you can about the three featured people.

1.

MODÈLE: *Je m'appelle Andrée. J'habite à Orléans. J'ai les cheveux bruns. J'aime beaucoup les sports. (Etc.)*

2.

Numbers from 0 to 10

zero	**trois**	**cinq**	**sept**	**neuf**
un, une	**quatre**	**six**	**huit**	**dix**
deux				

F. **Faisons les additions.** Do the following simple arithmetic problems.

MODÈLE: 2 + 3 =
Deux et trois font cinq.

1. 3 + 6 =
2. 4 + 6 =
3. 7 + 1 =
4. 2 + 5 =
5. 5 + 3 =
6. 2 + 7 =

The indefinite and definite articles

Indefinite	**Definite**
un, une, des (negative: **de**)	**le, la, l', les**

Ex. G: ⇄

G. **Est-ce que tu voudrais?** Ask a friend if he/she would like a beverage or food from the first category given. He/she will indicate that he/she doesn't like food or drinks of that kind and will ask for something from the second category. Follow the model.

MODÈLE: les sandwiches / les omelettes
— *Est-ce que tu voudrais un sandwich au fromage?*
— *Non, je n'aime pas les sandwiches. Je voudrais une omelette au fromage.*

1. les choses sucrées / les choses salées
2. les boissons chaudes / les boissons froides
3. les sandwiches / les omelettes

H. **Faisons connaissance!** In order to get to know one of your classmates better, ask him/her a series of yes/no questions. Use the elements suggested below, being careful to distinguish between nouns that require the definite article **le, la, l', les** and nouns that require the indefinite article **un, une, des.** Your classmate will answer your questions.

MODÈLES:

avoir / voiture
Tu as une voiture?
Oui, j'ai une voiture. ou:
Non, je n'ai pas de voiture.

aimer / sports
Tu aimes les sports?
Oui, j'aime beaucoup les sports. ou:
Non, je n'aime pas les sports.

1. avoir / frères / soeurs?
2. habiter / dans / appartement?
3. aimer / animaux?
4. aimer mieux / chiens / ou / chats?
5. avoir / chien (chat)?
6. aimer / musique?
7. préférer / rock / funk / jazz / musique classique?
8. avoir / disques / ou / cassettes?

The irregular verb *avoir*

j'**ai**	nous **avons**
tu **as**	vous **avez**
il, elle, on **a**	ils, elles **ont**

The irregular verb *faire*

je **fais**	nous **faisons**
tu **fais**	vous **faites**
il, elle, on **fait**	ils, elles **font**

Information questions

où (est-ce que)
combien de . . . est-ce que
qu'est-ce que
pourquoi est-ce que

I. **Des légendes.** *(Captions.)* Complete the captions for the following drawings, using one of these expressions: **avoir faim, avoir soif, avoir raison, avoir tort.**

MODÈLE:
Oui les enfants, vous avez . . . (raison/tort)
Oui les enfants, vous avez raison.

1. *Les voyageurs ont . . .*
(faim/soif)

2. *Nous avons . . .*
(faim/soif)

3. *Pierre a . . .*
(raison/tort)

Now complete the captions for the following drawings using the expression **avoir besoin de.**

MODÈLE:
Vincent a besoin de . . .
(radio-réveil/magnétoscope)
Vincent a besoin d'un radio-réveil.

1. *Monique a besoin de . . .*
(machine à écrire/calculatrice)

2. *J'ai besoin de . . .*
(clés/portefeuille)

3. *Jacques a besoin de . . .*
(taille-crayon/croque-monsieur)

J. **Où est-ce que ta soeur habite?** When you ask your French friends where their relatives live, they answer with the name of the city. You then ask them what their relatives do. This time they give an occupation.

Ex. J: ⇄

MODÈLE:

ta sœur

— *Où est-ce que ta soeur habite?*
— *Elle habite à Rouen.*
— *Qu'est-ce qu'elle fait à Rouen?*
— *Elle est architecte.*

1. *ton oncle*

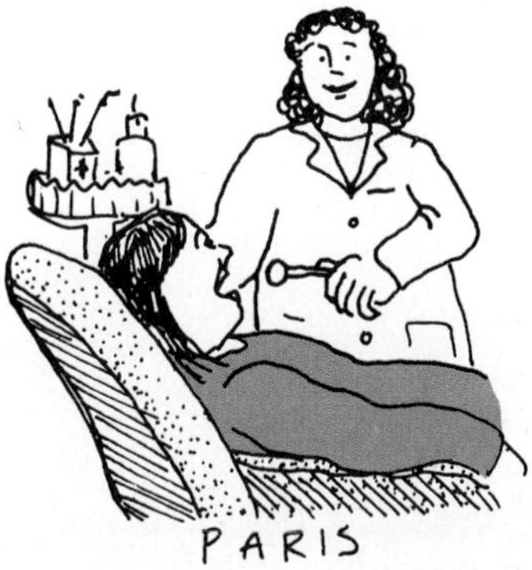

2. *la mère de François*

3. *ton oncle et ta tante*

4. *Michel et Dominique, vous*

5. *Annick, tu*

K. **Un nouvel ami.** *(A new friend.)* A French exchange student whom you have just met is telling you about his family and his life in France. Each time he makes a statement, you ask a follow-up question using **où, combien de. . . , qu'est-ce que** or **pourquoi.**

MODÈLE: J'ai une famille nombreuse. J'ai beaucoup de frères et de soeurs.
Combien de frères et de sœurs est-ce que tu as?

1. Nous sommes de Paris. Mais nous n'habitons pas à Paris.
2. Nous habitons dans un petit village qui s'appelle Lusignan.
3. Ma mère et mon père travaillent tous les deux.
4. Je suis élève dans un petit lycée. Il n'y a pas beaucoup d'élèves dans mon école.
5. J'étudie les mathématiques, le français et l'anglais.
6. Je n'étudie pas les sciences.
7. J'aime mes professeurs et mes camarades de classe, mais j'aime mieux le week-end. Je fais beaucoup de choses avec mes frères.
8. Nous faisons du ski.

J'étudie les mathématiques, le français et l'anglais.

Possessive adjectives

mon, ma, mes	**notre, nos**
ton, ta, tes	**votre, vos**

The possessive adjective agrees in gender (masculine or feminine) and number (singular or plural).

L. **Où est mon. . .?** You are continually losing your belongings at school. When you ask someone if something is yours, he/she says it belongs to Janine. When you ask Janine, she tells you that the item belongs to someone else. Follow the model.

MODÈLE: livre
— *C'est mon livre?*
— *Non, ce n'est pas ton livre. C'est le livre de Janine.*

— *C'est ton livre?*
— *Non, ce n'est pas mon livre. C'est le livre de Jean-Claude.*

1. cahier
2. calculatrice
3. clés
4. gomme
5. stylo
6. devoirs

Ex. L: △

Variation, Ex. L: Use actual objects from the class. Get something (e.g., **un cahier**) from a student. Have him/her look away while you mix it in with objects belonging to two other students. Then have the three students question each other. Objects: **livres, stylos, calculatrices, sacs à dos, clés, argent.**

Point d'arrivée

(Activités orales et écrites)

M. **Faisons connaissance!** Get to know another student by exchanging information. Find out:

1. his/her name
2. where he/she lives (and is from)
3. the size and makeup of his/her family
4. his/her interests (sports, music, etc.)
5. his/her possessions
6. his/her likes and dislikes (activities)

He/she will ask the same information of you.

Ex. M: ⇄. Pair students who have not worked together on an **échange** type exercise in this chapter.

Suggestion, Ex. N: If the class is large, have students practice giving their presentations in small groups, then choose (or have the group choose) someone to make his/her presentation to the class.

N. **Je suis. . .** Present yourself to the class. Using the French you've learned so far, give as much information as you can about your family, your interests, your activities, and your possessions.

Ex. O: △. You can circulate, playing the role of the **garçon.**

O. **Le déjeuner au café.** You go to a café for lunch with a person whom you've just met. When you arrive, you see a friend of yours. Along with two other members of the class, play the roles of the students in this situation. During the conversation, make introductions, order lunch, and find out as much as possible about each other.

Variation, Ex. P: Have the student construct his/her partner's family tree on the basis of what the partner tells him/her and what he/she asks the partner.

P. **L'arbre généalogique.** *(The family tree.)* Construct your family tree and explain to a classmate the relationships among you and the other family members. Give several bits of information for each person—where he/she lives, what he/she does and has, and what he/she likes or dislikes. If possible, bring a family photo to class.

Ex. Q: ⇄. Students will need time to prepare this exercise.

Q. **Un dialogue des contraires.** *(A dialogue of opposites.)* Imagine that you and another student have a relationship similar to that of the two people in the dialogue on p. 85. The two of you are friends, despite great differences in family background (where you are from, where you live, the size of your family, your parents' occupations, etc.), possessions, and interests. Invent the details of your two lives and present them to the class in the form of a dialogue of opposites.

POURQUOI?

Your family has agreed to host a French exchange student for a few months. All that you know about your guest is her name (Colette Hulot), where she lives (Nîmes), and what she does (she's a student at the Collège Saint-François de Sales). Your older brother, who is a senior in college and has studied French for several years, quickly volunteers to meet Colette at the airport. When he meets her plane from France, he is both surprised and disappointed. Why?

a. He was expecting a girl, and Colette is a boy.
b. She is much younger than he thought she would be.
c. Females in France are very shy and rarely speak to people they don't know.
d. She comes from a part of France where everyone speaks a dialect. As a result, your brother can't understand a word she says.

Answer, Pourquoi?: b. A **collège** is a junior high school, not a *college* in the American sense. She could be as young as 13 or 14.

Written Work: See Workbook.

J'ai les cheveux bruns et les yeux bruns aussi. J'aime la musique rock et le tennis. Alors, bien sûr, dans ma chambre j'ai une raquette de tennis, un poster de Sting et beaucoup de disques.

Michel Maillet

FRANCE

Unité trois

On se renseigne

Planning Strategy: See Workbook.

Audio Tape and/or Video: See Teaching Guide.

Objectives

In this unit, you will learn:

- to identify and locate places in a city;
- to ask for and give directions;
- to give orders and suggest activities;
- to tell time;
- to make plans;
- to indicate possession;
- to read a tourist brochure.

Chapitre sept:	**Faisons connaissance de la ville!**
Première étape:	Les bâtiments publics
Deuxième étape:	Où peut-on aller pour s'amuser?
Troisième étape:	Le centre ville
Chapitre huit:	**Où se trouve . . . ?**
Première étape:	C'est loin d'ici?
Deuxième étape:	Pardon, Monsieur. Où est . . . ?
Chapitre neuf:	**Allons au festival!**
Première étape:	Nous voudrions voir . . .
Deuxième étape:	Rendez-vous à 10h.

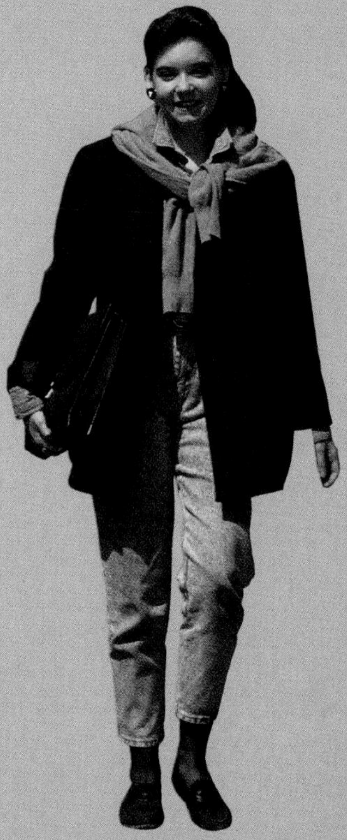

Véronique Béziers
Tarascon, France

Chapitre sept

Faisons connaissance de la ville!

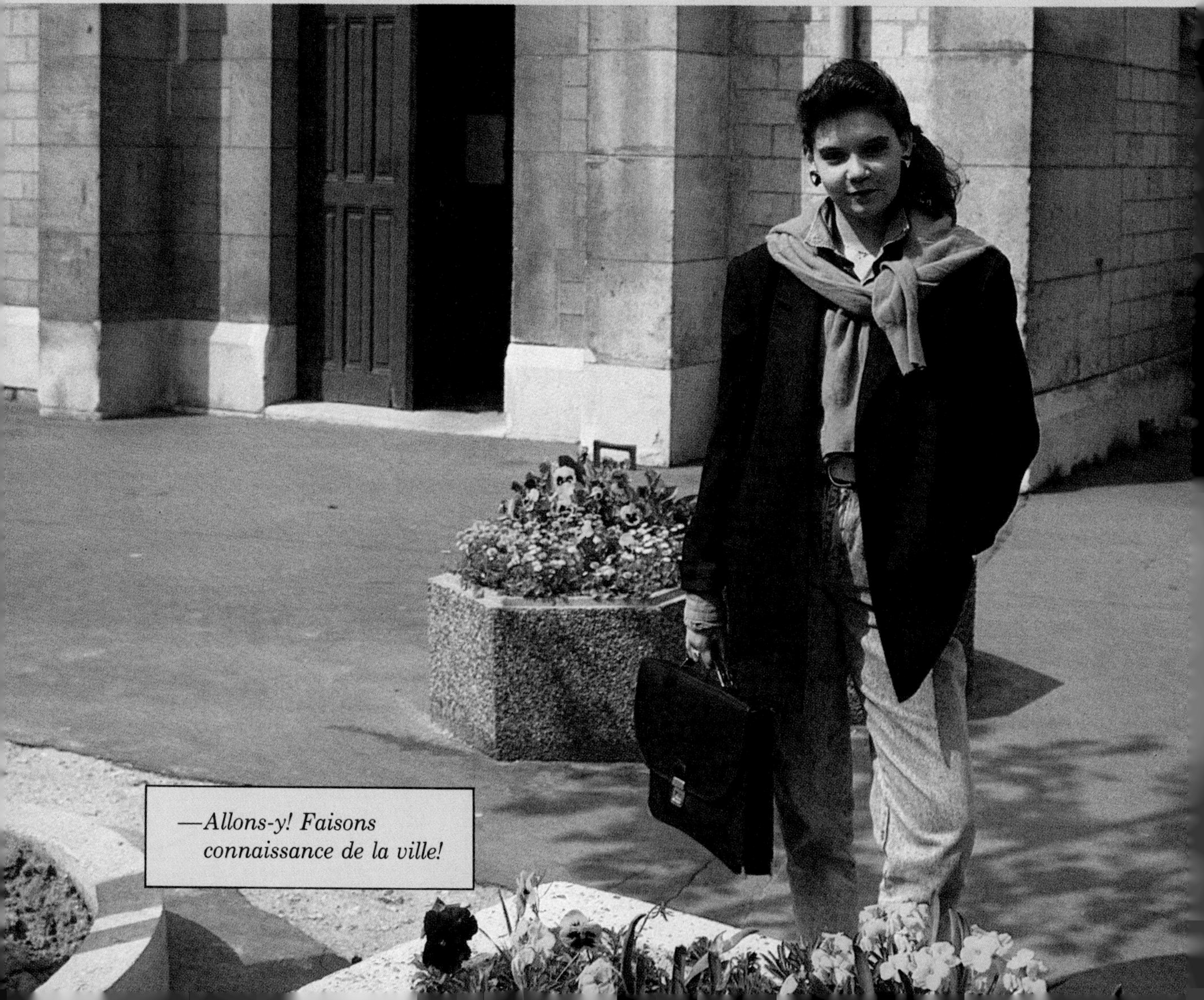

—Allons-y! Faisons connaissance de la ville!

Première étape

Point de départ:

Les bâtiments publics

Faisons connaissance de la ville: Let's get to know the city

Dans notre **ville** il y a

un aéroport	une cathédrale	une **bibliothèque**	library
une **gare**	une **église**	un **bureau de poste**	train station / church / post office
	une synagogue		
une **école**	une université	**un hôtel de ville**	school (general or elementary) / town hall
un **lycée**	un hôpital	**un commissariat de police**	high school / police station

À vous!

A. **Qu'est-ce que c'est?** Identify each building or place.

Vocabulary activities

Transparency, Ex. A; public buildings

MODÈLE:
C'est une cathédrale.

1.

2.

3.

4.

5.

6.

7.

8.

B. **Où est. . . ?** You have just arrived in town and are looking at a map. Using the appropriate form of the definite article **(le, la, l', les),** ask someone where each building or place is located.

MODÈLE: école
Où est l'école?

1. gare
2. hôtel de ville
3. aéroport
4. cathédrale
5. synagogue
6. hôpital
7. lycée
8. église
9. bibliothèque
10. université
11. commissariat de police
12. bureau de poste

Ex. C: ⇄

C. **Il est là.** *(It is there.)* Now that you are familiar with the map of the town, other newcomers come up and ask you where certain buildings and places are. Using **il est** or **elle est** and the expression **là,** indicate the various locations on the map.

MODÈLE: la gare
— *Où est la gare?*
— *La gare? Elle est là.*

1. la cathédrale
2. le bureau de poste
3. l'université
4. l'hôpital
5. le lycée
6. la synagogue
7. l'aéroport
8. le commissariat de police
9. l'école
10. l'hôtel de ville
11. l'église
12. la bibliothèque

STRUCTURE

Suggestion, aller: (1) Have students repeat conjugation while you write pronouns on the board in four groups: **je / tu, il, elle, on / ils, elles / nous, vous.** (2) Repeat with negative. (3) Add written forms to pronouns on board.

The present tense of the irregular verb ***aller***

Comment **vas-tu?**	How *are you?*
Marie va à Paris.	*Marie is going* to Paris.
Ils ne vont pas à Nice.	*They are not going* to Nice.

Nous allons *à Marseille.*

The verb **aller** (*to go*-in some expressions dealing with health can also mean *to be*) is irregular. Its present tense forms are:

aller	
je **vais**	nous **allons**
tu **vas**	vous **allez**
il, elle, on **va**	ils, elles **vont**

Application

D. Replace the subject in italics and make the necessary changes.
1. *Henri* va à Londres. (je / nous / M. et Mme Duplessis / Chantal)
2. Est-ce que *Jeanne* va en ville? (tu / Éric / vous / Paul et son frère)
3. *Ils* ne vont pas à la bibliothèque. (Michèle / je / nous / on)

Ex. E: ⇄

E. **À la gare.** You are at the railroad station with a group of friends who are all leaving to visit cathedrals in different French cities. Each time you ask if someone is going to a certain cathedral, you find out that you are wrong. Ask and answer questions following the model.

MODÈLE: Alex / à Paris (à Rouen)
— *Alex va à Paris?*
— *Mais non, Alex ne va pas à Paris. Il va à Rouen.*

1. Thérèse / à Strasbourg (à Bourges)
2. tu / à Poitiers (à Chartres)
3. Jean-Paul et François / à Marseille (à Albi)
4. vous / à Angers (à Reims)
5. Michel / à Lille (à Lyon)

Suggestion, Note grammaticale, Adverbs: Put on board a continuum from **toujours** to **ne . . . jamais.** Use **aller à la bibliothèque** with different people and frequencies.

NOTE GRAMMATICALE

Adverbs used with **aller**

These adverbs are frequently used with **aller:**

toujours *(always)*	**de temps en temps** *(from time to time)*
souvent	**quelquefois** *(sometimes)*
rarement	**ne . . . jamais** *(never)*

De temps en temps and **quelquefois** usually begin or end the sentence. The shorter adverbs directly follow the verb. **Ne . . . jamais** is a negative expression. **Ne** precedes the verb and **jamais** follows it, just as with **ne . . . pas:**

De temps en temps nous allons en ville.	*From time to time* we go into town.
Il va **souvent** à l'église.	He *often* goes to church.
Je **ne** vais **jamais** à la bibliothèque.	I *never* go to the library.

F. **Une enquête.** *(A survey.)* Ask three other students the questions below and take note of their answers. The students do not need to answer with complete sentences. (When answering with **ne . . . jamais,** if there is no verb, you do not need to use **ne.**)

Ex. F: The examples in this and succeeding exercises in this **étape** avoid **au.**

Ex. F: □

MODÈLE: — Est-ce que tu vas souvent à l'aéroport?
— *Rarement.*
— *De temps en temps.*
— *Jamais.*

1. Est-ce que tu vas souvent à la bibliothèque?
2. Est-ce que tu vas souvent à l'église ou à la synagogue?
3. Est-ce que tu vas souvent à l'hôpital?
4. Est-ce que tu vas souvent à l'hôtel de ville?

G. **Les résultats.** *(The results.)* Now report your findings from Exercise F to other members of your class. This time use complete sentences.

Ex. G: ○

MODÈLE: *De temps en temps Éric va à la bibliothèque, Janine va rarement à la bibliothèque, mais Martine va très souvent à la bibliothèque.*

DÉBROUILLONS-NOUS!

H. **Échange.** Ask another student the following questions. He/she will answer them on the basis of his/her knowledge and personal situation.

Review of the **étape**

Ex. H: ⇄

1. Est-ce qu'il y a un aéroport dans notre ville? Un hôpital? Un bureau de poste? Une cathédrale?
2. Est-ce que tu vas souvent à l'école? À l'église ou à la synagogue? À la gare? À l'hôtel de ville?

I. **Dans la rue.** You run into a classmate in the street. Greet each other. Then find out where he/she is going and whether he/she goes there often.

Suggestion, Ex. I: Have students choose a destination. They circulate in class, competing to see who can meet the most friends.

MODÈLE: — *Salut, . . . Ça va?*
— *Oui, ça va. Et toi?*
— *Oui, ça va très bien. Où est-ce que tu vas?*
— *Je vais à la bibliothèque.*
— *Est-ce que tu vas souvent à la bibliothèque?*
— *Oui, assez souvent* (fairly often).

Written Work: See Workbook.

Deuxième étape

Point de départ:

Où peut-on aller pour s'amuser?

peut-on: can one (we)

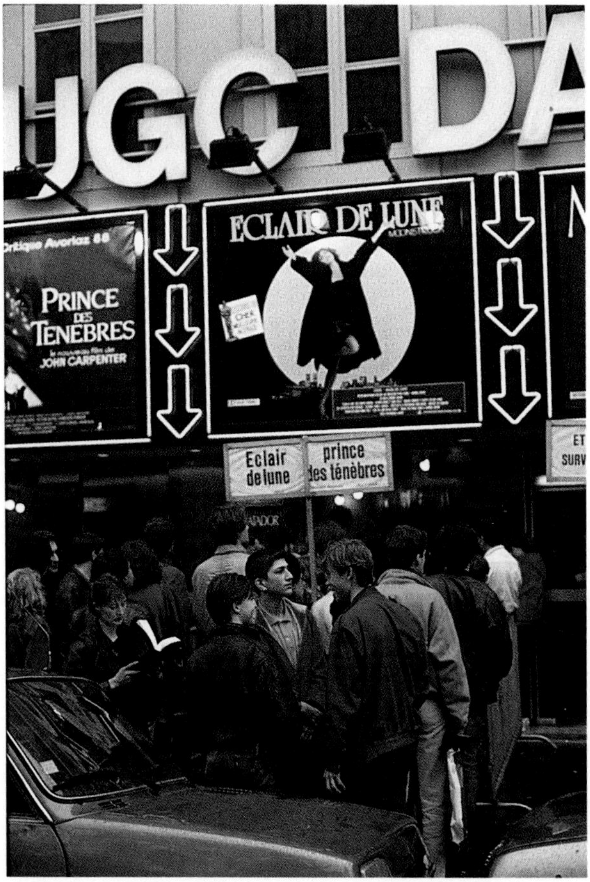

Pour s'amuser, dans notre ville il y a

un café	un cinéma	un parc
un restaurant	un théâtre	une discothèque
un fast-food	un **musée**	un **stade**
		une **piscine**

museum / stadium
swimming pool

À vous!

Vocabulary activities

A. **Qu'est-ce que c'est?** Identify each building or place.

Transparency, Ex. A; entertainment buildings

1.

2.

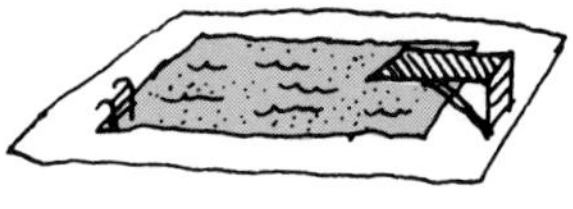

3.

4.

5.

6.

B. **Est-ce qu'il y a un(e) . . . dans le quartier?** *(Is there a . . . in the neighborhood?)* Ask a passerby if the following places are in the area. The passerby will answer affirmatively and indicate the street where each can be found.

Ex. B: ⇄

MODÈLE: restaurant / dans la rue Clemenceau
— *Pardon, Madame (Monsieur). Est-ce qu'il y a un restaurant dans le quartier?*
— *Oui. Il y a un restaurant dans la rue Clemenceau.*

1. parc / dans la rue Bellevue
2. discothèque / dans la rue d'Orléans
3. théâtre / dans l'avenue Jean Mermoz
4. musée / dans l'avenue de la Libération
5. cinéma / dans la rue Mazarin
6. piscine / dans la rue Jean-Jacques
7. fast-food / dans l'avenue de Paris

Transparency, Ex. C; map of Cassis

C. **Qu'est-ce qu'il y a à Cassis?** Using the map of Cassis, indicate what there is and what there is not in this little Mediterranean town.

MODÈLE: *À Cassis il y a des cafés, mais il n'y a pas de fast-food.*

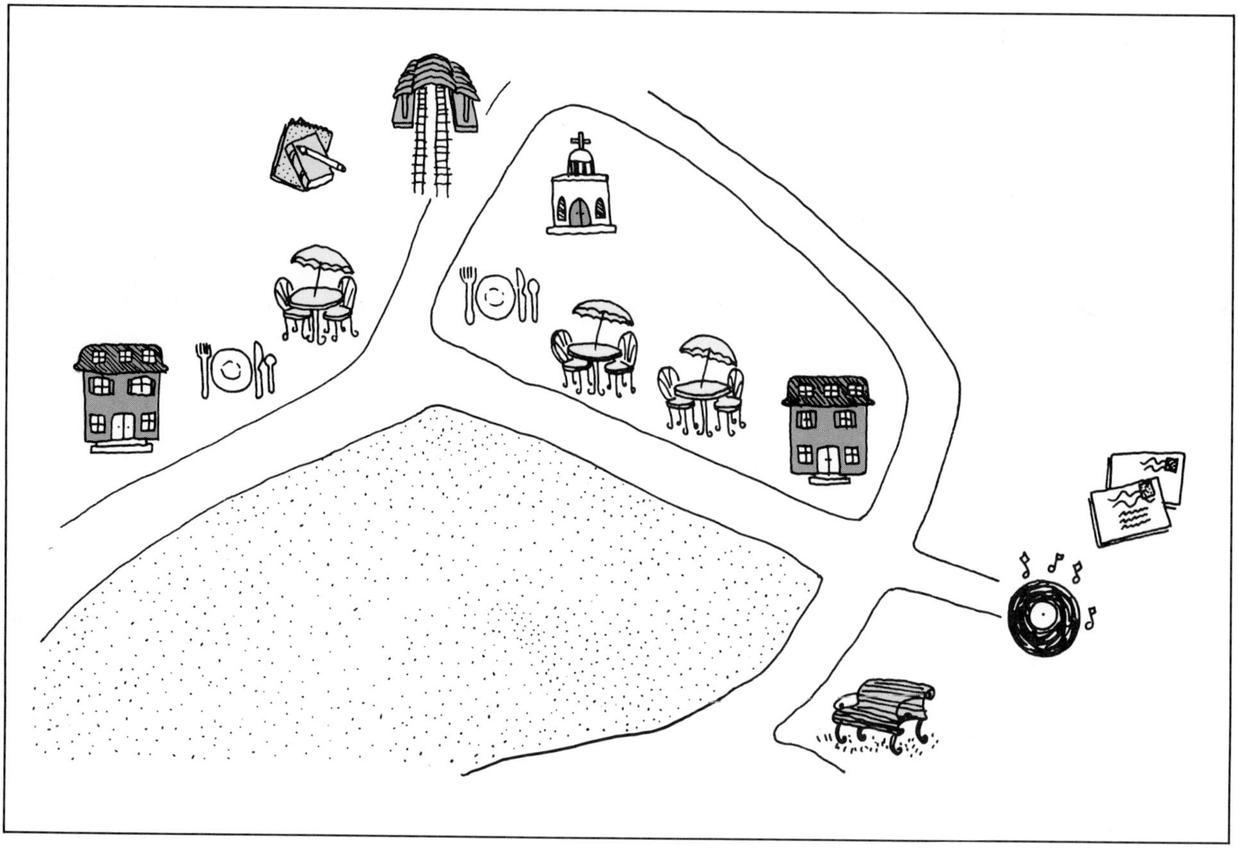

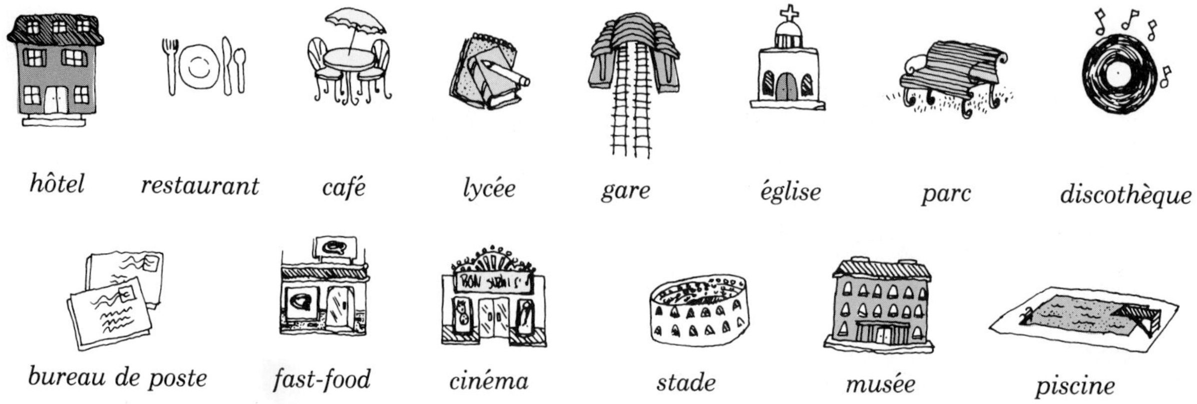

Prononciation: *The combination* ***gn***

In French, the combination **gn** is pronounced much like the **ny** in the English word *canyon* **[ɲ]-: gagner, ligne.**

Pratique

D. Read each word aloud, being careful to pronounce the **gn** combination as [ɲ]:

1. espagnol
2. on se renseigne
3. magnifique
4. magnétique
5. signe
6. Agnès
7. Champagne
8. Charlemagne
9. montagne
10. champignon

REPRISE

E. **Où vont-ils?** Thierry and his family have gone into Lyon for the day. Because they all want to see different things, they decide to split up. Using the drawings, give Thierry's explanation of where each person is headed.

mon oncle

MODÈLE: *Mon oncle va à la cathédrale.*

1. mes parents

2. ma sœur et moi

3. mes cousins

4. *moi*

5. *toi*

Suggestion, À + definite article: Use the transparencies of buildings; begin with **à la** and **à l',** then proceed to **au.** Switch to people: **parler à la mére de . . . , l'oncle de,** then **le père de . . .** and **les frères (soeurs) de . . .**

STRUCTURE

The preposition à and the definite article

Nous sommes **à la** piscine.	We're *at the* swimming pool.
Mon frère travaille **à l'**aéroport.	My brother works *at the* airport.
Nous allons **au** cinéma ensemble.	We're going *to the* movies together.
Elle parle **aux** médecins.	She's talking *to the* doctors.

When followed by **la** or **l',** the preposition **à** *(to, at, in)* does not change. However, **à** followed by **le** contracts to form **au** and **à** followed by **les** contracts to form **aux:**

à + la	→ **à la**	**à la** maison
à + l'	→ **à l'**	**à l'**église
à + le	→ **au**	**au** café
à + les	→ **aux**	**aux** professeurs

The **x** of **aux** is silent, except when it precedes a vowel or a vowel sound. Then, in liaison, it is pronounced as a **z: aux‿étudiants.**

Application

F. Replace the word in italics and make the necessary changes.

1. Il va à la *cathédrale.* (maison / bibliothèque / gare / piscine)
2. Elles sont à *l'hôpital.* (université / église / aéroport / hôtel de ville)
3. Est-ce que tu vas au *café?* (restaurant / musée / bureau de poste / fast-food)
4. Je parle aux *professeurs.* (médecins / avocats / ingénieurs)

G. Replace the words in italics and make the necessary changes.

1. Ma sœur travaille *au musée.* (bureau de poste / hôtel de ville / gare / théâtre)
2. Nous allons souvent *au café.* (église / parc / bibliothèque / cinéma / piscine)
3. Est-ce que nous sommes déjà *au restaurant?* (cathédrale / hôpital / musée / bureau de poste / stade)
4. Il parle *au garçon.* (professeur / avocat / étudiants / médecins)

H. **Tu vas au musée, toi?** A group of young people join you in front of a map of a town. Find out where each one is headed, being careful to use the appropriate form of **à** and the definite article.

Ex. H: ⇄

MODÈLE: musée / hôpital
— *Tu vas au musée, toi?*
— *Non, je vais à l'hôpital.*

1. église / cathédrale
2. école / piscine
3. gare / aéroport
4. théâtre / cinéma
5. bureau de poste / parc
6. café / discothèque

I. **D'abord... ensuite...** *(First... then...)* After lunch, you and your friends are discussing your plans. Using the verb **aller** and the appropriate form of **à** + the definite article, find out where each person is headed.

Ex. I: ⇄

MODÈLE: Anne-Marie (piscine / bibliothèque)
— *Anne-Marie, où est-ce que tu vas?*
— *D'abord, je vais à la piscine et ensuite je vais à la bibliothèque.*

1. Élisabeth (église / théâtre)
2. Pierre et Sylvie (restaurant / cinéma)
3. Monique (bureau de poste / bibliothèque)
4. Jean-Jacques et François (gare / aéroport)
5. Simone (musée / parc)
6. Henri et Alain (stade / café)

→ **Le savez-vous?**

When the French use the term *le foot,* what are they referring to?
a) a part of the body
b) American football
c) soccer

réponse →

J. **Après les classes, nous jouons...** *(After school, we play...)* What do you and your friends play after school? How about you and your family? Choose games from the following list to complete the sentences. Notice that the verb **jouer** *(to play)* is followed by **à** before a noun. Be sure to make the appropriate contraction.

le basket	le volley	les échecs *(chess)*
le football *(soccer)*	le baseball	le flipper *(pinball)*
le football américain	le tennis	le Monopoly

Supplementary vocabulary, Games: **le golf, le hockey (sur glace), les cartes, les dames, le scrabble**

MODÈLE: Mes amis et moi, nous jouons toujours. . .
Mes amis et moi, nous jouons toujours au basket.

1. Mes amis et moi, nous jouons souvent. . .
2. Quelquefois nous jouons. . .
3. Nous jouons rarement. . .
4. Nous ne jouons jamais. . .
5. Ma famille et moi, nous jouons souvent. . .
6. Nous ne jouons jamais. . .

Note Culturelle

Traditionally, the French have preferred to watch sports rather than participate in them. This may be changing somewhat among the younger generations, who seem to be particularly interested in such sports as cycling, soccer, and jogging. For those who prefer more solitary or tranquil outdoor activities, hunting, fishing, and **boules (pétanque)** are still the most popular sports in France.

Boules is usually played in teams of two. The object of the game is to toss heavy metal balls as close as possible to a small wooden ball that has previously been thrown about ten yards from the players. This game can be played anywhere and is a favorite among both school-age youngsters and elderly men.

➡ c

DÉBROUILLONS-NOUS!

K. **Échange.** Ask the following questions of another student, who will answer them.

Review of the **étape**

Ex. K: ⇄

1. Est-ce qu'il y a un restaurant dans ton quartier? Un cinéma? Un parc?
2. Est-ce que tu dînes souvent au restaurant?
3. Est-ce que tu vas souvent au musée? Au parc? À la discothèque? Au théâtre?
4. Est-ce que tu joues au tennis? Au volley? Au football? Aux échecs? Aux boules?

L. **Dans la rue.** While heading for a place in town (your choice), you bump into a friend. Greet your friend, find out how he/she is and where he/she is going. If you are going to the same place, propose that you go there together **(On y va ensemble!).** If not, say good-bye and continue on your way.

Ex. L: ⇄. Students choose destinations, then circulate.

Written Work: See Workbook.

Troisième étape

Point de départ:

Le centre ville

Dans notre ville il y a

une **librairie**	une banque	une **boucherie**
un **bureau de tabac**	un hôtel	une **épicerie**
une pharmacie		une **boulangerie**

bookstore / butcher shop
tobacco store (also sells stamps, newspapers) / grocery store
bakery (bread, rolls)

À vous!

Vocabulary activities

Transparency, Ex. A; commercial buildings

A. **Qu'est-ce que c'est?** Identify each building or place.

1.

2.

3.

4.

5.

6.

B. **Près d'ici.** *(Near here.)* You ask a passerby whether certain stores and places are nearby. The passerby will answer affirmatively and indicate the street where each can be found.

Exs. B and C: ⇄

MODÈLE: banque / dans l'avenue Schuman
— *Pardon, Monsieur (Madame). Est-ce qu'il y a une banque près d'ici?*
— *Oui, il y a une banque dans l'avenue Schuman.*

1. pharmacie / dans l'avenue du Maréchal Joffre
2. hôtel / dans la rue de la Montagne
3. boulangerie / dans la rue de Strasbourg
4. bureau de tabac / dans la rue Vauban
5. épicerie / dans l'avenue Aristide Bruant
6. librairie / dans la rue du Manège

C. **Où est-ce qu'on va d'abord?** *(Where are we going first?)* Whenever you run errands with your friend, you like to know where you are headed first. However, each time you suggest a place, your friend has another idea.

MODÈLE: banque / bureau de tabac
— *Où est-ce qu'on va d'abord? À la banque?*
— *Non, d'abord on va au bureau de tabac. Ensuite on va à la banque.*

1. boucherie / épicerie
2. bureau de tabac / librairie
3. bureau de poste / banque
4. pharmacie / boulangerie
5. bibliothèque / briocherie
6. gare / bureau de tabac

Prononciation: *The consonant s*

The consonant **s** represents the sound **[z]** when it occurs between two written vowels **(visage, rose)**. In all other cases, the consonant **s** represents the sound **[s]: sœur, masse, disque.**

Pratique

D. Read each pair of words aloud, being careful to distinguish between the **[s]** of the first word and the **[z]** of the second.

1. dessert, désert 2. poisson, poison 3. coussin, cousin 4. russe, ruse

E. Read each word aloud, being careful to distinguish between **[s]** and **[z].**

1.	désire	5.	brésilien	9.	maison
2.	souvent	6.	suisse	10.	professeur
3.	croissant	7.	classique	11.	musée
4.	Mademoiselle	8.	église	12.	passer

REPRISE

Recycling activity

Variation, Ex. F: If students have difficulty doing all sentences at once, split the task into two or three parts: either have different students work with each cue or work with one set of cues (e.g., **travailler**) all the way through (1–6), then go back and do **aimer** and finally **aller.**

F. **Les parents de vos amis.** Your parents are curious about your friends. Tell them where your friends' parents work and what they like to do.

MODÈLE: le père de Janine (hôpital / les livres / bibliothèque)
Le père de Janine travaille à l'hôpital. Il aime beaucoup les livres et il va souvent à la bibliothèque.

1. le père de Christine (gare / les films / cinéma)
2. la mère de Vincent (hôtel de ville / la nature / parc)
3. le père de Jean-Alex (bureau de poste / l'art / musée)
4. la mère de Philippe (bibliothèque / manger / restaurant)
5. le père de Jacqueline (musée / danser / discothèque)
6. la mère de Denise (université / chanter / théâtre)

Suggestion, Numbers: Present progressively: 11; 11, 12; etc. Then reverse: 20; 20, 19; etc.

STRUCTURE

The numbers from 11 to 29

11	**onze**	18	**dix-huit**	24	**vingt-quatre**
12	**douze**	19	**dix-neuf**	25	**vingt-cinq**
13	**treize**	20	**vingt**	26	**vingt-six**
14	**quatorze**	21	**vingt et un**	27	**vingt-sept**
15	**quinze**	22	**vingt-deux**	28	**vingt-huit**
16	**seize**	23	**vingt-trois**	29	**vingt-neuf**
17	**dix-sept**				

The **t** of **vingt** is not pronounced, except in liaison: **ving~~t~~ livres,** but **vingt élèves.** However, in the numbers from 21 through 29, the **t** of **vingt** is always pronounced: **vingt-cinq.**

Application

G. 1. Comptez de 11 à 20, de 20 à 11, de 0 à 20, de 20 à 0.
   2. Comptez de 21 à 29, de 0 à 29, de 29 à 0.
   3. Donnez les nombres pairs de 0 à 28.
   4. Donnez les nombres impairs de 1 à 29.

H. **Faisons des sommes!** *(Let's do some addition!)*

MODÈLE: 2 + 2
— *Combien font deux et deux?*
— *Deux et deux font quatre.*

1. 3 + 6	4. 2 + 5	7. 3 + 10	10. 6 + 5	13. 11 + 17
2. 7 + 9	5. 14 + 3	8. 9 + 9	11. 19 + 1	14. 15 + 6
3. 11 + 4	6. 8 + 12	9. 12 + 7	12. 4 + 9	15. 17 + 9

NOTE GRAMMATICALE

Quel âge as-tu?

To ask someone's age in French, use **avoir:**

Quel âge as-tu?
How old are you?

Quel âge a ta sœur?
How old is your sister?

To answer the questions, use **avoir . . . ans.** Note that **ans** must always be included in French even though *years* may be left out in English:

J'ai quinze ans.	*I'm fifteen years old.*
Elle a trois ans.	*She's three.*

Variation, Ex. I: Books closed; write numbers 11–20 on board, point to number and have student respond.

I. **Quel âge. . .?** In the process of getting to know your friends, you find out how old they are. Remember to use the verb **avoir** and the word **ans.**

MODÈLE: Quel âge a Philippe? (13)
Il a treize ans.

1. Sylvie, quel âge as-tu? (14)
2. Éric, quel âge as-tu? (12)
3. Marie-Claire et Denise, quel âge avez-vous? (15)
4. Quel âge a Robert? (16)
5. Quel âge a Caroline? (17)
6. Quel âge a Bruno? (22)

DÉBROUILLONS-NOUS !

Ex. J: ⇄

J. **Échange.** Ask the following questions to a classmate, who will answer you.

1. Quel âge as-tu?
2. Est-ce que tu as des frères et des sœurs? Comment est-ce qu'ils s'appellent? Quel âge a . . . ? et . . . ?
3. Est-ce qu'il y a une épicerie dans ton quartier? Une boulangerie? Une pharmacie? Une banque?

Ex. K: ⇄. Students choose their destinations before beginning exercise. There will probably only be enough time for one or two conversations.

K. **Au café.** On the way to a store to do an errand (your choice of store), you stop in a café for something to drink. You see a friend there. Greet your friend, find out how many brothers and/or sisters he/she has, and their names and ages. When you leave, find out where your friend is going and tell him/her where you are going.

Written Work: See Workbook.

Lexique

Pour se débrouiller

Pour demander un renseignement

Pardon, . . .
Où est . . . ?
Est-ce qu'il y a un(une) . . . près d'ici?

Pour donner un renseignement

dans l'avenue
dans la rue

Pour demander et indiquer l'âge

Quel âge avez-vous (as-tu)?
J'ai . . . ans.

Thèmes et contextes

Les bâtiments commerciaux

une banque
une boucherie
une boulangerie
un bureau de tabac
un cinéma
une discothèque
une épicerie
un hôtel
une librairie
une pharmacie
un restaurant
un théâtre

Les bâtiments et les lieux publics

l'aéroport *(m.)*
la bibliothèque
le bureau de poste
une cathédrale
une école
une église
le commissariat de police
la gare
l'hôpital
l'hôtel de ville
un lycée
un musée
un parc
une piscine
un stade
une synagogue
une université

Les jeux

le baseball
le basket
les boules *(f.pl.)*
les échecs *(m.pl.)*
le flipper
le football (américain)
le Monopoly
la pétanque
le tennis
le volley

Vocabulaire général

Noms

la ville

Verbes

aller

Autres expressions

d'abord
de temps en temps
ensuite
là-bas
ne . . . jamais
quelquefois
rarement
souvent
toujours

Chapitre huit

Où se trouve . . . ?

—*Où se trouve le cinéma?*
—*Il est dans la rue du Château.*

Première étape

Point de départ:

C'est loin d'ici?

Transparency, Point de départ; streets and buildings

se trouve: is (located)

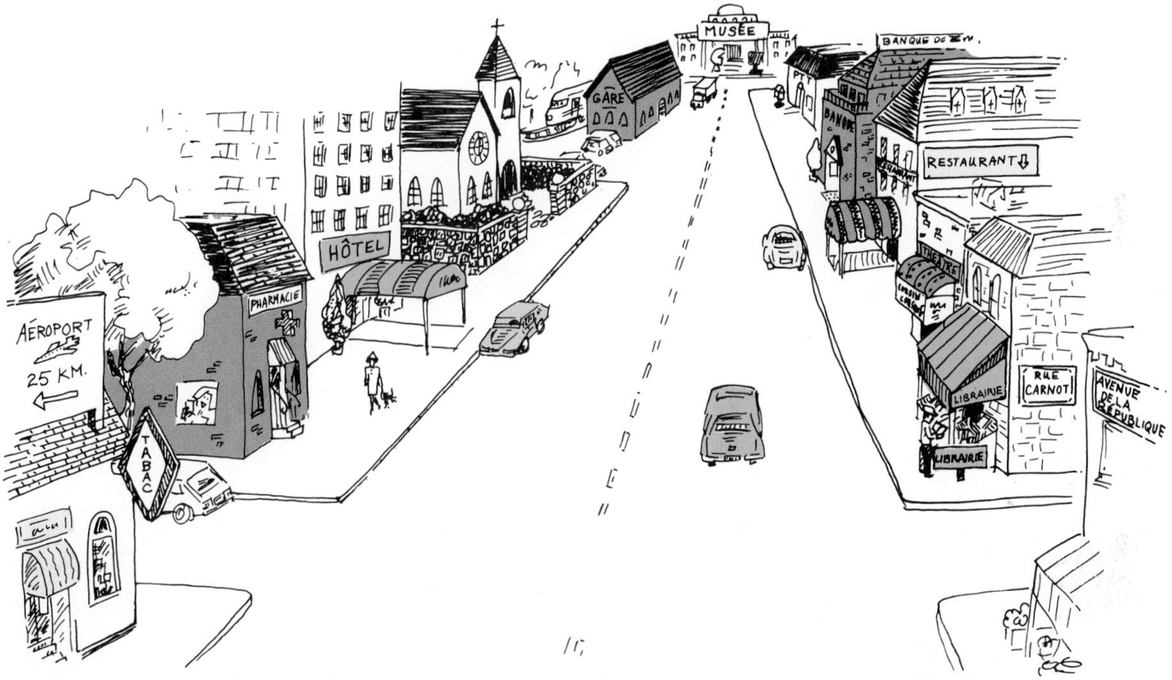

Où se trouve l'aéroport?	Il est **loin de** la ville.	far from
Où se trouve la gare?	Elle est **près de** l'église.	near
Où est le bureau de poste?	Il est **en face de** la gare.	across from
Où est la pharmacie?	Elle se trouve **à côté de** l'hôtel.	next to
Où est le musée?	Il est **au bout de** l'avenue de la République.	at the end of
Où se trouve le bureau de tabac?	Il est **au coin de** la rue Carnot et de l'avenue de la République.	on the corner of
Où est la voiture de Georges?	Elle est **dans** un parking, **derrière** l'église.	in / behind
Où est la voiture de Monique?	Elle est **dans** la rue, **devant** le restaurant.	in / in front
Mais où se trouve la banque?	Elle est **entre** le restaurant et le bureau de poste.	between

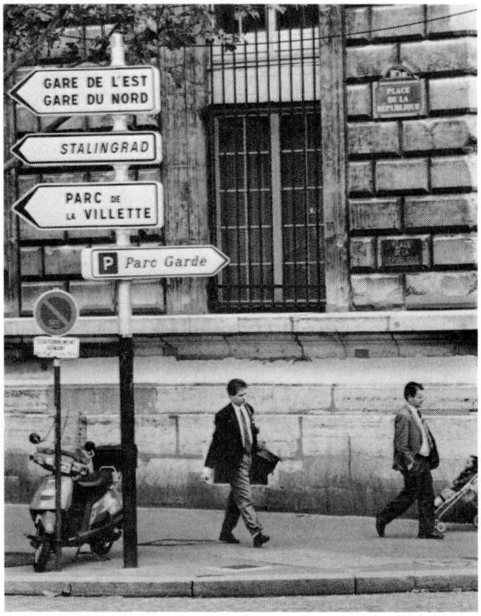

À vous!

Vocabulary activities

A. **La ville.** When someone asks you about the town pictured on p. 155, you answer using the suggested expressions.

MODÈLE: Où est la gare? (près de l'église)
Elle est près de l'église.

1. Où est l'hôtel? (à côté de la pharmacie)
2. Où est la banque? (en face de l'église)
3. Où est l'aéroport? (loin de la ville)
4. Où est le bureau de poste? (près de la banque)
5. Où est le musée? (au bout de l'avenue de la République)
6. Où est la pharmacie? (au coin de la rue Carnot et de l'avenue de la République)
7. Où est la gare? (à côté du musée)
8. Où est le restaurant? (entre le théâtre et le bureau de poste)

Variation, Ex. B: Books closed; ask questions, then give slightly erroneous statements:
—Où est l'hôtel? Il est à côté de la gare?
—Non, à côté de l'église.

B. **La ville (suite).** This time, correct the erroneous statements made to you about the city pictured on p. 155.

MODÈLE: L'aéroport est près de la ville, n'est-ce pas? (loin de)
Mais non, il est loin de la ville.

1. Le restaurant est à côté de l'église, n'est-ce pas? (en face de)
2. La gare est loin du musée, n'est-ce pas? (près de)
3. Le théâtre est en face de la librairie, n'est-ce pas? (à côté de)

4. Le bureau de tabac est au bout de l'avenue de la République, non? (au coin de)
5. Le musée est à côté de la banque, non? (au bout de)
6. La voiture de Monique est dans le parking, derrière l'église? (dans la rue, devant la banque)
7. La banque est en face de la librairie et du bureau de poste? (entre)

C. **On fait la queue.** *(We wait in line.)* While waiting to get into the movies, your brother points out some of his friends to you. He does so by indicating each person's place in line. Use the drawing to give your brother's answers.

Variation, Ex. C: Books closed. Ask: **Jacqueline est devant Frédéric? Non, elle est devant Jean-Loup.**

Jean-Loup **Jacqueline** **Marc** **Frédéric** **Simone** **Francis**

MODÈLE: Simone / derrière
Simone? Elle est derrière Francis.

1. Jacqueline / devant
2. Frédéric / derrière
3. Marc / entre
4. Jean-Loup / derrière
5. Francis / devant

Prononciation: *The consonant* ***t***

The **t** in French is usually pronounced like the **t** in the English word *stay:* **hôtel, Vittel, hôpital.** The **th** combination in French is also pronounced **[t].** Compare:

English	**French**
theater	**th**éâtre
Ca**th**olic	ca**th**olique

Pratique

D. Read each word aloud, being sure to pronounce both **t** and **th** as **[t].**

1. thé
2. tes
3. tante
4. menthe
5. étudiant
6. cathédral
7. habiter
8. omelette
9. à côté
10. Athènes
11. mythe

REPRISE

E. **Combien de fois par mois. . .?** *(How many times a month. . . ?)* Indicate how frequently you go to the following places. You may also respond that you go there rarely or never.

MODÈLE: Combien de fois par mois est-ce que vous allez à la boucherie?
D'habitude, je vais à la boucherie trois fois par mois. ou:
Je vais rarement à la boucherie. ou:
Je ne vais jamais à la boucherie.

1. Combien de fois par mois est-ce que vous allez à la pharmacie?
2. Et à la banque?
3. Et à la librairie?
4. À l'épicerie?
5. Au bureau de tabac?
6. À la boulangerie?
7. À la piscine?
8. Au bureau de poste?

Reminder: Students might like to make a rough comparison between French and American grades— A or 90's (17–20 sur 20), B or 80's (14–16 sur 20); C or 70's (11–13 sur 20).

Variation, Ex. F: Books closed Have numbers written on board.

F. **Quelle note?** *(What grade?)* In French schools, students are usually graded on the basis of twenty, and ten out of twenty is a passing grade. When giving a grade, the French use the preposition **sur** (on, out of): **dix sur vingt.** Play the role of the teacher and announce the grades of the following students.

MODÈLE: Hervé Maréchal: 12/20
— *Hervé Maréchal?*
— *Douze sur vingt.*

1. Colette Marchand: 14/20
2. Véronique Dupuis: 18/20
3. Françoise Lévarèque: 9/20
4. Mireille Tavernier: 13/20
5. Henri Saulnier: 11/20
6. Jean Leblanc: 15/20
7. Jean-Claude Goidin: 17/20
8. Éric Ménétrier: 16/20

STRUCTURE

*The preposition **de** and the definite article*

Elle arrive **de la** gare.	She arrives *from the* station.
Quelle est l'adresse **de l'**hôtel?	What is the address *of the* hotel?
Voilà la voiture **du** professeur.	There is the teacher*'s* car.
Nous parlons **des** élèves.	We are talking *about the* students.

When followed by **la** or **l',** the preposition **de** *(of, about, from)* does not change. However, **de** followed by **le** contracts to form **du** and **de** followed by **les** contracts to form **des:**

de + la	⟶ **de la**	**de la** pharmacie
de + l'	⟶ **de l'**	**de l'**hôtel
de + le	⟶ **du**	**du** musée
de + les	⟶ **des**	**des** élèves

The **s** of **des** is silent, except when it precedes a vowel or a vowel sound. Then, in liaison, it is pronounced as a **z: des‿églises.**

Suggestion, De + definite article: Begin with **la** and **l'.** Have students ask **Quel est le nom de . . . ?** or **Quelle est l'adresse de . . . ?**

Application

G. Replace the word in italics and make the necessary changes.

1. Quel est le nom du *restaurant?* (épicerie / banque / musée)
2. Où est l'entrée du *lycée?* (parc / bibliothèque / église)
3. Est-ce que tu as l'adresse du *bureau de tabac?* (hôtel / restaurant / librairie)
4. Non, elle ne parle pas du *professeur.* (médecins / élèves / avocat)

Le savez-vous?

Which of the following can you *not* buy in a *bureau de tabac?*
a) stamps
b) bus and subway tickets
c) cigarettes
d) soft drinks

réponse ➡

Où se trouve la librairie?

Suggestion, Note grammaticale, place prepositions: Use the transparency of buildings and streets to stress contractions.

NOTE GRAMMATICALE

De with prepositions of place

Many of the prepositions of place presented in the **Point de départ** of this **étape** are followed by **de:**

près de *(near)*	**à côté de** *(next to)*
loin de *(far from)*	**au bout de** *(at the end of)*
en face de *(across from)*	**au coin de** *(at the corner of)*

This **de** follows the usual rules for contraction:

La voiture est en face **de la** maison.	Nous sommes près **du** musée.
Tu habites à côté **de l'**hôtel?	Le parc est au bout **du** boulevard.

➡ d

H. Replace the words in italics and make the necessary changes.

1. La banque est *près de* la gare. (à côté / en face / loin)
2. Nous habitons *en face de* l'avenue Leclerc (près / au bout / loin)
3. Est-ce que la pharmacie est *loin du* restaurant? (en face / près / à côté)
4. L'hôtel est près de *la cathédrale.* (université / musée / parc / gare)
5. Le café est en face de *l'épicerie.* (théâtre / boulangerie / bureau de poste / hôtel de ville)

I. **La ville (suite).** Using the map on p. 155, answer these questions that strangers ask about the city. Be as precise as possible.

MODÈLE: Pardon, Monsieur. Le théâtre, s'il vous plaît?
Le théâtre? Il est dans l'avenue de la République, en face de l'hôtel.

1. Pardon, Madame. Le restaurant, s'il vous plaît?
2. Pardon, Monsieur. Où se trouve l'église, s'il vous plaît?
3. Pardon, Mademoiselle. Où est la pharmacie?
4. S'il vous plaît, le musée?
5. La banque, s'il vous plaît?
6. Où est le bureau de poste, s'il vous plaît?
7. Est-ce qu'il y a un bureau de tabac près d'ici?
8. Pardon, Monsieur. L'hôtel, est-ce qu'il est près de l'aéroport?

J. **Moi, je joue du. . .** What musical instruments do you, your friends, and your relatives play? Choose instruments from the drawings and talk about the people mentioned. Notice that the verb **jouer** is followed by **de** before a musical instrument. (The preposition **à** is used only with games.) Be sure to make the appropriate contraction.

Supplementary vocabulary, Instruments: **le hautbois, le violoncelle, le tuba, l'harmonica**

le piano

le violon

la guitare

la flûte

le saxophone

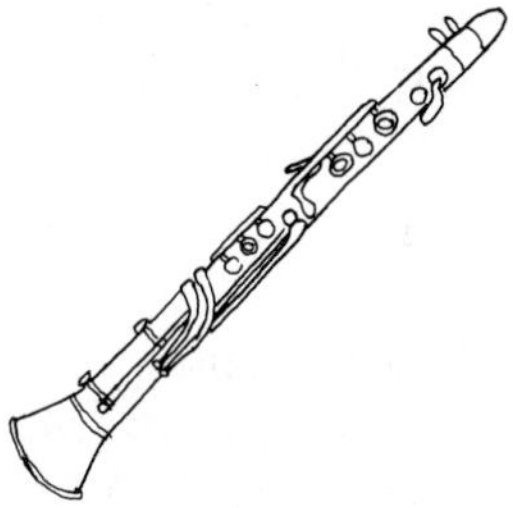

la clarinette

la trompette

la batterie

le trombone

MODÈLE: votre frère
Mon frère joue de la clarinette. ou:
Mon frère ne joue pas d'un instrument de musique.

1. vous
2. votre père
3. votre mère
4. vos frères et vos sœurs
5. votre ami
6. votre amie

DÉBROUILLONS-NOUS !

Review of **étape**

Ex. K: ⇄

K. **Échange.** Ask the following questions of a classmate, who will answer you.

1. Est-ce que tu vas à l'aéroport de temps en temps? Est-ce qu'il est près de la ville? Près du lycée?
2. Est-ce que tu vas souvent au cinéma? Est-ce qu'il y a un cinéma près de ta maison? Qu'est-ce qu'il y a à coté du cinéma?
3. Est-ce qu'il y a une boulangerie près de ta maison? Qu'est-ce qu'il y a en face de la boulangerie?
4. Qu'est-ce qu'il y a entre ta maison et l'école? Une épicerie? Une banque? Une bibliothèque? Des maisons?
5. Qu'est-ce qu'il y a devant l'école? Derrière l'école?

Ex. L: Divide class into French and English speakers. Do conversation, then reverse roles and change partners.

Written Work: See Workbook.

L. **S'il vous plaît?** You are walking down the street in your town when a French-speaking stranger stops you and asks where a certain place (movie theater, bank, train station, drug store, etc.—his/her choice) is located. You indicate the street or avenue and then try to describe the area (such as what is near, next to, across from, behind, between, etc.).

Deuxième étape

Transparency, Point de départ; streets and itinerary

Point de départ:

Pardon, Monsieur. Où est. . . ?

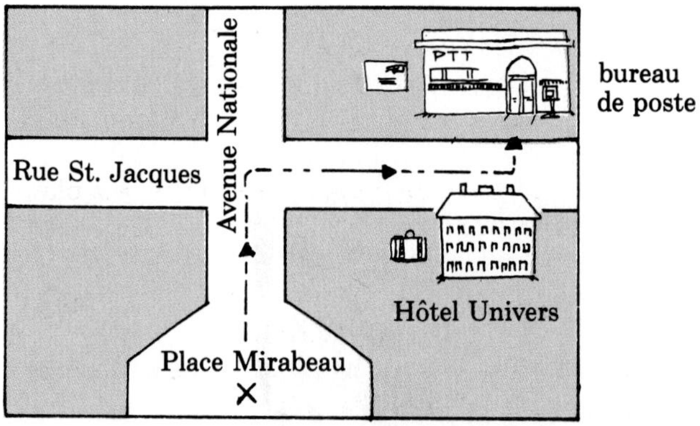

— Pardon, Monsieur. Est-ce qu'il y a un bureau de poste près d'ici?
— Oui, Madame. Dans la rue Saint-Jacques.
— Mais . . . où est la rue Saint-Jacques?
— Bon, vous **traversez la place** et vous allez **tout droit** dans l'avenue Nationale. Continuez **jusqu'à** la rue Saint-Jacques et **tournez à droite.** Le bureau de poste est en face de l'Hôtel Univers, **sur votre gauche.**
— Merci bien, Monsieur.
— Je vous en prie, Madame.

cross the square / straight ahead until (up to) / turn right on your left

Note Culturelle

Many American cities are laid out in fairly regular patterns: streets often meet at right angles, run north and south or east and west, and have numbers (Second Avenue, Seventeenth Street) rather than names. In French cities, streets rarely form regular patterns, and they are usually given the name of a landmark **(le boulevard de la Gare),** a famous person **(la rue Balzac),** or a historical event **(l'avenue de la Libération).**

As a result, Americans and French people have different ways of giving directions. Americans often express distance in terms of city blocks and compass points: "Go three blocks east and turn left." But the French don't use the notion of city blocks. Instead, they indicate the cross street on which to turn: **"Vous allez jusqu'à la rue Pascal et vous tournez à gauche."**

À vous!

A. Replace the words in italics. Notice that French uses the preposition **sur** to talk about a square or a boulevard **(sur la place, sur le boulevard)** and the preposition **dans** to talk about streets and avenues **(dans la rue, dans l'avenue).**

Vocabulary activities

1. Traversez *la rue.* (la place / le boulevard / l'avenue)
2. Vous tournez à droite *dans l'avenue Mitterrand.* (dans la rue Ste-Catherine / sur le boulevard des Italiens / sur la place Notre-Dame)
3. Vous continuez tout droit *jusqu'à la rue Jean-Baptiste.* (jusqu'à la place de la Révolution / jusqu'à l'avenue Clemenceau / jusqu'au boulevard Garibaldi).
4. Allez tout droit *jusqu'à l'avenue de la Gare.* (jusqu'au coin / jusqu'au bout de la rue Victor Hugo / jusqu'à la cathédrale)
5. Tournez à gauche *dans la rue Ste-Anne.* (dans l'avenue de la Marine / sur le boulevard Masséna / sur la place Stanislas)

Transparency, Ex. B; city map

Suggestion, Ex. B: Do the first destination with the class, using the transparency of the city map. Then have students work with pairs. You may wish to go over their work, using the transparency again.

B. **Pardon, Monsieur/Madame.** Play the role of the police officer on duty at the place de la Libération (see the map on p. 165). Explain how to get to the following places.

MODÈLE: le Lycée Camus
— *Pardon, Monsieur (Madame). Le Lycée Camus, s'il vous plaît?*
— *Vous traversez la place de la Libération. Vous continuez sur le boulevard Victor Hugo jusqu'à la rue Notre-Dame. Tournez à gauche et le lycée est en face de la Bibliothèque Municipale.*

1. la gare
2. la pharmacie Girard
3. la Bibliothèque Municipale
4. l'Hôtel Nelson

REPRISE

Recycling activity

Ex. C: ⇄

C. **S'il vous plaît. . . ?** Some tourists stop you in the street to ask where certain places are located. Using the map, locate as precisely as possible the places that they are looking for.

MODÈLE: le Théâtre Municipal
— *Le Théâtre Municipal, s'il vous plaît?*
— *Il est en face du parc, à côté du Café du Parc.*

1. la Banque Nationale de Paris (BNP)
2. le bureau de poste
3. le Restaurant Chez Jacques
4. la Boucherie Roger
5. le Cinéma Royal
6. l'Hôtel National
7. la Librairie Catholique
8. le Musée des Beaux-Arts
9. le Stade Municipal
10. l'hôtel de ville

La Boucherie Roger, s'il vous plaît?

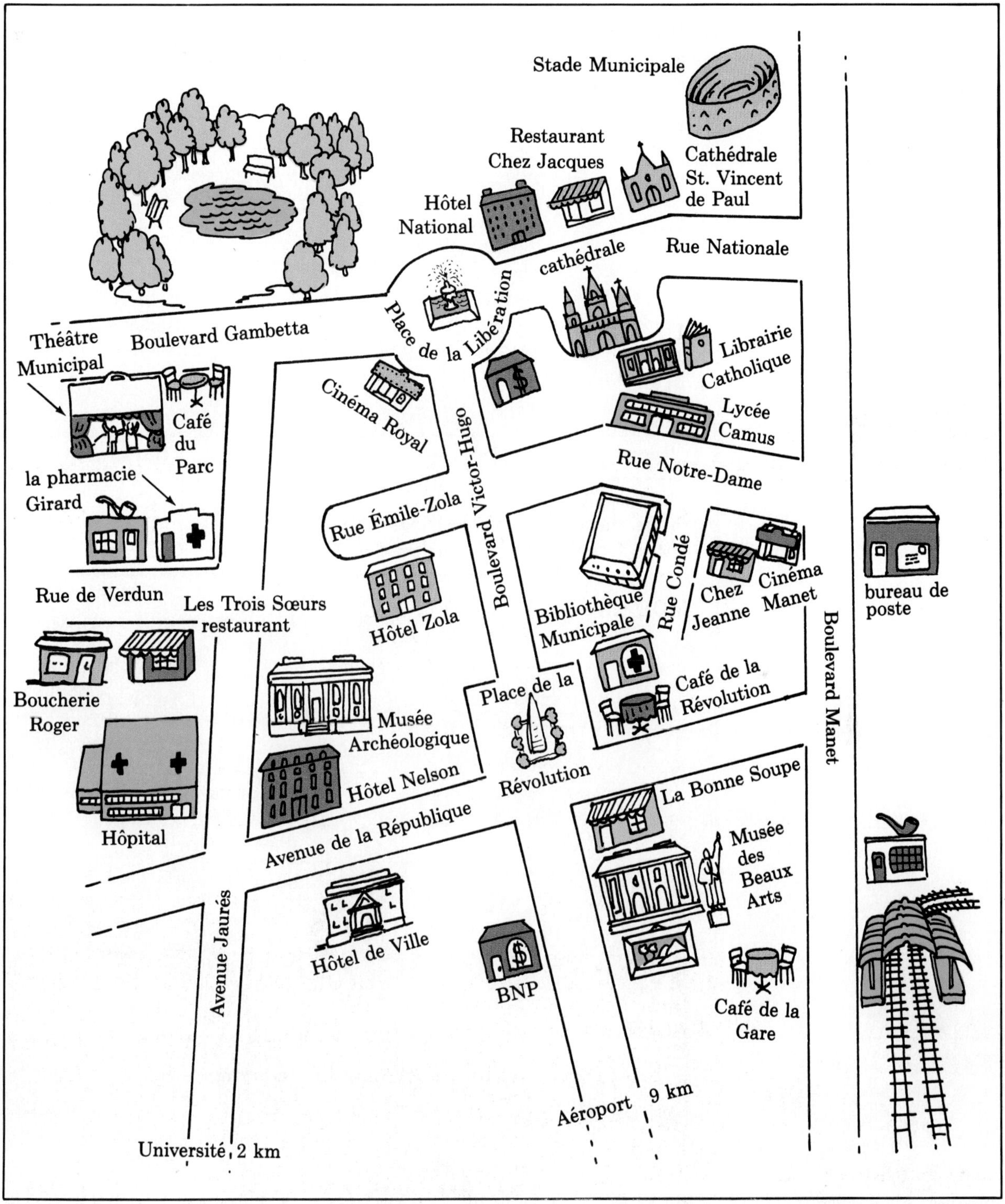
Stade Municipale
Restaurant Chez Jacques
Hôtel National
Cathédrale St. Vincent de Paul
Rue Nationale
cathédrale
Place de la Libération
Boulevard Gambetta
Théâtre Municipal
Café du Parc
la pharmacie Girard
Librairie Catholique
Lycée Camus
Cinéma Royal
Boulevard Victor-Hugo
Rue Notre-Dame
Rue Émile-Zola
Rue de Verdun
Les Trois Sœurs restaurant
Hôtel Zola
Bibliothèque Municipale
Rue Condé
Chez Jeanne
Cinéma Manet
bureau de poste
Boulevard Manet
Boucherie Roger
Hôpital
Musée Archéologique
Hôtel Nelson
Place de la Révolution
Café de la Révolution
La Bonne Soupe
Musée des Beaux Arts
Avenue de la République
Hôtel de Ville
BNP
Café de la Gare
Avenue Jaurès
Aéroport 9 km
Université 2 km

Suggestion, Imperative: Using the verb **regarder,** establish the three forms of the imperative: (1) speak to one student, (2) to several students, (3) involve the whole class. Then show on board the relationship between **tu regardes, vous regardez, nous regardons** and the imperative forms.

STRUCTURE

The imperative

Écoute! — *Listen!*
Faites attention! — *Be* careful! (*Pay* attention!)
Allons en ville ensemble! — *Let's go* downtown together!

Imperative, or command, forms of the verb are used to give orders, directions, and suggestions. The three forms of the imperative—**tu** (familiar), **vous** (formal or plural), and **nous** (plural, including yourself)—are based on the present tense. The subject pronoun is omitted and the verb is used alone. In written French, the **s** of the **tu** form is dropped for regular **-er** verbs and for **aller:**

Present tense	Imperative	Present tense	Imperative
tu travailles vous travaillez nous travaillons	**travaille!** **travaillez!** **travaillons!**	tu vas vous allez nous allons	**va!** **allez!** **allons!**

To form the negative imperative, place **ne** before the verb and **pas** after it:

Ne parlez pas anglais! — *Don't speak* English!
Ne mange pas! — *Don't eat!*

The verbs **avoir** and **être** have irregular imperative forms:

avoir	être
aie! **ayez!** **ayons!**	**sois!** **soyez!** **soyons!**

Application

D. Give the three imperative forms of the following verbs.

MODÈLE: regarder
Regarde!
Regardez!
Regardons!

1. chanter
2. ne pas parler anglais
3. aller au bureau de poste
4. avoir de la patience
5. être sage *(be good, said to a child)*

E. **Dites à. . .** *(Tell . . .)* Use the appropriate command form to get the following people to do what you want.

Dites à votre petit frère de:

MODÈLE: écouter
Écoute!

1. aller à l'école
2. ne pas regarder la télévision
3. faire attention
4. être sage

Dites à vos amis de:

MODÈLE: chanter
Chantez!

5. regarder
6. ne pas écouter
7. faire un voyage
8. aller au théâtre

Proposez à vos amis de:

MODÈLE: danser
Dansons!

9. aller à la boulangerie
10. faire une promenade
11. ne pas parler anglais
12. ne pas manger de sandwiches

Ex. F: O. Encourage students to vary the form **(tu, vous, nous).**

F. **Allez-y!** *(Go on and do it!)* Using the suggested verbs, tell one or two of your classmates to do something. They are obliged to obey you! Verbs:

regarder, écouter, chanter, danser, parler, aller, faire des devoirs, chercher, commander

MODÈLE: *Charles et Henri, chantez!*
Anne, parle à Monique!
Éric, dansons!

DÉBROUILLONS-NOUS !

Review of **étape**

Ex. G: ⇄

G. **On va à l'école.** Explain to another student how you get from where you live to your school. If you go on foot, use **je;** if you ride to school, use **nous.** Include in your explanation the verbs **aller, traverser, tourner,** and **continuer.**

Ex. H: △ or □. If possible, place photos of these cities around the class; if not, put labels on walls or board. Have students circulate in groups of three or four.

H. **Au musée.** You and your friends are at an exposition of photographs of famous cities where French is spoken (Montréal, Bruxelles, Genève, Dakar, Alger). You and your friends argue about which sets of photos to look at next. Follow the model.

MODÈLE: — *J'aime les photos de Dakar.*
— *Moi, je préfère les photos de Bruxelles. Ne regarde pas les photos de Dakar.*
— *C'est ça. Regardons les photos de Bruxelles.*

Note Culturelle

La francophonie is the term used to designate those countries outside of France itself where French is either the official language or a dominant means of communication. In 1988, some 100 million **francophones** were scattered throughout the world. Over 65 million live in Europe (in Switzerland, Belgium, Luxembourg, for example), some 12 million in the Americas (Canada, the Caribbean, portions of the United States—Louisiana, New England), approximately 20 million in Africa (mainly Northern Africa and the West Coast), as well as another two million in the Pacific (Polynesia and the Far East) and the Middle East.

Written Work: See Workbook.

Lexique

Pour se débrouiller

Pour demander un renseignement

Où se trouve . . . ?
. . . , s'il vous plaît?

Pour donner un renseignement

à côté de
au bout de
au coin de
derrière
devant
en face de
entre
loin de
près de

Pour expliquer comment aller quelque part

continuer tout droit
jusqu'à . . .
dans l'avenue
dans la rue
sur (dans) le boulevard
sur la place
tourner à droite
à gauche
traverser

Thèmes et contextes

Les instruments de musique

la batterie
la clarinette
la flûte
la guitare
le piano
le saxophone
le trombone
la trompette
le violon

Vocabulaire général

Noms

le plan

Autres expressions

je ne sais pas
par mois

Chapitre neuf

Allons au festival!

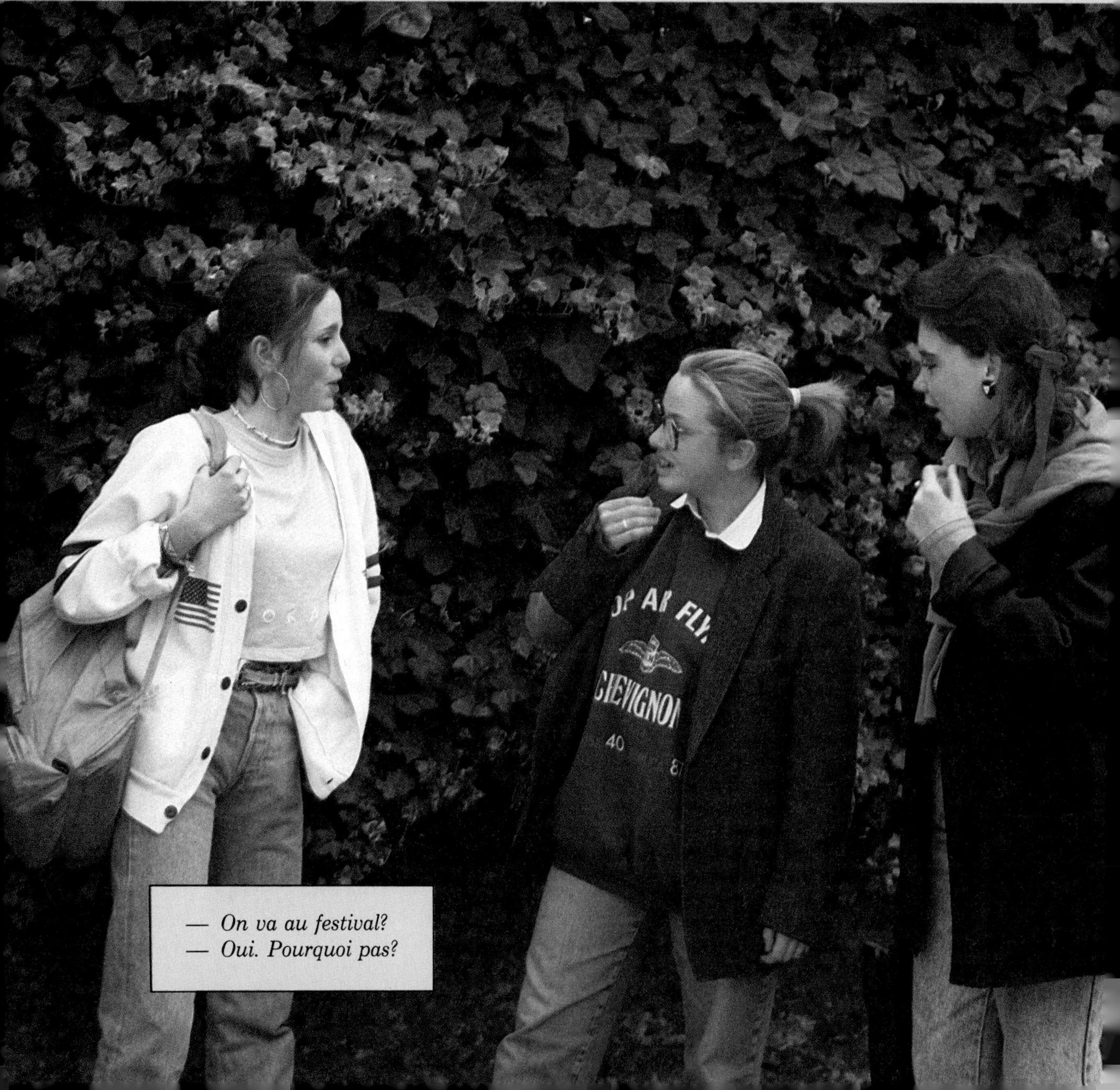

— On va au festival?
— Oui. Pourquoi pas?

Première étape

Point de départ:

Nous voudrions voir. . .

Transparency, Point de départ; poster for Tarascon Fête des fleurs

Nous voudrions voir: We would like to see

Christine Abello habite à Tarascon, dans le **sud** de la France. **Tous les ans** il y a un festival, la Fête des **Fleurs,** à Tarascon. Christine regarde une affiche annonçant le festival de **cette année.**

south / every year
flowers
this year

FÊTE DES FLEURS

Tarascon

samedi 27 juin

10h30	**Défilé:** la Grande Cavalcade (Bd. Victor Hugo, Bd Gambetta, Bd Itam)
11h–12h	Danses folkloriques (place de la Mairie)
12h–14h	**Dégustation:** spécialités de la région **(au bord du Rhône)**
13h–15h	Concert de rock: Louis Bertgani et «Les Visiteurs» (place de la Mairie)
14h–18h	Sports: tennis, judo, volley ball (stade municipal)
14h–18h	Exposition de peintures (musée des Beaux-Arts)
16h–18h	Concert d'**orgue** (église Ste-Marthe)
19h–21h	Dégustation: spécialités de la région (au bord du Rhône)
21h30	Spectacle **son et lumière** (devant le **château**)
22h30	**Feux d'artifice** (au bord du Rhône)
23h	**Bal** populaire (devant le château)

Saturday
Parade
(food) tasting / on the banks of the Rhône river
organ
Sound and Light / castle
Fireworks
Dance

À vous!

Vocabulary activities

Reminder Ex. A: You may wish to take a moment to talk about the use of official time in France (transportation, radio and TV, movies, concerts, etc.) and to have students practice converting from official time to conversational time.

A. **Où? À quelle heure?** *(Where? At what time?)* You are staying in Tarascon at the time of the festival. You run into a group of American tourists who do not speak French and are confused by the schedule of events. Answer their questions. Reminder: In France, many public events are listed according to official time (that is, using a 24-hour clock rather than the 12-hour clock used to express time in conversation).

MODÈLE: Where are the fireworks? And when?
On the banks of the Rhone river. They start at 10:30 p.m.

1. Where are the folk dances? What time?
2. When does the parade start? Where will it go?
3. If we get hungry, is there food to eat? Where? When?
4. My husband and I love classical music. Are there any concerts? Where? When?
5. Our children hate classical music. Is there anything for them? When? Where?
6. What time does the dancing begin?
7. The little boys would like to watch some sporting events. Where can they go? All day?
8. We heard there was a historical pageant with music and lights. What time does that start? Where do we go to see it?

Ex. B: ⇄

B. **Qu'est-ce que vous voudriez faire?** You and your French friends are talking about the festival. Ask the people indicated below what they would like to do or see. A classmate will answer with the information provided. In the questions and answers, use the appropriate form: **je voudrais, tu voudrais, vous voudriez,** or **nous voudrions.**

MODÈLES: Martin / voir le défilé
— *Martine, qu'est-ce que tu voudrais faire?*
— *Je voudrais voir le défilé.*

Paul et René / aller à l'exposition de peintures
— *Paul et René, qu'est-ce que vous voudriez faire?*
— *Nous voudrions aller à l'exposition de peintures.*

1. Giselle / voir les danses folkloriques
2. Gérard / aller au concert d'orgue
3. Renée et Isabelle / aller au concert de rock
4. Isabelle et David / voir le défilé
5. Alain / regarder le judo au stade municipal
6. Véronique / manger des spécialités de la région
7. Marc et Sylvie / aller au bal
8. Christiane et Monique / voir le son et lumière

REPRISE

C. **Est-ce qu'il y a. . . ?** You are at the American Embassy in the African city of Bamako, the capital of Mali (see the map below. Find out if certain places are nearby.

Among the places you might be looking for are **une pharmacie, un bureau de tabac, un bureau de poste, une épicerie, le commissariat de police, une boulangerie, un café, un restaurant, une boucherie, une banque, un hôtel, l'hôpital.**

MODÈLE: boucherie
— *Pardon. Est-ce qu'il y a une boucherie près d'ici?*
— *Non, il n'y a pas de boucherie près d'ici, mais il y a une boucherie dans l'avenue de la Liberté.*

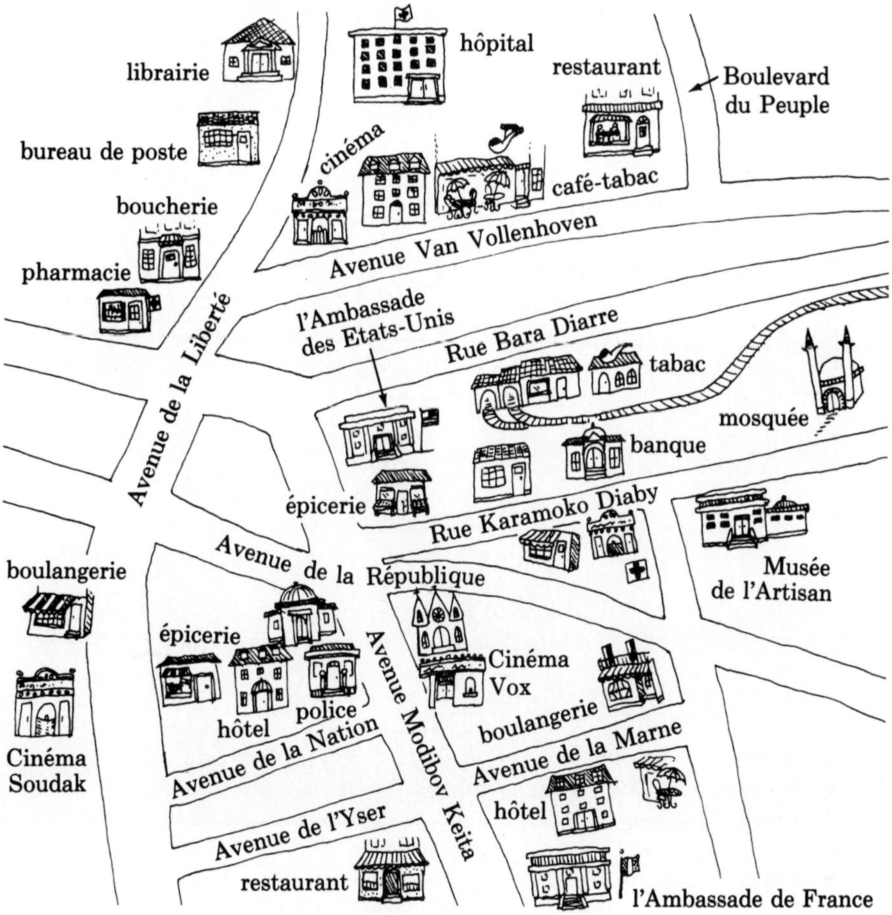

Transparency, Ex. C; map of Bamako

Recycling activities

Ex. C: ⇄

Le savez-vous?

Why would someone go to a *syndicat d'initiative?*
a) to get tourist information
b) to obtain a business loan
c) to ask for protection

réponse

Suggestions, time: Use a model clock. Begin by having students repeat the hours from **une heure** until **midi** (contrast with **minuit**). Then have them repeat the time every five minutes from **trois heures** until **quatre heures.**

a

STRUCTURE

Quelle heure est-il?

Il est une heure.

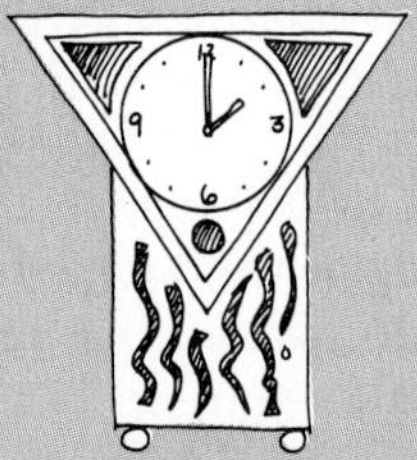

Il est deux heures.

Il est deux heures dix.

Il est deux heures et quart.

Il est deux heures et demie.[1]

Il est trois heures moins vingt.

Il est trois heures moins le quart.

Il est midi.

Il est minuit et demi.[1]

To distinguish between A.M. and P.M., use the expressions **du matin** *(in the morning)*, **de l'après-midi** *(in the afternoon)*, or **du soir** *(in the evening)*.

9:12 A.M.	**neuf heures douze du matin**
2:30 P.M.	**deux heures et demie de l'après-midi**
8:40 P.M.	**neuf heures moins vingt du soir**

[1]The word **heure** is feminine; consequently, the word **demie** ends in **-e.** However, since **midi** and **minuit** are masculine, no **-e** is added when **demi** follows these two expressions.

Application

D. Give the time for every three minutes between **9h** and **10h.**

E. **Quelle heure est-il?** Find out the time from a classmate. Indicate whether it is morning **(du matin),** afternoon **(de l'après-midi),** or evening **(du soir).**

MODELE: 2h20
— *Quelle heure est-il?*
— *Il est deux heures vingt de l'après-midi (du matin).*

1. 8h20
2. 12h00
3. 3h10
4. 1h30
5. 10h55
6. 11h45
7. 4h15
8. 5h35
9. 7h45
10. 10h25

NOTE GRAMMATICALE

Questions about time

To ask someone *what time* something happens, use **À quelle heure. . . ?** The response to this question requires either the preposition **à** (if you give an exact time) or the preposition **vers** (if you give an approximate time).

— **À quelle heure** est-ce qu'on mange?	— *What time* do we eat?
— **À 6h15.**	— *At 6:15.*
— **Vers 6h.**	— *Around 6 o'clock.*

To ask someone *when* something occurs, use **quand.** To indicate that something happens *between* two times, use either **entre. . . et. . .** or **de. . . jusqu'à. . .**

— **Quand** est-ce que tu fais ton français?	— *When* do you do your French?
— **Entre 8h et 9h.**	— *Between 8 and 9 o'clock.*
— **Quand** est-ce que ta mère travaille?	— *When* does your mother work?
— Elle travaille **de 4h jusqu'à minuit.**	— She works *from 4 until midnight.*

F. **On va au festival de Tarascon.** You want to find out when you and your friends are going to do certain things the day of the festival. Answer the questions using the information provided.

MODÈLE: Quand est-ce qu'on va à l'exposition de peintures? (vers 3h)
On va à l'exposition vers 3h.

1. À quelle heure est-ce qu'on va au défilé? (vers 10h)
2. À quelle heure commence *(begins)* le concert de rock? (à 1h)
3. Quand est-ce qu'on mange? (entre midi et 2h)
4. Quand est-ce que nous avons la possibilité de regarder le judo? (de 2h jusqu'à 6h)
5. À quelle heure est-ce qu'on va au son et lumière? (vers 9h)
6. À quelle heure commencent les feux d'artifice? (à 10h30)
7. Quand est-ce qu'on fait des danses folkloriques? (entre 11h et midi)
8. À quelle heure est-ce que le bal commence? (vers 11h)

DÉBROUILLONS-NOUS!

Ex. G: ⇄

G. **Où es-tu d'habitude?** Find out from a classmate where he/she usually is at the following times. Some possible answers: **à la maison, à l'école, en ville, au travail, chez mon ami(e),** etc.

1. En semaine *(during the week),* où es-tu à 9h du matin? À midi? À 5h de l'après-midi? À 8h du soir?
2. Le samedi *(on Saturdays),* où es-tu à 8h du matin? À 11h du matin? À 3h de l'après-midi? À 9h du soir?
3. Le dimanche *(on Sundays),* où es-tu à 9h30 du matin? À 11h30? À 2h de l'après-midi? À 6h du soir?

Ex. H: Have students change partners two or three times. You may wish to assign activities for variety.

H. **Au festival de Tarascon.** Imagine that your class is in Tarascon for the annual **Fête des Fleurs.** Ask your classmates what they would like to see. Then find out at what time the activity begins and where you go.

MODÈLE: — *Janet, qu'est-ce que tu voudrais faire?*
— *Moi, je voudrais voir les danses folkloriques.*
— *À quelle heure commencent les danses?*
— *À 11h.*
— *Où est-ce qu'on va?*
— *On va à la place de la Mairie.*

POURQUOI?

Answer, Pourquoi?: d

While driving in France, an American tourist arrives at a three-way intersection slightly ahead of a truck and a small Renault. He has a stop sign, as do the other two vehicles. The American stops, makes sure that the truck and the car also stop, then starts out across the intersection. Suddenly, his car is struck on the right side by the truck. When the American gets out to see what has happened, both the trucker and the driver of the Renault scream at him in French. What is the problem?

Suggestion: Point out stereotypical nature of answers b and c as well as the difference between French and American rules of the road **(la priorité à droite).**

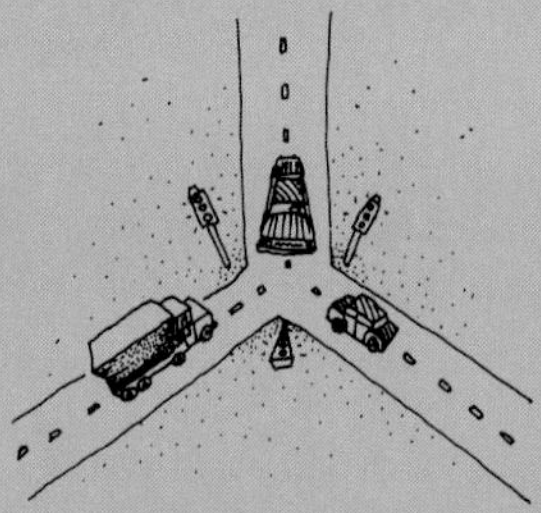

a. Trucks always have the right of way in France.
b. Most French drivers do not like Americans.
c. The truck driver was not paying attention and didn't see that the American got to the intersection first.
d. The vehicle farthest to the right always has the right of way in France.

Written Work: See Workbook.

C'est quand, la Fête des Fleurs?

Le chateau de Tarascon

Deuxième étape

Point de départ:

Rendez-vous: meeting

Rendez-vous à 10h

Suggestion, Point de départ: Discuss with students what has to be decided when making plans (Where to go? When and where to meet?). Then have them listen to the dialogue (Teacher Tape) and answer the above questions (in French or in English).

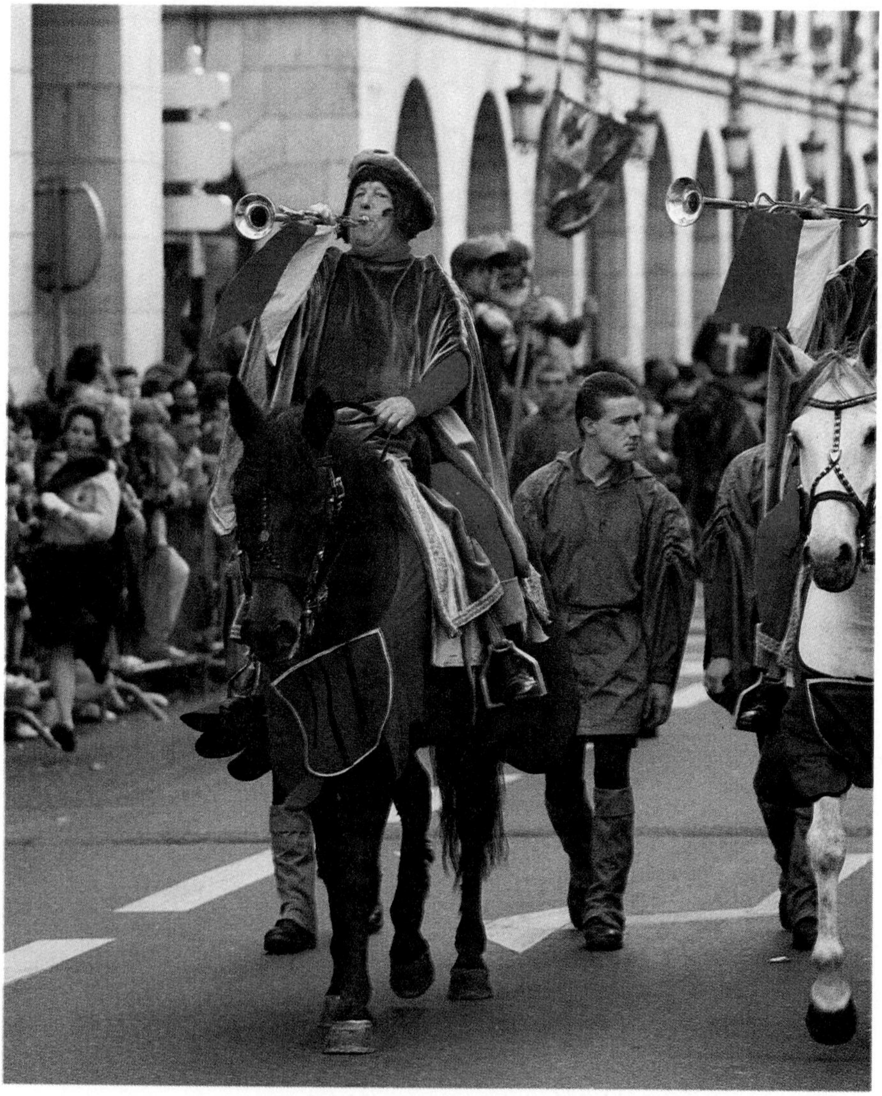

Christine et ses amis parlent du festival.

CHRISTINE:	**Alors,** qu'est-ce qu'on fait?	so
JEAN-LOUP:	Allons voir le défilé!	
CÉCILE:	**D'accord. Bonne idée!**	OK! / Good idea!
PATRICIA:	Oui. Pourquoi pas?	
DAVID:	Mais moi, je voudrais faire du tennis.	
CHRISTINE:	Pas de problème! D'abord, on va voir le défilé et ensuite on va au stade faire du tennis. Ca va?	
DAVID ET LES AUTRES:	Oui, ça va.	
CÉCILE:	Où est-ce qu'**on se retrouve?**	we meet
DAVID:	Et à quelle heure?	
CHRISTINE:	Sur le boulevard Gambetta, devant le parking, vers 10h. D'accord?	
LES AUTRES:	D'accord.	
PATRICIA:	Alors, **c'est décidé.** Rendez-vous à 10h devant le parking sur le boulevard Gambetta.	it's settled

À vous!

A. **Qu'est-ce qu'on fait?** You and a classmate are planning to attend the **Fête des Fleurs** at Tarascon. Ask your classmate what he/she wants to do at the festival. When your classmate suggests an activity, indicate your agreement by saying, **"D'accord. Bonne idée!"** or **"Oui. Pourquoi pas?"**

Vocabulary activities

Ex. A: ⇄

MODÈLES: aller voir le défilé
— *Alors, qu'est-ce qu'on fait?*
— *Allons voir le défilé!*
— *D'accord. Bonne idée!*
— *Bon. C'est décidé. On va voir le défilé.*

regarder le judo
— *Alors, qu'est-ce qu'on fait?*
— *Regardons le judo!*
— *Oui. Pourquoi pas?*
— *Bon. C'est décidé. On regarde le judo.*

1. écouter le concert de rock
2. manger des spécialités de la région
3. aller au bal populaire
4. aller voir le son et lumière
5. regarder le tennis
6. aller voir les feux d'artifice

Le savez-vous?

Gothic cathedrals, such as Reims and Chartres, were built in what time period?
a) twelfth and thirteenth centuries
b) sixteenth century
c) nineteenth century

réponse

Ex. B: ⇄

B. **Mais moi, je voudrais. . .** When you propose an activity to your classmate, he/she has a different idea. Settle the disagreement by suggesting that first **(d'abord)** you do one activity and then **(ensuite)** you do the other.

MODÈLE: aller voir les danses folkloriques / écouter le concert de jazz
— *Alors, qu'est-ce qu'on fait?*
— *Allons voir les danses folkloriques!*
— *Mais moi, je voudrais écouter le concert de jazz.*
— *D'abord, on va voir les danses folkloriques et ensuite on écoute le concert de jazz.*
— *Bon. D'accord.*

→ a

1. aller voir le défilé / manger des spécialités de la région
2. écouter le concert de rock / regarder le judo
3. regarder le tennis / écouter le concert d'orgue
4. manger des spécialités de la région / aller voir le son et lumière
5. aller voir les feux d'artifice / aller au bal populaire

Ex. C: ⇄

C. **À quelle heure est-ce qu'on se retrouve? Et où?** You and your classmate have decided where to go. Now you need to arrange a time and place to meet.

MODÈLE: 10h / devant le parking sur le boulevard Gambetta
— *À quelle heure est-ce qu'on se retrouve?*
— *À 10h.*
— *Et où?*
— *Devant le parking sur le boulevard Gambetta.*
— *D'accord. Rendez-vous à 10h devant le parking sur le boulevard Gambetta.*

1. 11h / à la place de la Mairie
2. 3h / au stade
3. 4h / à l'église Sainte-Marthe
4. 9h / devant le château

REPRISE

D. **Quelle heure est-il?** Answer according to the cues.

MODÈLE: 2h30
— *Quelle heure est-il?*
— *Il est deux heures et demie.*

1. 7h25
2. 11h52
3. 10h15
4. 3h30
5. 8h10
6. 1h45
7. 4h40
8. 12h05
9. 8h33
10. 9h16

E. **Moi, je voudrais écouter le concert d'orgue.** You have met some students who are staying at the **Hôtel Terminus** in Tarascon. As each of the students tells you what he/she would like to do, tell him/her where to go and how to get there. Reminder: In giving directions to a student, use the familiar forms: **tu vas, tu continues, tu tournes, tu traverses,** etc.

Ex. E: ⇄

Transparency, Ex. E; map of Tarascon

MODÈLE: écouter le concert d'orgue / l'église Sainte-Marthe
— *Moi, je voudrais écouter le concert d'orgue.*
— *Eh bien, tu vas a l'église Sainte-Marthe.*
— *Elle est près d'ici?*
— *Oui, tu vas au boulevard Victor-Hugo, tu tournes à gauche, tu continues sur le boulevard Victor-Hugo jusqu'au boulevard du Château, tu tournes à droite et l'église Sainte-Marthe est sur ta droite, en face du château.*

1. aller au concert de jazz / la place de la Mairie
2. regarder le tennis / le stade municipal
3. voir l'exposition de peintures / le musée des Beaux-Arts
4. voir les feux d'artifice / le château

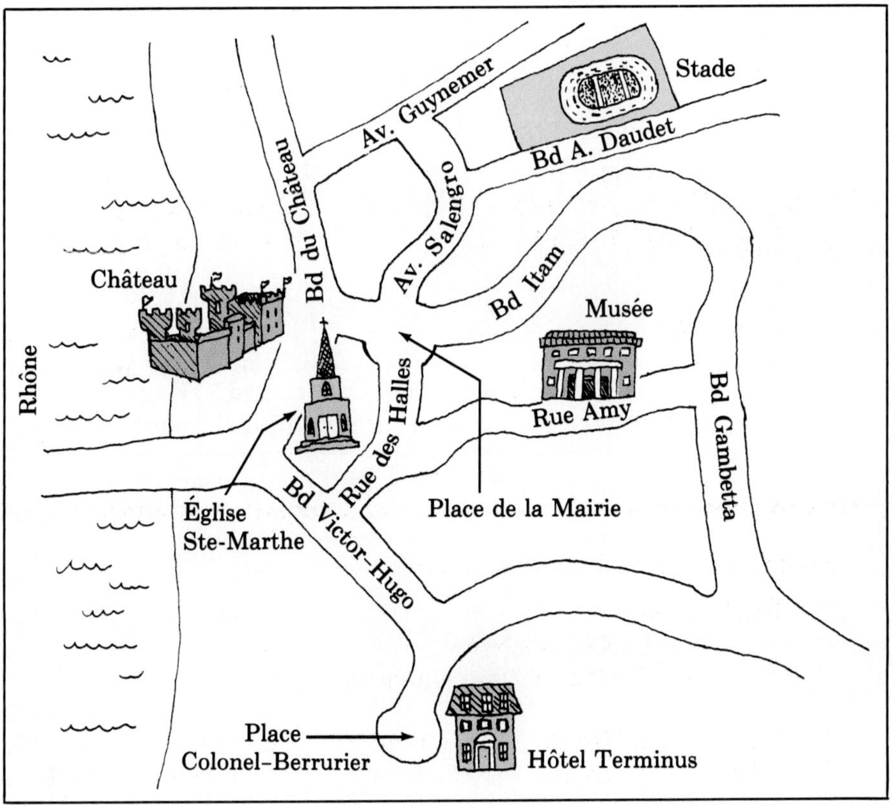

Suggestion, Possessive adjectives: Present as in Unit 2, Ch. 5. This time do not speak directly to owner. **Voici le livre. C'est livre de Paul?** Visually reinforce use of **son, sa, ses** for masculine and feminine; **leur(s),** for singular and plural.

STRUCTURE

Possessive adjectives—third person

— C'est le vélo de Bénédicte? — Oui, c'est **son** vélo.	— It's Bénédicte's bike? — Yes, it's *her* bike.
— Où est la chambre de Mathieu? — **Sa** chambre est là-bas.	— Where is Mathieu's room? — *His* room is over there.
— Tu aimes les amis de ta sœur? — Oui, en général, j'aime **ses** amis.	— Do you like your sister's friends? — Yes, generally I like *her* friends.
— Où sont les disques de Jeanne et de Monique? — Voici **leurs** disques.	— Where are Jeanne and Monique's records? — Here are *their* records.

The third-person singular forms of the possessive adjectives are **son, sa,** and **ses.** Like the first- and second-person possessive adjectives (**mon, ta, nos, votre,** etc.), these adjectives agree with the noun they modify. The third-person plural of the possessive adjective has only two forms: **leur** (with singular nouns) and **leurs** (with plural nouns).

Subject	Masculine singular	Feminine singular	Masc. and fem. plural	English equivalent
il/elle/on	**son**	**sa**	**ses**	*his* or *her*
ils/elles	**leur**	**leur**	**leurs**	*their*

When a feminine noun begins with a vowel or a vowel sound, the masculine form **(son)** is used: **son‿auto, son‿amie.**

The **s** of **ses** and **leurs** is silent, except before a noun beginning with a vowel or a vowel sound. Then liaison takes place: **ses livres,** but **ses‿amis; leurs vélos,** but **leurs‿avocats.**

NOTE GRAMMATICALE

Because a possessive adjective agrees with the noun that it modifies and *not* with the person who possesses, the gender of the possessor must be determined from the context, not from the adjective.

son père — *his father* or *her father*
son vélo — *her bike* or *his bike* (**Vélo** is masculine.)

sa mère — *his mother* or *her mother*
sa chambre — *her room* or *his room* (**Chambre** is feminine.)

ses amis — *her friends* or *his friends* (**Amis** is plural.)

Application

Exs. F, G, H:

These first three mechanical exercises are designed to fix the structures (F,G) and to underline the agreement with the object rather than the possessor.

F. Replace the word in italics and make the necessary changes.

1. Voilà son *stylo.* (cahier / appartement / amie / vélo)
2. Où est sa *chambre?* (maison / calculatrice / clé / télévision)
3. Ce sont ses *clés?* (disques / cahiers / amis / stylos)
4. Où est leur *appareil-photo?* (transistor / voiture / hôtel / appartement)
5. Voici leurs *livres.* (clés / amies / crayons / disques)

G. Replace the word in italics and make the necessary changes.

1. Voici son *crayon.* (maison / appartement / ami / amie / disques / amis)
2. Voilà leur *maison.* (chambre / voiture / clés / amis / ordinateur)

H. Answer the questions affirmatively.

MODÈLE: C'est le cahier de Pierre?
Oui, c'est son cahier.

1. C'est le cahier d'Anne-Marie?
2. C'est la chambre de Robert?
3. C'est la chambre d'Annick?
4. Ce sont les clés d'Éric?
5. Ce sont les clés de Véronique?
6. Ce sont les clés de Pascale et de Roger?
7. C'est la chambre de Guy et de Chantal?
8. C'est l'amie de Claire?
9. C'est l'amie de Jean-Luc?
10. Ce sont les amis d'Yvonne?

Ex. I: △

I. **À qui est. . .?** *(Whose . . . ?)* Find out to whom the objects belong.

Dominique *Le professeur* *M. et Mme Pagnol*

Follow-up, Ex. I: Choose four students to play the roles of Dominique, le professeur, M. et Mme Pagnol. Repeat Ex. G: A: **À qui est la chaîne stéréo?** B: **C'est la chaîne stéréo de Dominique.** C: **Dominique, c'est ta chaîne stéréo?** Dominique: **Oui, c'est ma chaîne stéréo.** B: *(pointing at Dominique)* **Oui, c'est sa chaîne stéréo.**

MODÈLE: la chaîne stéréo
— *À qui est la chaîne stéréo?*
— *C'est la chaîne stéréo de Dominique.*
— *Oui, c'est sa chaîne stéréo.*

1. le cahier
2. la voiture
3. les chiens
4. le vélo
5. les livres
6. l'appareil-photo
7. la maison
8. les clés
9. la chambre

DÉBROUILLONS-NOUS !

Review of **étape**

Ex. J: ⇄

J. **Échange.** Ask the questions of another student, who will answer using a possessive adjective **(son, sa, ses, leur, leurs)** when possible.

1. Où est-ce que ta famille habite? Et la famille de ton ami(e)?
2. Où est-ce que tes parents travaillent? Et les parents de ton ami(e)?
3. Quel est ton nom de famille? Et le nom de famille de ton ami(e)?

Ex. K: ⇄

Written Work: See Workbook.

K. **Qu'est-ce qu'on fait?** Make plans with one or more of your classmates to do something. Agree on an activity. Then arrange a time and place to meet. Possible activities: **aller au cinéma, aller à un concert, faire une promenade, regarder la télé, écouter des disques.**

Lexique

Pour se débrouiller

Pour organiser une activité

Qu'est-ce que tu voudrais faire?
vous voudriez voir?
Je voudrais voir...
Nous voudrions aller...
Allons...
Faisons...

D'accord. Bonne idée.
Oui. Pourquoi pas?

Pour fixer un rendez-vous

À quelle heure est-ce qu'on se retrouve?
Où est-ce qu'on se retrouve?
On se retrouve à...
Rendez-vous à...

Pour demander et donner l'heure

Quelle heure est-il?
Il est une heure.
une heure et quart.
une heure et demie.
deux heures moins le quart.
midi.
minuit.

Pour établir la possession

A qui est ... ?
C'est le (la, l', les) de ...
C'est (Ce sont) son (sa, ses) ...
leur (leurs) ...

Vocabulaire général

Noms

un bal
un concert d'orgue
de rock
un défilé
les danses folkloriques *(f.pl.)*
la dégustation
un festival
les feux *(m.pl.)* d'artifice
un spectacle son et lumière
une spécialité de la région

Autres expressions

alors
C'est décidé.
tous les ans

Mise au point

Prereading: Have students discuss what features might go into a paragraph for a brochure designed to attract tourists to their town or city.

Lecture: *Visitez Fougères!*

Read the following tourist brochure published by the tourist office of Fougères, a city in eastern Brittany. Use the many cognates to do Exercise A *without* looking at the definitions that follow the reading.

"Nulle part en France
le voyageur ne rencontre
de contraste aussi grandiose ...
La Bretagne est là
dans sa fleur"

Balzac.

FOUGÈRES Ville d'Art

Citadelle du Duché de Bretagne

Visitée et chantée par les grands écrivains[1] de l'époque romantique, FOUGÈRES offre aux touristes, aux historiens, aux peintres, avec le souvenir vivant de son passé et de son site incomparable, le spectacle de ses monuments d'architecture militaire avec son château et ses fortifications urbaines, de foi[2] médiévale avec ses magnifiques églises.

Riche de son passé, FOUGÈRES est de nos jours[3] un centre industriel et agricole très important.

[1] writers
[2] faith
[3] nowadays

Compréhension

A. **La brochure.** After your first reading of the passage, list as many facts about the city of Fougères as you can. Then read the passage again, consulting the definitions at the end, and add to your list any attractions or ideas that you missed.

B. **Visitez Fougères!** Fill in the text for this poster encouraging tourists to visit Fougères.

C. **Visitez. . . !** Create a poster, similar to the one for Fougères, aimed at attracting French-speaking tourists to your town or area.

REPRISE

D. **Qu'est-ce qu'on fait cet après-midi?** You and a classmate are trying to decide what to do after school this afternoon **(cet après-midi).** When your classmate proposes an activity, agree and then arrange a time and place to meet.

Recycling activities

Ex. D: ⇄

MODÈLE: manger quelque chose / au Macdo, 3h30
— *Alors, qu'est-ce qu'on fait cet après-midi?*
— *Moi, je voudrais manger quelque chose.*
— *Pourquoi pas? Où est-ce qu'on se retrouve?*
— *Au Macdo. À trois heures et demie.*
— *Bon. D'accord. Rendez-vous à trois heures et demie au Macdo.*

1. manger quelque chose / au Burger King, 3h45
2. regarder la télé / chez moi (toi), 4h
3. aller au cinéma / au cinéma, 5h30
4. faire une promenade / devant l'école, 3h

E. **Non, ce n'est pas ça.** *(No, that's not right.)* Your brother has some mistaken ideas about the families of your new friends. Correct his mistakes, using the appropriate possessive adjectives **(son, sa, ses, leur, leurs)**

MODÈLE: Le frère de François habite à Toulon. (à Toulouse)
Non, ce n'est pas ça. Son frère habite à Toulouse.

1. La sœur de Jacques habite à Nîmes. (à Nice)
2. La sœur de Denise travaille à Cherbourg. (à Strasbourg)
3. Le frère de Daniel travaille à Rouen. (à Rennes)
4. Le frère de Chantal travaille à Nantes. (à Nancy)
5. Les cousins de Janine sont de Lyon. (de Lille)
6. Les cousins de Marcel sont de Grenoble. (de Genève)
7. Les parents de Béatrice sont professeurs. (avocats)
8. Les parents de Didier et de Maurice sont médecins. (ingénieurs)

RÉVISION

In this **Révision,** you will review:

- the irregular verb **aller;**
- **à** + definite article;
- the numbers from 11 to 29;
- **de** + definite article;
- place prepositions and adverbs;
- the imperative;
- telling time;
- the possessive adjectives.

The irregular verb *aller*

je **vais**	nous **allons**
tu **vas**	vous **allez**
il, elle, on **va**	ils, elles **vont**

à + definite article

à + la ⟶ **à la**
à + l' ⟶ **à l'**
à + le ⟶ **au**
à + les ⟶ **aux**

Numbers from 11 to 29

onze	quinze	dix-neuf
douze	seize	vingt
treize	dix-sept	vingt et un
quatorze	dix-huit	vingt-deux, *etc.*

Ex. F: ⇄

F. **On va en ville.** Your brothers and sisters are all heading into town to do errands. Ask where each is going.

Librairie Moderne, 12 rue Bordet Boulangerie Ancienne, 19 bd Mouchy Boucherie Campion, 15 avenue des Bois Pharmacie du Moulin, 14 rue du Moulin Tabac Royal, 16 bd de la Plaine Épicerie de la Ville, 11 avenue d'Orléans Café des Sports, 28 rue Legrand

MODÈLE: — *Où est-ce que tu vas?*
— *Je vais à la Pharmacie du Moulin.*
— *Où est-ce qu'elle se trouve?*
— *14 rue du Moulin.*

1. Où est-ce que Henri va?
2. Et Martine?
3. Et Jean-Pierre et Isabelle?
4. Et vous deux, Éric et Patrice?

***De* + definite article**		**Place prepositions and adverbs**	
de + la →	**de la**	**près (de)**	**devant**
de + l' →	**de l'**	**loin (de)**	**derrière**
de + le →	**du**	**à côté (de)**	**entre**
de + les →	**des**	**en face (de)**	
		au bout (de)	
		au coin (de)	

G. **Au service des renseignements.** You are working at the information bureau at the railroad station. When a traveler asks for help, you look at your map (p. 165) and give precise information, including the exact name of the place. Ex. G: ⇄

MODÈLE: café / près du parc
— *Pardon. Est-ce qu'il y a un café près du parc?*
— *Oui, sur le boulevard Gambetta, à côté du théâtre.*
— *Quel est le nom du café?*
— *C'est le Café du Parc.*

1. hôtel / près de la place de la Libération
2. cinéma / près de la gare
3. restaurant / près de l'hôpital
4. boulangerie / près du bureau de poste
5. restaurant / près du Lycée Camus
6. café / près du Musée Archéologique

The imperative

The imperative is usually formed by using the present-tense form **(tu, vous, nous)** of the verb without the subject (**avoir** and **être** are exceptions). Remember that the **-s** of the **tu** form is dropped for regular **-er** verbs and for **aller:**

regarder	aller	faire	avoir	être
regarde! regardez! regardons!	va! allez! allons!	fais! faites! faisons!	aie! ayez! ayons!	sois! soyez! soyons!

Ex. H: ⇄

H. **Écoute! Écoutez! Écoutons!** Using the verbs suggested, give five commands or suggestions to each of the following people or groups. Select from the verbs provided. Use both affirmative and negative forms.

1. Vous parlez à votre petit frère. (écouter, regarder, faire attention, être sage, manger, parler, chanter)

   MODÈLE: *Écoute!*

2. Vous parlez à un groupe de touristes. (écouter, aller, regarder, traverser, tourner, parler, manger, visiter)

   MODÈLE: *Écoutez!*

3. Vous parlez à vos amis. (écouter, aller, regarder, manger, danser, visiter, travailler, étudier)

   MODÈLE: *N'écoutons pas la radio!*

Telling Time

Quelle heure est-il? **Il est huit heures (8h).**
huit heures dix (8h10).
huit heures et quart (8h15).
huit heures et demie (8h30).
neuf heures moins vingt (8h40).
neuf heures moins le quart (8h45).
midi (12h).
minuit (12h).

To distinguish between A.M. and P.M., specify morning **(du matin)**, afternoon **(de l'après-midi)**, or evening **(du soir)**.

Quelle heure est-il?

I. **Une réunion familiale.** Your family has organized a big reunion, and relatives are arriving from all over the country at various times of the day and night. Using the indicated information, explain to the French exchange student who is staying with you at what time the following people are arriving. When appropriate, distinguish between A.M. and P.M.

MODÈLE: ton oncle Jim / 3:00 P.M.
— *À quelle heure arrive ton oncle Jim?*
— *Il arrive à trois heures de l'après-midi.*

1. ta tante Sara / 7:00 A.M.
2. ton oncle Bill / 10:45 P.M.
3. ton grand-père / 12:20 P.M.
4. ta cousine de New York / 6:30 P.M.
5. tes cousins de San Francisco / 4:15 P.M.
6. ta grand-mère / 12:50 A.M.
7. tes cousins de Chicago / 1:10 P.M.
8. ta tante Kathy / 5:30 A.M.

Possessive adjectives

Remember that the possessive adjective in French agrees with the object possessed, not with the possessor.

mon	**ma**	**mes**
ton	**ta**	**tes**
son	**sa**	**ses**
notre	**notre**	**nos**
votre	**votre**	**vos**
leur	**leur**	**leurs**

Mon, ton, son are also used with feminine nouns that begin with a vowel or a vowel sound.

Ex. J: □

Ex. L: ⇄

J. **Non, ce n'est pas...** The questioner tries to identify the owner of each object. Each group member denies ownership and attributes it to one or two other students in the group. Finally, the questioner admits that it belongs to him/her.

MODÈLE: livre
ÉLÈVE A: *C'est ton livre?*
ÉLÈVE B: *Non, ce n'est pas mon livre. C'est son livre.*
ÉLÈVE C: *Mais non, ce n'est pas mon livre. C'est leur livre.*
ÉLÈVE D: *Non, ce n'est pas notre livre. C'est son livre.*
ÉLÈVE A: *Oui, c'est vrai. C'est mon livre.*

1. vélo
2. maison
3. disques
4. calculatrice
5. clés
6. ordinateur

Point d'arrivée

Ex. K: ⇄

Suggestion, Ex. K: Students should be made to distinguish between asking for a specific place **(Où est l'hôtel Zola?)** and a generic place **(Est-ce qu'il y a un restaurant près de . . . ?)**

K. **On se renseigne.** You have been living in the town on p. 165 for several months. A stranger stops you in the street and asks directions. Help the stranger find the desired destination.

You are at	**The stranger is looking for**
the railroad station	the Hôtel Zola
the Hôtel Nelson	the Librairie Catholique
the cathedral	a restaurant (near the hospital)
the archeological museum	a bank

Suggestion, Ex. L: Have students prepare at home. Give presentations in small groups, then choose one or two to be presented to class.

L. **Mon ami(e).** Make a presentation to the class about a friend of yours. Among the information you might provide are the person's name, interests, family background, possessions, likes, and dislikes.

Ex. M: ⇄

M. **Au Café de la Révolution.** You and an Austrian pen pal have just arrived in the town on p. 165. While having lunch at the Café de la Révolution, you talk about your families, your interests, and the like. Then you look at the map and discuss the best way to get to your next destination. You are going to the park and your pen pal is meeting his/her family in front of the cathedral.

N. **Au festival de Tarascon.** You and one or more of your classmates are in Tarascon for the festival. Using the poster on p. 171, plan your activities for the day. You will probably want to do some activities together. However, each person should have one activity that he/she will do alone. You can then make plans to meet again later in the day.

Ex. N: O

Written Work: See Workbook.

J'habite dans la ville de Tarascon, au sud de la France, non loin d'Avignon. Notre appartement se trouve dans la rue des Halles, en face de l'Hôtel de Ville et tout près du château.

Véronique Béziers

CHAT NOIR

Unité quatre

On va en ville

Planning Strategy: See Workbook.

Audio Tape and/or Video: See Teaching Guide.

Objectives

In this unit, you will learn:

- to make plans to do various activities in town;
- to use the Paris subway;
- to talk about the future;
- to give directions for using the Paris subway;
- to read a short informational text about transportation.

Chapitre dix:	**Tu voudrais aller en ville avec moi?**
Première étape:	Pour quoi faire?
Deuxième étape:	Quand est-ce qu'on y va?
Troisième étape:	Comment est-ce qu'on y va?
Chapitre onze:	**Prenons le métro!**
Première étape:	Quelle direction?
Deuxième étape:	Au guichet
Chapitre douze:	**On y va à pied? Non!**
Première étape:	Prenons la voiture de ton père!
Deuxième étape:	Je veux prendre un taxi!

Massyla Fodéba
Dakar, Sénégal

Chapitre dix

Tu voudrais aller en ville avec moi?

— *Tu voudrais aller en ville avec moi?*
— *Oui, j'ai une course à faire.*

Première étape

Point de départ:

Pour quoi faire?

en ville: to town, downtown

pour quoi faire?: in order to do what?

Transparency, Point de départ: people and activities

Suggestion, Point de départ: Ask students questions using the new expressions, moving from the drawings **(Où est-ce qu'il va retrouver ses amis?)** to the personal **(Est-ce que vous retrouvez vos amis en ville? Où? Est-ce que vous avez rendez-vous avec un[e] ami[e] après la classe?)**

— *Je vais en ville pour* ***retrouver*** *des amis.*
— *Ah, tu* ***as rendez-vous avec*** *des amis.*

— *Je vais en ville pour* ***faire des achats.***
— *Ah, tu voudrais* ***acheter*** *quelque chose.*

retrouver: to meet (arranged in advance)

as rendez-vous avec: have a date to meet with

faire des achats: to go shopping

acheter: to buy

— *Je vais en ville pour aller au cinéma.*
— *Ah, tu* ***as envie d'****aller au cinéma.*

— *Je vais en ville pour* ***faire une course. Je dois*** *aller au bureau de poste pour ma mère.*
— *Ah, tu* ***as une course à faire.***

as envie: feel like

faire une course: to do an errand / *Je dois:* I have to

as une course à faire: have an errand to do

to go window-shopping

have nothing to do

— *Je vais en ville pour* ***faire du lèche-vitrine.***
— *Ah, tu* ***n'as rien à faire.***

Une scène

— François, est-ce que tu voudrais aller en ville avec moi?
— Pour quoi faire?
— J'ai une course à faire pour mon père. Je dois aller à la banque.
— **Justement,** je voudrais acheter un feutre. **Allons-y!**
— D'accord. Allons-y!

As a matter of fact / let's go!

Vocabulary activities

À vous!

A. **Je dois. . . , mais j'ai envie de. . .** In each case, indicate what you have to do **(je dois)** and what you feel like doing **(j'ai envie de).**

MODÈLE: aller au bureau de poste / retrouver mes amis
Je dois aller au bureau de poste, mais j'ai envie de retrouver mes amis.

1. aller à la banque / faire du lèche-vitrine
2. acheter quelque chose pour ma mère / aller au cinéma
3. retrouver mes amis / faire des achats
4. faire des courses pour mon père / retrouver mes amis au café
5. aller au cinéma avec mes parents / rester à la maison avec mes amis

Reminder: You may want to point out to students, using the **Point de départ** as an example, that there is usually more than one way to express the same basic idea. You can then do a follow-up to Ex. B by having two different students respond to each item: e.g., **Elle va en ville pour retrouver une amie. / Oui, elle a rendez-vous avec une amie.**

B. **Pourquoi est-ce qu'elle va en ville?** Your teacher wants to know why each of the following students are going downtown. On the basis of the drawings, explain why.

MODÈLE:
Pourquoi est-ce que Chantal va en ville?
Elle va en ville pour retrouver une amie.

1. Pourquoi est-ce que Vincent va en ville?

2. Pourquoi est-ce que Michèle va en ville?

3. Pourquoi est-ce que Monique va en ville?

4. Pourquoi est-ce que Liliane va en ville?

5. Pourquoi est-ce que Roger va en ville?

6. Pourquoi est-ce que Christian et Marc vont en ville?

Ex. C: ⇄

C. **Tu veux aller en ville avec moi?** You are going downtown and invite a friend to go along. When you explain (on the basis of the drawings below) the reason for going, your friend decides to accompany you.

MODÈLE:
— *Tu veux aller en ville avec moi?*
— *Pour quoi faire?*
— *Je vais aller au bureau de poste.*
— *Bon. D'accord. Allons-y!*

1.

2.

3.

4.

5.

6.

STRUCTURE

The immediate future

Je vais aller en ville.	*I'm going to go* downtown.
Nous allons regarder la télé.	*We're going to watch* TV.
— Qu'est-ce que **tu vas faire** ce soir?	— What *are you going to do* tonight?
— **Je vais rester** à la maison.	— *I'm going to stay* home.

What you have learned to say in French so far refers mainly to the present or to a general situation. It is now time to learn how to talk about the future. One way to express a future action, especially one that will occur in the not-too-distant future, is to use a present-tense form of **aller** and an infinitive. This structure is the equivalent of the English phrase *going to + verb.*

aller + ***infinitive***	***English equivalent***
Je vais danser.	*I'm going to dance.*
Tu vas parler français.	*You're going to speak* French.
Est-ce qu'elle va rester ici?	*Is she going to stay* here?
Nous allons regarder un film.	*We're going to watch* a film.
Vous allez manger.	*You're going to eat.*
Ils vont faire un voyage.	*They're going to take a trip.*

In the negative, **ne . . . pas** is placed around the conjugated form of **aller:**

Je ne vais pas aller en ville.	*I'm not going to go* downtown.
Elle ne va pas faire les courses.	*She's not going to run the errands.*

Suggestion, Immediate future: (1) Review conjugation of **aller.** (2) Have students generate conjugation of **aller danser ce soir.** (3) Repeat in negative. (4) Have one student give the present **(je danse),** another the immediate future **(je vais travailler).**

Application

D. Replace the subject in italics and make all necessary changes.

1. *Suzanne* va faire une promenade ce soir. (Jean-Paul / nous / je / les Mauclair / tu / vous)
2. *Marc* ne va pas aller en ville. (Annick / je / mes amis / vous / tu / nous)
3. Est-ce que *Nicolas* va rester à la maison? (tu / Georges et sa sœur / vous / on / Paulette / nous)

E. **Qu'est-ce qu'on va faire samedi après-midi?** You are trying to find out what your friends are going to do Saturday afternoon **(samedi après-midi).** A classmate will answer the questions using the expressions in parentheses.

MODÈLE: Marcelle, qu'est-ce que tu vas faire samedi après-midi? (aller au cinéma)
Je vais aller au cinéma.

1. Charles, qu'est-ce que tu vas faire samedi après-midi? (faire une course en ville)
2. Et Jean-Pierre, qu'est-ce qu'il va faire? (aller au musée)
3. Et Michèle et son amie? (faire leurs devoirs à la bibliothèque)
4. Sylvie, qu'est-ce que tu vas faire samedi après-midi? (retrouver des amis en ville)
5. Et Éric, qu'est-ce qu'il va faire? (faire des achats)
6. Et Jacques et Isabelle? (faire du lèche-vitrine)
7. Et vous deux? (rester à la maison)

Follow-up, Ex. E: Ask students what they are planning to do **samedi aprés-midi.**

F. **Comment aller à l'école.** Mme Vallon is explaining to her ten-year-old son Gérard how to get to his new school. Play the role of Mme Vallon and adapt the model to the following situations. Change all verbs to the immediate future.

MODÈLE: *Bon, tu quittes* (leave) *la maison, tu vas tout droit jusqu'à l'avenue de St-Cloud, tu tournes à gauche, tu traverses le boulevard de la Reine et voilà, tu entres dans ton école.*

1. Mme Vallon explique à Gérard ce qu'il va faire demain matin *(tomorrow morning): Bon, demain matin, tu vas quitter la maison, . . .*
2. Mme Vallon explique à M. Vallon ce que Gérard va faire demain matin: *Bon, demain matin, Gérard va quitter la maison, . . .*
3. Mme Vallon explique à Gérard et à sa sœur Sophie ce qu'ils vont faire demain matin: *Bon, demain matin, vous allez quitter la maison, . . .*
4. Mme Vallon explique à M. Vallon ce que Gérard et Sophie vont faire demain matin: *Bon, demain matin, Gérard et Sophie vont quitter la maison, . . .*

DÉBROUILLONS-NOUS!

Review of **étape**

Ex. G: ⇄

G. **Échange.** Ask the following questions of a classmate, who will answer them.

1. Est-ce que tu vas souvent en ville? Qu'est-ce que tu fais?
2. Est-ce que tu fais des courses pour tes parents? Où est-ce que tu vas?

3. Où est-ce que tu retrouves tes amis en ville?
4. Qu'est-ce que tu fais quand *(when)* tu n'as rien à faire?
5. Qu'est-ce que tu vas faire ce soir *(tonight)?* Est-ce que tu as envie de faire autre chose *(something else)?*
6. Qu'est-ce que tu vas faire samedi après-midi?

H. **Tu veux aller en ville avec moi?** Decide why you want to go downtown, then find two or three other students who are willing to go with you. (If someone does not want to go with you, that person can explain what he/she is going to do instead.)

Ex. H: O. Divide the class in two groups. Have one group do the inviting for a few minutes, then have the second group do it. Encourage students to speak with different people the second time.

Written Work: See Workbook.

Deuxième étape

Point de départ:

Quand est-ce qu'on y va?

Aujourd'hui **Demain**

today / tomorrow

Ce matin, *je vais aller à l'école.*

Demain matin, je vais ***faire la grasse matinée.***

Ce matin: this morning

faire la grasse matinée: sleep late

Cet après-midi, *je vais faire mes devoirs.*

Demain après-midi, je vais aller en ville.

Cet apres-midi: this afternoon

Ce soir: this evening

Ce soir, *je vais rester chez moi.* *Demain soir, je vais aller au cinéma.*

Une scène

— Tu voudrais aller en ville avec moi? Je dois aller au bureau de poste.
— Justement, moi aussi, j'ai une course à faire. Quand est-ce que tu voudrais y aller? Ce matin?
— Non, c'est impossible. **Je ne peux pas.** Je dois rester à la maison. Cet après-midi? **Ça va?**
— Oui, ça va. On va en ville cet après-midi.

I can't
is that OK?

Vocabulary activities

À vous!

A. **Quand est-ce qu'il va aller en ville?** Based on the drawings, indicate when the following activities take place. Today's date is the fourteenth.

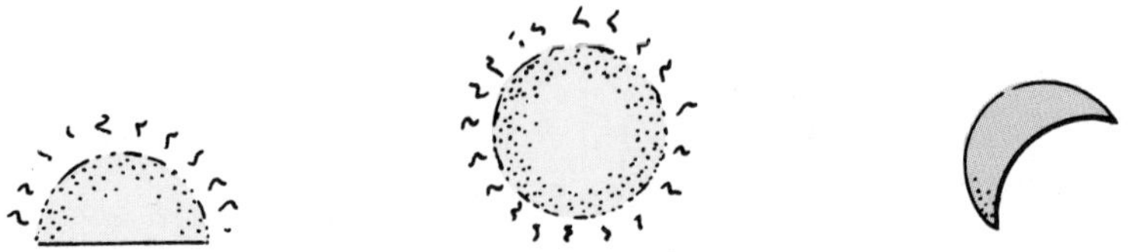

matin après-midi soir

MODÈLE: Quand est-ce qu'Henri va aller en ville?
Il va aller en ville ce soir.

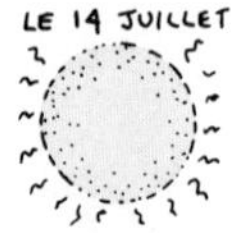

1. Quand est-ce que Francine va aller en ville?

2. Quand est-ce que vos parents vont aller au cinéma?

LE 14 JUILLET

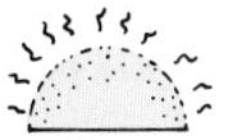

3. Quand est-ce que votre sœur va faire les courses?

LE 15 JUILLET

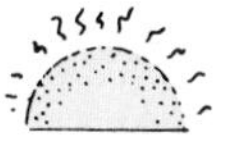

4. Quand est-ce que Michel va téléphoner à son amie?

LE 14 JUILLET

5. Quand est-ce que vous allez retrouver vos amis?

LE 15 JUILLET

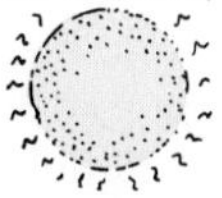

6. Quand est-ce que Janine et Louise vont faire leurs achats?

B. **Quand est-ce que tu voudrais y aller?** Using the information provided, imitate the model dialogues. Ex. B: ⇄

MODÈLE: aller au cinéma, ce soir / oui
— *Est-ce que tu voudrais aller au cinéma avec moi?*
— *Oui. Quand est-ce que tu voudrais y aller?*
— *Ce soir. Ça va?*
— *Oui, ça va. On va aller au cinéma ce soir.*

1. aller en ville, ce soir / oui
2. faire un tour à vélo, demain matin / oui
3. aller à la piscine, demain après-midi / oui

MODÈLE: aller en ville, cet après-midi / non (travailler), demain après-midi
— *Est-ce que tu voudrais aller en ville avec moi?*
— *Oui, quand est-ce que tu voudrais y aller?*
— *Cet après-midi? Ça va?*
— *Non, c'est impossible. Je ne peux pas. Je dois travailler. Demain après-midi? Ça va?*
— *Oui, ça va. On va aller en ville demain après-midi.*

4. aller au musée, cet après-midi / non (faire une course), demain après-midi
5. faire une promenade, ce matin / non (étudier), cet après-midi
6. aller au théâtre, ce soir / non (rester à la maison), demain soir

Reminder, Prononciation: Modern usage no longer distinguishes between **im, in / um, un.** The same phonetic symbol [ɛ̃] is used for both sounds.

Suggestion, Prononciation: Point out to students that the rule given here includes cases where **m** and **n** are followed by other consonants that are *also silent.*

Prononciation: *The final consonants* m *and* n

Like most final consonants in French, **m** and **n** are not pronounced at the end of a word. However, the presence of a final **m** or **n** frequently signals that the preceding vowel is nasalized—that is, that air passes through the nose as well as through the mouth. Depending on which vowel precedes the final **m** or **n,** three different nasal sounds are possible:

-am (champ), **-an** (tant), **-em** (temps), **-en** (gens) → [ɑ̃]

-om (nom), **-on** (sont) → [ɔ̃]

-aim (faim), **-ain** (saint), **-ien** (bien), **-éen** (européen), **-um** (parfum), **-un** (un) → [ɛ̃]

Pratique

C. Read each word aloud, being careful to nasalize the vowel without pronouncing the final consonant(s).

1. citron
2. allemand
3. Jean
4. appartement
5. boisson
6. demain
7. quand
8. canadien
9. souvent
10. jambon
11. combien
12. nous avons
13. vingt

REPRISE

Recycling activities

D. **Qui voudrait aller en ville avec moi?** Choose an activity card. On the basis of the information on the card, try to find three or four people who are willing to go downtown with you (that is, people who have activities that are compatible with yours).

Ex. E: ○

Follow-up, Ex. E: It is important to have students work on recognizing the time frame of questions (present, general or specific, future). Continue asking students double questions: **Vous faites les courses avec vos parents? Vous allez faire les courses ce soir?** Suggested expression: **faire des achats, écouter des disques, étudier votre français, regarder la télévision, acheter des livres.**

E. **Questions.** Your teacher will play the role of an exchange student who has just arrived at your school. He or she wants to get to know you. Answer his or her questions, paying close attention to whether each question is gèneral and therefore requires the present tense, or whether it deals with a specific future time and thus calls for **aller** + infinitive.

1. Est-ce que vous étudiez beaucoup? Est-ce que vous allez étudier ce soir?
2. D'habitude, qu'est-ce que vous faites le soir *(in the evening)?* Qu'est-ce vous allez faire ce soir?

3. Est-ce que vous allez souvent en ville? Qu'est-ce que vous faites en ville? Est-ce que vous allez . . . demain?
4. Est-ce que vous étudiez le français? Le russe? Le chinois? Est-ce que vous allez étudier une autre langue?
5. Est-ce que vous faites souvent des promenades? Est-ce que vous allez faire une promenade ce soir?

STRUCTURE

The days of the week

— **Quel jour est-ce aujourd'hui?**	— *What day is it today?*
— C'est **mercredi.**	— It is *Wednesday.*
Jeudi je vais aller au théâtre.	*On Thursday* I'm going to the theater.
Dimanche nous allons faire une promenade.	*Sunday* we are going to take a walk.

In French, the days of the week are:

lundi *(Monday)*
mardi *(Tuesday)*
mercredi *(Wednesday)*
jeudi *(Thursday)*
vendredi *(Friday)*
samedi *(Saturday)*
dimanche *(Sunday)*

The French consider the week to begin on Monday and end on Sunday. The names of the days are masculine and are not capitalized.

Suggestion, days of the week: (1) Have students repeat the days of the week. (2) Write today's date plus the dates for the next six days. Ask: **Quel jour est-ce aujourd'hui? Ah, c'est aujourd'hui le (lundi 9). Et le 10, c'est mercredi? Ah, bon, c'est mardi.** Etc.

Le savez-vous?

On what days do French schoolchildren (elementary and secondary) *not* have school?
a) Saturday and Sunday
b) Sunday only
c) Wednesday and Sunday

réponse: →

Application

F. **C'est aujourd'hui. . .** Answer using the day **following** the day mentioned in the question.

MODÈLE: C'est aujourd'hui lundi?
Non, ce n'est pas lundi. C'est aujourd'hui mardi.

1. C'est aujourd'hui jeudi?
2. C'est aujourd'hui samedi?
3. C'est aujourd'hui mercredi?
4. C'est aujourd'hui dimanche?
5. C'est aujourd'hui vendredi?
6. C'est aujourd'hui mardi?

G. **Ils arrivent jeudi.** Some students from France are going to visit your school. They come from different cities and will arrive on different dates. Using the calendar below, indicate on what day of the week the various students are getting here.

MODÈLE: Jean-Michel va arriver le 18.
Ah, il arrive jeudi.

1. Renée va arriver le 15.
2. Maurice et Olivier vont arriver le 17.
3. Bruno va arriver le 21.
4. Marie et Jeanne vont arriver le 20.
5. Henri va arriver le 16.
6. Tous les autres *(all the others)* vont arriver le 19.

JANVIER

L	M	M	J	V	S	D
1	2	3	4	5	6	7
8	9	10	11	12	13	14
15	16	17	18	19	20	21
22	23	24	25	26	27	28
29	30	31				

→ c

NOTE GRAMMATICALE

In French, the days of the week are not usually accompanied by either an article or a preposition. Thus, **jeudi** means *on Thursday* as well as just *Thursday.* To indicate a repeated occurence, the French use the definite article **le.** Thus, **le dimanche** is the equivalent of *on Sundays* or *every Sunday.*

Le dimanche, ma famille et moi allons en ville.	*On Sundays,* my family and I go downtown.
Le vendredi, je vais au cinéma avec mes amis.	*On Fridays,* I go to the movies with my friends.

H. **Quel(s) jour(s)?** *(What day[s]?)* Some French exchange students are asking you questions about your life in the United States. In particular, they want to know when you do certain things.

MODÈLE: Quel jour est-ce que tu vas au cinéma?
D'habitude, je vais au cinéma le vendredi ou le samedi.

1. Quels jours est-ce que tu vas à l'école?
2. Quels jours est-ce que tu ne vas pas à l'école?
3. Quel(s) jour(s) est-ce que tu vas en ville?
4. Quels jours est-ce que ton père travaille?
5. Ta mère, elle travaille aussi? Quels jours?
6. Quel(s) jour(s) est-ce qu'on fait les courses chez toi?

DÉBROUILLONS-NOUS!

Review of **étape**

I. **Je ne peux pas.** Using the same (or a different) activity card, try to find two or three people who want to go downtown with you. This time, start by trying to get people to go with you today. However, if necessary, be willing to switch to tomorrow.

Ex. I: O. Divide the class into four groups. Have students from group 1 invite students from group 2, students from group 3 invite students from group 4. Then reverse and switch: group 2 invites group 3, group 4 invites group 1.

Written Work: See Workbook.

Troisième étape

Point de départ:
Comment est-ce qu'on y va?

Transparency, Point de départ: means of transportation

Pour se déplacer en ville — to get around town

Suggestion, Point de départ: (1) Have students repeat while looking at the transparency of means of transportation. Then, have them correct your statements: **Mme Valentin prend son vélo? Mme Dufour prend le métro?** Etc. (2) Have students repeat and read the short scene.

*M. Valentin **prend** le métro.* — takes

Mme Valentin prend sa voiture.

Mme Dufour prend l'autobus.

M. Dufour prend un taxi.

Jacqueline prend son vélo.

Claude y va[1] à pied.

Une scène

Gabrielle, qui habite à Nantes, est à Paris avec sa cousine Andrée.

ANDRÉE: Tu voudrais aller au Musée Rodin aujourd'hui?
GABRIELLE: Mais oui. J'adore les sculptures de Rodin. On y va à pied?
ANDRÉE: Non, non. C'est trop loin. Prenons le métro.
GABRIELLE: Bon, d'accord. On va prendre le métro.

Vocabulary activities

À vous!

A. **Comment est-ce qu'ils y vont?** Based on the drawing, tell how each person gets around town.

MODÈLE: Valérie prend . . .
Valérie prend son vélo.

[1]With the verb **aller,** it is usually necessary to specify where one is going. When the place is not indicated in the sentence, the pronoun **y** *(there)* is used with the verb. Examples: **On y va. Allons-y! Quand est-ce que tu voudrais y aller?**

1. Francine prend. . .

2. Mme de Noël prend. . .

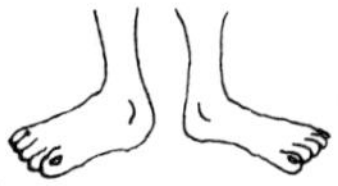

3. Béatrice y va. . .

4. Georges prend. . .

5. M. Janvier prend. . .

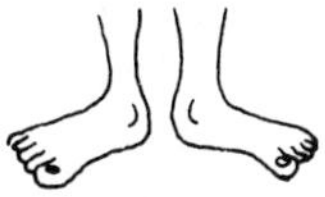

6. Jacques et sa sœur y vont. . .

7. M. Lanvin prend. . .

B. **Nous y allons?** Suggest to a friend how the two of you will go somewhere. Use either **allons** or **prenons** as the verb form.

MODÈLE: autobus
Prenons l'autobus!

1. métro
2. à pied
3. taxi
4. voiture
5. autobus
6. vélos

C. **Tu voudrais aller. . . ?** You invite a friend to go somewhere with you. He/she responds affirmatively, saying either **mais oui, bien sûr** *(certainly),* **je voudrais bien,** or **pourquoi pas?** Your friend then suggests a way of going there, but you have a different idea. Follow the model.

Ex. C: ⇄

MODÈLE: musée / métro / à pied
— *Tu voudrais aller au musée?*
— *Bien sûr. On prend le métro?*
— *Non, non. Allons à pied!*
— *D'accord. On y va à pied.*

1. au cinéma / à pied / autobus
2. en ville / autobus / voiture
3. à la cathédrale / taxi / métro
4. au parc / voiture / à pied

REPRISE

D. **Non, c'est impossible.** You suggest an activity to a friend. He/she is interested but cannot do it on the day you have proposed. You then suggest a different day, which is fine with your friend. Follow the model.

Recycling activity

Ex. D: ⇄

Preparation, Ex. D: (1) Review the days of the week. (2) Then ask students: **Quel jour est-ce aujourd'hui? C'est samedi? Quels jours est-ce que nous avons notre classe de français? Quels jours est-ce que vous restez à la maison?**

MODÈLE: faire un tour à vélo, demain / travailler / samedi
— *Faisons un tour à vélo demain.*
— *Non, c'est impossible.* (ou: *Non, je ne peux pas.*) *Je dois travailler.*
— *Samedi? Ça va?*
— *Oui. Allons faire un tour à vélo samedi.*

1. aller en ville, ce soir / aller au cinéma avec mes parents / demain soir
2. aller en ville, samedi / travailler / dimanche
3. faire une promenade, cet après-midi / faire mes devoirs / samedi
4. faire du lèche-vitrine, samedi / aller en ville avec ma mère / dimanche
5. aller au cinéma, demain / faire des courses / vendredi
6. aller à la bibliothèque, aujourd'hui / rester à la maison / mardi

Suggestion, prendre: (1) Have students repeat conjugation while you write pronouns in three groups—**je, tu, il, elle, on / ils, elles / nous, vous.** (2) Repeat in negative. (3) Add written forms to pronouns, distinguishing between **je, tu / il, elle, on.**

STRUCTURE

The present tense of the irregular verb **prendre**

Je prends *le petit déjeuner.*
I eat (have) breakfast.

Elle prend le train.	*She takes* the train.
Tu ne prends pas ton temps.	*You're not taking* your time.
Nous prenons un café.	*We're having* a cup of coffee.
Prenez la rue Monge.	*Take* Monge Street.
Ils prennent un billet.	*They are buying* a ticket.

The irregular verb **prendre** has several English equivalents: *to take; to have* or *to eat* or *to drink* when referring to meals, food, or beverages; and *to buy* when referring to tickets. The present-tense forms are:

prendre	
je **prends**	nous **prenons**
tu **prends**	vous **prenez**
il, elle, on **prend**	ils, elles **prennent**

Application

E. Replace the subject in italics and make all necessary changes.

1. *Marie-Hélène* prend le déjeuner. (Jacques / tu / nous / vous / Hervé et son cousin / je)
2. *Gérard* ne prend pas le métro d'habitude. (je / nous / Chantal / Michèle et ses amis / tu)
3. Est-ce que *Jean-Pierre* prend les billets? (tu / nous / tes parents / je / vous / Jacqueline)

F. **Ah, c'est intéressant!** By asking questions, you learn some interesting things about your new French friends.

MODÈLE: Est-ce que tu prends le petit déjeuner? (toujours)
Oui, je prends toujours le petit déjeuner.

1. Est-ce qu' Étienne prend toujours le petit déjeuner? (rarement)
2. Et tes parents? (assez souvent)
3. Et ta sœur? (ne . . . jamais)

MODÈLE: Comment est-ce que Martine va à l'école? (le métro)
Elle prend le métro.

4. Comment est-ce que vous allez à l'école? (l'autobus)
5. Et Jean-Jacques? (son vélo)
6. Et vos professeurs? (le métro)

MODÈLE: Quelle rue est-ce que Didier prend pour rentrer à la maison? (la rue du Bac)
Il prend la rue du Bac.

7. Quelle rue est-ce que tu prends pour rentrer à la maison? (l'avenue de l'Armée)
8. Et tes amis? (le boulevard de l'Ouest)
9. Et Geneviève? (la rue Champollion)

MODÈLE: Qu'est-ce que Jean-Luc prend d'habitude au café? (un café)
Il prend un café.

10. Qu'est-ce que Michèle prend d'habitude au café? (un diabolo citron)
11. Et vous deux? (une limonade)
12. Et les autres? (un Coca)

NOTE GRAMMATICALE

Apprendre and *comprendre*

Two other verbs conjugated like **prendre** are **apprendre** *(to learn)* and **comprendre** *(to understand):*

Elle apprend l'italien.	*She is learning* Italian.
Nous apprenons le portugais.	*We are learning* Portuguese.
Je ne comprends pas.	*I don't understand.*
Vous comprenez?	*Do you understand?*

G. **Et Nathalie? Et Yves?** Answer the questions on the basis of the drawings.

MODÈLE: Quelle langue est-ce que vous apprenez?
Nous apprenons le chinois.

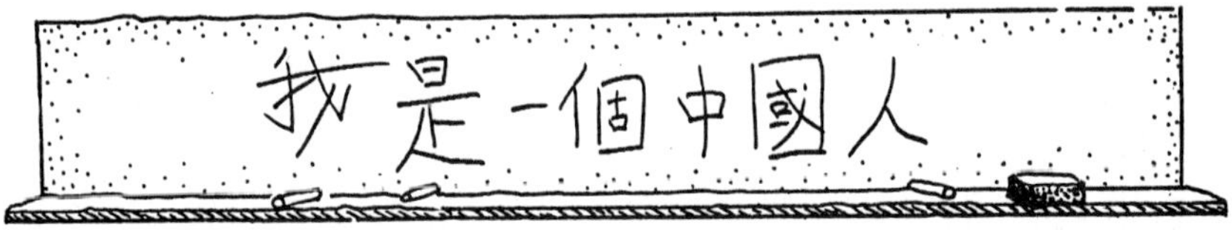

1. Quelle langue est-ce que Nathalie apprend?

2. Et Yves?

3. Et toi, Pierre?

Ich verstehe nicht!

4. Et les amis de Brigitte?

¡Buenos días, Pablo!

5. Et nous?

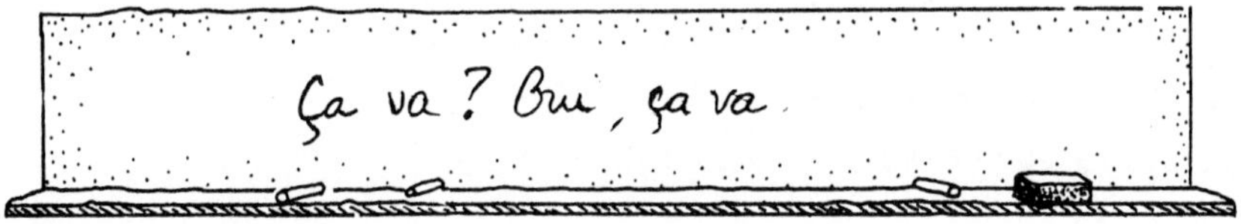
Ça va? Oui, ça va.

H. **Vous comprenez?** Say whether or not the people mentioned understand Italian. Ex. H: ⇄

MODÈLE: Est-ce que vous comprenez, oui ou non? (oui)
Oui, nous comprenons.

6. Est-ce-que Charles comprend, oui ou non? (oui)
7. Et toi, Michèle? (non)
8. Et vous autres? (non)
9. Et Renée? (oui)
10. Et les élèves? (non)

apprendre une langue
c'est aussi un art
de vivre

DÉBROUILLONS-NOUS!

Review of **étape**

I. **Échange.** Ask the following questions of a classmate, who will answer them.

1. Est-ce que tu prends toujours le petit déjeuner? Est-ce que tu vas prendre le petit déjeuner demain matin?
2. Est-ce que tu prends l'autobus pour aller à l'école?
3. Est-ce que tu travailles rapidement ou est-ce que tu prends ton temps?
4. Est-ce que tu apprends le russe? Est-ce que tu voudrais apprendre le russe? Quelle langue est-ce que tu voudrais apprendre?
5. Est-ce que tu comprends toujours les questions du professeur?

Ex. J: ⇄. You may wish to assign a specific situation: i.e., accompany you on an errand, go to a specific kind of movie, or go shopping. You can complicate the situation by requiring that three people agree on the day and the means of transportation.

Written Work: See Workbook.

J. **Tu voudrais y aller?** Invite a classmate to do something with you. When you get an affirmative response, arrange a day and a time, and agree on a means of transportation.

Lexique

Pour se débrouiller

Pour dire oui ou non à une proposition

d'accord
je ne peux pas
c'est impossible

Pour organiser une excursion en ville

On prend
 l'autobus.
 le métro.
 un taxi.
 sa voiture.
 son vélo.
On y va à pied.
Quand est-ce qu'on y va?
Quand est-ce que tu voudrais y aller?
 aujourd'hui
 ce matin
 cet après-midi
 ce soir
 demain (matin, après-midi, soir)

Pour quoi faire?

avoir rendez-vous avec
avoir une course à faire
faire des achats
faire du lèche-vitrine
faire une course
je dois
n'avoir rien à faire
retrouver quelqu'un

Pour parler de ses projets

aller + infinitive
avoir envie de + infinitive

Pour demander le jour qu'il est

C'est aujourd'hui . . . ?

Thèmes et contextes

Les jours de la semaine

lundi
mardi
mercredi
jeudi
vendredi
samedi
dimanche

Vocabulaire général

Verbes

apprendre
comprendre
entrer (dans)
prendre
quitter
rester

Autres Expressions

justement

Chapitre onze

Prenons le métro!

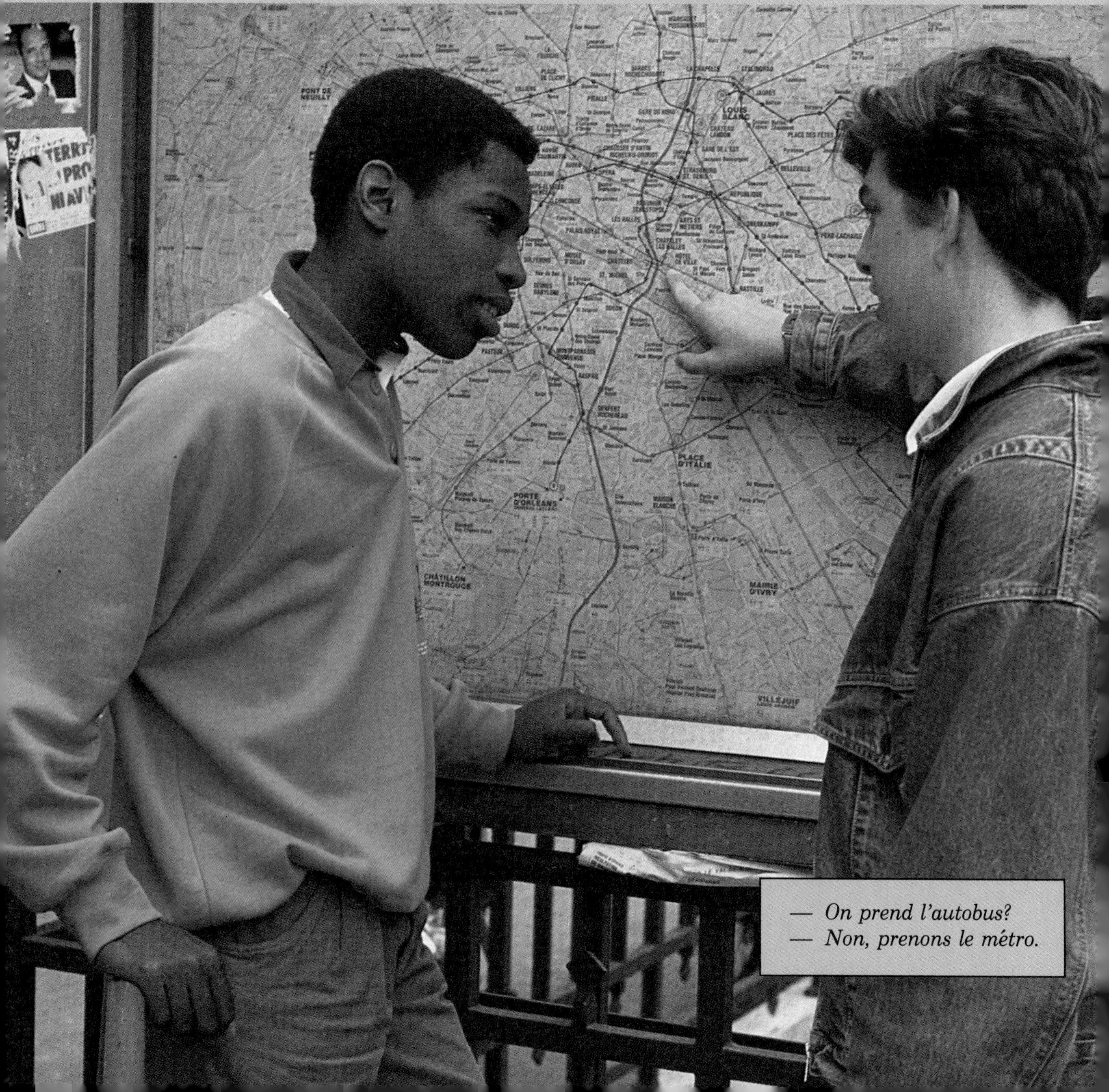

— *On prend l'autobus?*
— *Non, prenons le métro.*

Première étape

Point de départ:

Quelle direction?

Transparency, Point de départ; Paris metro map

Suggestion, Point de départ: Show the places and routes mentioned in the dialogue on the transparency of the métro map.

Andrée et sa cousine Gabrielle vont prendre le métro pour aller au Musée Rodin. L'appartement d'Andrée est près de la place d'Italie, où il y a une station de métro. Les deux jeunes filles regardent le **plan de métro** qui se trouve devant l'entrée de la station.

plan de métro: métro map

ANDRÉE:	Bon. Nous sommes là, place d'Italie.	
GABRIELLE:	Où est le Musée Rodin?	
ANDRÉE:	Il est près de la Station Invalides. Là.	
GABRIELLE:	**Alors,** qu'est-ce qu'on fait?	so (then)
ANDRÉE:	C'est **facile.** Nous prenons la direction Charles de Gaulle-Étoile.	easy
GABRIELLE:	C'est direct ou est-ce qu'**il faut prendre une correspondance?**	is it necessary to change trains?
ANDRÉE:	Il faut prendre une correspondance. Nous changeons à La Motte-Picquet, direction Créteil.	
GABRIELLE:	Et nous **descendons**[1] à Invalides. C'est ça?	get off
ANDRÉE:	Oui, c'est ça. Bon. Allons-y!	

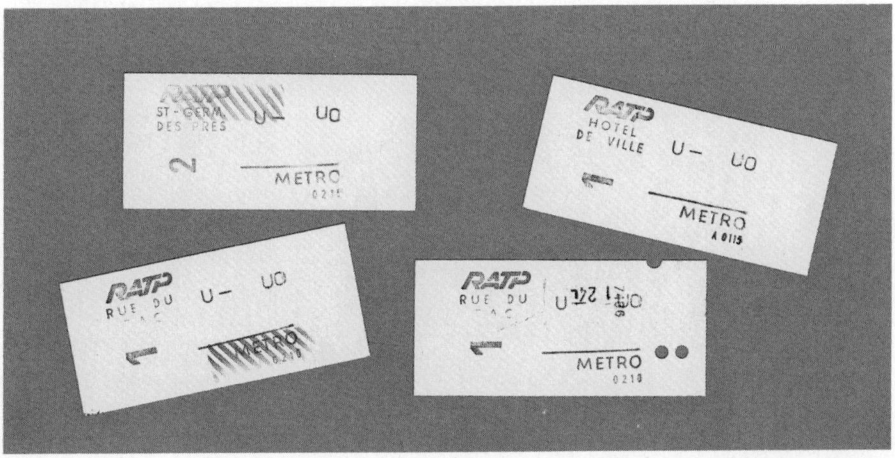

[1] **Descendre** is a regular **-re** verb, a category that you will not meet formally until later in your study of French. For the moment, learn these forms: **je descends, tu descends, nous descendons, vous descendez.**

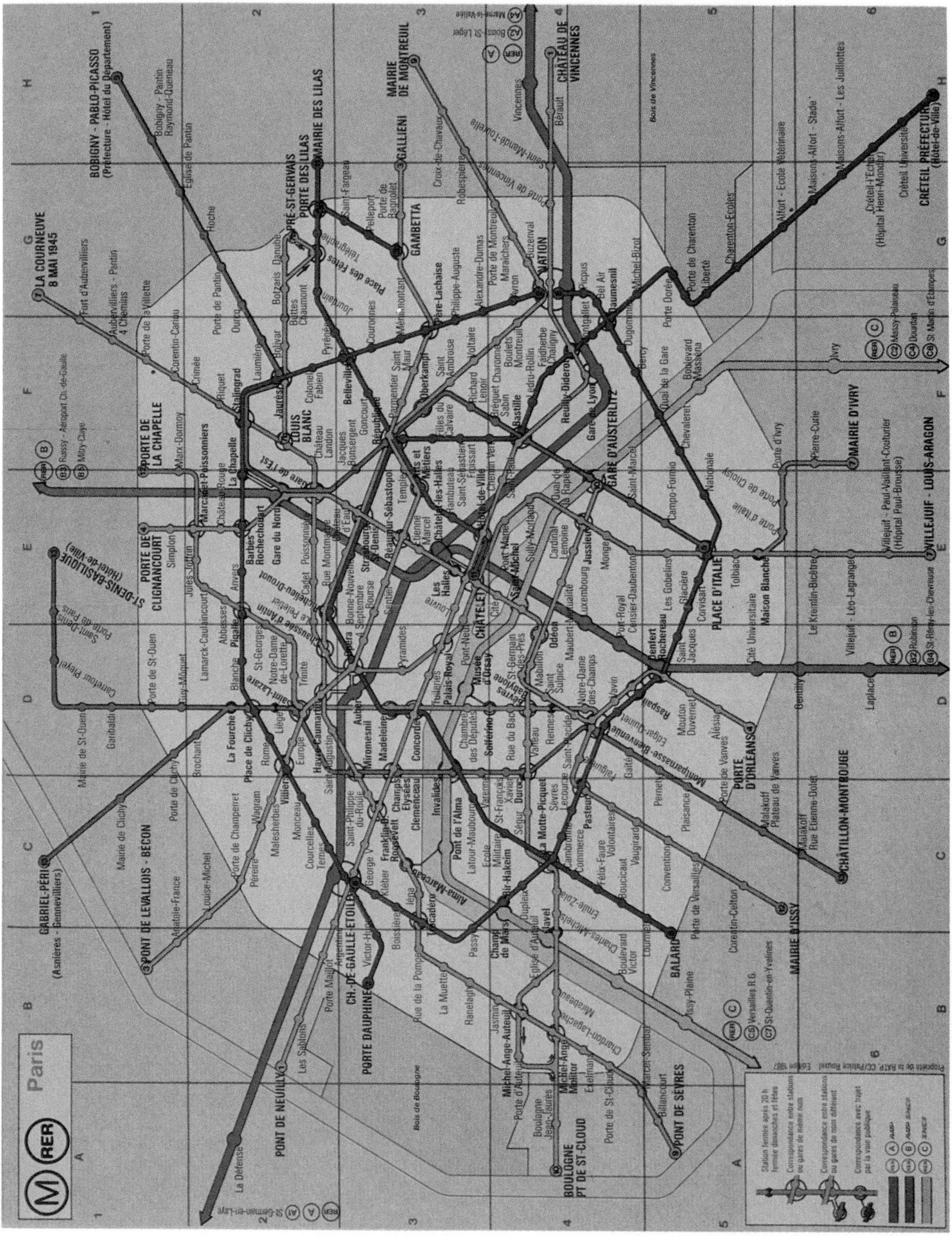

plan de métro

Note Culturelle

Le métro (the Paris subway) is one of the best-developed subway systems in the world. There are sixteen lines, organized so that it is possible to go almost anywhere in Paris with a minimum number of **correspondances** (changes of line). Each line has a number. However, most often the lines are designated by the **directions** (stations at each end of the line). Thus, Line 1 is called **Château de Vincennes-Pont de Neuilly** (sometimes abbreviated to **Vincennes-Neuilly)**, Line 4 is **Porte d'Orléans-Porte de Clignancourt (Orléans-Clignancourt)**, and so forth.

To determine your route, you look at **un plan de métro** (map) like the one on p. 220. These maps are found on the street near **les bouches de métro** (station entrances), inside the stations, and on the platforms. There are also pocket-sized maps that you can carry with you. On the map, find the station where you want to get off and the station at the far end of the line (for example, **la direction Orléans)**. Then follow the signs for that **direction.** If you need to change trains, find the new **direction** (from the map) and look for signs indicating **correspondance** and **direction.** Do not confuse the subway lines with the **R.E.R.** lines (trains that run between Paris and its suburbs).

Le savez-vous?

The Paris *métro* has a worldwide reputation. Many people do not know, however, that there is more than one subway system in France. What other city (or cities) has (have) a *métro?*

a) Bordeaux
b) Marseille
c) Lyon
d) Lille

réponse →

À vous!

Vocabulary activities

Preparation, Exs. A and B: Three verbs **(prendre, changer, descendre)** are required to do the **métro** exercises. You may wish to review briefly the **je, tu, nous, vous** forms before doing the exercises.

Ex. A: ⇄

A. **On change à... On descend à...** Based on the cues, answer each person's questions about where he/she should change lines and where he/she should get off the subway. Follow the model.

MODÈLE: Concorde / Palais-Royal / tu (je)
— *Est-ce qu'il faut changer?*
— *Oui, tu changes à Concorde.*
— *Et où est-ce que je descends?*
— *Tu descends à Palais-Royal.*

1. Châtelet / Rue de Rennes / tu (je)
2. Montparnasse-Bienvenüe / Trocadéro / vous (nous)
3. Sèvres-Babylone / Notre-Dame des Champs / vous (nous)
4. Saint-Lazare / place de Clichy / tu (je)

B. **Prenons le métro!** Following the models and using the **métro** map on p. 220, explain how to use the subway. The number-letter combinations (shown in parentheses after the name of each station) correspond to the grid coordinates on the map and will help you locate the stations.

MODÈLES: Alain / Saint-Lazare (D2) → Bastille (F4)
Alain, tu prends la direction Mairie d'Issy, tu changes à Concorde, direction Château de Vincennes, et tu descends à Bastille.

M. Genois / Montparnasse-Bienvenüe (D4) → Opéra (D3)
M. Genois, vous prenez la direction Porte de Clignancourt, vous changez à Châtelet, direction La Courneuve, et vous descendez à Opéra.

1. Jacqueline / Charles de Gaulle-Étoile (C3) → Raspail (D4)
2. Albert / Gare du Nord (E2) → Gare de Lyon (F4)
3. Mme Fantout / Louvre (E3) → Trocadéro (C3)
4. Isabelle et Jean-Luc / Odéon (D4) → place de Clichy (D2)

Prononciation: *The consonants **m** and **n** in the middle of a word*

There are three possible contexts for **m** and **n** in the middle of a word:

b, c, and **d**

1. If **m** or **n** falls between two vowels, the **m** or **n** is pronounced: **ami, imiter**
2. If **m** or **n** is followed by another **m** or **n,** the double consonant is pronounced as a single **m** or **n: dommage, ennemi**
3. If **m** or **n** is followed by a consonant other than **m** or **n,** the preceding vowel is nasalized and the **m** or **n** is *not* pronounced: **i~~m~~possible, cha~~n~~ter**

Pratique

C. Read each word aloud, being careful to distinguish between **m** or **n** between vowels, **m** or **n** in combination with another **m** or **n,** and **m** or **n** followed by a consonant.

1. Londres
2. camping
3. banque
4. commande
5. sandwich
6. japonais
7. oncle
8. cinéma
9. immédiatement
10. limonade
11. tante
12. impossible
13. Orangina
14. omelette
15. changer
16. sciences
17. inutile

REPRISE

D. **D'habitude, . . .** Some members of your family follow a regular routine. On a certain day of the week, they always do the same thing. Describe where they go and how they get there, based on the drawings below.

Recycling activity

MODÈLE:
votre mère
Le lundi ma mère va à l'épicerie.
Elle y va à pied.

1. *votre grand-père*

2. *votre cousin*

3. *votre sœur*

4. *votre tante et votre oncle*

5. *vos cousines*

6. *vos parents*

Follow-up, Ex. D: Review the first- and second-person forms of **prendre** by asking personal questions, such as **Où est-ce que vous allez le samedi après-midi? Est-ce que vous prenez l'autobus?** Etc. **Où est-ce que vous allez avec vos parents? Quel(s) jour(s)? Comment est-ce que vous y allez?**

Suggestion, Adverbs: (1) Write on board today's date, plus dates for this week and next; write also the present year and next year. (2) Review and introduce adverbs by using the dates. Begin with the present and move to the future.

Supplementary vocabulary: le mois prochain.

STRUCTURE

Adverbs that designate the present and the future

Ma mère travaille **aujourd'hui.**	My mother is working *today.*
Demain elle ne va pas travailler.	*Tomorrow* she's not going to work.
Où est-ce qu'ils sont **maintenant?**	Where are they *now?*
Lundi matin je vais aller à l'école.	*Monday morning* I'm going to school.
Elles vont arriver **la semaine prochaine.**	They are going to get here *next week.*

You have already learned several adverbs that express present or future time:

aujourd'hui
cet après-midi
ce matin
ce soir

demain
demain après-midi
demain matin
demain soir

Here are some additional expressions:

maintenant *(now)*
cette semaine *(this week)*
cette année *(this year)*
la semaine prochaine *(next week)*
l'année prochaine *(next year)*

In addition, the expressions **matin, après-midi, soir,** and **prochain** can be combined with the days of the week: **lundi matin, samedi après-midi, dimanche soir, mardi prochain.** Time expressions are usually placed at the very beginning or end of the sentence.

Application

E. Replace the words in italics and make the necessary changes.

1. Où est-ce que tu vas *aujourd'hui?* (maintenant / cet après-midi / vendredi soir / cette semaine)
2. *Cet après-midi* je vais aller au cinéma. (ce soir / aujourd'hui / samedi matin / jeudi après-midi / demain)
3. Elles vont aller à Paris *mercredi prochain.* (cette année / la semaine prochaine / l'année prochaine / vendredi prochain)

F. **Pas ce soir. . .** Your mother is always asking about people's activities, but then she gets them all confused. Correct her statements, using the information given.

MODÈLE: Toi et Jean, vous allez au cinéma ce soir? (demain soir)
Pas ce soir. Nous allons au cinéma demain soir.

1. Toi et Jean, vous allez en ville mercredi soir? (mercredi après- midi)
2. Ton père va faire les courses demain matin? (samedi matin)
3. Marcel va faire du ski cette semaine? (la semaine prochaine)
4. Ton frère apprend l'espagnol cette année? (l'année prochaine)
5. Toi et Marie, vous allez au cinéma ce soir? (vendredi soir)
6. Ta sœur va prendre la voiture cet après-midi? (dimanche après-midi)
7. Tes grand-parents vont arriver aujourd'hui? (jeudi prochain)
8. Est-ce que tu vas faire tes devoirs maintenant? (ce soir)

G. **L'emploi du temps des Verdun.** *(The Verduns' schedule.)* Answer questions about the Verdun family's activities during the month of February. Choose the appropriate time expressions, assuming that *today* is the morning of February 15.

Transparency, Ex. G: Verdun family calendar

LUNDI	MARDI	MERCREDI	JEUDI	VENDREDI	SAMEDI	DIMANCHE
1	2	3	4	5 Restaurant	6	7 église
8	9	10	11	12 Restaurant	13	14 église
15 M. et Mme. en ville théâtre (soir)	16 M. jouer au tennis	17 M. travail (soir)	18 Mme. Musée	19 Mme. travail (matin) restaurant	20 Mme. cours de Russe (apres-midi)	21 église
22 Cathédrale	23 Les Michaud	24 Les Michaud	25 Les Michaud	26 Restaurant Les Michaud	27	28 église

MODÈLE: Quand est-ce que Mme Verdun va aller au musée?
Jeudi.

1. Quel soir est-ce que M. Verdun va travailler?
2. Quand est-ce que les Verdun vont visiter la cathédrale?
3. Quand est-ce que les Verdun dînent au restaurant?
4. Quand est-ce qu'ils vont avoir la visite des Michaud?
5. Quand est-ce que M. Verdun va jouer au tennis?
6. Quel matin est-ce que Mme Verdun va travailler?

MODÈLE: Qu'est-ce que M. Verdun va faire mercredi soir?
Il va travailler.

7. Qu'est-ce que les Verdun vont faire ce soir?
8. Où est-ce que M. et Mme Verdun vont le dimanche?
9. Qu'est-ce que Mme Verdun va faire samedi après-midi?
10. Qu'est-ce que les Verdun et les Michaud vont faire vendredi prochain?

DÉBROUILLONS-NOUS!

Review of **étape**

Ex. H: ⇄. You will probably want to model this exercise first. Alternate problem: hotel near St-Sulpice, going to the airlines terminal at Porte Maillot.

Written Work: See Workbook.

H. **Il faut prendre quelle direction?** You and your family are staying in Paris at a hotel near the place de l'Odéon (D4). You need to go to the American Express office near the Opéra (D3). You are newly arrived in Paris and don't understand the subway system yet, so you ask the desk clerk for help. When he/she explains how to get there, you repeat the instructions to make sure you have understood. (Another student will play the role of the desk clerk.) Consult the **métro** map on p. 220.

Deuxième étape

Point de départ:
Au guichet

au guichet: at the ticket window

Andrée et Gabrielle entrent dans la station de métro et vont au guichet.

GABRIELLE: Je prends un billet de **seconde?**
ANDRÉE: Non, tu prends un **carnet** de dix billets. C'est **moins cher.**
GABRIELLE: Et toi, tu ne prends pas de billet?
ANDRÉE: Non, j'ai une carte orange. **Je peux** prendre le métro ou l'autobus pour **tout un mois.**
GABRIELLE: C'est bien, ça. *(Au guichet:)* S'il vous plaît, Madame. Un carnet de seconde.
L'EMPLOYÉE: Vingt-sept francs cinquante, Mademoiselle.

second class
book (of tickets) / less expensive
I can
a whole month

Le savez-vous?

What do Franklin D. Roosevelt, George V, Voltaire and Victor Hugo have in common?
a) They are all former heads of state.
b) They are all famous writers.
c) They all spent most of their lives in Paris.
d) They are all names of Paris *métro* stations.

réponse

Note Culturelle

French subway cars **(voitures)** are divided into first-class cars **(voitures de première)** and second-class cars **(voitures de seconde).** The first-class cars, found in the middle of the train, are usually less crowded and more comfortable, but first-class tickets cost more. Since 1984, people are allowed to ride in first class with a second class ticket from 7:30 to 9:00 A.M. and from 5:30 to 7:00 P.M., during **les heures de pointe** *(rush hour).*

Métro tickets can be bought singly **(un billet)** or in groups of ten **(un carnet).** You can also buy a four-day or seven-day tourist ticket **(un billet de tourisme, quatre jours** or **sept jours),** or a full-month commuter ticket **(une carte orange).** These tickets can all be used on buses as well as on the subway.

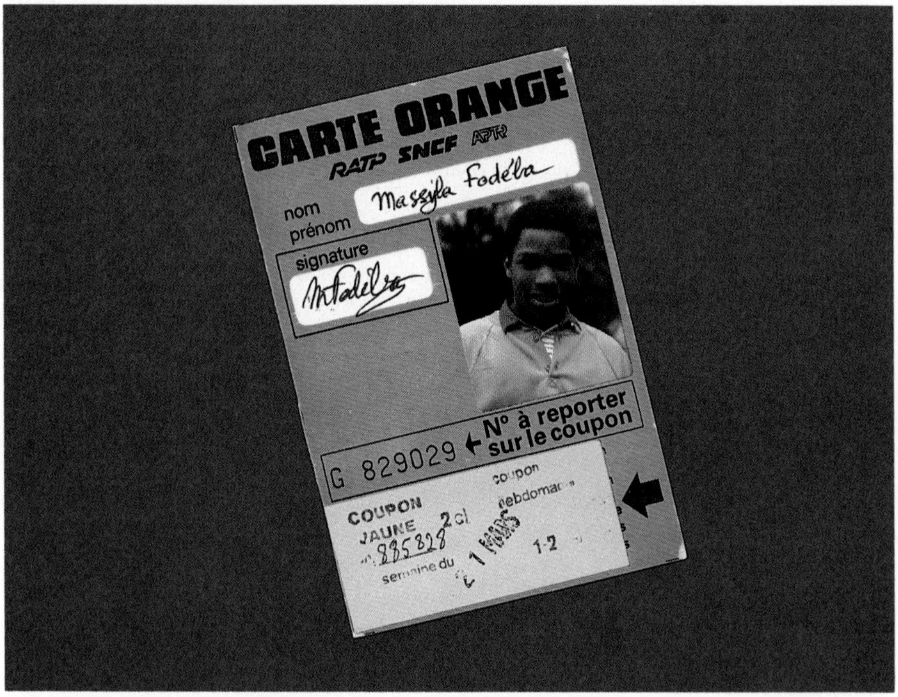

d

Vocabulary activities

À vous!

A. **Au guichet.** Buy the indicated **métro** tickets.

MODÈLE: a book of first-class tickets
Un carnet de première, s'il vous plaît.

1. one first-class ticket
2. one second-class ticket
3. a book of ten second-class tickets
4. a ticket that allows you to travel for a week
5. a ticket that allows you to travel for a month

B. **Prenons le métro!** Explain to each person how to take the subway. Specify the kind of ticket to buy. Consult the **métro** map on p. 220. (Map coordinates are given in parentheses.)

MODÈLE: *Tu vas (vous allez) à la Station Monceau, tu prends (vous prenez) un carnet de seconde, tu prends (vous prenez) la direction. . . , etc.*

1. Olga, your German friend, is in Paris for a couple of days. Her hotel is near the Odéon Station (D4). She wants to go see a church near the Madeleine Station (D3).

2. Mr. and Mrs. Van D'Elden, Dutch friends of your family, are spending three weeks in Paris. Their hotel is near the Palais-Royal Station (D3). Their first day in the city they want to go to a store near the Montparnasse-Bienvenüe Station (D4).
3. A stranger passing through Paris is trying to get from the airline terminal at Porte Maillot (B2) to the Gare du Nord (E2).

REPRISE

C. **Ce que je fais?** Using the adverbs of time provided, tell your classmates about your usual activities **(le samedi, le lundi matin,** etc.) and then about your upcoming plans **(samedi prochain, lundi matin,** etc.).

Recycling activity

MODÈLE: le lundi / lundi prochain
— *Le lundi je vais à l'école d'habitude.*
— *Lundi prochain je vais aller à l'école comme d'habitude.*
— ou: *Lundi prochain je vais rester à la maison.*

1. le samedi après-midi / samedi prochain
2. le vendredi soir / vendredi prochain
3. le dimanche matin / dimanche prochain
4. le lundi matin / lundi prochain
5. cette année, le samedi soir / l'année prochaine, le samedi soir

Qu'est-ce que tu fais d'habitude le lundi matin?

Suggestion, vouloir: (1) Review ordering in a café substituting **vouloir** for **désirer** or **prendre: Qu'est-ce que vous voulez? (Une limonade.) Ah, vous voulez une limonade. Georges veut une limonade.** Etc. (2) Write pronouns on board in three groups: **(je, tu, il, elle, on / ils, elles / nous, vous).** (3) Write forms in four groups **je, tu / il, elle, on / ils, elles / nous, vous).** (4) To review verb + infinitive, ask students: **Vous voulez aller en ville?**

STRUCTURE

The present tense of the irregular verb ***vouloir***

Tu veux un Coca?	*Do you want* a Coke?
Elle ne veut pas de café.	*She doesn't want* any coffee.
Ils veulent aller au cinéma.	*They want* to go to the movies.
Est-ce que vous voulez faire une promenade?	*Do you want* to take a walk?

The verb **vouloir** is used to indicate something one *wants* to have or do. Its present-tense forms are:

vouloir	
je **veux**	nous **voulons**
tu **veux**	vous **voulez**
il, elle, on **veut**	ils, elles **veulent**

Application

D. Replace the subjects in italics and make the necessary changes.

1. *Je* veux habiter à Paris. (nous / mes sœurs / Jacques / tu)
2. Est-ce que *Michel* veut aller en ville? (tu / Martine / vos parents / vous)
3. *Anne-Marie* ne veut pas de frites. (je / les autres / nous / Michel / on)

Ex. E: ⇄

E. **Ils veulent tous faire autre chose.** *(They all want to do something else.)* Your father asks you if you're going to the movies with your friends. Explain to him that your friends all seem to have other plans.

MODÈLE: Suzanne / aller au concert
— *Est-ce que tu vas au cinéma avec Suzanne?*
— *Non, elle veut aller au concert.*

1. Alain / faire du ski
2. tes frères / aller au restaurant
3. Geneviève / aller à la bibliothèque
4. tes cousins / faire un tour en voiture
5. Denise / faire des achats
6. Jean et Catherine / regarder la télévision

Follow-up, Ex. E: Have one student ask several other students to go somewhere with him/her. Have the other students all indicate another preference. (e.g., **Bill, demandez à Susan d'aller au cinéma samedi.) —Susan, tu veux aller au cinéma samedi? —Non, merci. Je veux aller au restaurant. —Elle ne veut pas aller au cinéma; elle veut aller au restaurant. (Eh bien, demandez à Frank et à Louise.** Etc.)

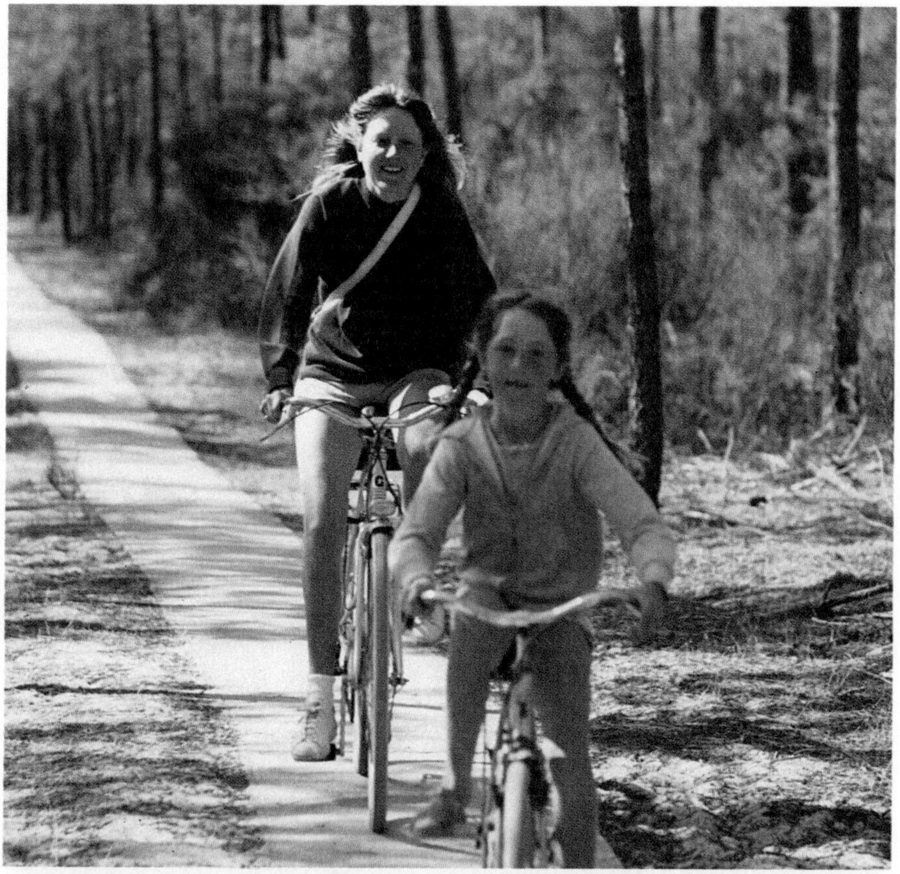

Tu veux faire un tour à vélo?

NOTE GRAMMATICALE

You are already familiar with **je voudrais** and **tu voudrais,** as well as with **nous voudrions** and **vous voudriez.** These are all polite forms of **vouloir** that you use when you wish to offer or request something.

Tu voudrais y aller aussi?	*Would you like* to go too?
Nous voudrions parler au professeur.	*We would like* to speak to the teacher.

The idiomatic expression **vouloir bien** is an informal way of indicating *OK, gladly, with pleasure:*

— **Tu veux** faire un tour à vélo?	— *Do you want* to take a bike ride?
— Oui, **je veux bien.**	— Yes, *I'd like to.*

Suggestion, Note grammaticale, Polite forms: (1) Remind students of the **je, tu** forms; then write the **nous/vous** forms on board. (2) Ask students: **Qu'est-ce que vous voudriez faire ce soir?** (3) Remind students of levels of language. Contrast **Tu veux aller en ville? Oui, je veux bien.** with **Vous voudriez dîner chez nous? Avec plaisir.**

Ex. F: ⇄

Follow-up, Ex. F: Have students invite you to do something. Then have them invite a friend to do the same thing.

F. **Des invitations.** Invite a friend or friends to go somewhere or to do something with you. When your friend(s) accept(s), suggest a way of getting there. Use the appropriate forms of **vouloir** and **vouloir bien.**

MODÈLE: aller en ville / autobus
— *Tu veux aller en ville?*
— *Oui, je veux bien.*
— *Prenons l'autobus.*
— *D'accord. C'est une bonne idée.*

1. aller au cinéma / métro
2. faire un tour en voiture / ma voiture
3. dîner en ville / autobus
4. visiter la cathédrale / à pied
5. faire des courses en ville / nos vélos

Now invite some people you know less well to do something or to go somewhere. When they accept, suggest a day. This time, instead of using **vouloir bien** (which is appropriate for more informal situations), use **avec plaisir.**

MODÈLE: aller au théâtre avec nous / samedi
— *Est-ce que vous voudriez aller au théâtre avec nous?*
— *Oui, avec plaisir.*
— *Samedi, c'est possible?*
— *Oui, c'est très bien.*

6. aller au concert avec moi / jeudi
7. dîner chez nous / mardi
8. faire une promenade avec nous / dimanche
9. aller au musée avec moi / samedi

DÉBROUILLONS-NOUS !

Review of **étape**

Ex. G: ⇄. Have the students playing the group leader repeat the instructions that the American students give them.

Written Work: See Workbook.

G. **S'il vous plaît. . .** You've now become an expert on the Paris **métro.** While you are waiting at the Porte Maillot Air Terminal (B2) for a bus to take you to the airport for your trip home, a group of Japanese tourists, just arriving in Paris, ask you for help in getting to their hotel near the place d'Italie (E5). (One of your classmates will play the role of the group leader for the tourists.)

Lexique

Pour se débrouiller

Pour proposer de faire quelque chose ensemble

Tu veux (tu voudrais) . . . ?
Vous voulez (vous voudriez) . . . ?
  Mais oui.
  Bien sûr.
  Avec plaisir.
  C'est une bonne idée.
Pourquoi pas?
  C'est impossible.
  Je ne peux pas.

Pour se débrouiller dans le métro

changer
descendre
Quelle direction?
prendre

Thèmes et contextes

Le métro

un billet
  de première
  de seconde
  de tourisme
une bouche de métro
un carnet
une carte orange
une correspondance
le guichet
un plan de métro
une station de métro

Vocabulaire général

Noms

cette année
l'année prochaine
cette semaine
la semaine prochaine

Adjectifs

cher (chère)

Autres expressions

maintenant

Chapitre douze

On y va à pied? Non!

— *On y va à pied?*
— *Non. On peut prendre ma voiture.*

Première étape

Point de départ:

Prenons la voiture de ton père!

Les **marques** de voiture — makes

Les voitures françaises

une Renault	une Peugeot	une 2-CV

Les voitures européennes

une Fiat	une Golf	une Mercédès

Les voitures japonaises

une Datsun	une Toyota	une Honda

Les voitures américaines

une Ford	une Cadillac	une Chevrolet

Le permis de conduire

le permis de conduire: driver's license

En France, quand on a dix-huit ans, **on peut passer un examen** pour avoir un permis de conduire. On va à une **auto-école** pour apprendre à **conduire.** L'examen est très difficile. Si on **échoue,** il faut retourner à l'école et repasser l'examen. Quand on a son permis de conduire, il est **valable pour la vie.**

you can take the test
driving school / to drive
fails
valid (good) for life

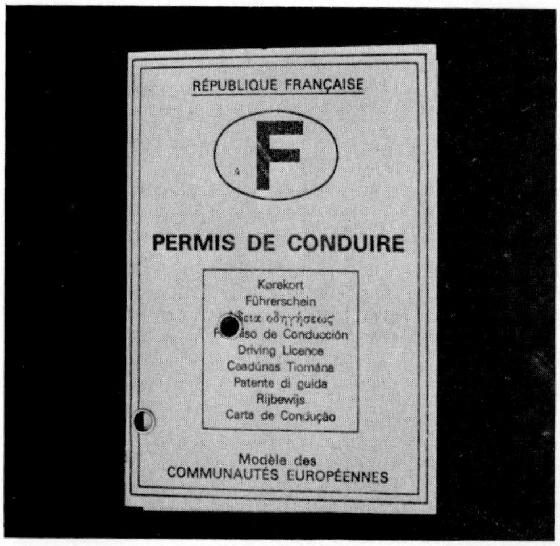

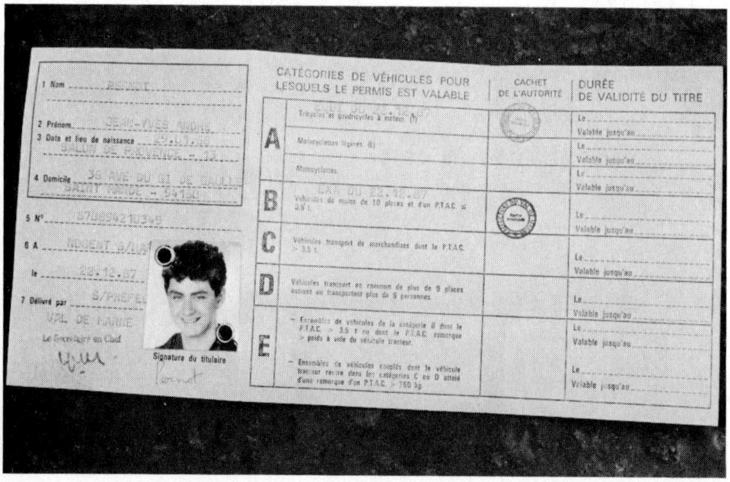

Vocabulary activities

À vous!

A. **Qu'est-ce qu'ils ont comme voiture?** *(What kind of a car do they have?)* Tell what make of car each person owns.

MODÈLE: Qu'est-ce que les Féraud ont comme voiture? (Fiat)
Ils ont une Fiat.

1. Qu'est-ce que Jean-Pierre a comme voiture? (Renault 5)
2. Qu'est-ce que M. et Mme Clandon ont comme voiture? (Mercedes)
3. Est-ce que Simone a une Golf? (Toyota)
4. Qu'est-ce que les Magnin ont comme voiture? (Peugeot)
5. Qu'est-ce que Lucienne a comme voiture? (Golf)
6. Est-ce que Claude a une Fiat? (2-CV)

B. **Et vous?** Answer the following questions about you and your family.

1. Qu'est-ce que vos parents ont comme voiture?
2. Est-ce que vous avez une voiture? (Est-ce que vous voudriez avoir une voiture un jour?)
3. Quelle marque de voiture est-ce que vous aimez le mieux? Quelle marque de voiture est-ce que vous voudriez avoir?
4. Est-ce que vous avez votre permis de conduire? Quel âge avez-vous maintenant? À quel âge est-ce qu'on peut avoir un permis de conduire dans votre état (*state*)? Est-ce que vous allez avoir votre permis de conduire dans deux ans?
5. Est-ce qu'il faut passer un examen pour avoir un permis de conduire? Comment est l'examen—facile, assez difficile, très difficile?

Prononciation: *The consonants **m** and **n** followed by the vowel **e***

The presence of a mute **e** at the end of a word causes the preceding consonant, which in many cases would be silent, to be pronounced. In the case of **m** and **n**, pronouncing the consonant denasalizes the vowel:

Sim**on**	améric**ain**	**un**	**an**
Sim**one**	améric**aine**	**une**	**âne**

Pratique

C. Read each pair of words aloud, being careful to pronounce the **m** or **n** in the first word and keep the **m** or **n** silent in the second.

1. américaine, américain
2. mexicaine, mexicain
3. cousine, cousin
4. prochaine, prochain
5. Christiane, Christian
6. une, un
7. Jeanne, Jean

D. Read each word aloud, distinguishing between words in which the final consonant is silent (nasal vowel) and those in which it is pronounced.

1. Madame
2. marine
3. Pékin
4. direction
5. fume
6. chaîne
7. garçon
8. machine
9. Rome
10. Lyon
11. crème
12. italien

Le savez-vous?

French young people are eligible to get a drivers license at the age of 18. What additional restriction is placed on them during the first year after they have their license?

a) They cannot drive faster than 90 kilometers an hour (56 mph).

b) They cannot drive at night.

c) They must be accompanied by an older licensed driver at all times.

réponse

REPRISE

Recycling activity

Ex. E: O

E. **Demande aux autres.** *(Ask the others.)* Tell the person next to you to ask the other members of your group the following questions. After asking each group member individually, the questioner will report back to you.

1. Demande aux autres s'ils veulent aller à la bibliothèque.
   Est-ce que tu veux aller à la bibliothèque? Et toi, . . . ?
2. Demande aux autres ce qu'ils veulent acheter.
   Qu'est-ce que tu veux (voudrais) acheter?
3. Demande aux autres la ville qu'ils veulent visiter un jour.
   Quelle ville est-ce que tu veux (voudrais) visiter un jour?
4. Demande aux autres ce qu'ils veulent faire samedi.
   Qu'est-ce que tu veux faire samedi?

STRUCTURE

The numbers from 30 to 69

30	**trente**	50	**cinquante**
31	**trente et un**	51	**cinquante et un**
32	**trente-deux**	52	**cinquante-deux**
33	**trente-trois,** etc.	53	**cinquante-trois,** etc.
40	**quarante**	60	**soixante**
41	**quarante et un**	61	**soixante et un**
42	**quarante-deux**	62	**soixante-deux**
43	**quarante-trois,** etc.	63	**soixante-trois,** etc.

a

Application

F. Do the following exercises.

1. Comptez de 30 jusqu'à 69.
2. Donnez les nombres impairs *(odd)* de 1 jusqu'à 69.
3. Donnez les nombres pairs *(even)* de 2 jusqu'à 68.
4. Comptez de 10 jusqu'à 60 par 10.
5. Comptez de 69 jusqu'à 3 par 3.
6. Lisez: 31, 47, 54, 62, 41, 33, 68, 55, 61, 29, 66, 57, 44, 32, 51, 39.

Follow-up, Ex. G: Speed math drill. Write on board problems, such as: **6 × 10 − 9 − 3 + 16 = ?** Students give results of each calculation: **60, 51, 48, 64.**

G. **Trois fois vingt font. . . ?** Do the following multiplication problems in French.

MODÈLE: 3 × 20 = ? *Trois fois vingt font soixante.*

1. 2 × 15 = ?	4. 7 × 8 = ?	7. 3 × 7 = ?
2. 4 × 9 = ?	5. 4 × 10 = ?	8. 2 × 24 = ?
3. 3 × 19 = ?	6. 6 × 11 = ?	9. 5 × 5 = ?

DÉBROUILLONS-NOUS!

Review of **étape**

Ex. H: O. You will want to model this conversation before having students work in groups.

Written Work: See Workbook.

H. **Vous voulez aller au bal avec nous?** Invite some classmates to go to the big dance **(au bal)** with you and your friend. Discuss what cars your parents have. Then decide whose car you will go in and who will drive **(Qui va conduire?).**

Deuxième étape

Point de départ:

Je veux prendre un taxi!

Suggestion, Point de départ: Do a mini-planning strategy about taking a taxi. Have students generate the need to know the address, how long the trip will take, and how much it will cost.

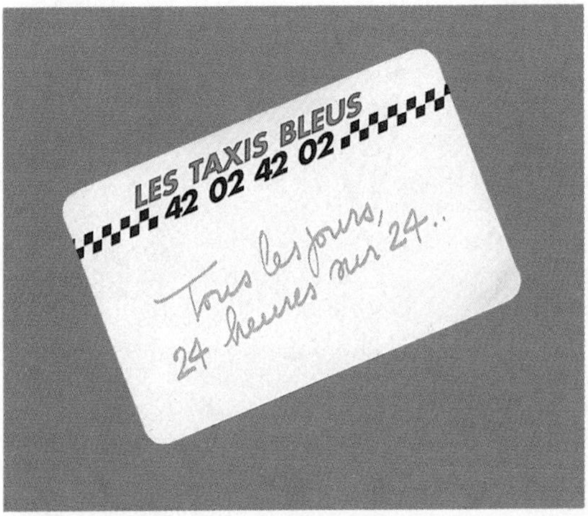

Andrée et Gabrielle visitent le Musée Rodin et ensuite elles veulent dîner dans un petit restaurant près du Palais de Chaillot. Gabrielle veut prendre un taxi.

ANDRÉE: Taxi! Taxi!
LE CHAUFFEUR: Mesdemoiselles? Où est-ce que vous allez?

Elles **montent dans** le taxi. — get in

ANDRÉE: 46, avenue de New York, s'il vous plaît. **Il faut combien de temps pour y aller?** — How long does it take to go there?
LE CHAUFFEUR: Dix minutes... quinze, au maximum.

Elles arrivent au restaurant. Gabrielle descend. C'est Andrée qui va payer.

ANDRÉE: **Je vous dois combien,** Monsieur? — How much do I owe you?
LE CHAUFFEUR: Dix-sept cinquante, Mademoiselle.
ANDRÉE: Voilà un **billet de 20. Gardez la monnaie,** Monsieur. — a 20-franc bill / Keep the change
LE CHAUFFEUR: Merci, Mademoiselle. Au revoir.

Suggestion, Note culturelle, French money: If you have some coins and bills, show them to the students and get them to identify them. Explain to students that in Canada, the form of currency used is the dollar.

Note Culturelle

French money, like currency in the United States, is based on the decimal system. The main unit, the **franc,** is divided into 100 centimes. Coins **(les pièces de monnaie)** are issued by the French government. Bills **(les billets)** are issued by the **Banque de France.** Here are examples of French money:

une pièce de	**5 centimes**	**un billet de**	**10 francs**
	10 centimes		**20 francs**
	20 centimes		**50 francs**
	50 centimes		**100 francs**
	1 franc		**500 francs**
	5 francs		**1.000 francs**
	10 francs		

Prices in French are written either with a comma **(22,50 — vingt-deux cinquante)** or with an **F (22F50 — vingt-deux francs cinquante).**

À vous!

Vocabulary activities

Ex. A: ⇄

A. **Il faut combien de temps pour y aller?** As you make plans with your friends, you discuss how long it will take to get to your destination. The answer will depend on the means of transportation you choose. Notice that in French the preposition **en** is used in the expressions **en voiture, en autobus, en métro,** and **en taxi,** but **à** is used in **à pied** and **à vélo.** Follow the model.

MODÈLE: au parc / en autobus (10 minutes) / à pied (30 ou 35 minutes)
— *Il faut combien de temps pour aller au parc?*
— *Pour y aller en autobus, il faut dix minutes.*
— *Et pour y aller à pied?*
— *À pied? Il faut trente ou trente-cinq minutes.*

1. à la bibliothèque / à pied (25 minutes) / à vélo (10 minutes)
2. à la cathédrale / en métro (20 minutes) / en autobus (25 ou 30 minutes)
3. à l'aéroport / en taxi (45 minutes) / en métro (30 ou 35 minutes)
4. à la gare / en voiture (20 minutes) / en métro (10 minutes)
5. en ville / à pied (35 minutes) / en autobus (15 minutes)

Le savez-vous?

Berlioz, Racine, Delacroix and Voltaire have their pictures on various denominations of French paper money. What do these four men have in common?
a) They were all well-known political figures.
b) They were all famous scientists.
c) They were all associated with the arts (literature, music, painting, etc.).
d) They were all famous generals.

réponse

B. **Je vous dois combien?** You ask the taxi driver how much you owe. You give him/her some money (small French bills come in denominations of 10, 20, and 50) and then either tell him/her to keep the change **(Gardez la monnaie)** or you take the change and give back a tip **(Et voilà pour vous).**

Ex. B: ⇄

MODÈLE: 36F
— *Je vous dois combien?*
— *Trente-six francs, Monsieur (Mademoiselle).*
— *Voilà un billet de cinquante... Et voilà pour vous.*
— *Merci, Monsieur (Mademoiselle). Au revoir.*

1. 18F
2. 42F
3. 27F
4. 31F
5. 48F

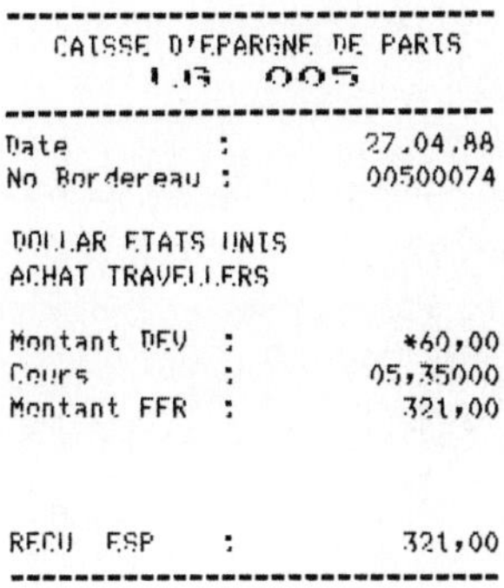
CAISSE D'EPARGNE DE PARIS
LG 005

Date	:	27.04.88
No Bordereau	:	00500074

DOLLAR ETATS UNIS
ACHAT TRAVELLERS

Montant DEV	:	*60,00
Cours	:	05,35000
Montant FFR	:	321,00
RECU ESP	:	321,00

REPRISE

Recycling activities

Ex. C: ⇄

Follow-up, Ex. C: As a listening practice for numbers, students ask you: **Je vous dois combien?** You give a number **(7F50).** Student gives you an appropriate bill **(Voilà un billet de 10F.)** You give correct (or incorrect) change **(Voilà 2F50** or **Voilà 1F50).** Be sure that the original price does not contain centimes lower than 35 (so that students are not forced to try to use numbers they haven't learned when making change).

C. **Combien?** You and your friends are going over how much money you have paid for certain things. Each time you say the price, your friend asks for confirmation, so you repeat more clearly.

MODÈLE: 12,50
— *Douze cinquante.*
— *Combien?*
— *Douze francs cinquante.*

1. 3,25	3. 51,65	5. 47,30	7. 26,50
2. 16,40	4. 39,15	6. 13,60	8. 65,45

D. **Qui va conduire?** As you and several friends plan an outing, you discuss who is going to drive. Choose one of the suggestions based on your reaction to the car each person owns. Follow the model.

MODÈLE: Qui va conduire—le père de Richard (Peugeot) ou le père de Jean-Jacques (Toyota)?
Le père de Richard. Il a une Peugeot et j'aime mieux les Peugeot. ou:
Le père de Jean-Jacques. Il a une Toyota et j'aime mieux les Toyota.

➡ c

1. Qui va conduire—Henri (2CV) ou Chantal (Renault 5)?
2. Qui va conduire—la mère de Françoise (Peugeot) ou la mère de Nelly (Ford)?
3. Qui va conduire—le père d'Annick (Mercedes) ou le père de Jean-Philippe (Cadillac)?
4. Qui va conduire—le frère d'Hervé (Fiat) ou la sœur de Michel (Datsun)?

Suggestion, espérer and **avoir l'intention de:** (1) Have students discuss in English the difference between **je veux aller** and **je vais aller.**
(2) Introduce **j'espère aller** and **j'ai l'intention d'aller.** Have students situate in relation to the first two expressions.
(3) Have students react with one of the four expressions to **faire mes devoirs, aller au cinéma, avoir une Fiat,** etc. You may wish to include **avoir envie de** in the list of expressions for discussing future plans.

STRUCTURE

Expressions for discussing plans ***(espérer, avoir l'intention de)***

J'espère acheter une Renault l'année prochaine.	*I hope* to buy a Renault next year.
Mon père a l'intention de prendre la voiture ce soir.	*My father intends* to take the car tonight.

You have already learned two ways to talk about future actions: what you *want* to do **(vouloir)** and what you *are going* to do **(aller).** You can make the exact state of your plans more specific by telling what you *hope* to do **(espérer)** or what you *intend* to do **(avoir l'intention de).** In all four expressions, the action verb is in the infinitive form.

In the following examples, note how the meanings of these expressions progress from the least certain to the most certain:

vouloir + infinitive	**Je voudrais aller** en ville ce soir. *I would like to go* downtown tonight.
espérer + infinitive	**J'espère aller** en ville ce soir. *I hope to go* downtown tonight.
avoir l'intention de + infinitive	**J'ai l'intention d'aller** en ville ce soir. *I intend to go* downtown tonight.
aller + infinitive	**Je vais aller** en ville ce soir. *I'm going to go* downtown tonight.

These expressions can also be used in the negative:

Je n'ai pas l'intention de rester ici.	*I don't intend to stay* here.

Application

E. Replace the verb in italics and make any necessary changes.

1. Je *veux* aller en France. (vais / espère / n'ai pas l'intention / voudrais)
2. Nous *allons* faire un voyage. (voudrions / avons l'intention / espérons / voulons)
3. Est-ce que tes parents *vont* voyager en Afrique? (espèrent / ont l'intention / veulent)

F. **Un jour.** Indicate how each person indicated feels about doing the following activities someday.

MODÈLE: voyager en Europe (votre père / vos amis / vous)
Mon père ne veut pas voyager en Europe.
Mes amis espèrent voyager en Europe un jour.
Moi, j'ai l'intention de voyager en Europe l'année prochaine.

1. aller à Paris (votre mère / vos frères [sœurs, amis] / vous)
2. voyager en Asie (votre amie / vos parents / vous)
3. être président(e) (vous et vos amis / votre père / votre sœur [frère, ami])
4. avoir une Mercédès (votre père / vos amis / vous)

DÉBROUILLONS-NOUS!

Review of the **étape**

Ex. G: ⇄

G. **Échange.** Ask the following questions of a classmate, who will answer them.

1. Qu'est-ce que tu as l'intention de faire ce soir?
2. Qu'est-ce que tu vas faire samedi après-midi?
3. Qu'est-ce que tu as envie de faire samedi?
4. Qu'est-ce que tu veux faire dimanche?
5. Qu'est-ce que tu as l'intention de faire l'année prochaine?
6. Qu'est-ce que tu espères faire un jour?

Suggestion, Ex. H: ⇄. Divide the class into pairs; have each pair choose a card. Students playing the role of the American look at side 1 of the card for the address, then give the card to their partner, who looks at side 2 for time and price. You will probably wish to model the dialogue once before dividing into pairs.

Written Work: See Workbook.

H. **Il faut prendre un taxi.** You are in Paris with your parents, who don't speak French. They want to go from their hotel (the Paris Sheraton) to Notre-Dame Cathedral. They don't like the subway, so they ask you to go with them in a taxi. Hail a taxi and tell the driver where you want to go. Then ask if it's nearby and how long the trip will take. Remember to pay for the ride when you reach your destination. (A classmate will play the role of the taxi driver.)

Lexique

Pour se débrouiller

Pour organiser une excursion en ville

Il faut combien de temps pour y aller
en autobus?
en métro?
à pied?
en taxi?
en voiture?
à vélo?

Pour parler de ses projets

aller
avoir envie de
avoir l'intention de
espérer
vouloir
un jour

Pour payer

C'est combien?
Je vous dois combien?
Voilà pour vous.

Thèmes et contextes

L'argent (m.)

un billet
un centime
un franc
une pièce de monnaie

Les voitures (f.pl.)

l'auto-école (f.)
la marque
un permis de conduire

Vocabulaire général

Verbes

conduire
monter (dans)

Mise au point

Prereading: Ask students what they would like to know about public transportation in a city they will visit for the first time.

Lecture: *Histoire de billets*

In addition to recognizing the many cognates in French and English, you must be able to make intelligent guesses about the meanings of words you don't know. Often the context—that is, the words and expressions (and illustrations) that surround the word you are trying to understand—will be of help.

Read the following cartoon passage, taken from a brochure distributed by the **RATP (Régie Autonome des Transports Parisiens)** for people who are unfamiliar with the transportation system in Paris. Do **not** look at the definitions at the end. Once you have a sense of the passage's general meaning, do the first comprehension exercise, which deals with guessing from context.

disent: say *déplacement:* movement *lui permettra:* will allow him *environs:* surrounding area *faire les achats:* to go shopping *magasins:* stores

Compréhension

Postreading: Have students create a simple brochure, aimed at French-speaking visitors, dealing with public transportation in the town or city where you live.

A. **Devinez!** *(Guess!)* For each boldfaced word, choose the meaning that seems to best fit the context. In items 1-3, you will be given several choices. In the remaining items, it is up to you and your classmate(s) to suggest the possibilities and then select the best one.

1. John Busy est arrivé à Paris **sans** sa "Rolls" parce qu'il préfère voyager dans sa "deuxième voiture" (le métro). *(choices: with / without / in / on)*
2. Avec un **seul** ticket, John Busy peut aller à toutes les stations dans le métro. *(choices: special / only / lonely / single)*
3. Le métro est en service de **l'aube** jusqu'à après **minuit.** *(choices: east, west / dawn, midnight / sunrise, sunset / suburbs, city center)*
4. Son **réseau** consiste en 359 stations.
5. 20 km **en dehors de** Paris, le métro devient le RER.
6. A certaines stations du RER, il peut même **louer** un vélo.
7. Pour **rentrer** à son hôtel, John Busy prend le bus à un des 5.656 **arrêts d'autobus.**
8. John Busy a déjà préparé ses **projets** pour demain.

B. **Vous allez à Paris?** Reread the text, this time looking at the definitions found at the end. Pick out at least five items of information that would be very useful to know for an American tourist going to Paris for the first time.

REPRISE

Recycling activity

C. **Et vous?** Based on the drawings, tell what each person hopes to or is planning to do. Then, using expressions such as **je vais, j'espère, je veux (voudrais), j'ai l'intention de,** or their negatives, tell what you hope to or plan to do.

MODÈLE: Qu'est-ce que Monique a l'intention de faire samedi?
— *Elle a l'intention de rester à la maison.*
— *Moi aussi, j'ai l'intention de rester à la maison.* ou: *Moi, je n'ai pas l'intention de rester à la maison. Je vais aller en ville.*

1. Qu'est-ce que Jean-Loup a l'intention de faire ce soir?

2. Qu'est-ce que Mireille espère faire l'année prochaine?

3. Qu'est-ce que Nadine et René vont faire dimanche après-midi?

4. Qu'est-ce que François veut acheter un jour?

5. Qu'est-ce que Michel et sa sœur espèrent faire l'année prochaine?

RÉVISION

In this **Révision,** you will review:

- Means of transportation;
- The immediate future;
- The days of the week;
- Adverbs designating the present and the future;
- The irregular verb **prendre;**
- Numbers from 30 to 69;
- The irregular verb **vouloir;**
- Expressions for making plans.

Means of transportation

D. **La famille Chénier.** Home again after a stay with a family in France, you tell your parents about the activities of your French family. Using the information given below, indicate *where* each person goes, the *means of transportation* he/she uses, and *how long* it takes to get there.

MODÈLE: M. Chénier / au travail / métro / 15 minutes (en métro)
M. Chénier va au travail. Il prend le métro. Il faut 15 minutes pour y aller en métro.

1. Mme Chénier / au travail / métro / 20 minutes (en métro)
2. Isabelle / à l'université / autobus / 30 minutes (en autobus)
3. Alain / au lycée / à pied / 10 minutes (à pied)

4. Jean-Claude / au lycée / vélo / 5 minutes (à vélo)
5. la famille / chez les parents de Mme Chénier / voiture / 1h (en voiture)
6. la famille / chez les parents de M. Chénier / train / 5h (par le train)

The immediate future (*aller* + the infinitive)

je **vais danser**
tu **vas chanter**
il, elle, on **va parler**
nous **allons travailler**
vous **allez faire du ski**
ils, elles **vont aller en ville**

The days of the week

(le) lundi
(le) mardi
(le) mercredi
(le) jeudi
(le) vendredi
(le) samedi
(le) dimanche

Remember that **le** plus a day of the week indicates repetition: **le mardi** *(on Tuesdays).*

Adverbs designating the present and the future

maintenant	**demain**
aujourd'hui	**demain matin**
ce matin	**demain après-midi**
cet après-midi	**demain soir**
ce soir	**vendredi prochain**
cette semaine	**la semaine prochaine**
cette année	**l'année prochaine**

Remember that these time adverbs are usually placed either at the beginning or at the end of a sentence.

E. **Ils sont très actifs!** Jacques Chapon, his sister Caroline, and his parents (M. et Mme Chapon) lead very busy lives. Based on their activity calendar, indicate what will be happening on each day shown. Give your answers from Jacques' point of view (that is, Jacques = **je)** and use **aller** and an infinitive to indicate what is going to happen. Today is May 10.

MODÈLE: *Ce soir, mes parents vont dîner au restaurant.*
Demain, je vais manger au Quick.

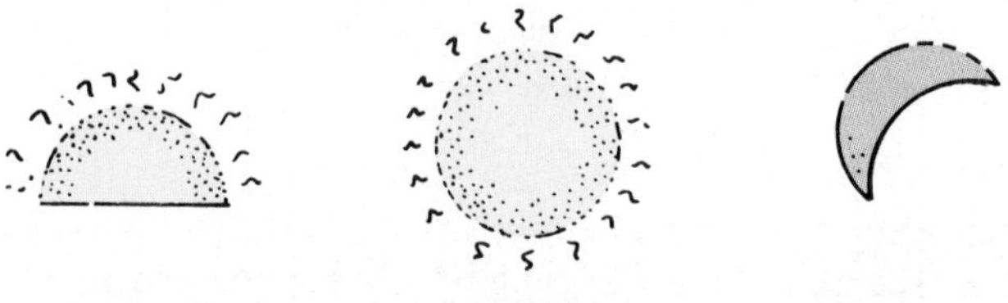

matin **après-midi** **soir**

F. **Et le samedi?** Using the suggested expressions (or others that you know), tell what each person *usually* does each day of the week. Suggested expressions: **travailler (au bureau** *[at the office]*, **à la maison), aller à l'école (à l'université), rester à la maison, aller en ville, faire un tour.**

MODÈLE: votre père
D'habitude, le lundi, le mardi, le mercredi, le jeudi et le vendredi mon père travaille au bureau. Le samedi matin il fait des courses. Le samedi après-midi et le dimanche il regarde la télé.

1. votre mère
2. vos frères (sœurs, amis)
3. vous
4. votre père

The irregular verb *prendre*

je **prends**	nous **prenons**
tu **prends**	vous **prenez**
il, elle, on **prend**	ils, elles **prennent**

Numbers from 30 to 69

trente, trente et un, trente-deux, . . .
quarante, . . .
cinquante, . . .
soixante, . . .

G. **Prenons l'autobus!** The following people like to take the bus in Paris. Indicate where each goes and the number of the bus (or buses) that each takes to get there.

MODÈLE: Gilles / au travail / 46
Pour aller au travail, Gilles prend le 46.

1. Nicole / à l'école / 62
2. André et sa femme / au travail / 47, 28
3. nous / à l'université / 54
4. tu /en ville / 33
5. moi, je / au cinéma / 35, 50
6. Philippe / au bureau / 49, 66

The irregular verb *vouloir*

je **veux**	nous **voulons**
tu **veux**	vous **voulez**
il, elle, on **veut**	ils, elles **veulent**

Expressions for making plans

aller + infinitive *(to be going to . . .)*
espérer + infinitive *(to hope to . . .)*
avoir l'intention de + infinitive *(to intend to . . .)*
vouloir + infinitive *(to want to . . .)*

Ex. H: ○

H. **Qu'est-ce qu'ils veulent?** For each of the following situations, find out what the other members of your group want to do or order or buy. Then report back to the class about the results. Include yourself in the report.

MODÈLE: au Quick / Qu'est-ce que tu veux?
Jim veut un Giant. Maggie et Peter veulent des BigCheese. Sarah et moi, nous voulons des frites et des milk-shakes à la vanille.

1. au café / Qu'est-ce que tu veux?
2. au Salon de l'Automobile *(Automobile Showroom)* / Qu'est-ce que tu veux (voudrais) acheter?
3. samedi / Qu'est-ce que tu veux faire ce soir?
4. dimanche / Qu'est-ce que tu veux faire cet après-midi?

Ex. I: ⇄

I. **Pourquoi est-ce qu'il fait ça?** Based on the drawings, suggest why the people are doing what they are doing. Use an appropriate form of **aller, vouloir, espérer,** or **avoir l'intention de** and an infinitive in each answer.

MODÈLE:
Pourquoi est-ce que Pierre veut rester à la maison?
Parce qu'il a l'intention de faire ses devoirs. ou:
Parce qu'il va faire ses devoirs.

1. Pourquoi est-ce qu'Isabelle fait ses devoirs vendredi soir?

2. Pourquoi est-ce que Claude et Michèle étudient l'anglais?

3. Pourquoi est-ce que Louis va à la librairie?

4. Pourquoi est-ce que Frédérique étudie les sciences?

5. Pourquoi est-ce que Juliette va en ville?

6. Pourquoi est-ce que Catherine et Bruno vont à l'auto-école?

Answer, Pourquoi? d. All stops are **facultatifs;** i.e., the driver will only stop if someone is getting off or if someone waves (signals) to the driver.

POURQUOI?

You are staying with a French family on the outskirts of Paris. You decide to go into the city one day, by yourself, to visit a museum. Your French "mother" tells you that the 52 bus will take you where you want to go. You go to the bus stop and wait about 20 or 25 minutes. It is a cold and rainy day. Because no one else is waiting, you start to worry that you might be at the wrong spot, but finally you see the 52 bus coming down the street. To your dismay, instead of stopping, it keeps right on going toward Paris. What is wrong?

a. Paris bus drivers are naturally unpleasant. They like to see people stand outside in bad weather.
b. The bus was probably full. Drivers cannot allow anyone to stand.
c. Paris bus drivers don't like to stop for a single passenger.
d. You didn't signal the driver to stop.

Point d'arrivée

Ex. J: ⇄

Variation, Ex. J: Have each pair of students write out the directions. Then exchange them with another group and try to follow the instructions received on the **métro** map.

J. **Une visite-éclair de Paris.** *(A lightning-fast visit of Paris.)* You and a friend have only a few hours between planes in Paris. Discuss how you will make use of the **métro** in order to see the following sights. Use such expressions as **Nous allons à la station. . . , Nous prenons la direction. . . , Nous changeons à. . . , Nous descendons à. . . , Ensuite nous allons. . .** Begin and end your tour at the **Gare du Nord (E2),** which has trains connecting with the airport. Refer to your **métro** map on p. 220.

1. la Cathédrale de Notre-Dame (métro: Cité—E4)
2. l'Arc de Triomphe (métro: Charles de Gaulle-Étoile—C3)
3. la Tour Eiffel (métro: Trocadéro—C3)
4. Montmartre (métro: place de Clichy—D2)

Ex. K: ⇄

K. **Au café.** You have just met a young traveller who speaks no English. You and your new friend are in a café on the rue Dauphine. Order something. Discuss your families, your activities, and the like. Using the **métro** map on p. 220, explain to your new friend how to take the subway from the Saint-Germain-des-Prés (D4) **métro** station to the place d'Italie (E5).

L. **Allons en ville!** You and a friend are making plans to do something downtown over the weekend. Decide what you want to do, when you want to do it, and how you will get there. Then try to persuade two other friends to join you.

Ex. L: ⇄

M. **Mes projets.** *(My plans.)* Discuss your future plans with some friends. Talk about next year **(l'année prochaine)** and the years following **(dans deux ans, dans cinq ans, dans dix ans,** etc.). Suggestion: Consider what you definitely intend to do **(J'ai l'intention d'aller à l'université),** what you would like to do **(Je voudrais aller à Paris),** and what you hope to do **(J'espère avoir trois enfants).**

Ex. M: ○

Implementation, Ex. M: Vocabulary could well be a problem here. You may wish *first* to ask questions of the class in preparation for doing this exercise in smaller groups. You can thus identify vocabulary words students will want and need.

Variation, Ex. M: Have students prepare a short oral presentation; have them give their talks to the class or in small groups.

Written Work: See Workbook.

Quand je suis à Dakar, je prends l'autobus pour aller en ville. Mais quand je suis à Paris, je prends le métro. Il est très efficace et il ne coûte pas très cher.

Massyla Fodéba

Unité cinq

On visite Paris

Planning Strategy: See Workbook.

Audio Tape and/or Video: See Teaching Guide.

Unit 5 is the reading unit in *ON Y VA!*, Level 1. Most new vocabulary is glossed in the margins to provide students with ready access. Students are not expected to learn this vocabulary for production, however, only for receptive purposes. Many of the words treated receptively here will be presented for production in Levels 2 and 3. In this unit, the only vocabulary to be used for production is presented in the **Structures.**

The KIT contains additional reading materials about Paris.

Objectives

In this unit, you will learn:

- to understand short descriptions of various sights in Paris;
- to get information about various activities in Paris;
- to talk about events in the past;
- to talk about past, present, and future activities.

Chapitre treize: **Ah bon, tu veux connaître Paris!**

Première étape: Paris à vol d'oiseau
Deuxième étape: La rive gauche et l'île de la Cité
Troisième étape: La rive droite

Chapitre quatorze: **Qu'est-ce qu'il y a à voir?**

Première étape: Paris ancien
Deuxième étape: Paris moderne

Chapitre quinze: **Qu'est-ce qu'on peut faire à Paris?**

Première étape: Paris branché
Deuxième étape: Les distractions

Claire Maurant, Strasbourg, France

Chapitre treize

Ah bon, tu veux connaître Paris!

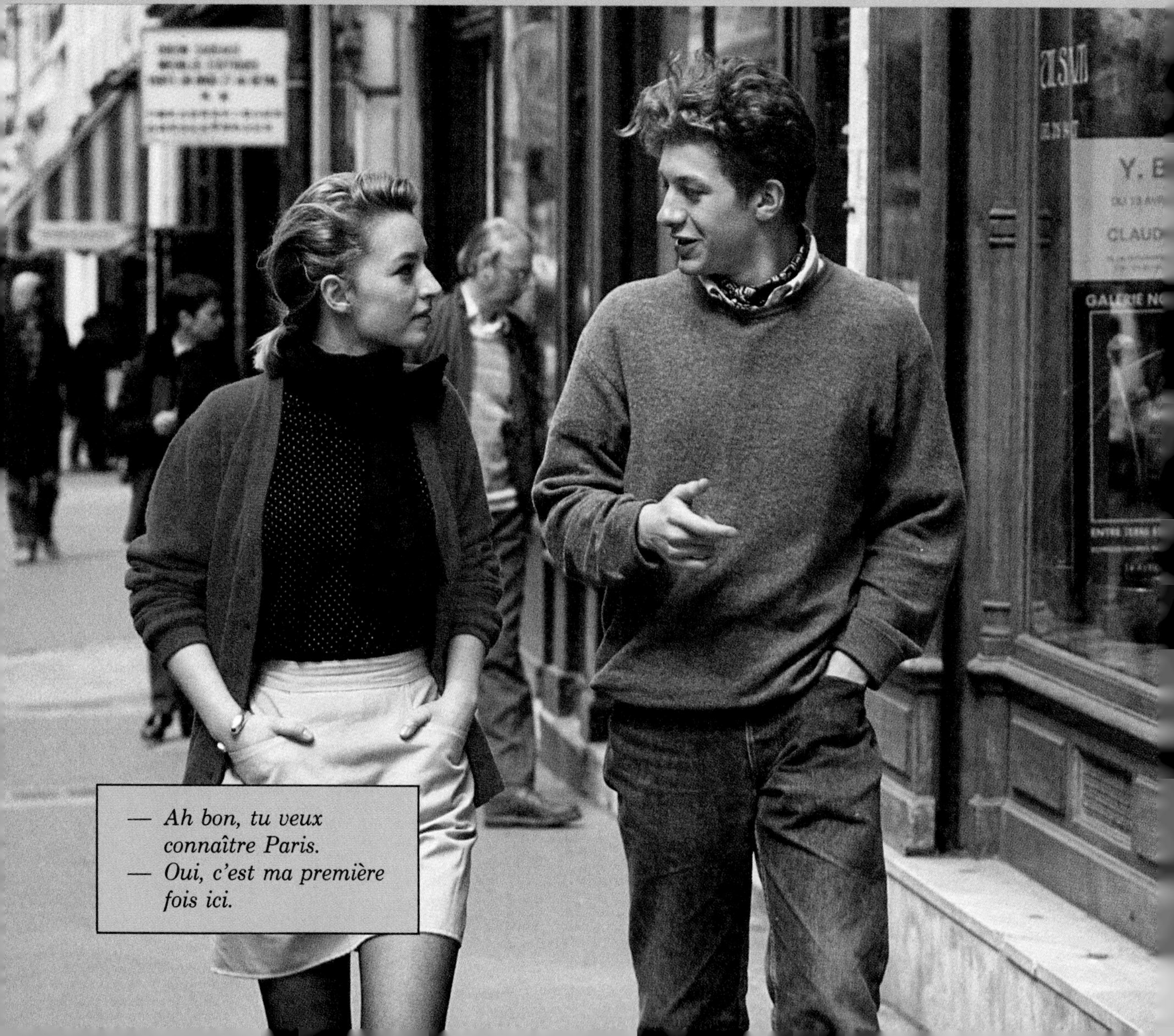

— *Ah bon, tu veux connaître Paris.*
— *Oui, c'est ma première fois ici.*

Première étape

The material in this unit has been written to help you develop your reading skills. That means that each chapter begins with short descriptions that have various aspects of Paris as their theme. When you read each paragraph, remember that you want to concentrate on the general meaning, not on the meaning of each word. Try to read as smoothly as possible and to use some of the reading techniques you've already learned. You'll find out that recognizing cognates (words that have the same meaning as in English) and guessing meaning from context will help you understand a text without having to look up many words.

Ah bon, tu veux connaître Paris: So you want to get to know Paris

Prereading: Ask students to talk about their own town, what the major buildings, sights, and monuments are. This will bring out some of the vocabulary that will be dealt with in these readings on Paris.

Lecture: *Paris à vol d'oiseau*

Paris à vol d'oiseau: A bird's-eye view of Paris

Although Paris is not representative of all of France, it has always been and remains today the center of attention for French people and foreigners alike. In this unit, you will learn about Paris starting with some general information about the city. As you progress through each **étape** and chapter, you will get a closer look at the sights of one of the most beautiful cities in the world.

Implementation: It is not necessary that all paragraphs be done during the same class period. In fact, you may wish to do one or two paragraphs in class followed by general comprehension questions and vocabulary work, and then assign the other paragraphs for homework. These latter paragraphs would then be discussed during the next class period.

Suggestion: Give students one minute to read (silently) each of the three sections in the **Lecture.** Do one section at a time, then ask them what the main ideas are and ask them to point out some of the cognates. You can also ask them to tell you if they had any problems understanding any aspects of the reading.

Suggestion: In Chapter 13, the word study is based on cognates. For specific cognates, consult the Teaching Guide.

La géographie

Paris est une ville de 2 176 243, mais la région parisienne a plus de 10 millions d'*habitants.* Paris est la capitale politique, industrielle et commerciale de la France. La ville est traversée par un *fleuve* qui s'appelle **la Seine.** Elle divise la ville en deux parties—**la rive gauche** et **la rive droite.** *Au milieu de* la Seine se trouvent deux *petites îles* —**l'île de la Cité** et **l'île Saint-Louis.**

inhabitants
river
in the middle of
small islands

Transparency: Complete map of Paris

L'organisation de la ville

Du point de vue administratif, Paris est organisé en vingt **arrondissements;** du point de vue culturel, la ville est divisée en **quartiers.** Chaque quartier est comme une petite ville, avec ses magasins, ses écoles, ses églises, ses cafés et restaurants.

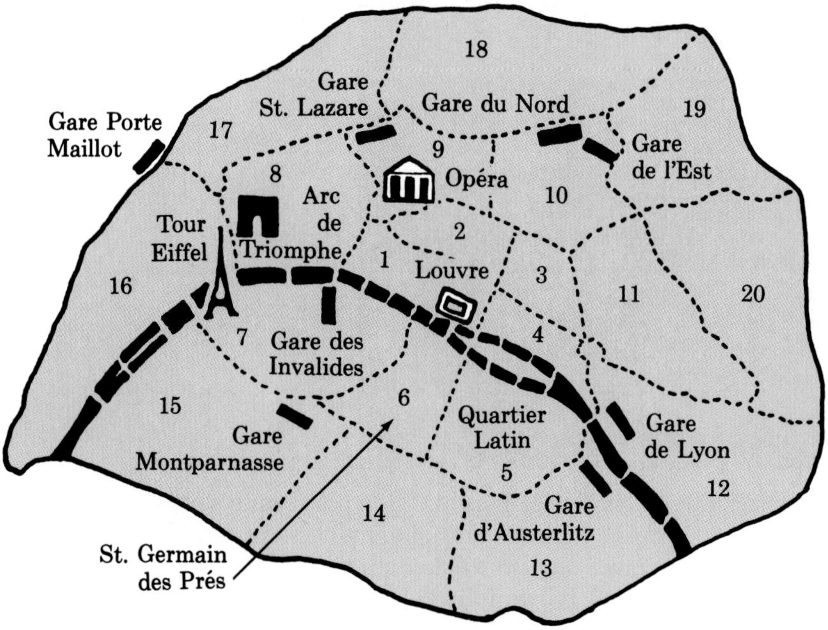

Les boulevards et les avenues

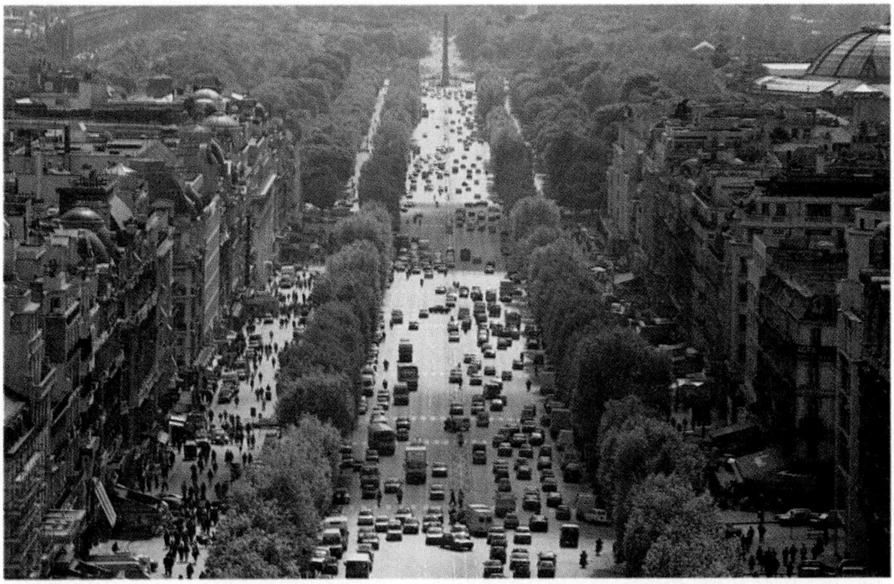

l'avenue des Champs-Elysées

Comme les grandes villes des États-Unis, Paris est traversé de boulevards et d'avenues *célèbres* dans le monde entier. Il y a **le boulevard Saint-Michel** qui traverse le quartier des étudiants, **le boulevard Saint-Germain** et, surtout, **l'avenue des Champs-Élysées.** *Large de* 71 mètres, l'avenue des Champs-Élysées est un centre de commerce et de tourisme. C'est là qu'*ont lieu* de grands *événements* de caractère national—le défilé du 14 juillet (la fête nationale française) et l'arrivée du Tour de France (une *course* à vélo).

famous
with a width of
take place
events
race

Exercices de familiarisation

A. **On visite Paris.** You and your friends are going to visit Paris. Because you know quite a bit about the city, you give them some information before you get there. Complete each statement by choosing the appropriate information among the various choices provided.

1. Paris has over (5 million, 4 million, 2 million, 3 million) inhabitants.
2. The Parisian region has over (13 million, 17 million, 10 million, 14 million) inhabitants.
3. The river that flows through Paris is called the **(Garonne, Seine, Loire, Rhine).**
4. The city is divided into two parts, called (the left and right banks, the north and south quarters, the industrial and political quarters).
5. One of the islands in the middle of the river is called (the **île droite,** the **île de la Cité,** the **île de la Seine**).
6. From an administrative point of view, Paris is organized into twenty (**quartiers,** small cities, **arrondissements**).
7. From a cultural point of view, the city is divided into (**arrondissements, quartiers,** small cities).
8. The boulevard that is associated with the student neighborhood is called the **(boulevard Saint-Germain, avenue des Champs-Élysées, boulevard Saint-Michel).**
9. The Champs-Élysées attracts a lot of (tourists, workers, students).
10. If you're in Paris on July 14, you can see a parade on the **(boulevard Saint-Michel, avenue des Champs-Élysées, boulevard Saint-Germain).**

Suggestion, Ex. B: This activity can be done either in small groups or by the class as a whole. If done in small groups, there should be a follow-up during which students can share their ideas.

B. **Imaginons!** Imagine that you are a Parisian explaining to someone (in English) why you think Paris is the greatest city in the world. Using the facts you have learned and common knowledge (culture, food, history, etc.), present a favorable picture of Paris.

Structure: The **passé composé** is presented with emphasis on the past participle. This allows it to be treated as a regular tense: i.e., once the student has learned the past participle, conjugation of this tense is relatively simple.

STRUCTURE

The ***passé composé*** *with* ***avoir***

J'ai habité à Paris.	*I lived* in Paris.
Ils n'ont pas trouvé le musée.	*They didn't find* the museum.
Où est-ce qu'**elle a acheté** les souvenirs?	Where *did she buy* the souvenirs?
Nous avons déjà **visité** le Louvre.	*We* already *visited* the Louvre.

In French, to talk about actions that you carried out in the past, you use the past tense called the **passé composé** *(compound past).* This tense is called "compound" because it is made up of two parts: a helping verb, that agrees with the subject of the sentence, and a past participle. For most French verbs, the helping verb is **avoir.**

	helping verb **(avoir)**	past participle	
	↓	↓	
Nous	**avons**	**visité**	Paris.

The key to using the **passé composé** is learning the past participles. The past participle of an **-er** verb sounds exactly like the infinitive; however, the written form ends in **-é** rather than in **-er:**

Infinitive		**Past participle**
voyager	⟶	voyag**é**
quitter	⟶	quitt**é**
habiter	⟶	habit**é**
travailler	⟶	travaill**é**
visiter	⟶	visit**é**
parler	⟶	parl**é**
commencer	⟶	commenc**é**
danser	⟶	dans**é**
manger	⟶	mang**é**
étudier	⟶	étudi**é**
regarder	⟶	regard**é**

Suggestions, Past with **avoir:** (1) Present using **D'habitude je quitte la maison à 8h.** Substitute: **Demain matin je vais quitter la maison à 9h.** Then, **Ce matin j'ai quitté la maison à 7h30.** (2) Review conjugation of **avoir.** (3) Present concept of past participle for regular **-er** verbs. (4) Have students generate conjugations of several verbs in **passé composé** from the past participle you give them. (5) Have students contrast present and past, then immediate future and past.

Application

C. Replace the past participle in italics with those given in parentheses.

1. Est-ce que tu as *voyagé?* (travaillé / regardé la télé / visité Paris)
2. J 'ai *cherché* le livre. (trouvé / commencé / aimé / acheté)
3. Hier soir, nous avons beaucoup *dansé.* (parlé / mangé / étudié)

D. Replace the subject in italics and make all necessary changes.

1. *Paul* a traversé la rue. (Anne / nous / ils / je / vous / tu)
2. *Chantal* a déjà visité Paris. (Marc / tu / vous / elles / nous / je)
3. *J* 'ai regardé la télévision. (nous / elle / tu / ils / vous / je)

E. **Bien sûr!** Your parents are always checking up on you to see that you did the things you were supposed to do. As you're being questioned, answer in the affirmative.

MODÈLE: Est-ce que tu as parlé à Jean?
Oui, bien sûr! J'ai parlé à Jean.

1. Est-ce que tu as commencé tes devoirs?
2. Est-ce que tu as mangé quelque chose *(something)?*
3. Est-ce que tu as parlé à ton professeur?
4. Est-ce que tu as étudié pour ton examen?
5. Est-ce que tu as cherché ta calculatrice?

NOTE GRAMMATICALE

To form the negative of the **passé composé,** simply insert **ne** before the helping verb and **pas** after the helping verb. Remember that **ne** becomes **n'** before a vowel.

n' **pas**
Ils ∨ ont ∨ trouvé le musée.
Ils **n'**ont **pas** trouvé le musée.

To ask a question in the past tense, use any of the interrogative forms that you've already learned.

Tu as regardé la télévision?	*Did you watch* television?
Est-ce que vous avez visité la Tour Eiffel?	*Did you visit* the Eiffel Tower?
Quand est-ce qu'elle a quitté la maison?	*When did she leave* the house?

F. Replace the subject in italics and make all necessary changes.

1. *Je* n'ai pas mangé la salade. (nous / elle / vous / ils / tu / je)
2. *Elles* n'ont pas dansé. (tu / nous / il / je / vous / elles)
3. Est-ce que *vous* avez visité Paris? (tu / elle / ils / vous)
4. Quand est-ce que *tu* as quitté la maison? (vous / elles / il / tu)

G. **Oui et non.** You spent the evening at a friend's house. The next day your other friends want to know how you spent the evening. Tell them what you did and did not do.

MODÈLES: Est-ce que tu as parlé à Simone? Et à Francine?
J'ai parlé à Simone mais je n'ai pas parlé à Francine.

Est-ce que vous avez dansé? (étudier)
Nous avons dansé mais nous n'avons pas étudié.

1. Est-ce que vous avez téléphoné à Paul? Et à Marie?
2. Est-ce que vous avez écouté la radio? (danser)
3. Est-ce que tu as mangé un sandwich? Et des fruits?[1]
4. Est-ce que tu as regardé la télévision? (étudier)
5. Est-ce que tu as parlé aux parents de Sylvie? Et à sa sœur?

H. **Pourquoi est-ce que vous êtes en retard?** You and your friend arrive late at a party. Use the drawing and the verbs to explain what happened.

MODÈLE: *Nous avons quitté la maison à 8h15, nous avons traversé la rue . . .*

Variation, Ex. H: Another student explains why the people in the drawing were late **(Ils ont quitté la maison.** Etc.).

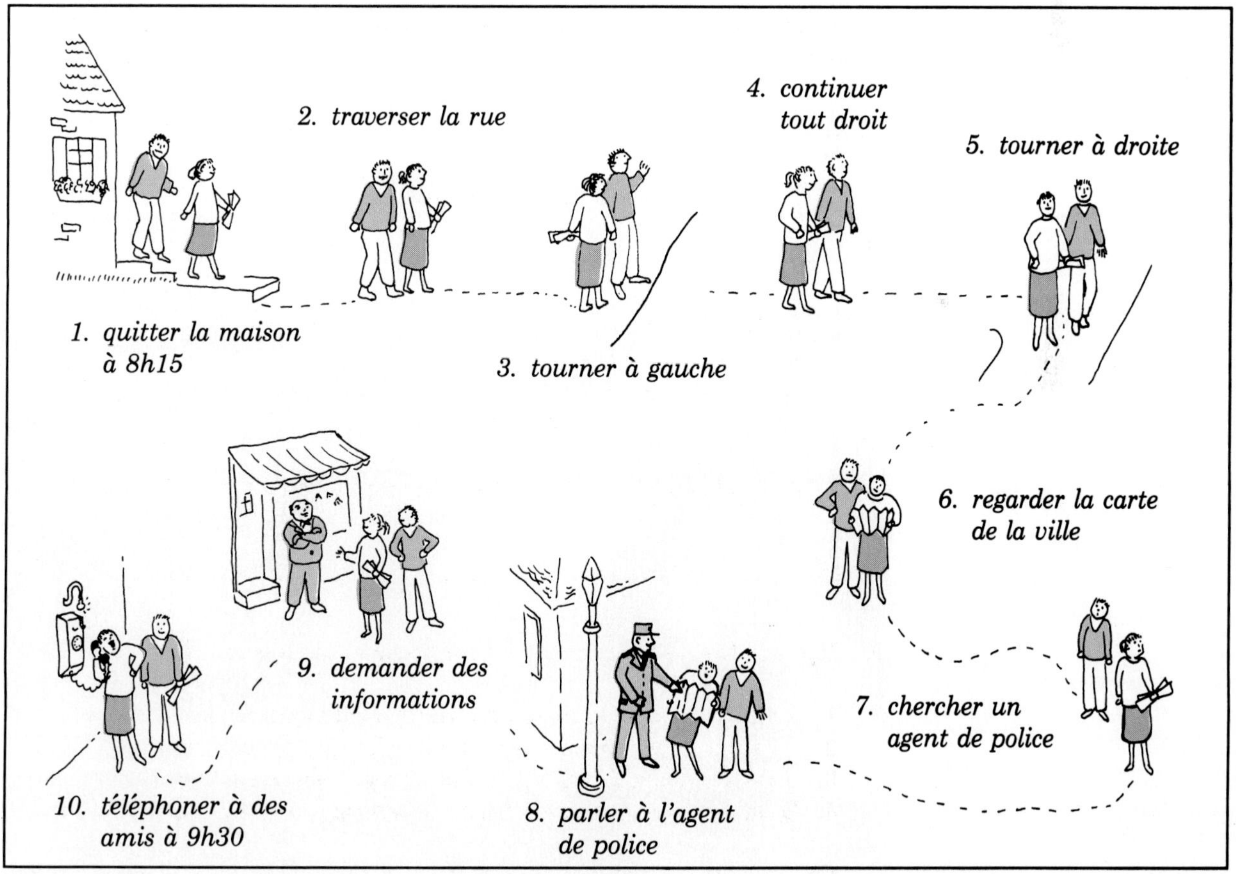

[1]Remember that the indefinite articles **un, une, des** become **de** after a negative:
Tu as acheté **une** voiture? Non, je n'ai pas acheté **de** voiture.

Transparency, Ex. H: activity map

DÉBROUILLONS-NOUS!

Review of the **Étape**

Ex. I: ⇄

I. **Échange.** Ask the following questions of a classmate, who will answer them.

1. Est-ce que tu as étudié hier soir?
2. Est-ce que tu as quitté la maison de bonne heure *(early)* ce matin?
3. Est-ce que tu as déjà *(already)* visité Paris? Et Rome? Et Québec?
4. Est-ce que tu as téléphoné à tes amis hier soir?
5. Est-ce que tu as mangé quelque chose pour le petit déjeuner?

Ex. J: ⇄

J. **Mon week-end.** It's Monday morning and you and your friend are telling each other what you did and did not do over the weekend. Choose from among the verbs provided and be sure to use the **passé composé** in your conversation. Suggested verbs: **travailler, regarder la télévision, parler, téléphoner à, danser, manger, étudier, visiter, écouter la radio.**

Written Work: See Workbook.

Deuxième étape

Transparency: Refer back to the transparency of the map of Paris..

Lecture: *La rive gauche et l'île de la Cité*

LA RIVE GAUCHE

Le Quartier latin

Prereading: In English, ask students how their town or city is divided: e.g. how are the different neighborhoods identified, what makes them unique? If you are in a small town, ask them to talk about neighboring towns and the associations they have with them. The important thing is to stress the notion of neighborhood so that they will easily understand the idea of the Parisian **quartier.**

le boulevard Saint-Michel

Nous commençons notre visite de la **rive gauche** par le quartier des étudiants. Au **Quartier latin,** les cafés, les restaurants, les cinémas et les librairies *attirent* des étudiants de nationalités variées. La rue principale du quartier est **le boulevard Saint-Michel;** les étudiants l'appellent «le Boul' Mich'». Ici, les étudiants *se réunissent* dans les cafés pour étudier et pour discuter. C'est un quartier très animé non seulement le jour, mais aussi la nuit.

attract

meet

Lecture: There are four short sections in this **Lecture.** You can have all students read one paragraph at a time (approx. one minute each) and then ask them for the main ideas and to identify some of the cognates. Or, you can divide the class into four groups, and each group is assigned one of the paragraphs. When the paragraph is done, each group has to tell the others what the reading was about. Then you can give them additional time to read the remaining sections.

Saint-Germain-des-Prés

le Café Aux Deux Magots

Nous continuons notre visite de la rive gauche dans un *vieux* quartier situé à *l'ouest* du Quartier latin. Les cafés, les restaurants et les *magasins d'antiquités* du **Quartier Saint-Germain-des-Prés** sont fréquentés par les Parisiens chics et par les touristes. Si vous voulez manger une *bonne glace,* vous *pouvez* aller au **Café Aux Deux Magots,** un café très célèbre et très chic.

old

west / antique shops

good ice cream / can

Montparnasse

la Tour Maine-Montparnasse

very
worlds / there
high buildings / business

Situé *tout* près de Saint-Germain-des-Prés et du Quartier latin, **Montparnasse** est un quartier paradoxal: deux *mondes y* coexistent, l'un à côté de l'autre. Le jour on est conscient surtout des *hauts bâtiments,* du centre *d'affaires,* des parkings—signes de l'urbanisme moderne. Mais le soir, on a la possibilité de visiter les restaurants, les théâtres et les music-halls où l'on continue la tradition artistique et bohémienne de Stravinsky, de Lénine, de Chagall et de Hemingway. Aujourd'hui, le quartier est dominé par un haut bâtiment, **la Tour Maine-Montparnasse.** *Cette* construction moderne (elle date de 1973) a plus de 200 mètres de *hauteur.* C'est le plus haut *immeuble* d'Europe.

This
height / office (apartment) building

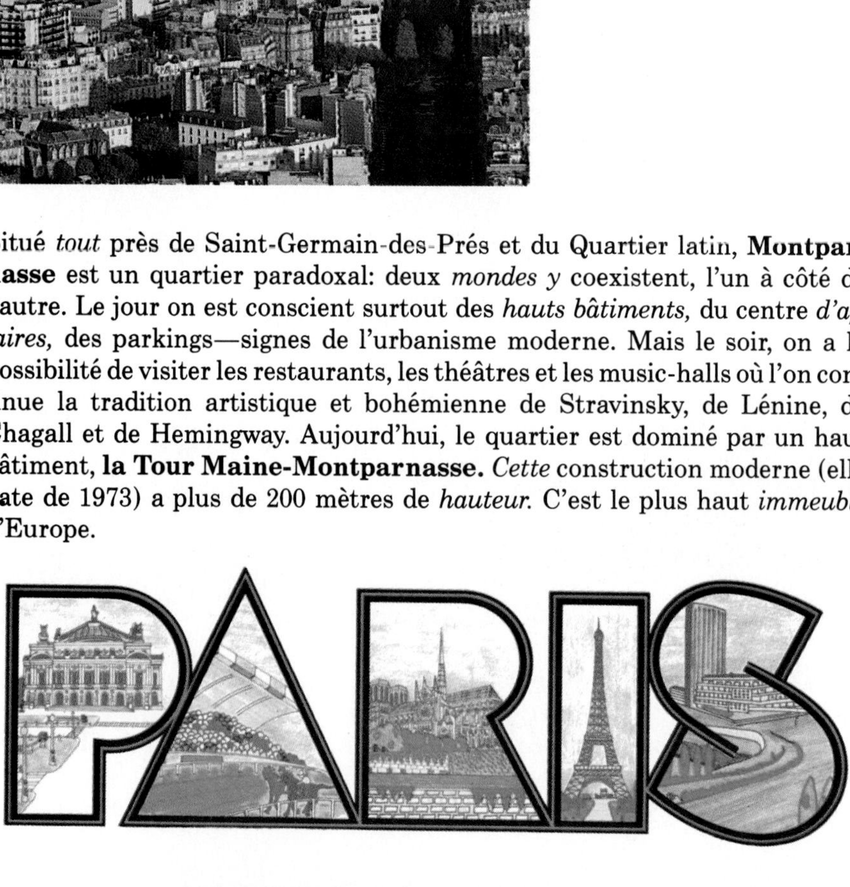

L'île de la Cité

Nous continuons notre visite de Paris. Nous traversons la Seine et nous sommes dans l'île de la Cité. On appelle l'île de la Cité «le *berceau* de Paris» parce que c'est là que Paris *est né. Avant la naissance* de Jésus-Christ, l'île *était* déjà habitée par des Gaulois. Son nom était **Lutèce**—*mot* celtique qui signifie «habitation au milieu des eaux». L'île de la Cité est *reliée* à la rive gauche et à la rive droite par neuf *ponts.* Le plus célèbre et le plus ancien, c'est **le Pont Neuf.**

cradle
was born / Before the birth / was
word
connected
bridges

Exercices de familiarisation

A. **C'est quel quartier?** A friend of yours shows you six drawings of different sections of Paris. Unfortunately, the captions are missing and your friend cannot identify the **quartier.** Help him out by telling him whether the drawings represent (a) the **Quartier latin,** (b) **Saint-Germain-des-Prés,** (c) **Montparnasse,** or (d) **l'île de la Cité.**

Variation, Ex. A: In addition to the drawings, you can read key sentences from the different selections and have students identify the **quartier.** This reinforces their listening comprehension skills.

MODÈLE: *C'est le Quartier latin.*

1.

2.

3.

4.

5.

6.

Implementation, Ex. B: This exercise is done in English so that students have the chance to express themselves without the linguistic limitations they are still experiencing in French. This also helps to relieve some of the frustrations language learners feel at a stage when their productive skills are not at the level of their ideas.

B. **Où aller?** Your friends are about to leave for Paris and they tell you the kinds of things they're interested in seeing or doing. As they describe their interests to you, tell them which of the four **quartiers** they should visit.

MODÈLE: I'm interested in seeing how students spend their day.
You should go to the ***Quartier latin.***

1. I love antique stores.
2. I would like to see the place where Hemingway spent much of his time.
3. I want to see the place where Paris was first established.
4. I would like to see what a modern French apartment and office building looks like.
5. I'm particularly interested in Parisian university life.
6. What I like about cities are the large, busy boulevards.

Prononciation: *The vowels **a** and **i***

In French, the letters **a** and **i,** when not combined with another vowel or with the consonants **m** or **n,** are pronounced as follows:

The French **a** sound is between the **a** sounds in the English words *fat* and *father.* It is pronounced with the mouth rounded.

The French **i** sound is similar to the *i* sound in the English word *machine.* It is pronounced with the lips spread wide, as in a smile.

Pratique

C. Read each word aloud, being careful to open your mouth to pronounce **a** and to spread your lips (smile!) when saying **i.**

1. la
2. Ça va?
3. gare
4. papa
5. ici
6. livre
7. dîne
8. ville
9. Paris
10. mari
11. Italie
12. pharmacie
13. capitale
14. politique
15. rive
16. île
17. divisé
18. habiter

REPRISE

Recycling activity

D. **Un séjour à Paris.** *(A stay in Paris.)* Here is a paragraph from a letter you wrote to a friend last year explaining your plans for a visit to Paris. Now that you've returned from your trip, you want to tell your friend that you fulfilled your plans. Redo the following paragraph by changing the italicized verbs to the **passé composé.** Start your story with **L'année dernière, j'ai visité Paris. . .** *(Last year I visited Paris . . .).*

L'année prochaine, je *vais visiter* Paris. Avant de quitter les États-Unis, mes parents et moi nous *allons étudier* le plan de la ville et mon père *va acheter* les billets. Je *vais* aussi *chercher* des informations sur Paris à la bibliothèque de mon école. Ma famille et moi nous *allons quitter* New York le 25 juin et nous *allons traverser* l'Atlantique en avion. À Paris, nous *allons commencer* notre visite sur l'avenue des Champs-Élysées. Moi, je *vais visiter* le quartier des étudiants. Le soir, mon père et ma mère *vont visiter* Saint-Germain-des-Prés et moi, je *vais regarder* la télévision. Nous *allons* aussi *manger* beaucoup de choses délicieuses. Nous *allons* beaucoup *aimer* Paris.

Structure: We have omitted the irregular verb **vouloir** from the **passé composé** section because it changes meaning *(to try)* and because it is not likely to be used frequently by students.

STRUCTURE

*The **passé composé** with **avoir** (irregular past participles)*

L'année dernière, j'**ai fait** un voyage à Paris.	Last year, I *took* a trip to Paris.
J'ai pris l'avion.	I *took* the plane.
Pendant mon séjour, nous **avons eu** beaucoup d'aventures.	During my stay, we *had* a lot of adventures.

When you talk about events in the past using the **passé composé,** you will often need irregular verbs. The past participles of irregular verbs do not follow the same pattern as those of **-er** verbs. Among the verbs you have already learned, the following have irregular past participles:

Infinitive		Past participle
avoir	⟶	**eu**
être	⟶	**été**
faire	⟶	**fait**
prendre	⟶	**pris**
apprendre	⟶	**appris**
comprendre	⟶	**compris**

Application

E. Replace the subject in italics and make all necessary changes.

1. *Sylvie* n'a pas fait ses devoirs. (Jean-Luc / tu / vous / elles / nous / je)
2. Est-ce que *tu* as appris les verbes? (vous / elles / il / tu)
3. *J'*ai eu un très bon été. (nous / ils / vous / elle / je)
4. *Il* a été à Paris. (elles / nous / tu / je / vous / elle)
5. *Nous* avons fait un séjour en France. (je / elles / il / vous / tu / nous)

F. **Des questions.** For everything you are told, ask a follow-up question using the verbs in parentheses. Be sure to use the **passé composé.**

MODÈLE: J'ai fait un séjour en France. (prendre l'avion)
Est-ce que tu as pris l'avion?

1. Ils ont passé leurs vacances à Paris. (apprendre beaucoup de choses)
2. Nous avons visité beaucoup de quartiers. (être à Montparnasse)

3. Il a mangé au restaurant. (aimer le repas *[meal]*)
4. J'ai regardé la télévision française. (comprendre les émissions *[programs]*)
5. Elles ont visité les musées. (prendre le métro)
6. Nous avons passé quinze jours à Paris. (faire des excursions)

G. **Le week-end.** Your friends want to know what you did over the weekend. They ask you questions using the words provided. You answer **oui** or **non.**

Follow-up, Ex. G: Question/answer drill based on **Qu'est-ce que vous avez fait?** Indicate either orally or on the board the verbs to be used in the responses. MODÈLE: **(étudier)—Qu'est-ce que vous avez fait?—J'ai étudié.** (To another student):**—Est-ce qu'il a regardé la télévision?—Non, il n'a pas regardé la télévision, il a étudié.**

MODÈLE: téléphoner / parents
—Est-ce que tu as téléphoné à tes parents?
—Oui, j'ai téléphoné à mes parents. ou:
—Non, je n'ai pas téléphoné à mes parents.

1. avoir / accident de voiture
2. faire / promenade
3. faire / devoirs
4. regarder une vidéo
5. apprendre / quelque chose
6. être / chez Jean
7. téléphoner / amis
8. manger / restaurant

DÉBROUILLONS-NOUS!

H. **Mon après-midi.** Using the drawings and the verbs as guides, explain to your parents how you spent the afternoon.

Review of the **Étape**

MODÈLE: *J'ai quitté l'école avec Patrick.*

quitter

1. prendre

2. faire les devoirs

3. faire une promenade

4. écouter des disques

5. quitter

6. acheter

7. manger

Follow-up, Ex. H: Have other students say how the people in the drawings spent their afternoon (using **il** or **elle,** and **ils**).

Written Work: See Workbook.

Troisième étape

Lecture: *La rive droite*

Transparency: Refer back to the map of Paris to help students situate the various places mentioned in the reading.

Continuons notre visite de Paris! Notre guide nous *amène* sur la rive droite. — takes

LA RIVE DROITE

Prereading: Have students point out some of the more interesting sights in their town or a town they know well. This should be done in English.

Nous commençons au Louvre.

Le Louvre

Lecture: This **Lecture** contains six short selections. You can have students read them one at a time, giving you the main idea and identifying some of the cognates. They should also associate the text with the photographs.

Ancienne résidence des *rois* de France (jusqu'au 17e *siècle*), **le Louvre** est *depuis* 1793 un musée. Ses galeries *réunissent* des collections variées: *antiquités* égyptiennes, grecques et romaines; sculptures et peintures du *moyen âge* jusqu'au 19e siècle. L'entrée du Louvre a changé de *visage*. La pyramide en verre et en acier, *conçue* par l'architecte I.M. Pei, attire l'attention des Parisiens et des touristes. Cette structure très controversée fait partie d'un ensemble de rénovations inspiré par l'architecture moderne.

former / kings / century
since / bring together
relics
Middle Ages / look (expression)
conceived

Entre le palais du Louvre et l'Arc de Triomphe de l'Étoile *s'étend* une très belle perspective qu'on appelle la *Voie* Triomphale. Elle *comprend* le jardin des Tuileries, la place de la Concorde, les Champs-Élysées et la place Charles de Gaulle.

stretches out
Way (route) / includes

Le jardin des Tuileries

banks / this / the work / gardener
flowers / way

Situé sur les *bords* de la Seine, *ce* grand parc est *l'œuvre* du célèbre *jardinier* Le Nôtre. C'est un autre bel exemple d'un jardin à la française—bassins, allées, statues, plantes et *fleurs* disposés de *façon* géométrique.

La place de la Concorde

gift
old

C'est sur cette immense place qu'on a guillotiné le roi Louis XVI en 1793. Au centre de la place se trouve **l'obélisque de Louksor,** *cadeau* du gouvernement égyptien. L'obélisque, *vieux* de trente-trois siècles, est couvert d'hiéroglyphes.

La place Charles de Gaulle

Entre la place de la Concorde et **la place Charles de Gaulle** s'étend l'avenue des Champs-Élysées. *En montant vers* la place Charles de Gaulle, on découvre des boutiques, des restaurants, des cafés et clubs, et des *salons d'automobile.* Au centre de la place Charles de Gaulle, nommée *aussi* la place de l'Étoile, se trouve **l'Arc de Triomphe,** construit par Napoléon en l'honneur de ses armées. L'arc *abrite* le tombeau du Soldat *Inconnu.*

going up toward
car showrooms
also
houses / Unknown

Visitons maintenant le quartier le plus pittoresque de Paris—Montmartre.

Montmartre

Situé sur une *butte* qui domine la ville, **Montmartre** *était* au 19e *siècle* un centre artistique et bohémien. Le boulevard de Clichy, entre la place Blanche et la place Pigalle, est le centre de la vie de *nuit.* On visite le Moulin Rouge, café-cabaret *rendu* célèbre par le peintre Toulouse-Lautrec. Pour monter sur la Butte Montmartre, on *peut* prendre le *funiculaire,* le Montmartrobus, ou, si on est très sportif, on peut prendre les *escaliers!*

hill / was / century
night
made
can / rail cars
stairs

La Basilique du Sacré-Cœur

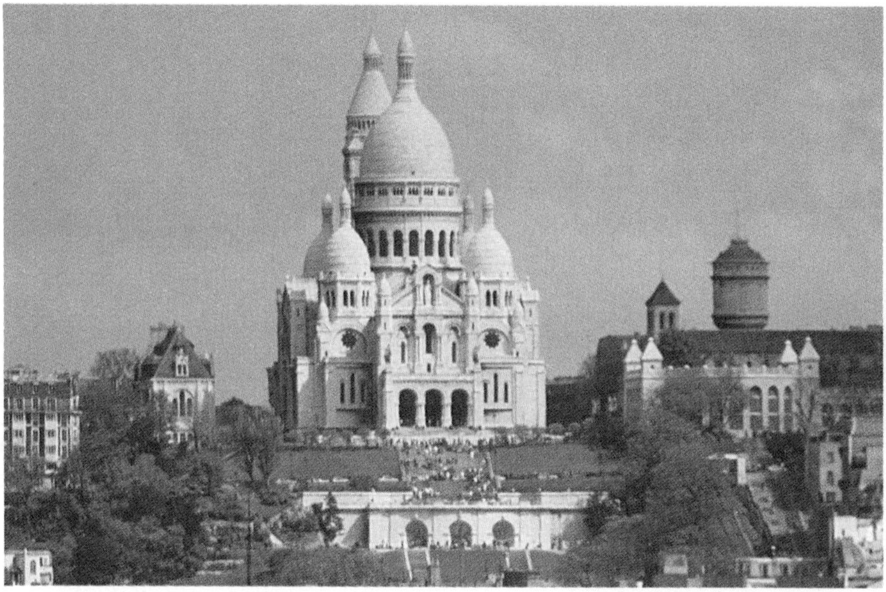

end

Perchée sur la Butte Montmartre, l'église date de la *fin* du 19e siècle. Son style romano-byzantin distingue l'église des autres monuments religieux de la ville.

Exercices de familiarisation

A. **Une mauvaise mémoire.** *(A bad memory.)* Your traveling companion has a difficult time remembering what you have seen on the Right Bank. Remind him/her.

1. Le Louvre est un _____.
2. La Voie Triomphale comprend _____, _____, _____ et _____.
3. Le grand parc sur les bords de la Seine s'appelle _____.
4. L'obélisque de Louksor se trouve sur _____.
5. L'arc qui abrite le tombeau du Soldat Inconnu s'appelle _____.
6. L'église sur la Butte Montmartre s'appelle _____.

B. **Pourquoi?** You've just come back from a trip to Paris and your friends want to know why they should see certain places in the city. Answer them (in English), using the information from the reading selections.

1. Why should I go to the Tuileries?
2. What can I see at the Louvre?
3. What's so special about Montmartre?
4. What is there to see along the Voie Triomphale?
5. What's so special about the place de la Concorde?

REPRISE

C. Based on the drawing, describe the activities you see. Give a description of all activities for each subject.

Recycling Activity

Transparency, Ex. C: itinerary map

MODÈLE: je
J'ai quitté la maison, j'ai tourné à gauche dans la rue Maubert . . .

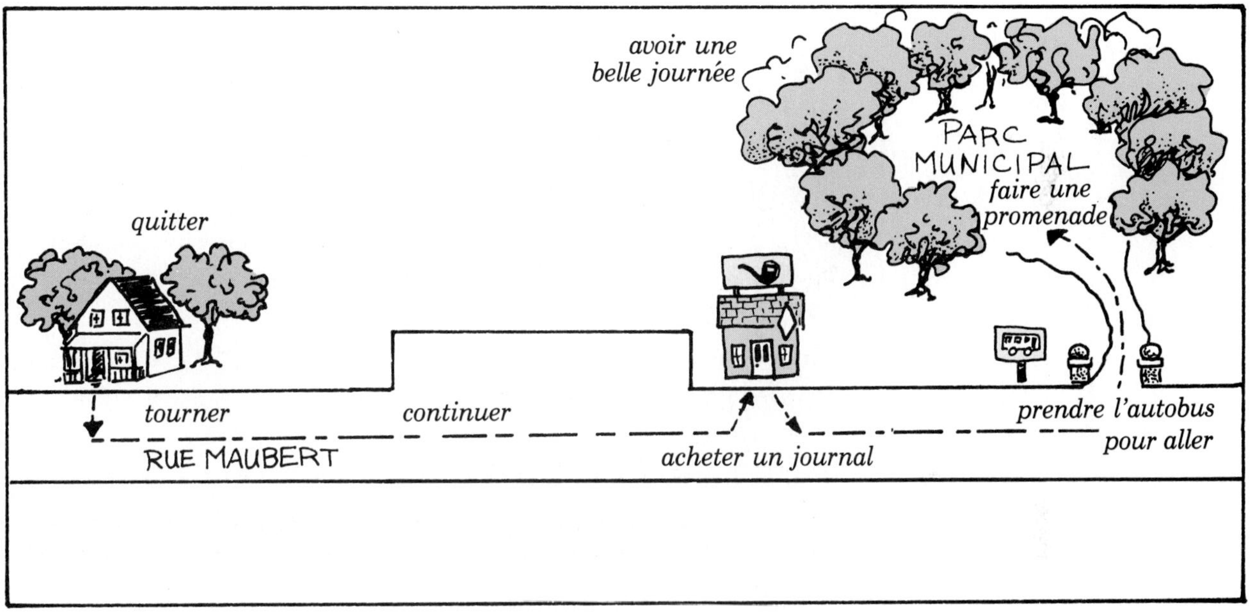

1. je
2. Louise
3. mon ami(e) et moi, nous
4. M. et Mme Giroud
5. Jean-Claude
6. Yves et toi, vous

Suggestion, Adverbs: Write on board today's date plus dates for last week; write years—present and past.

STRUCTURE

Adverbs and prepositions used to designate the past

La semaine dernière, j'ai visité Montmartre.	*Last week,* I visited Montmartre.
Nous avons dîné au restaurant **hier.**	We ate at a restaurant *yesterday.*

The following time expressions are used to talk about an action or a condition in the past.

hier	*yesterday*
hier matin (après-midi, soir)	*yesterday morning (afternoon, evening)*
mercredi (samedi, etc.) dernier	*last Wednesday (Saturday, etc.)*
le week-end dernier	*last weekend*
la semaine dernière	*last week*
le mois dernier	*last month*
l'année dernière	*last year*

The following expressions will enable you to express for how long you did something and how long ago something happened:

pendant une heure (deux jours, six ans[2])	*for an hour (two days, six years)*
il y a une heure (deux mois, cinq ans)	*an hour (two months, five years) ago*

Time expressions are usually placed at the beginning or at the end of the sentence.

J'ai travaillé **pendant une heure.**	I worked *for an hour.*
Je suis allé en France **il y a deux ans.**	I went to France *two years ago.*

[2]There are two French equivalents for *year.* The word **année** is used with an adjective **(l'année prochaine)**; the word **an** is used with a number **(un an, trois ans).** The same rule applies to **jour/journée.**

Application

D. Replace the words in italics with the words in parentheses.

1. *Hier* nous avons eu un accident. (la semaine dernière / jeudi dernier / hier soir / l'année dernière)
2. Qu'est-ce que tu as fait *samedi dernier?* (hier après-midi / le mois dernier / la semaine dernière / il y a huit jours)
3. Ils ont été à Paris *la semaine dernière.* (il y a trois ans / le mois dernier / pendant deux semaines / il y a quinze jours)

E. **Quand?** Use the expressions in parentheses to explain when you and your friends did the following things.

MODÈLE: Quand est-ce que Paul a terminé les devoirs?
(il y a une heure)
Il a terminé les devoirs il y a une heure.

1. Quand est-ce qu'Anne-Marie a appris le russe? (l'année dernière)
2. Quand est-ce que vous avez habité à Paris? (il y a trois ans)
3. Quand est-ce que la classe a commencé? (il y a cinq minutes)
4. Quand est-ce que les Leroux ont acheté leur voiture? (la semaine dernière)
5. Quand est-ce que vous avez parlé à vos grands-parents? (dimanche dernier)

6. Quand est-ce que ton frère a trouvé ses clés? (hier matin)
7. Quand est-ce que ta sœur a téléphoné? (il y a une heure)
8. Pendant combien de temps est-ce que Georges a été à Montréal? (pendant deux mois)

Follow-up, Ex. F: Question/answer drill based on **pourquoi / parce que.** MODELE:—**Pourquoi est-ce que vous n'allez pas visiter la cathédrale? —Parce que j'ai visité la cathédrale hier/la semaine dernière/il y a trois jours.** Suggestions: **acheter du chocolat, étudier à la bibliothèque, visiter le musée, prendre le (petit) déjeuner, parler à votre ami(e), téléphoner à vos grands-parents.**

F. **Mais non!** Use the expressions in parentheses to contradict what your friends are saying.

MODÈLES: Gérard a habité à Paris pendant trois ans. (un an)
Mais non! Il a habité à Paris pendant un an.

Claire va visiter la cathédrale demain. (hier)
Mais non! Elle a visité la cathédrale hier.

1. Hervé a été à Paris il y a quatre jours. (trois semaines)
2. Françoise va parler à ses parents cette semaine. (la semaine dernière)
3. Vous avez travaillé pendant cinq heures. (une heure)
4. M. et Mme Beaulieu vont acheter une maison. (l'année dernière)
5. Ils vont visiter le Louvre. (mardi dernier)
6. Tu vas étudier ce soir. (hier soir)
7. Elles ont téléphoné hier. (il y a huit jours)

DÉBROUILLONS-NOUS!

Review of the **Étape**

Ex. G: ⇄

G. **Échange.** Ask a classmate the following questions.

1. Est-ce que tu as fait des devoirs hier soir?
2. Qu'est-ce que tu as acheté le week-end dernier?
3. Est-ce que tu as parlé à tes grands-parents récemment? Quand?
4. Qu'est-ce que tu as fait l'été dernier?
5. Est-ce que tu as visité Paris? Quand?

Written Work: See Workbook.

Lexique

Pour se débrouiller

Pour situer une action dans le passé

hier
hier matin
hier après-midi
hier soir
lundi (mardi, etc.) dernier
le week-end dernier
la semaine dernière
le mois dernier
l'année dernière
il y a une heure (deux mois, cinq ans)

Vocabulaire général

Noms

un accident
un agent de police
une aventure
un centre de culture
une chose
une émission
un fruit
une heure
les informations *(f.pl.)*
une promenade
un quartier
un séjour
un souvenir
les vacances *(f.pl.)*
la variété
un voyage

Verbes

commencer
téléphoner à
trouver
visiter
voyager

Adjectifs

bon/bonne
intéressant(e)
international(e)
parisien(ne)

Autres expressions

quelque chose
pendant

Chapitre quatorze

Qu'est-ce qu'il y a à voir?

— *Tu veux visiter le palais du Luxembourg?*
— *Qu'est-ce qu'il y a à voir?*

Première étape

Lecture: *Paris ancien*

Qu'est-ce qu'il y a à voir?: What is there to see?

Il *serait* impossible de continuer notre visite de Paris sans apprécier le *côté* historique de cette *belle* ville. Notre itinéraire nous *mène* donc à cinq monuments admirés pour leur beauté architecturale et leur importance dans l'histoire de la France.

would be / side
beautiful / leads

Prereading: Ask students to talk about whom we honor in the U.S. through our monuments and buildings. For example, how do we honor writers, artists, composers? What kinds of monuments do we have for political figures, statesmen, etc.? Do we display the tombs of famous people?

Lecture: This reading contains four paragraphs of about equal length, each accompanied by a photograph. You may wish to treat the selections one at a time, allowing students about one minute per selection for silent reading, then asking them to give you the main idea of each selection.

Once you have completed this basic comprehension activity, you can move on to word study.

Note: In Ch. 13, the word study was based on cognates. In this chapter you can either continue this emphasis on cognates if you feel that students need more practice, or you can concentrate on words of the same family.

Le Panthéon

Situé dans la rue Soufflot, non loin du boulevard Saint-Michel, le Panthéon a été construit sous le *roi* Louis XV au 18e siècle. L'inscription sur la façade proclame: «Aux grands hommes, la *patrie reconnaissante*». C'est sous le dôme de cet édifice impressionnant que se trouvent les tombeaux de grands *écrivains* français: Voltaire, Rousseau, Hugo, Zola et *d'autres*.

king
homeland (nation) / grateful
writers / others

VOLTAIRE

ROUSSEAU

La Conciergerie

La Conciergerie est la partie médiévale du Palais de Justice de Paris. Au 14e siècle elle *est devenue* une prison. Pendant la Révolution de 1789, la *reine* Marie-Antoinette y a passé deux mois avant d'être guillotinée sur la place de la Révolution (aujourd'hui la place de la Concorde). On *peut* encore *voir* son *cachot* où se trouvent des objets personnels de la reine: son crucifix et des lettres. La Conciergerie a joué un rôle très sinistre dans l'histoire de la France.

became / queen

can / see
prison cell

Les Invalides

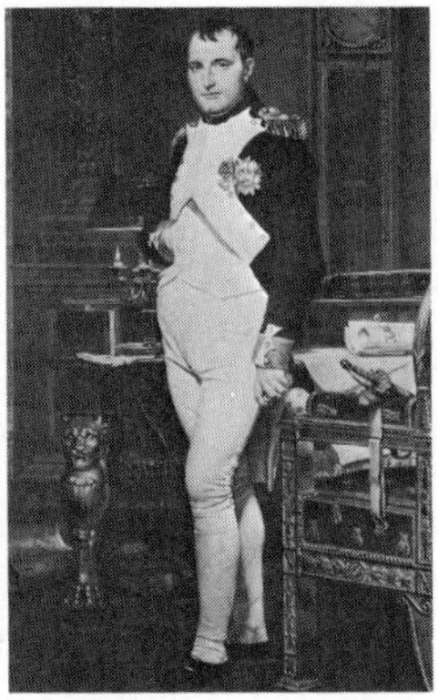

L'Hôtel des Invalides a été construit par Louis XIV au 17e siècle pour les soldats *blessés* (invalides) pendant les *guerres.* Aujourd'hui on y trouve le musée de l'Armée et le tombeau de Napoléon. Napoléon a été l'empereur des Français entre 1804 et 1815. Sa grande armée *a été battue* par les Anglais à Waterloo, l'empereur a été exilé et il *est mort* en 1821.

wounded / wars

was beaten
died

Notre-Dame de Paris

Nous voilà arrivés à une des plus belles cathédrales gothiques d'Europe. Ses roses, ses *arc-boutants* et ses *gargouilles* font de la cathédrale un magnifique exemple de l'architecture du 13e siècle. Le visiteur courageux peut monter les 387 *marches* sur la tour nord de Notre-Dame. De là, il a une vue spectaculaire sur les rues et les ponts de Paris. L'intérieur de la cathédrale est immense. Neuf mille personnes *peuvent s'asseoir* quand il y a une messe ou une grande cérémonie.

flying buttresses / gargoyles

steps (of stairs)

can sit down

Exercices de familiarisation

A. **Comment s'appelle ce bâtiment?** After a long and tiring day spent looking at historical monuments, your friends can't remember the names of the buildings they visited. As they describe each place to you, help them out by providing the name of the building.

1. Il y a le tombeau de Napoléon et aussi le musée de l'Armée.
2. C'est une cathédrale qui date du 13e siècle.
3. Dans ce bâtiment il y a les tombeaux de Voltaire, Rousseau, Hugo et Zola.
4. C'est dans cette prison que Marie-Antoinette a passé deux mois avant d'être guillotinée.

B. **Paris historique.** For each of the centuries given, name the monument.

1. le 13e siècle 2. le 18e siècle 3. le 14e siècle 4. le 17e siècle

Suggestion, Ex. B: Although students have not learned the ordinal numbers, you can tell them how to read them with the word **siècle.** This foreshadowing will make it all the more simple when they arrive at ordinal numbers later on in the book.

REPRISE

Recycling activity

Postreading: Have students write a composition on a Paris monument that has *not* been treated in this chapter. They can go to an encyclopedia, find the most important information, and imitate the short reading passages as they occur in the chapter. To reduce the likelihood of error, tell them to use some of the same sentences they found about other monuments.

Suggested buildings and monuments in Paris and surrounding areas: **la colonne Vendôme, l'Opéra, l'église de la Madeleine, Père-Lachaise, le Palais-Royal, le Palais de l'Élysée, l'Obélisque de Luxor, le Palais de Justice, Malmaison, le palais de Versailles, Fontainebleau, l'Observatoire, l'Hôtel de Ville, l'Église Saint-Germain-des-Prés, Bibliothèque nationale**

C. Répondez aux questions.

1. Est-ce que vous étudiez beaucoup? Est-ce que vous avez étudié hier soir? Est-ce que vous allez étudier ce soir?
2. Est-ce que vous aimez voyager? Est-ce que vous avez fait un voyage l'année dernière? Est-ce que vous allez faire un voyage l'année prochaine?
3. Est-ce que vous prenez le petit déjeuner d'habitude? Est-ce que vous avez pris le petit déjeuner ce matin? Est-ce que vous allez prendre le petit déjeuner demain matin?

STRUCTURE

The **passé composé** *with* **être**

Je suis allé au concert hier soir.	*I went* to the concert last night.
Est-ce que **tu es arrivé** à l'heure?	*Did you arrive* on time?
Oui, et après, **Jeanne est rentrée** avec moi.	Yes, and afterwards, *Jean came home* with me.
Nous sommes arrivés chez nous à minuit.	*We arrived* home at midnight.

Sylvaine est allée à la station de métro.

To talk about past events, you have already learned to use the **passé composé** with the auxiliary verb **avoir.** In addition, some verbs use **être** as their auxiliary verb in the **passé composé.** The past participles of many of these verbs are formed in the regular manner (i.e., **-er** becomes **-é**). Note, however, that **descendre** has **descendu** as a past participle. Here are some verbs conjugated with **être:**

Infinitive		Past participle
aller	⟶	**allé**
arriver	⟶	**arrivé**
descendre	⟶	**descendu**
entrer	⟶	**entré**
monter	⟶	**monté**
rester *(to remain)*	⟶	**resté**
rentrer *(to go/come home)*	⟶	**rentré**
retourner	⟶	**retourné**
tomber	⟶	**tombé**

When a verb is conjugated with **être,** the past participle of that verb becomes like an adjective. This means that it agrees in gender (masculine or feminine) and in number (singular or plural) with the subject of the verb. The basic spelling possibilities are:

Masculine singular	⟶	allé
Feminine singular	⟶	allée
Masculine plural	⟶	allés
Feminine plural	⟶	allées

Now study the complete conjugation of the verb **aller** and remember that the past participle will vary according to the gender and number of the subject:

aller	
je suis **allé (allée)**	nous sommes **allés (allées)**
tu es **allé (allée)**	vous êtes **allé (allée, allés, allées)**
il est **allé**	ils sont **allés**
elle est **allée**	elles sont **allées**
on est **allé**	

Structure: The **passé composé** with **être** is best introduced orally, with books closed, so that students don't immediately see the added problem of past participle agreement. In fact, it may be wise to delay exposure to the written form as long as possible. The most important aspect is to know which verbs are conjugated with **être.** Once there is some control in this area, the writing will follow fairly easily. (1) Using gestures, tell students what you did yesterday afternoon, after school: **Après l'école, je suis allé(e) au supermarché. Après, je suis rentré(e). Je suis arrivé(e) à la maison à 5 heures. Je suis allé(e) dans la cuisine. Ensuite, je suis monté(e) dans ma chambre. Ensuite, je suis descendu(e) et je suis entré(e) dans la cuisine. Je suis resté(e) dans la cuisine pendant une heure.** (2) Then move to questions/answers: **Après l'école, je suis allé(e) au supermarché. Et vous, où est-ce que vous êtes allé(e)?** Students then keep repeating **Je suis allé(e) . . .** until they are used to the form. Continue the questions based on your original narrative. (3) Now tell them that some verbs are conjugated with **être** to form the **passé composé**. Remind them of the verbs and make sure they know the meanings. (4) Move on to Exs. D and E. (5) Introduce the notion of past participle agreement. you may now wish to do Exs. D and E again with books open, so students can see how the agreement words. (6) Do Ex. F.

Application

D. Replace the subject in italics and make all necessary changes.

1. *Hervé* est allé au cinéma. (Jeanne / je / nous / les autres / vous / tu)
2. *Yvonne* n'est pas arrivée. (Marc / Sylvie et Alain / nous / je / tu / vous)
3. Est-ce que *vous* êtes descendu à Châtelet? (Monique / vos amis / elles / tu / Éric)

E. **Oui ou non?** You're part of a student group on a tour of Paris. All of the students have dispersed and you're the only one left to answer the group leader's questions about the others. Answer **oui** or **non** according to the indications in parentheses.

1. Est-ce que Gérard est allé au musée? (oui)
2. Est-ce que Madeleine est allée à la Tour Eiffel? (non)
3. Est-ce que Didier est resté dans sa chambre? (oui)
4. Est-ce que Bénédicte est déjà rentrée? (non)
5. Est-ce que Philippe et sa sœur sont arrivés? (non)
6. Est-ce qu'Anne et Chantal sont montées dans leur chambre? (non)
7. Est-ce que Sylvie est allée au théâtre? (oui)
8. Est-ce que Marie-Claire et Françoise sont allées à la piscine? (oui)

Florence et Jeanne sont allées au Musée d'Orsay. Et toi, où est-ce que tu es allé(e)?

F. Answer each of the questions, indicating that the activities were carried out yesterday.

MODÈLE: Est-ce qu'elles vont aller à la piscine demain?
Non, elles sont allées à la piscine hier.

1. Est-ce que Françoise va rester à la maison demain?
2. Est-ce que tu vas aller en ville demain?
3. Est-ce que tes amies vont arriver demain?
4. Est-ce que Paul et Jacques vont rentrer à Paris demain?
5. Est-ce qu'elles vont aller au théâtre demain?
6. Est-ce qu'il va retourner à New York demain?

NOTE GRAMMATICALE

Now that you've studied the **passé composé,** you know that most verbs are conjugated with the helping verb **avoir** and that some verbs are conjugated with the helping verb **être.** From now on, every time you learn a new verb, you need to determine whether **avoir** or **être** is the proper helping verb:

J'**ai** parlé avec mes amis.
Je **suis** allé au musée.

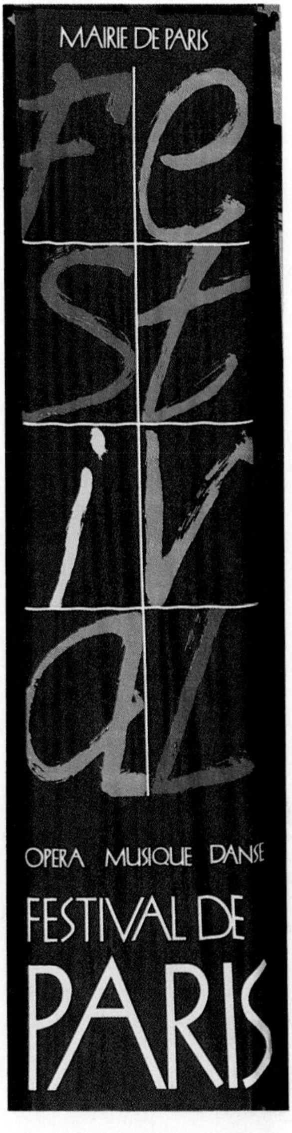

G. **La journée de Claire.** Use the verbs provided to tell what Claire did yesterday. Be careful to distinguish the verbs conjugated with **être** from those conjugated with **avoir.**

MODÈLES: quitter la maison
Elle a quitté la maison.

aller au bureau de tabac
Elle est allée au bureau de tabac.

1. aller à la station de métro
2. prendre le métro
3. descendre à l'île de la Cité
4. visiter le Palais de Justice
5. rester au musée jusqu'à deux heures
6. rentrer à la maison
7. monter dans sa chambre
8. téléphoner à son amie

DÉBROUILLONS-NOUS!

Review of the Étape

Ex. H: ⇄

H. **Échange.** Ask the following questions of a classmate.

1. Est-ce que tu es allé(e) en ville hier?
2. Est-ce que tu as acheté quelque chose?
3. Qu'est-ce que tu as acheté?
4. Est-ce que tu es resté(e) à la maison le week-end dernier?
5. Qu'est-ce que tu as fait le week-end dernier?

Ex. I: O

Written Work: See Workbook.

I. **Les monuments de Paris.** Look at the monuments featured on this map of Paris. Choose three monuments, identify them, say where they're located, and give two facts about each one. You may do this exercise in English.

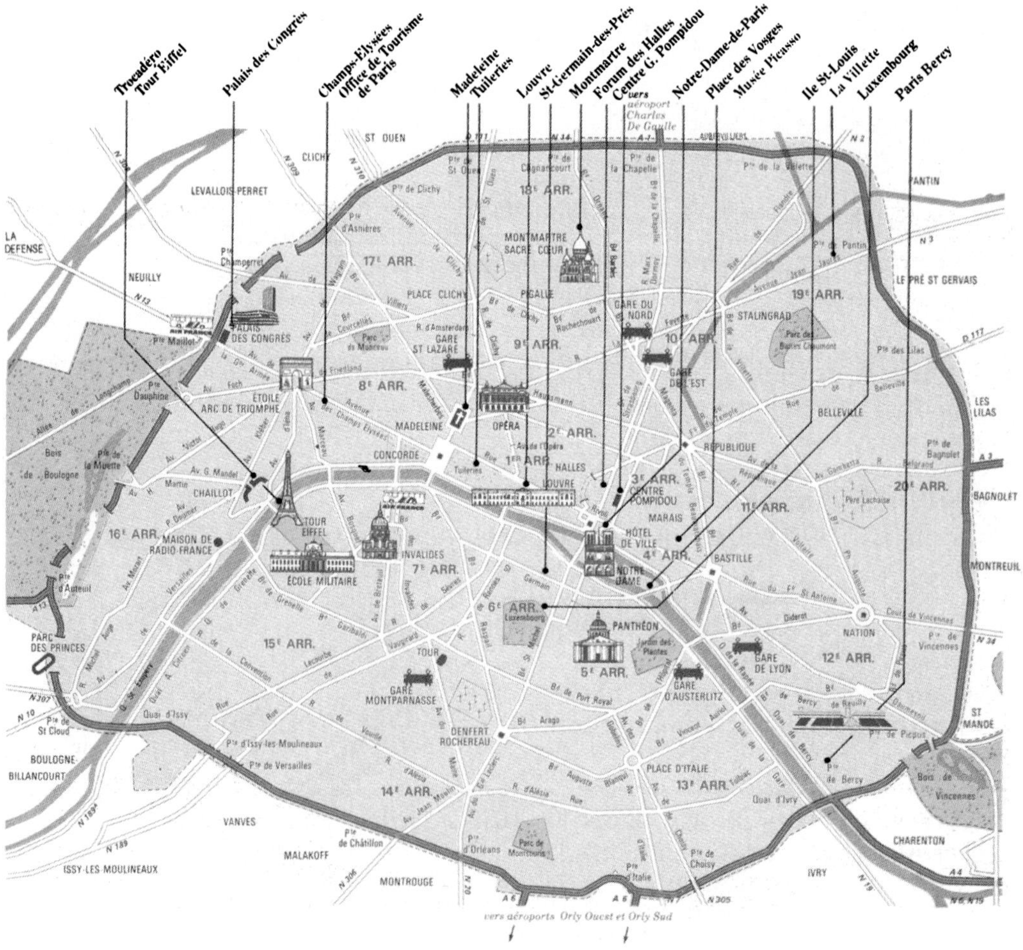

Deuxième étape

Lecture: *Paris moderne*

Pour explorer le côté moderne de Paris, nous visitons la Tour Eiffel, qui *nous* donne une perspective impressionnante des constructions modernes de la ville.

us

Prereading: Have students discuss what they like and dislike about modern architecture. Ask them for their definition of the word *modern.* Do Americans have a different definition for this word than the French? For the French, the modern period begins with the 16th century **(la France moderne).** If they want to refer to the France of today, they are more likely to say **la France contemporaine.** Show students that the length of one's history is likely to affect one's idea of the world and one's use of words.

La Tour Eiffel

La Tour Eiffel est le symbole de Paris. On la *voit* de très loin. À ses pieds, on se sent vraiment minuscule, et quand on *lève* la tête vers le sommet, on a un peu le *vertige.*

La tour a été construite entre 1887 et 1889. Sept cents architectes ont présenté leurs *dessins* et c'est l'ingénieur Gustave Eiffel qui *a gagné* le *concours.*

La tour mesure 320 mètres, elle *pèse* 7 000 tonnes et 2 500 000 *boulons* maintiennent les 12 000 pièces *d'acier.* Tous les sept ans on *fait sa toilette* avec 52 tonnes de *peinture.*

Pour monter les trois étages, il y a un ascenseur ou bien ... les *jambes* (c'est la solution des grands sportifs *car* il y a 1652 marches!). Chaque année, 3 millions de touristes visitent la tour.

sees
raises
dizziness
drawings (plans) / won
contest (competition)
weighs / bolts
steel / cleans it up
paint
legs
for (because)

Adapted from *Paris* (les petits bleus), Hachette Guides Bleus, 1984

La Villette: La cité des sciences et de l'industrie

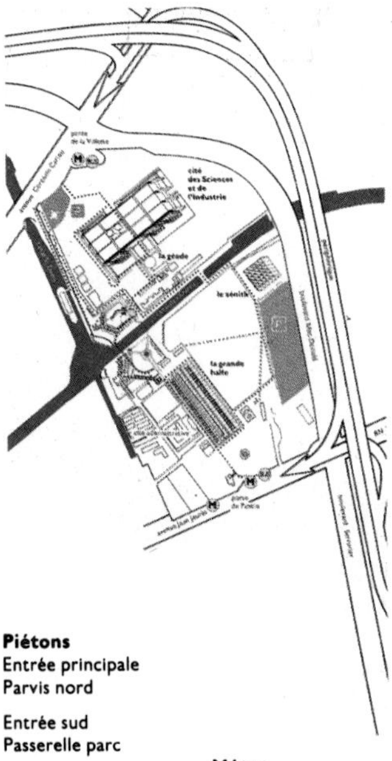

Piétons
Entrée principale
Parvis nord

Entrée sud
Passerelle parc

Véhicules tourisme
Boulevard Macdonald
Avenue Corentin Cariou

Autocars-taxis
Boulevard Macdonald

Gare des cars
Accès S1

Métro
Porte de la Villette
ligne n° 7 Mairie d'Ivry-Villejuif
Fort d'Aubervilliers

Autobus
150 – 152 – 250A – PC

Parking
Accès étage S2

explora
une exploration du monde des sciences des techniques et de l'industrie contemporaines.
L'aventure humaine individuelle et sociale, économique et culturelle est retracée dans quatre grands secteurs d'activité.

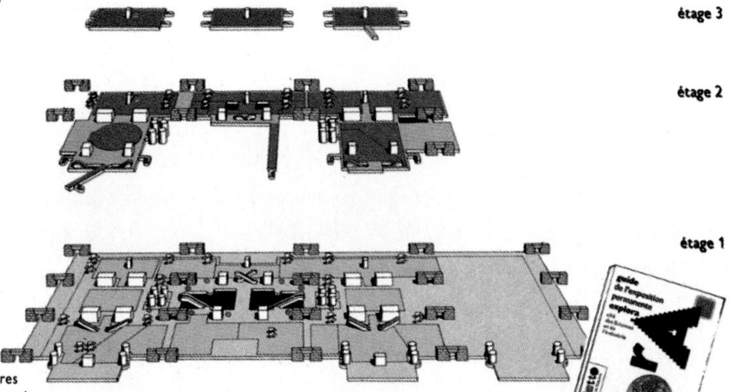

• panneaux index explora
• accueil des secteurs

l'aventure de la vie
(étages 1, 2, 3)
de la complexité des êtres vivants à celle des milieux de vie et des sociétés humaines, les questions posées aux sciences de la vie.

de la terre à l'univers
(étages 1, 2, 3)
un voyage dans l'espace, l'océan, et au centre de la terre : à la recherche de nouveaux savoirs, de ressources et de limites nouvelles.

langages et communication
(étages 1, 2)
des expériences sur les sons, les images, l'informatique, les comportements humains pour en découvrir toutes les facettes : scientifiques, techniques, culturelles, artistiques et historiques.

la matière et le travail de l'homme
(étages 1, 2, 3)
une grande enquête sur la nature profonde de la matière, les fonctionnements économiques, l'évolution des technologies, des nouveaux matériaux, de la robotique, de l'énergie ou des transports.

Le guide d'explora est en vente dans les boutiques de la cité

En mars 1986, le président de la République, François Mitterrand, a inauguré ce musée des sciences. L'architecture ultramoderne de la Villette est destinée à attirer les Parisiens et les touristes de toutes les parties du monde.

Beaubourg

Le Centre National d'Art et de Culture Georges Pompidou s'appelle d'habitude le Centre Pompidou ou, tout simplement, Beaubourg (il se trouve sur la place Beaubourg). L'architecture du Centre provoque des réactions violentes: les uns aiment son style ultramoderne; les autres trouvent qu'il ressemble à une *usine*. — factory

> «Beaubourg est transparent. La construction est en *verre* et en acier. Les 28 *poteaux* qui la soutiennent sont *remplis* d'eau; ils maintiennent fermement le bâtiment. Beaubourg *pèse* 15 000 tonnes. Les *tuyaux* sont de couleurs différentes et *chacun* joue son rôle: dans les bleus passe l'air, dans les jaunes les *fils* électriques, dans les verts *coule* l'eau, et les rouges servent au mouvement, comme les ascenseurs et les *escaliers*.»

glass
pillars / filled
weighs / pipes
each one
wiring / flows
here: escalators

From *Paris* (les petits bleus), Hachette Guides Bleus, 1984

Les programmes et les expositions du centre culturel ont pour sujet l'art, la musique et la littérature modernes.

La Défense

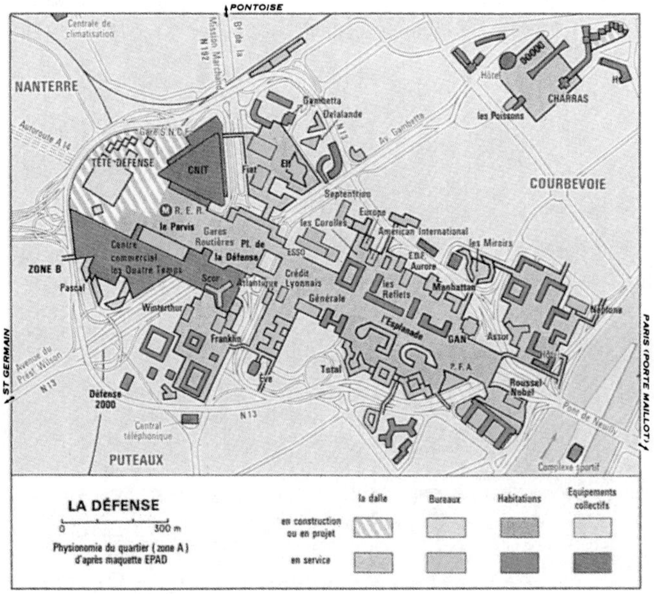

suburbs
business
above
pedestrians
company / moved in
apartment buildings / everything

Ce quartier ultramoderne se trouve dans la *banlieue* ouest de Paris. C'est un centre *d'affaires* et d'habitation qui a comme but de décongestionner le centre de Paris. La Défense a deux parties: la partie souterraine où on trouve les autoroutes, une gare, des parkings et le métro et *au-dessus,* la partie des *piétons* et des grandes tours. La plus haute tour a 45 étages (Fiat). La première *société* (Esso) *s'est installée* en 1964, et depuis ce temps-là, d'autres grandes sociétés ont établi leurs bureaux à la Défense (Mobil Oil, IBM, Fiat, des banques, etc.). Beaucoup des employés de ces sociétés habitent dans les *immeubles* construits très près de leur travail. Ils trouvent *tout ce dont* ils ont besoin dans ce quartier: grands magasins, boutiques, cinémas, théâtres, écoles.

Exercices de familiarisation

A. **Paris moderne.** One of your friends is particularly interested in modern architecture and tells you the kind of things he/she is interested in. For each statement, decide whether the person should go to **la Tour Eiffel,** to **la Défense,** to **Beaubourg,** or to **la Villette.**

1. I'm particularly interested in how you can separate pedestrian and automobile traffic.
2. I'd like to see an all-steel construction.

3. I'm particularly interested in scientific discoveries.
4. I'd like to see a building where all the pipes are visible from the outside.
5. I'm interested in seeing a structure that contains both work place and lodging.
6. Where can I go to find out about robots?
7. Where can I go to see a place that combines modern architecture, art, music, and literature?

B. **Où est-ce qu'ils sont?** Decide whether you are most likely to find the following people at **la Tour Eiffel, la Défense, Beaubourg,** or **la Villette.**

1. the president of a large corporation
2. a person doing research on sound
3. a person giving a lecture on modern art
4. a tourist who wants to have a good view of the city of Paris
5. students learning about important scientific discoveries
6. a person who is doing a survey on the effects of ultramodern living on the attitudes of people
7. a person who wants to learn about the latest trends in music

Prononciation: *The vowel u*

In French, the letter **u,** when not followed by another vowel or the consonants **m** or **n,** is always pronounced in the same fashion. To learn to make the sound represented by the letter **u,** first pronounce the letter **i** (remember to spread your lips in a smile). Then, keeping the interior of your mouth in the same tense position, move your lips forward as if to whistle.

Prononciation, The vowel **u:** Since this is one of the more difficult sounds for students to pronounce accurately, your tolerance level needs to be very high. It is unlikely that they will pronounce this sound consistently well right from the start. By now you have often corrected them, so little time needs to be spent on this segment. Only imitation and practice will eventually yield the desired results.

Pratique

C. Read each word aloud, being careful to pronounce the **u** sound with your lips as far forward as possible.

1. une
2. tu
3. fume
4. autobus
5. bureau
6. portugais
7. salut
8. vue
9. russe
10. musique
11. musée
12. sur
13. architecture
14. d'habitude

REPRISE

Recycling activity

D. Using the verbs in the drawing, describe what these people did yesterday.

MODÈLE: Je
J'ai quitté l'hôtel à 12h30, je suis allé au café . . .

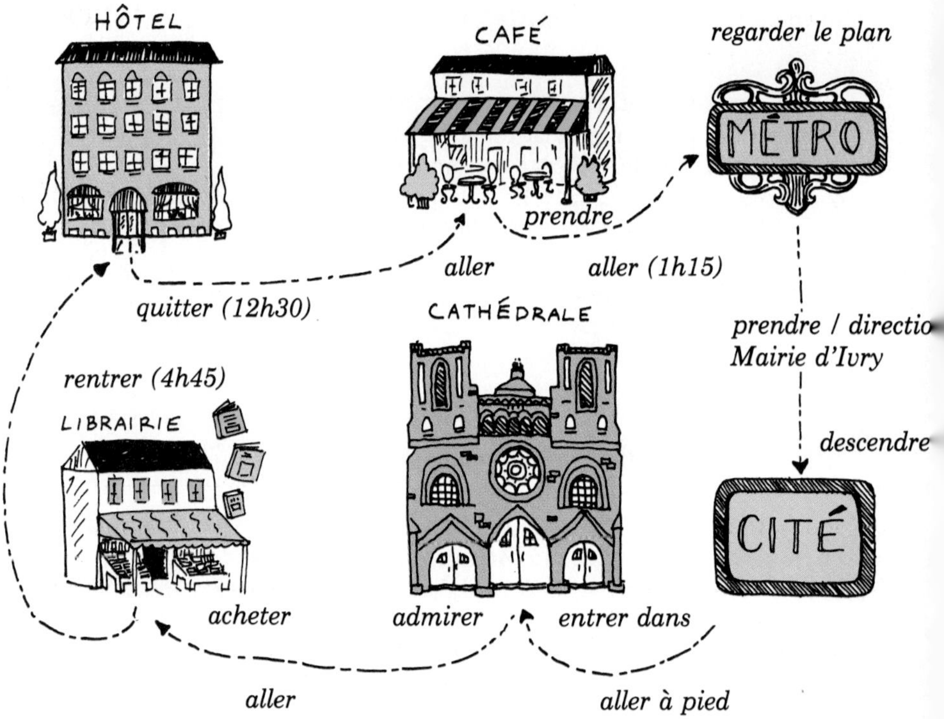

1. je
2. Jean-Jacques
3. ma sœur et moi, nous
4. mes amis

Ex. E: ⇄

E. **Échange.** Ask a classmate the following questions.

1. Est-ce que tu es allé(e) au cinéma le week-end dernier?
2. Est-ce que tu es allé(e) à Paris? Quand?
3. Est-ce que tu es allé(e) à la bibliothèque hier soir?
4. Est-ce que tu es arrivé(e) en classe avant ou après le professeur?
5. Est-ce que tu es rentré(e) hier après-midi avant ou après tes parents?

STRUCTURE

Expressions used to talk about actions in the past

D'abord, je suis allé au bureau de poste. **Ensuite,** j'ai fait une promenade dans le parc. **Enfin,** je suis rentré à la maison.

When talking about actions in the past, you will find the following expressions useful:

d'abord (premièrement)	*first*
ensuite (puis)	*then*
enfin	*finally*

These expressions are also useful when talking about future actions:

D'abord je vais aller au bureau de poste. **Ensuite,** je vais aller chez Monique. **Enfin,** nous espérons aller au cinéma.

Structure: These are lexical items rather than grammatical ones. The purpose of this **Structure** section is to lead students slowly but surely to the ability to form spoken paragraphs. These time indicators will be expanded upon throughout Unit 5. You may again wish to begin this presentation by enumerating the things you did. Then you can have students imitate your model before they go on to the exercises.

Suggestion: To make the idea of time transpositions clearer to students, you may wish to give them some examples in English before you give them the French.

Application

F. **Et qu'est-ce qu'il fait, Philippe?** Use the expressions in parentheses to tell what Philippe did at some point in the past.

1. Philippe a passé la journée à Paris. (samedi dernier)
2. Il est allé au café pour le petit déjeuner. (d'abord)
3. Il a visité la Tour Eiffel. (ensuite)
4. Il est allé à la Villette. (puis)
5. Il est rentré à la maison. (enfin)

Now tell what he is going to do at some point in the future.

6. Philippe va faire un voyage en Suisse. (le mois prochain)
7. Il va aller à Genève. (d'abord)
8. Il va visiter Lausanne. (ensuite)
9. Il va rentrer le 3 novembre. (enfin)

G. **D'abord. . . ensuite. . . enfin.** Describe the order of each set of three activities. Choose the verbs that are logical.

MODÈLE: nous / piscine / devoirs / cinéma
D'abord nous sommes allés à la piscine, ensuite nous avons fait les devoirs, et enfin nous sommes allés au cinéma.

1. ils / école / sandwich / télévision
2. je / bibliothèque / magasin / disque
3. nous / ville / jogging / radio
4. elle / petit déjeuner / métro / musée
5. il / devoirs / déjeuner / disques
6. elles / promenade / Coca / maison

H. **Le week-end dernier.** Invent excuses for why you didn't call your friend on Friday, Saturday, or Sunday. Use the appropriate time expressions and verbs of your choice. Suggested verbs: **aller, travailler, acheter, rentrer, rester, manger, étudier, parler, téléphoner.**

DÉBROUILLONS-NOUS !

Review of the Étape

I. **Un calendrier.** Look at Chantal's calendar for a week in September and answer the questions about her activities.

SEPTEMBRE

Lundi	8	
Mardi	9	chez le dentiste
Mercredi	10	librairie piscine cinema
Jeudi	11	théâtre
Vendredi	12	courses
Samedi	13	ville fête chez Paul
Dimanche	14	dîner en famille

MODÈLE: Qu'est-ce que Chantal a fait dimanche le 14 septembre?
Elle a eu un dîner en famille.

1. Qu'est-ce qu'elle a fait d'abord mercredi le 10 septembre? Et ensuite? Et enfin?
2. Qu'est-ce qu'elle a fait la veille *(day before)?*
3. Et le lendemain *(the next day)?*
4. Qu'est-ce qu'elle a fait pendant le week-end? Énumérez ses activités.
5. Qu'est-ce qu'elle a fait vendredi le 12?
6. Et le lendemain?

Written Work: See Workbook.

Lexique

Pour se débrouiller

Pour situer des actions dans le passé

un jour
lundi (mardi, etc.) dernier
lundi (mardi, etc.) matin, après-midi, soir
la semaine dernière
le mois dernier
l'année dernière
le lendemain
la semaine suivante
la veille

Pour énumérer une série d'actions

d'abord (premièrement)
ensuite (puis)
enfin

Vocabulaire général

Verbes

entrer
monter
rester
rentrer
retourner
tomber

Chapitre quinze

Qu'est-ce qu'on peut faire à Paris?

— *Tu veux sortir ce soir?*
— *Oui. Qu'est-ce qu'on peut faire à Paris?*

Première étape

Lecture: *Paris branché*

branché: current (up to date)

Prereading: Have students talk about the teen magazines they read, what is in them, why they read them. Also find out who the latest music celebrities are, what students think about them, and which performers they have seen or would like to see. Additional topic—television. When do they watch it, what do they watch, how do their parents feel about what they watch?

Lecture: You can divide this reading into two parts. Students should have one to two minutes to read each part silently. Then you can ask them to state the main ideas to demonstrate their basic comprehension. Because of the relatively large number of proper nouns in this **Lecture,** it is less important to work with vocabulary. Concentrate on the realia pieces and the exercises.

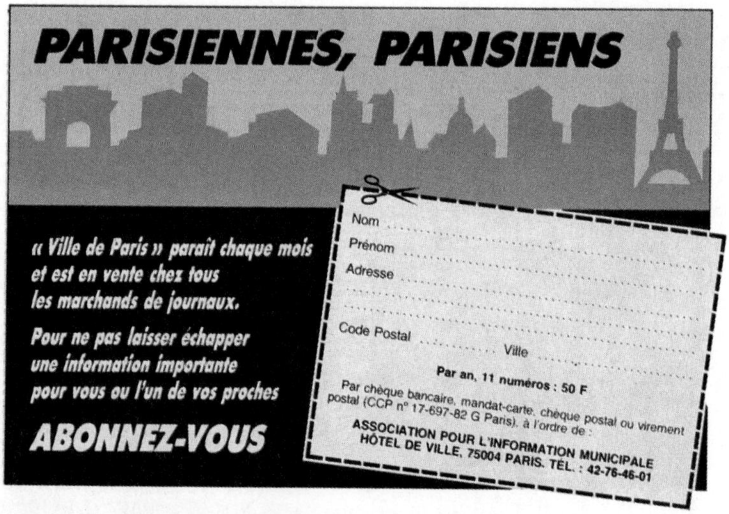

Radio, télévision, festivals, musées, cinémas, théâtres, à Paris c'est *l'embarras du choix.* Pour *se renseigner,* on peut consulter des magazines comme **Ville de Paris, Pariscope** ou **l'officiel des spectacles.** Ou bien, on peut aller à l'Office de Tourisme de Paris qui se trouve sur les Champs-Élysées.

l'embarras du choix: the difficulty of choosing
se renseigner: to inform oneself

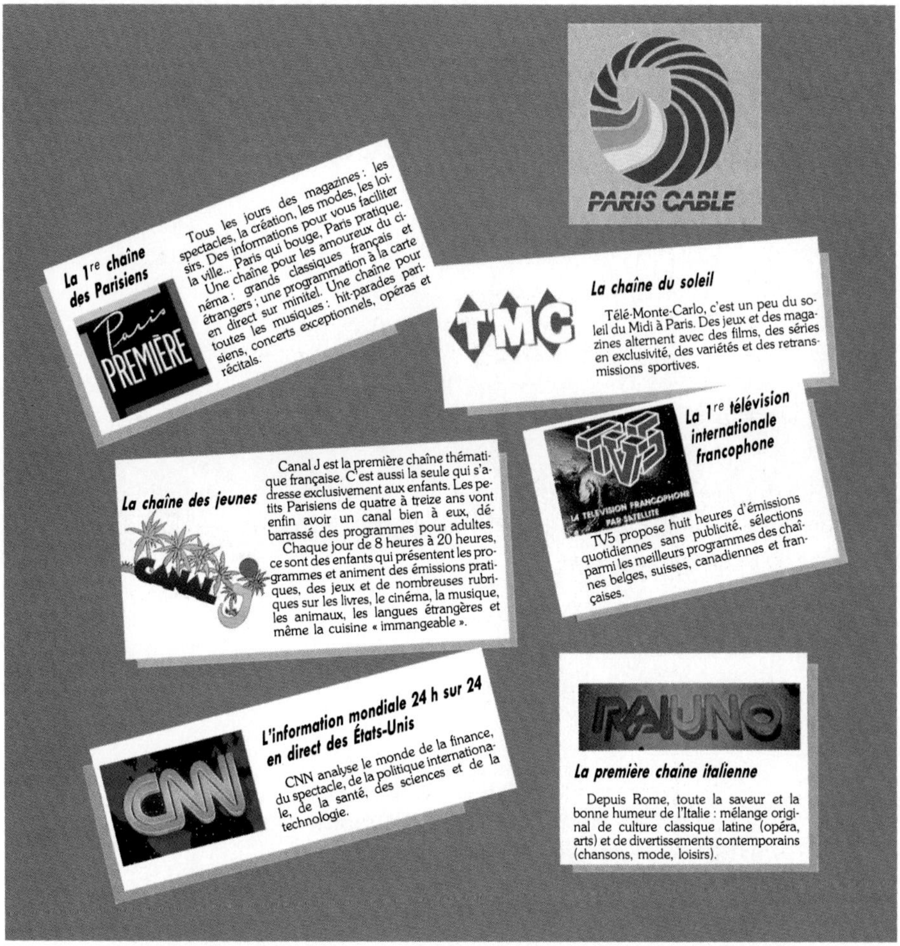

those

Pour *ceux* qui aiment le rock, les magazines des jeunes comme **Phosphore, Ok!** et **Salut!** annoncent les concerts. Par exemple, consultons le programme pour les mois de juin et de juillet.

Postreading: Have students write a series of announcements about concerts or TV programs that are to take place during the following week. They can also write an ad for a particular TV channel using the realia in the book as a guide.

Prince: les 15, 16 et 17 juin Paris Bercy. **U2:** le 15 juin Paris Zénith, le 4 juillet hippodrome de Vincennes. **Peter Gabriel:** du 5 au 8 juin Paris Bercy. **Genesis:** le 2 juin Paris Bercy, le 3 juin hippodrome de Vincennes. **Simply Red:** le 13 juin Paris Zénith. **Cameo:** le 8 juin Paris Zénith. **Iggy Pop:** le 9 juin Paris Zénith, le 17 juin Paris Élysée-Montmartre. **Hot Tuna:** le 13 juin Paris New Morning. **David Bowie:** le 3 juillet Paris La Courneuve. **Minimal Compact:** le 7 juin Paris Saint-Denis. **Stevie Wonder:** les 9, 10 et 11 juin Paris Bercy.

Adapted from *Phosphore,* No. 77, juin 1987

Exercices de familiarisation

A. **Paris Sélection.** You work at the **Office de Tourisme de Paris** and are explaining the advantages of having a **Paris Sélection** card. Answer the questions asked by your customers.

1. How much does the card cost and for how long is it valid?
2. What kinds of publications and documents will we receive as card holders?
3. How often do these publications appear?
4. What kinds of price reductions can we get for theater events and concerts?
5. Do we get any price reductions for museums?

B. **Télévision: Paris Câble.** While you're in Paris, you want to learn as much as you can. Television provides an opportunity to hear a lot of French and to find out a great deal about what is happening. Read the ads for the various channels available and, according to the interests stated, choose the channel you would turn to.

MODÈLE: I feel like watching a movie.
Paris Première

1. I want to learn something about fashions.
2. I want to watch a program from Belgium.
3. I feel like watching a children's program.
4. I want to keep up with the Parisian hit parade.
5. Which channel is most likely to give me the latest news about Paris?
6. I want to watch a sporting event.
7. I feel like watching a program with a variety of segments—games, movie clips, animals, etc.
8. I want to get some news from home.

C. **Allons au concert.** You and your friends are making plans to see a number of rock concerts in Paris. Consult the program for June and July in the reading and decide which performers you're going to see in which theaters. You can go to only one concert a day, so you'll have to make some choices.

Implementation, Ex. C: Note that students do not have to say the dates in this exercise. It is enough for them to recognize them.

MODÈLE: le 15 juin
Nous allons voir Prince au Bercy.

1. le 15 juin
2. le 2 juin
3. le 13 juin
4. le 3 juillet
5. le 7 juin
6. le 10 juin

REPRISE

D. **Un carnet.** *(A notebook.)* John kept a notebook of the monuments he and his family went to see. Based on his notes, explain where they went each day. If they saw several monuments on a given day, be sure to use the appropriate time indicators **(d'abord, ensuite, puis, enfin).** Use the verbs **aller** and **visiter.** Reminder: After **aller,** use **à, au, à la, à l', aux.**

MODÈLE: dimanche le 13 Invalides, Beaubourg, Tour Eiffel
D'abord, nous sommes allés aux Invalides; puis nous avons visité Beaubourg; enfin nous sommes allés à la Tour Eiffel.

lundi le 14	Notre-Dame, Tuileries, Panthéon, la Villette
mardi le 15	Arc de Triomphe, Louvre, jardin du Luxembourg
mercredi le 16	Beaubourg, Quartier Latin, Champs-Élysées
jeudi le 17	Sainte-Chapelle, Conciergerie, Tour Eiffel
vendredi le 18	Montmartre, Quartier Latin, Montparnasse

Structure: Since nothing in this **structure** is new, students have time to review and practice what they have already learned. You may want to begin again with a narrative of your own, this time mixing the **passé composé** with **avoir** and **être.** Then you can ask the class to imitate you by having each student contribute a sentence to the narrative.

STRUCTURE

The **passé composé** *with* **avoir** *and* **être**

Monique **est allée** en ville.	Monique *went* into town.
Elle **a acheté** des souvenirs.	She *bought* some souvenirs.
Ensuite elle **est rentrée** à l'hôtel.	Then *she went back* to the hotel.
Elle **a mangé** quelque chose.	She *ate* something.
Elle **est montée** dans sa chambre.	She *went up* to her room.
Elle **a regardé** la télévision.	She *watched* television.

As you have already seen, the **passé composé** is formed with either **avoir** or **être.** The correct choice depends on the main verb you want to conjugate in the past. The best way to learn the distinction is through repeated practice so that the appropriate auxiliary verb will automatically come to mind. However, two clues can help you to make a conscious decision until you become used to a particular verb combination:

1. By far the majority of French verbs are conjugated with the helping verb **avoir.** Your chances of selecting the right form are therefore very high if you use **avoir.**
2. The verbs conjugated with **être** tend to be verbs that move the subject physically from one place to another (**descendre, aller, arriver, rentrer, monter,** etc.).

Note: The verb **rester** *(to remain)* is also conjugated with **être,** although it does not show movement from one place to another.

Application

E. **Ce qu'ils ont fait hier.** *(What they did yesterday.)* Using the verbs indicated, explain what you, your friends and family did yesterday. Be careful to choose the right helping verb when forming the **passé composé.**

MODÈLE: frère / aller au cinéma
Mon frère est allé au cinéma.

1. Suzanne / aller en ville
2. père / faire du tennis
3. Paul et Véronique / rentrer à Paris
4. je / visiter le Sacré-Cœur
5. Françoise et Anne / écouter des disques
6. sœur / téléphoner à ses amis
7. je / retourner au travail
8. nous / aller au Louvre

F. **Pas aujourd'hui!** You and your friend have already spent a very hectic week in Paris and all you want to do now is relax at a café. Your friend, however, keeps suggesting that you do some more sightseeing. For every suggestion, say that you already did something similar last week. Use either **aller** or **visiter** depending on what makes most sense.

MODÈLE: Louvre / Beaubourg
Je voudrais aller au Louvre.
Pas aujourd'hui! Nous sommes déjà allé(e)s à Beaubourg la semaine dernière. ou:
Pas aujourd'hui! Nous avons déjà visité Beaubourg la semaine dernière.

1. place Charles-de-Gaulle / place de la Concorde
2. jardin des Tuileries / jardin du Luxembourg
3. Sainte-Chapelle / Notre-Dame
4. Tour Eiffel / Arc de Triomphe
5. Beaubourg / la Villette
6. boulevard Saint-Germain / boulevard Saint-Michel

DÉBROUILLONS-NOUS!

G. **Mon week-end.** Using the verbs you have already learned, describe to another student what you did last weekend. If you prefer, you can describe the weekend of a friend or a family member. Use both verbs conjugated with **avoir** and verbs conjugated with **être.** Remember the list of verbs that you know to this point that are conjugated with **être: aller, arriver, descendre, entrer, monter, rester, rentrer, retourner, tomber.**

Review of the **Étape**

Ex. G: ⇄

Written Work: See Workbook.

Deuxième étape

Prereading: Ask students what kinds of places they like to visit for fun. If you are not sure that they will focus on anything that will come up in the readings, you can ask them specific questions: **Est-ce que vous aimez faire des promenades? Est-ce que vous aimez les animaux?**

Lecture: This reading is divided into five short selections. Give students about thirty seconds to read each one silently and then ask them to identify the main ideas. Until now, students have worked with cognates and words of the same family. They are now ready to isolate the key words in each reading that are essential to the understanding of the text. For specific key words, see Teaching Guide.

Lecture: *Les distractions*

Moi, j'aime les plantes et les animaux...

Le jardin des plantes

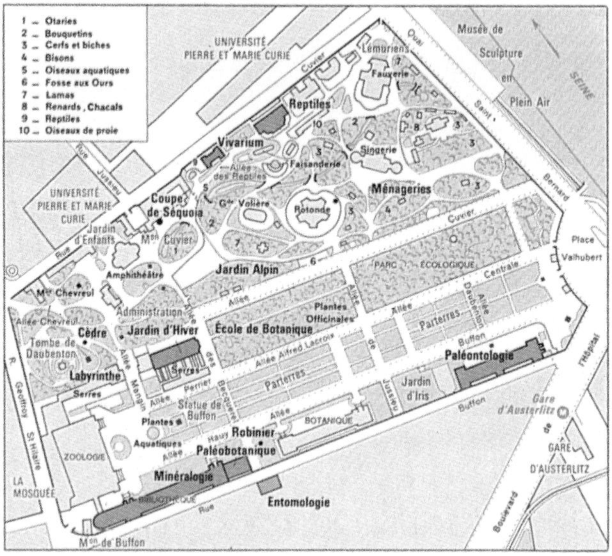

Métro: Austerlitz
Ouvert: de 9h à 17h

Au jardin des plantes, tu peux voir une grande variété de plantes et d'animaux. Il y a des plantes tropicales et désertiques, *aussi bien que* la flore de montagne et des régions polaires. Tu peux aussi voir de grands reptiles, des *oiseaux* et des animaux *sauvages.*

as well as
birds
wild

Jardin des Plantes (Muséum National d'Histoire Naturelle), 57, rue Cuvier, 43 36 54 26, Mº Jussieu ou Austerlitz. Ouvert t.l.j. sans exception de 7h15 (été) ou 8h (hiver) à la nuit. — **Ménagerie-Vivarium.** Ouvert de 9h à 17h (hiver) ou 18h (été). Rens. : 43.36.19.09. Ent. 20 F, réd. 10 F, scol. 5 F. **Serres Tropicales.** Ouvert de 13h30 à 17h sauf le mardi. Ent. 6,50 F. Tarif réduit 4,50 F. Groupes scolaires 2,20 F. **Ecole de Botanique.** Ouvert de 8h à 11h45 et de 13h30 à 17h sauf sam., dim. et j. fériés. Ent. libre.

Le zoo de Vincennes

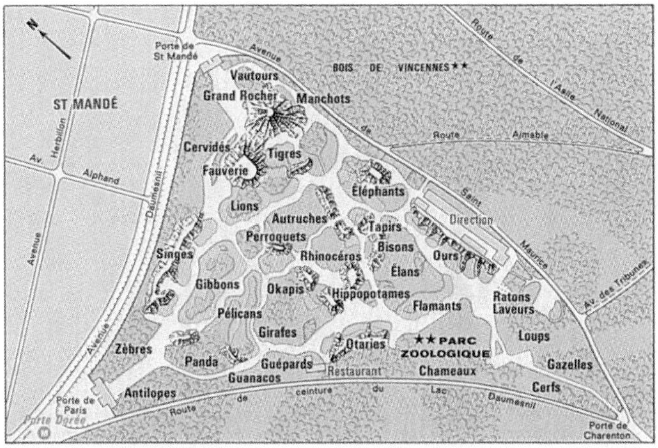

Métro: Porte-Dorée

Ouvert: de 9h à 17h30

Dans ce grand parc zoologique, tu peux voir 600 *mammifères* et 700 oiseaux. C'est une promenade agréable. *N'oublie pas* d'apporter ton appareil-photo!

mammals
Don't forget

Moi, j'aime faire des promenades. . .

Le Bois de Boulogne

À part tous les jardins publics que tu trouves dans la ville de Paris, tu peux aussi aller au Bois de Boulogne. Cette forêt a 95 kilomètres d'*allées,* deux lacs, des restaurants, des kiosques et des chalets. Tu peux y passer des journées très agréables.

Besides
country lane (lined with trees)

Postreading: Have students make a list of key words they associate with a topic of their choice. They will probably have to search for some words in the dictionary. This would therefore be a good time to have them learn how to use a dictionary effectively (e.g., cross-reference to check the accuracy of the word). Point out to them that they should be looking for nouns, adjectives, and verbs. You may wish to suggest some topics for them: **les voyages, l'école, les vacances, le travail, l'argent, la maison.** This exercise will help them to build their vocabulary, particularly if you ask them to share their findings with the class.

Moi, j'aime faire des promenades sur la Seine. . .

Les bateaux-mouches

way / to relax / legs

Tu peux prendre un bateau du Pont d'Alma, du Pont d'Iéna, du Square du Vert Galant ou du Quai de Montebello. Une promenade sur la Seine est une *façon* agréable de *te détendre* quand tes *jambes* sont fatiguées et quand tu désires avoir une vue différente de la ville de Paris.

HORAIRE

LEGENDE (*?) = se renseigner check up peut être annulé may be cancelled selon temps et saison subject to weather conditions

CONDITIONS MODIFIABLES - SE RENSEIGNER - CHECK UP
LOCATION 225 96 10 - 359 30 30 - 225 22 55 — TELEX 280898 NAVITOUR

DÉPART																							
	10h	10h30	11h	11h30	12h	13h30	14h	14h30	15h	15h30	16 h	16h30	17h	17h30	18h	18h30	19h	20h	20h30	21h	21h30	22h	22h30	23h
		(*?)		(*?)		(*?)								(*?)	(*?)	(*?)	(*?)	(*?)				(*?)	(*?)	(*?)
	20 F	20 F	20 F	20 F	20 F	20 F	20 F	20 F	20 F	20 F	20 F	20 F	20 F	20 F	20 F	20 F	20 F	25 F	25 F	25 F	25 F	25 F	25 F	25 F
DURÉE	1h15	1h15	1h15	1h15	1h15	1h15	1h15	1h15	1h15	1h15	1h15	1h15	1h15	1h15	1h15	1h15	1h15	1h15	1h15	1h15	1h15	1h15	1h15	1h15

Moi, j'aime les choses extraordinaires. . .

Les catacombes

subterranean / gravesite / several million / arranged / skulls / bones / frighten

Les galeries *souterraines* des catacombes sont des *ossuaires* où *plusieurs millions* de squelettes sont *rangés* contre les murs. Des *têtes de morts* et des *os* constituent une décoration macabre garantie de *faire peur* aux plus courageux!

Adapted from *Paris* (les petits bleus), Hachette Guides Bleus, 1984

Exercices de familiarisation

A. **Des associations.** In this exercise you have two columns of words. Column **A** contains the names of the places in Paris from the reading. Column **B** contains words that you can associate with these places. Match the words in each column.

A	B
le jardin des plantes	des os
le zoo de Vincennes	des lacs
le Bois de Boulogne	la flore tropicale
les catacombes	des mammifères
	des têtes de morts
	des serpents
	des chalets
	des galeries souterraines
	des oiseaux

B. **Des traits caractéristiques.** *(Character traits.)* Once you find out some character traits about each of the following people, suggest an appropriate activity for each person.

MODÈLE: J'aime avoir peur.
Il faut visiter les catacombes.

1. Nathalie est poète et aime contempler la nature.
2. Jean adore prendre des photos d'animaux.
3. Mes parents n'aiment pas aller à pied.
4. Nous étudions la botanique à l'école.
5. Jean-Paul n'aime pas les choses ordinaires.

Prononciation: *The combinations* ***ai*** *and* ***au***

The combinations **ai** and **au** are pronounced as single vowel sounds in French. The letters **ai** sound like the *ai* in the English word *wait* if they are the final sound of the word. However, if they are followed by a consonant sound (other than final **m** or **n**), they are pronounced like the *e* in the English word *melt.* The combination **au** is always pronounced like the *o* in the English word *hope.*

Pratique

C. Read each pair aloud, being careful to differentiate between the two sounds of **ai.**

1. j'ai, j'aime
2. français, française
3. anglais, anglaise
4. plaît, maître

D. Read each word aloud, being careful to pronounce the **au** combination as a single sound.

1. au
2. aussi
3. auto
4. autobus
5. de Gaulle
6. gauche
7. aujourd'hui

REPRISE

Recycling activity

Ex. E: ⇄

E. **Échange.** Ask a classmate questions about the last vacation he/she took. Your classmate will answer.

1. où / aller
2. avec qui / aller
3. comment / voyager
4. qu'est-ce que / faire
5. qu'est-ce que / acheter
6. où / manger
7. combien de temps / rester
8. quand / rentrer

F. **Confusion.** You're a detective who has been hired to follow someone. Although you've kept a log of the person's activities, when you go to report to the person who hired you, you discover that the pages have fallen out of your notebook and that the activities are all out of order. Put the following facts in the correct order.

Puis, il a fait une promenade sur le boulevard Saint-Michel.
Il a passé le week-end dernier à Paris.
Il est resté à l'hôtel toute la journée.
Ensuite il est allé au cinéma.
Samedi il est allé à l'hôtel.
Enfin il est rentré à l'hôtel.
Le lendemain, il a quitté l'hôtel et il est allé au Musée d'Orsay.

L'OFFICE DE TOURISME DE PARIS

Mairie de Paris
Chambre de Commerce
et d'Industrie de Paris

STRUCTURE

Structure: This review is intended to contrast past, present, and future time.

Past, present, and future time

Passé: Hier, je **suis allé** au Bois de Boulogne.
Présent: Aujourd'hui, je **vais** chez ma grand-mère.
Futur: Demain, je **vais aller** à la piscine.

Passé: Ce matin, il **a fait** une promenade.
Présent: Maintenant, il **fait** ses devoirs.
Futur: Plus tard, il **a l'intention de jouer** au football.

Passé: L'année dernière, nous **sommes allés** à Paris.
Présent: Cette année, nous **restons** à la maison.
Futur: L'année prochaine, nous **espérons aller** à Québec.

In this chapter, you have learned how to form the **passé composé** so that you can describe events in the past. You have also learned certain expressions that help situate events in the past, present, and future. Now it is important to review the verb structures that allow you to express yourself in past, present, and future time.

Present time: present tense

—Qu'est-ce que **tu fais?**
—**Je cherche** mes clés.

Past time: passé composé conjugated with the helping verbs **avoir** or **être**

—Qu'est-ce que **tu as fait** hier?
—**J'ai mangé** au restaurant et **je suis allé** au cinéma.

Future time: aller + infinitive
vouloir + infinitive
je voudrais + infinitive
avoir l'intention de + infinitive
espérer + infinitive

—Qu'est-ce que vous **allez faire** pendant les vacances?
—Moi, je **vais aller** en Californie.
—Et moi, je **voudrais visiter** New York.
—Paul **a l'intention de rester** à la maison.
—Simone **veut aller** à la plage.
—Moi, j'**espère retourner** à Genève.

Application

G. Replace the expression in italics with the expressions in parentheses and make all necessary changes.

1. *Demain* je vais étudier. (hier / aujourd'hui)
2. *Ce matin* il a pris le métro. (demain / maintenant)
3. *Cette année* nous étudions le français. (l'année dernière / l'année prochaine)
4. *Le mois dernier* ils ont visité la France. (ce mois / le mois prochain)
5. *Aujourd'hui,* elle fait les devoirs. (hier / demain)
6. *Hier soir,* Jean est allé au cinéma. (ce soir / la semaine prochaine)

H. **Explications.** For each set of drawings, explain what the people do normally **(d'habitude),** what they did in the past, and what they'll do in the future. Begin each explanation with **D'habitude. . . ,** continue it with **mais. . . ,** and finish it with **et. . . .**

d'habitude

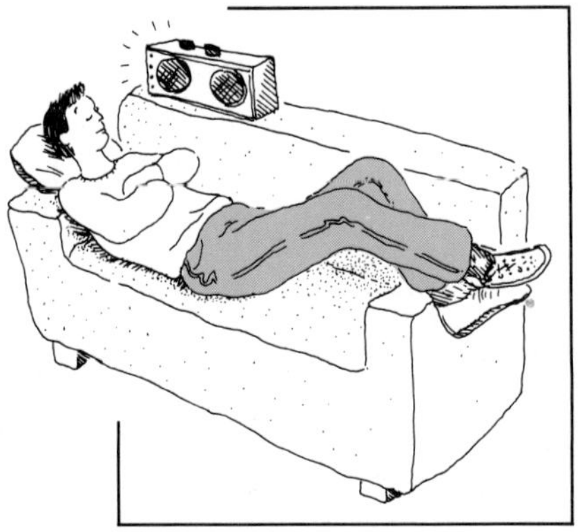

l'année dernière

l'année prochaine

MODÈLE: Qu'est-ce que tu fais pendant les vacances?
D'habitude je vais à la plage, mais l'année dernière je suis resté à la maison et l'année prochaine j'ai l'intention d'aller à Paris.

1. Qu'est-ce que vous faites le week-end?

d'habitude

le week-end dernier

le week-end prochain

2. À quel hôtel est-ce qu'elle descend quand elle est à Paris?

d'habitude

le mois dernier

le mois prochain

3. Qu'est-ce qu'elles mangent quand elles sont à l'école?

d'habitude

hier

demain

4. Qu'est-ce que tu fais le samedi soir?

d'habitude

samedi dernier

samedi prochain

Ex. I: ⇄

I. **Une interview.** You are being interviewed by a reporter from your school newspaper about your many travels. Answer the questions using the cues given in parentheses.

MODÈLES: Est-ce que vous espérez aller à Paris cette année? (non, l'année prochaine)
Non, je vais aller à Paris l'année prochaine.

Est-ce que vous avez l'intention d'aller à Rome? (non, l'année dernière)
Non, je suis allé(e) à Rome l'année dernière.

1. Est-ce que vous avez l'intention d'aller en vacances demain? (non, aujourd'hui)
2. Est-ce que vous avez déjà visité la France? (non, le mois prochain)
3. Est-ce que vous espérez aller à Madrid? (non, l'année dernière)
4. Est-ce que vous avez l'intention de visiter Paris? (oui, l'année prochaine)
5. Est-ce que vous avez l'intention d'aller à la Comédie-Française? (non, l'année dernière)
6. Est-ce que vous allez monter sur la Tour Eiffel? (non, la dernière fois)

DÉBROUILLONS-NOUS!

Review of the **Étape**

Ex. J: ⇄

J. **Échange.** Using the indicated verbs, ask questions to obtain the required information. When asking questions about the future, be sure to use some of the new expressions you have learned **(avoir l'intention de, espérer, aller,** and **vouloir + infinitive).**

1. **étudier:** Find out where your friend usually studies; whether he/she studied there last night; whether he/she is planning to study there tonight.

2. **aller au cinéma:** Find out if your friend likes going to the movies; if he/she went to the movies last week; whether he/she is going to the movies next week.

Suggestion, Map: You may wish to do a quick comprehension exercise using the information provided in this map of the monuments. For example, ask students to identify the main features of each of the sites.

Written Work: See Workbook.

3. **voyager:** Find out if your friend travels a lot; if he/she traveled last year and where he/she went; whether he/she hopes to travel next year and where he/she intends to go.

4. **aller/prendre:** Find out how your friend usually gets to school; if he/she got to school the same way this morning; whether he/she will get to school the same way next year.

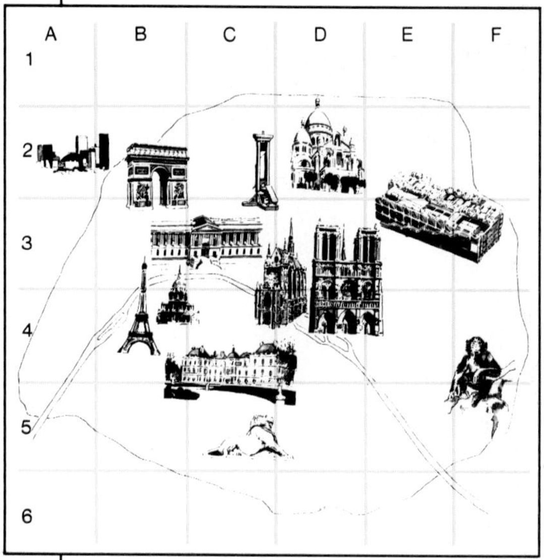

Monuments

La Tour Eiffel
B4 *métro Trocadéro*
→ 320,75 mètres

Les Invalides
C4 *métro Latour-Maubourg*
→ L'Hôtel des Invalides et ses musées
→ L'Église et le tombeau de Napoléon

L'Arc de Triomphe de l'Étoile
B3 *métro Ch. de Gaulle -Étoile*
→ Le tombeau du Soldat Inconnu
→ La vue !...

Musées

Centre Pompidou, *métro Châtelet-Halles, Hôtel de Ville, Rambuteau.*
E3 voir page 40

Louvre
D4 *métro Louvre* ou *Palais Royal*
→ Peintures, scupltures, dessins, etc.

Grévin
D3 *métro Richelieu-Drouot*
→ Personnages de cire : Histoire de France

Curiosités

Le C.N.I.T. et la Défense
A2 *métro La Défense RER*
→ Paris le plus moderne

Le Zoo de Vincennes
F5 *métro Porte Dorée*
→ 1 500 animaux vus chaque année par 1 500 000 visiteurs

Les Catacombes
C5 *métro Denfert Rochereau*
→ Paris le plus ancien : 6 millions de morts sous 10 millions de vivants

Parc du Luxembourg
D4 *métro Luxembourg*
→ bassins, marionnettes
→ tennis, jogging

Églises

Notre Dame de Paris
D4 *métro Cité*
→ Les tours, la crypte

La basilique du Sacré-Cœur
D2, *métro Anvers*
→ La vue panoramique

La Sainte Chapelle
D4 *métro Cité*
→ Les vitraux

Lexique

Pour se débrouiller

Pour exprimer des actions dans le futur

aller + infinitive
avoir l'intention de + infinitive
espérer + infinitive
vouloir + infinitive
je voudrais + infinitive

Mise au point

Lecture: *Le Tout-Paris acclame Prince*

Lecture: Give students a few seconds to look over the text. No words have been glossed, Then move on to Ex. A.

As you read this short announcement about the appearance of Prince in Paris, focus on the key words that indicate how the Parisians feel about the singer.

Le Tout-Paris acclame Prince

Le Tout-Paris (dont Catherine Deneuve, Stéphanie, Valérie Kaprisky, Jean-Louis Aubert, Axel Bauer, Jack Lang...), s'était déplacé pour assister à ce fameux concert de Prince au Zénith. C'est dans une ambiance délirante (et c'est peu dire !) et sous un flot de lumières irréelles, que l'idole a mis en moins de deux heures toute la capitale à ses pieds prouvant, malgré les controverses qu'il provoque, qu'il est bel et bien une superstar... au Zénith de sa carrière !

A. **Exercice de compréhension.** Read the short magazine announcement about Prince and answer the questions.

1. What do you think is meant by "le Tout-Paris"?
2. What words can you find in the text that indicate how Paris feels about Prince?
3. In which concert hall did Prince appear?
4. What play on words can you find based on the name of the concert hall?

REPRISE

Recycling Activity
Ex. B: ⇄

B. **Échange.** Ask a classmate the following questions. He/she will answer them.

1. Qu'est-ce que tu as fait hier soir? Qu'est-ce que tu vas faire ce soir?
2. Qu'est-ce que tu fais d'habitude le week-end? Qu'est-ce que tu as fait le week-end dernier?
3. Que font tes parents d'habitude le week-end? Qu'est-ce qu'ils ont fait le week-end dernier?
4. Est-ce que tu passes beaucoup de temps avec ta famille? Qu'est-ce que vous faites ensemble?
5. Qu'est-ce que tu as l'intention de faire après l'école secondaire?

RÉVISION

In this Révision you will review:

— places in Paris;
— the **passé composé** with **avoir** (including irregular past participles);
— the **passé composé** with **être;**
— verbs that are conjugated with **être;**
— expressions to talk about actions in the past.

The passé composé with *avoir*

j'**ai** étudié	nous **avons** étudié
tu **as** étudié	vous **avez** étudié
il, elle, on **a** étudié	ils, elles **ont** étudié

The passé composé with *avoir* (irregular past participles)

avoir	**eu**
être	**été**
faire	**fait**
prendre	**pris**
apprendre	**appris**
comprendre	**compris**

The passé composé with *être*

je **suis** rentré (rentrée)	nous **sommes** rentrés (rentrées)
tu **es** rentré (rentrée)	vous **êtes** rentré (rentrée, rentrés, rentrées)
il **est** rentré	ils **sont** rentrés
elle **est** rentrée	elles **sont** rentrées
on **est** rentré	

Verbs conjugated with *être*

aller
arriver
descendre (descendu)
entrer
monter
rester
rentrer
retourner
tomber

C. **I'm interested in . . .** Various friends and members of your family are going to visit Paris. Before leaving they tell you what they're interested in and ask your advice about what sights they could visit. Give them information using what you've learned in this unit. Ex. C: O

MODÈLE: I'm studying gothic art at the university.
You should visit Notre-Dame cathedral.

1. I want to find out what the French are doing in the field of science and technology.
2. I'd like to take some aerial photographs of Paris.
3. Are there any museums you can recommend?
4. I'd like to see the modern aspects of Paris. Which sights do you recommend?
5. I'm most interested in the historic Paris. What should I see?
6. Where would I go to find out more about Napoleon?
7. I would like to spend some of my time watching people go by. Where would I go to do this?

D. **La ronde de questions.** Using one of the suggested cues, each student in the group asks four questions. Each question should use a different pronoun—**tu, vous, il/elle,** or **ils/elles.** The other members of the group respond according to what they know or hear. Use the **passé composé** throughout the exercise.

MODÈLE: déjà manger

PAUL: *Sylvie, est-ce que tu as déjà mangé?*
SYLVIE: *Oui, j'ai déjà mangé.*
PAUL: *Marie et Éric, est-ce que vous avez déjà mangé?*
MARIE ET ÉRIC: *Oui, nous avons déjà mangé.*
PAUL: *Marie, est-ce que Sylvie a déjà mangé?*
MARIE: *Oui, Sylvie a déjà mangé.*
PAUL: *Sylvie, est-ce que Marie et Éric ont déjà mangé?*
SYLVIE: *Oui, ils ont déjà mangé.*

1. aller en ville
2. prendre le métro
3. rester à la maison le week-end dernier
4. avoir un accident
5. arriver en classe avant ou après le professeur

Suggestion: Have students look at the list of time indicators and point out the ones they can't remember. These are the ones that should then be reinforced.

Expressions to talk about actions in the past

hier (matin, après-midi, soir)
dernier (le weekend dernier, la semaine dernière, etc.)
pendant (une heure, deux jours, six ans, etc.)
il y a (une heure, trois mois, cinq ans, etc.)
d'abord (premièrement)
ensuite (puis)
enfin

Ex. E: ○

E. **Mon itinéraire.** Tell your friends what you did during your week in Paris. Use time expressions to be precise about when you did what. Here is a list of monuments you visited and things you did.

aller à l'hôtel / aller au café / le Centre Beaubourg / la Tour Eiffel / le jardin du Luxembourg / le boulevard Saint-Michel / prendre le bateau-mouche / Notre-Dame / acheter des souvenirs / le Panthéon / le Bois de Boulogne / les catacombes / la Défense / le Musée d'Orsay

MODÈLE: *Lundi matin, nous sommes allés au centre Beaubourg. Ensuite, nous avons acheté des souvenirs.* Etc.

Point d'arrivée

Ex. F: ○

F. **La semaine prochaine.** Explain to your classmates what you're going to do next week and in what order. They will ask you questions for clarification. Don't forget to use a variety of verbs to talk about the future and be sure to use appropriate time indicators.

Ex. G: ⇄

G. **Ton voyage à Paris.** Interview your classmate to find out what he/she did during his/her trip to Paris. Find out about what places he/she visited, what he/she did, etc. When you're done, report back to the class.

Ex. H: ○

H. **Notre itinéraire.** You and several classmates can spend only two days in Paris. Decide what you're going to do. When you have made your plans, share them with the rest of the class. Suggestions: What time do you leave the hotel in the morning? What monuments are you going to visit and in what order? When and where are you going to eat? What time do you get back to the hotel in the evening?

I. **Je suis le guide.** A French exchange student has just arrived in your town. Tell the person about your town, pointing out major attractions, places to visit, and the like. The exchange student will ask you questions for additional information.

Ex. I: ⇄

Suggestion: This paragraph about Claire Maurant summarizes what is known about her and expresses her feelings about her stay in Paris. Have students say what they know. **Elle est Alsacienne. Elle a passé les vacances avec son cousin à Paris. C'est son premier voyage à Paris. Claire et son cousin ont visité les monuments de Paris, ils sont allés au théâtre.** Have them enumerate other things they did according to the sights described in the unit. **Claire a beaucoup aimé Paris, mais elle est contente de rentrer en Alsace.** This summary will draw together what students have learned about Paris and obliges them to review the past tense. If you wish, you can also have them use some time indicators (**d'abord, ensuite, enfin**).

Written Work: See Workbook.

Je suis alsacienne et j'ai fait mon premier voyage à Paris cette année. J'ai un cousin qui est parisien et j'ai passé mes vacances chez sa famille. J'ai beaucoup aimé Paris. Nous avons visité des musées et des monuments, nous avons fait des promenades à pied, en voiture et en bateau-mouche sur la Seine. Le soir, nous sommes allés au théâtre et au cinéma. Mes trois semaines à Paris ont été formidables mais j'ai aussi été très contente de rentrer en Alsace!

Claire Maurant

LEGINOUX
06000 NICE
TÉL.: 93.83.00.12.
M.I.N. BOX N°63

Unité six

Planning Strategy: See Workbook.

Audio Tape and/or Video: See Teaching Guide.

Portrait: Ask students to give name of the teenager from Quebec and where he lives. Have them guess the color of his hair and eyes and invent some autobiographical details for him: family members, age, what type of lodging the family lives in, if he has a girlfriend, what's in his room, etc.

On fait les courses

Objectives

In this unit, you will learn:

to ask for information and make purchases in stores;
to know where to go to make various kinds of purchases;
to indicate quantities;
to understand information presented by salespeople;
to read ads.

Jean Hébert
Trois Rivières
Québec, Canada

Chapitre seize

Qu'est-ce qu'on va manger?

— *Regarde toutes ces bonnes choses!*
— *J'ai faim, moi! Qu'est-ce qu'on va manger ce soir?*

Première étape

Point de départ:

À la boulangerie-pâtisserie

Transparency, Note Culturelle: breads and pastries

Suggestion, Point de départ: You can present this short narrative in one of two ways: (1) Introduce students to the new vocabulary using the transparency of breads and pastries, read the text for them, and then have them read the text out loud. (2) Students have books closed while you tell them about Mme Thibaudet's trip to the **boulangerie-pâtisserie.** As you narrate, use the transparency to illustrate new vocabulary. *Note:* It's not necessary for students to learn all the vocabulary for the food items in this unit. For example, if they don't eat pork, they should recognize the words to avoid ordering it. But they are less likely to need it for production. When you test vocabulary, it should be open-ended enough so that students can work with their particular favorite foods.

Ce matin, Mme Thibaudet est allée en ville **faire ses courses.** D'abord elle est allée à la boulangerie. Elle a acheté[1] du **pain**—une baguette et un pain de campagne. Elle a aussi acheté trois croissants, trois pains au chocolat et six petits pains.

do her shopping
bread

Ensuite, elle a traversé la rue pour aller à la pâtisserie. Là elle a hésité: est-ce qu'il **vaut mieux** acheter une tarte, des tartelettes ou des pâtisseries?[2] Ses enfants adorent les tartes aux pommes et les tartes aux fraises. Son mari préfère les pâtisseries comme les religieuses, les éclairs et les mille-feuilles. Et elle? Elle préfère les tartelettes au citron.

is better

Enfin elle a pris sa décision. Elle a acheté une tarte, quelques pâtisseries et deux tartelettes. Et elle a aussi commandé un gâteau au chocolat pour l'**anniversaire** de son fils François.

birthday

[1]**Acheter** is conjugated like all other **-er** verbs, but an **accent grave** is added to some of the forms. In the present tense, the verb **acheter** is conjugated as follows: **j'achète; tu achètes; il, elle, on achète; nous achetons; vous achetez; ils, elles achètent.**

[2]The word **pâtisserie** may refer to either a pastry shop or the pastries made and sold there.

Supplementary vocabulary, Boulangerie: une ficelle, un pain de mie

Pâtisserie: un baba au rhum, un gâteau aux amandes, un gâteau mocca, des petits-fours, une tarte aux cerises, une tarte aux abricots

Note Culturelle

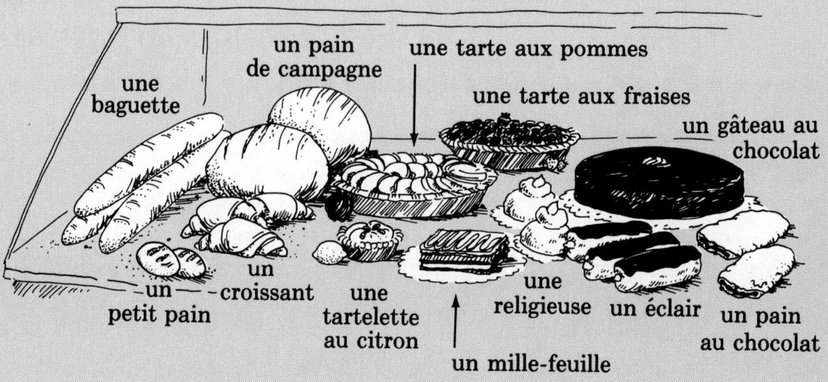

In France, bakery shops often specialize either in bread **(une boulangerie)** or in pastry **(une pâtisserie).** Many stores combine both **(une boulangerie-pâtisserie).** Since the French are known for their excellent bread and pastries, several of these shops are usually found in every neighborhood. Unlike the **briocherie,** pastry shops are not fast-food places, although you can, of course, go in to buy one pastry and eat it as you're strolling along. The **briocherie** is a sidewalk counter with a microwave oven **(four à micro-ondes)** and a limited choice of baked goods.

Bakery shops are usually open from 7 or 8 A.M. until 1 P.M. and then again in the afternoon from 4 P.M. until 7 P.M. They are often closed on Monday. Most bread is bought fresh every morning.

Vocabulary activities

À vous!

A. **Une baguette, s'il vous plaît.** Imagine that you're at a **boulangerie-pâtisserie** and ask for each item in the picture.

MODÈLE:
Une baguette, s'il vous plaît.

1.

2.

3.

4.

5.

6.

7.

8.

9.

B. **C'est combien?** Indicate how much you pay for each item in Exercise A.

MODÈLE: *Une baguette: deux francs cinquante.*[3]

C. **À la boulangerie-pâtisserie.** Use the cues to role play making purchases with one of your classmates. One of you is the customer, the other is the shopkeeper.

MODÈLES: 1 pain de campagne / 2F50
—Vous désirez?
—Je voudrais un pain de campagne. C'est combien?
—Un pain de campagne, c'est deux francs cinquante.

6 petits pains / 0,50 la pièce
—Vous désirez?
—Je voudrais six petits pains. C'est combien?
—Les petits pains, c'est cinquante centimes la pièce.

1. 3 mille-feuilles / 8F la pièce
2. 1 baguette / 2F30
3. 1 gâteau au chocolat / 49F
4. 5 éclairs / 6F50 la pièce
5. 1 tarte aux fraises / 70F
6. 3 religieuses / 7F50 la pièce

Ex. C: ⇄

Le savez-vous?

In France, the crusty French bread is eaten
a) only at breakfast
b) only at lunch as part of sandwiches
c) only at dinner
d) with every meal

réponse

Suggestion, Ex. C: Do one or two items with the class first before dividing students into pairs.

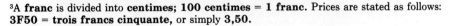

[3]A **franc** is divided into **centimes; 100 centimes = 1 franc.** Prices are stated as follows: **3F50 = trois francs cinquante,** or simply **3,50.**

Suggestion, quel: Begin by asking students questions using **quel: Quelle musique préférez-vous? Quel sport aimez-vous mieux, le baseball ou le football? Quel jour de la semaine sommes-nous aujourd'hui? Quelle est la date aujourd'hui?** Once students have heard the structure several times, write the forms of **quel** on the board along with one of the questions. Point out the construction **quel** + noun. Then use a similar procedure for **quel** + **être** + noun.

→ d

STRUCTURE

The interrogative expression **quel**

—**Quelles** pâtisseries est-ce que tu vas acheter?	*What (which)* pastries are you going to buy?
—Les éclairs et les religieuses.	

Quel, quelle, quels, quelles *(which, what)* are adjectives that are used in questions that ask someone to identify something **(Quel livre? Le livre de français.** *Which book? The French book.*). Because **quel** is an adjective, it must agree in gender and number with the noun it modifies. However, the pronunciation stays the same no matter how you spell it.

Quel can be used with both things and people, and it usually occurs in two types of questions:

1. Immediately before a noun (**quel** + noun):

Quelle pâtisserie?	*What* pastry?
Quel livre est-ce que tu cherches?	*What* book are you looking for?
Quels sports est-ce que tu aimes?	*What* sports do you like?
Quelles jeunes filles est-ce que tu as invitées?	*What* girls did you invite?

Note that when **quel** and the noun are followed by a **passé composé,** the past participle of the verb must agree in gender and number with the noun.

Quelle pâtisserie est-ce que tu as mangé**e**?
Quels disques as-tu acheté**s**?

2. Separated from the noun by the verb **être** (**quel** + **être** + noun):

Quelle est votre adresse?	*What* is your address?
Quels sont tes disques préférés?	*What* are your favorite records?

Application

Reminder, Exs. D–F: Make sure that students use the correct intonation pattern for these questions. Point out to them that the voice drops because **quel** forms information questions.

D. Use **quel** to form a question with each noun. Then spell the form of **quel** that you used. Remember that the pronunciation is the same for all spoken forms, but that each written form must agree in gender and number with the noun it modifies.

MODÈLE: livre
Quel livre? (Q-U-E-L)

1. chien
2. chambre
3. carnets
4. chaîne stéréo
5. filles
6. appartement
7. langue
8. peintures
9. portefeuilles
10. musique
11. cahiers
12. cassette
13. appareil-photo
14. pâtisseries
15. poster
16. voiture
17. vélo
18. disques
19. serviettes
20. hôtel

E. **Qu'est-ce que tu cherches?** Your friend has misplaced a lot of things. For each item lost, ask a question with **quel** to get more information.

MODÈLE: Je cherche le stylo.
Mais quel stylo est-ce que tu cherches?

1. Je cherche la clé.
2. Je cherche le cahier.
3. Je cherche les livres.
4. Je cherche les cassettes.
5. Je cherche le disque.
6. Je cherche une adresse.
7. Je cherche les posters.
8. Je cherche les plantes.

F. Ask one of your classmates questions with **quel** to get the required information. Use either **quel** + noun, or **quel** + **être** + noun.

Ex F: ⇄

MODÈLES: son nom
Quel est ton nom?

les sports qu'il/elle préfère
Quels sports est-ce que tu préfères?

1. son nom
2. la musique qu'il/elle préfère
3. son adresse
4. son numéro de téléphone
5. les cours qu'il/elle prend
6. sa saison préférée
7. les devoirs pour demain
8. son professeur préféré

DÉBROUILLONS-NOUS !

Review of the **étape**

G. **Échange.** Ask questions in French to obtain the following information from a classmate.

1. which music he/she likes
2. what his/her address is
3. what his/her telephone number is
4. what drink **(une boisson)** he/she prefers
5. what day of the week he/she likes best
6. what season he/she prefers

Ex. H: ⥂

H. **Le dessert.** You have been put in charge of buying some desserts for a party your class is having. You're in a **boulangerie-pâtisserie.**

1. Greet the salesperson.
2. Say that you want some pastries (name them).
3. Ask the price of the chocolate cake, the apple pies, and the lemon tarts.
4. Decide what and how much you're going to buy.
5. Pay, thank the salesperson, and say good-bye.

POURQUOI?

Answer, **Pourquoi?:** c

You're spending the summer with a French family. Because you live in a neighborhood that has a wide variety of food stores, your French family rarely goes to the supermarket. One day, however, your French "mother" asks you to go to the supermarket to buy bread. Why doesn't she send you to the **boulangerie** next door?

a. The **boulangerie** has gone out of business.
b. During the hottest part of the summer bread tends to spoil in shops that are not air-conditioned.
c. Many of the small food stores close for a one-month vacation in July or August.
d. The price of bread tends to go up in small shops during the tourist season.

Written Work: See Workbook.

Deuxième étape

Point de départ:

À la charcuterie

delicatessen

Transparency, Note Culturelle: food items found in the **charcuterie**

Suggestion, Point de départ: Present vocabulary using the transparency of the food items found in the charcuterie while you narrate the continuation of Mme Thibaudet's shopping trip. Then act out (you or a student) the dialogue (students have books closed). Then have students open the book while you read the dialogue again. Finally have different students play the roles.

Alternatively, you can begin by playing the dialogue from the Teacher Tape and have students answer very general questions in English: Where do you think the dialogue is taking place? How many people? What are some of the things Mme Thibaudet buys? Then proceed to dialogue.

Après la boulangerie-pâtisserie, Mme Thibaudet est allée à la charcuterie.

— Bonjour, Madame.
— Bonjour, Madame.
— Qu'est-ce que vous désirez aujourd'hui?
— D'abord, je voudrais du pâté—**assez** pour trois personnes. *enough*
— Très bien. Voilà. Et avec ça?
— **Donnez-moi** six **tranches** de jambon et une douzaine de tranches de saucisson. Des tranches très **fines.** C'est tout. *give me / slices* *thin*
— Bon. Le pâté, 12F; le jambon, 25F; et le saucisson, 15F. Ça fait 52F. Merci bien et au revoir, Madame.
— Au revoir, Madame.

du rôti de porc cuit: cooked roast pork

Note Culturelle

In France, **la charcuterie** is somewhat like an American delicatessen because you can buy a variety of prepared foods, particularly salad and some hot dishes. The **charcuterie** also sells ham and other cooked pork products, such as sausages, salami, ham, and pâté.

France uses the metric system of measurement. The basic unit of weight is the kilogram **(un kilo),** which equals one thousand grams **(une gramme).** Half a kilogram **(un demi-kilo)** is called **une livre** *(a pound).* However, because a kilogram is approximately 2.2 American pounds, a French **livre** is a little more than an American pound. The basic unit of measurement for liquids is the liter **(un litre),** which is roughly equivalent to a quart.

When shopping in a **charcuterie,** you can buy meats by the slice **(une tranche)** or you can simply let the salesperson know the number of people you're planning to serve. The **charcutier (charcutière)** is very good at helping you determine how much of something you should buy.

Vocabulary activities

À vous!

A. **J'ai besoin de. . .** *(I need . . .)* Use the cues to explain what you need to the shopkeeper.

MODÈLE: 1 livre / salade de concombres
J'ai besoin d'une livre de salade de concombres.

1. 1 poulet
2. 4 tranches / jambon
3. 10 tranches / saucisson
4. 6 saucisses
5. 1 livre / salade de thon
6. 1 livre / pâté

B. **Un très bon dîner.** Your parents are eating out tonight, and they have left you some money to buy your dinner at the **charcuterie.** For each of the amounts given, figure out what you can buy so that you have a balanced meal. Don't forget to buy your bread at the **boulangerie.**

MODÈLE: 50F
Je vais acheter une baguette, une livre de jambon, et une livre de salade de tomates.

1. 30F
2. 50F
3. 75F
4. 40F
5. 20F
6. 60F

Prononciation: *The vowel é*

The letter **é (été)** is pronounced much like the vowel sound in the English word *fail.* However, the French vowel is not a diphthong. That is, **é** is a single, steady sound, whereas the English sound tends to slide from one vowel to another.

Pratique

C. Read each word aloud, being careful to pronounce the **é** with enough tension to avoid making a diphthong.

1. thé
2. café
3. église
4. métro
5. éclair
6. cathédrale
7. été
8. écoute

REPRISE

D. **Échange.** Ask one of your classmates the following questions. He/she will answer you. Ex. D: ⇄

1. Est-ce que tu vas souvent à la boulangerie? Est-ce que tu aimes les croissants? Est-ce que tu as mangé des croissants récemment? Et du pain français?
2. Est-ce que tu aimes les pâtisseries? Lesquelles *(which ones)* est-ce que tu préfères? Est-ce que tu manges souvent des desserts? Quel dessert est-ce que tu préfères? Est-ce que tu as déjà mangé des pâtisseries francaises? Lesquelles?

Suggestion, Partitive: Present by asking class: **Qui aime le pain? Qui veut du pain? Qui a du pain?** Other items: **chocolat, soupe, eau minérale, argent, sandwiches, pâtisseries, fruits, bananes, oranges, tomates, concombres, café, thé, Coca.** Perhaps the most important thing to remember when presenting the partitive is to keep it as simple as possible. Experience has shown that the more one explains it, the more confused students become. Students should not be expected to control the partitive at this point.

In this unit, the partitive is used mainly with food. Point out to students that it is used also with abstract nouns, i.e. **Marie a de l'imagination. Jean a du tact.**

STRUCTURE

The partitive

Quand je vais à la charcuterie, j'achète toujours:

du pâté	*some* pâté
de la salade de thon	*some* salad
des saucisses	*some* sausages

Est-ce que vous avez **du** jambon?
Oui, et nous avons **des** saucisses aussi.

So far, you've learned two types of articles: the definite articles **le, la, l', les,** which mean *the* in English, and the indefinite articles **un, une, des,** which mean *a* or *an.*

Now you'll learn to use the partitive articles that allow you to express the idea of a certain amount or quantity, not the whole, of something. The partitive article has three singular forms and one plural form:

singular	masculine	**du**
	feminine	**de la**
	masculine or feminine before a vowel or a silent h	**de l'**
plural	masculine or feminine	**des**

Note that the **s** of **des** is silent except in liaison.

The partitive article is equivalent to *some* or *any* in English. In English, the partitive is often omitted; in French, it must be expressed.

Application

E. Replace the definite article with the partitive article.

MODÈLE: le pain
du pain

1. la salade
2. le pâté
3. les croissants
4. la limonade
5. la pâtisserie
6. le thé
7. les tartelettes
8. la crème
9. le lait
10. le café
11. l'eau minérale
12. les petits pains

F. Replace the word in italics with the words in parentheses. Remember to make the partitive article agree with each new word.

1. Marie-Jeanne achète du *pâté*. (jambon / saucisson / salade de thon / saucisses)
2. Je vais prendre du *thé*. (Coca / eau minérale / limonade / café)
3. Elle a acheté des *tartelettes*. (croissants / baguettes / religieuses / éclairs)

NOTE GRAMMATICALE

Both the partitive articles **(du, de la, de l', des)** and the indefinite articles **(un, une, des)** become **de** or **d'** after a negative expression, regardless of the gender and number of the noun. (The definite articles **le, la, l', les** remain the same.)

— Tu prends **du** café? — Non, je ne prends pas **de** café.	— Are you having coffee? — No, I'm not having coffee.
— Vous avez **de la** mayonnaise? — Non, nous **n'**avons **pas de** mayonnaise.	— Do you have *any* mayonnaise? — No, we do*n't* have *any* mayonnaise.
— Vous avez acheté **une** baguette? — Non, je **n'**ai **pas** acheté **de** baguette.	— Did you buy *a* baguette? — No, I did*n't* buy *a* baguette.
— Elle aime **les** fraises? — Non, elle **n'**aime **pas les** fraises.	— Does she like strawberries? — No, she does*n't* like strawberries.

G. **Merci, pas de. . .** Each time someone offers you something, you refuse politely. Remember that the partitive and indefinite articles become **de** after the negative.

MODÈLE: Du pain?
Merci, pas de pain.

1. Une banane?
2. Du pâté?
3. Un Coca?
4. Des croissants?
5. De la soupe?
6. Des oranges?
7. De la limonade?
8. Un café?
9. De la salade?
10. Des pâtisseries?

Exs. H, I, J: ⇄. You may wish to do one item with the entire class before breaking students into pairs.

H. Engage in short conversations based on the model. Remember to change the partitive articles to **de** after the negative. But don't change the definite articles!

MODÈLE: prendre / limonade / non / ne pas aimer
— *Tu prends de la limonade?*
— *Non, je ne prends pas de limonade.*
— *Pourquoi pas?*
— *Parce que je n'aime pas la limonade.*

1. prendre / pâté / non / ne pas aimer
2. vouloir / café / non / ne pas aimer
3. aller acheter / jambon / non / détester
4. aller manger / soupe / non / ne pas aimer
5. prendre / eau minérale / non / détester

NOTE GRAMMATICALE

J'aime beaucoup **le** pain, mais je préfère **les** croissants. — I like bread very much, but I prefer croissants.

When you want to make a statement about a general preference, use the definite articles **le, la, l', les.** For example, if you want to say that you like bread (bread in general), you'll say, "**J'aime le pain.**" The verbs of preference that take the definite article are **aimer, adorer, détester, préférer, aimer mieux, aimer bien.**

Remember that the indefinite articles **un** and **une** are used in the same way as the English *a* and *an*.

Donnez-moi **une** baguette et **une** tarte aux pommes, s'il vous plaît. — Give me *a* baguette and *an* apple pie, please.

I. Engage in short conversations based on the model. Distinguish between uses of the partitive and the indefinite articles.

MODÈLE: café / express
— *Vous désirez du café?*
— *Oui, je voudrais un express.*

1. thé / thé au citron
2. fruits / banane, orange
3. pâtisseries / religieuse, mille-feuille
4. pain / baguette, pain de campagne
5. café / café au lait

J. Engage in short conversations based on the model. Distinguish among uses of the partitive, the definite, and the indefinite articles.

MODÈLE: pain / baguette, pain de campagne
— *Vous aimez le pain?*
— *Oui, j'aime beaucoup le pain.*
— *Est-ce que vous avez acheté du pain hier?*
— *Oui, j'ai acheté une baguette et un pain de campagne.*

1. pâtisseries / tarte aux pommes, gâteau au chocolat
2. pâtisseries / religieuse, tartelette aux fraises
3. eau minérale / bouteille de Vittel, bouteille de Perrier
4. pain / pain au chocolat, petit pain

DÉBROUILLONS-NOUS!

K. **Un pique-nique.** You and your friends are planning a picnic. You have to decide what you want to buy, and you don't always agree with each other. For each suggestion one of you makes, the second person agrees but the third person disagrees.

Review of the **étape**

Ex. K: △

MODÈLE: jambon
— *Est-ce que nous allons acheter du jambon?*
— *Ah oui. J'adore le jambon.*
— *Non, je ne veux pas de jambon. Je déteste le jambon.*

1. pâté
2. saucisson
3. eau minérale
4. salade de concombres
5. Coca
6. croissants
7. saucisses
8. poulet
9. tartelettes au citron
10. pâtisseries
11. bananes
12. salade de thon

Le savez-vous?

A *marché aux puces* is
a) a kind of open-air supermarket
b) a place where you can buy antiques
c) a high-fashion specialty store
d) a discount record store

réponse

Written Work: See Workbook

Troisième étape

Transparency, Note Culturelle: meats in the butcher shop

Suggestion, Point de départ: You can begin the lesson in three ways: (1) Start with the **Note culturelle** and tell students (in English) about the difference between a **charcuterie** and a **boucherie.** Then use the transparency of meats in the butcher shop to present the vocabulary. Finally go to the dialogue. (2) Use the transparency to present the vocabulary through personalized questions about student likes and dislikes. Then move to the dialogue. Finally go to the **Note culturelle.** (3) Integrate the dialogue, the **Note culturelle,** and the transparency into one presentation. Use the transparency to give a narration about Mme Thibaudet's purchases at the butcher's. Say what she bought and didn't buy. Include some facts about the butcher shop.

Point de départ:

À la boucherie

➡ b

Après la charcuterie, Mme Thibaudet a traversé la rue pour prendre quelque chose à la boucherie.

— Bonjour, Madame Thibaudet.
— Bonjour, Monsieur Garant.
— Qu'est-ce que je peux faire pour vous aujourd'hui?
— Eh ben. . . Il me faut beaucoup de choses. Donnez-moi d'abord un rôti de porc. Assez pour six personnes.
— Très bien. Et avec ça? Regardez ces **beaux** biftecks. (beautiful)
— Oui, je vais prendre trois biftecks et aussi ce poulet-ci.
— Voilà. Et **quoi d'autre?** (what else)
— Peut-être un kilo de rosbif. Et voilà, c'est tout.
— Très bien, Madame. Le rôti de porc, 55F; les biftecks, 42F; le poulet, 32F; et le rosbif, 55F. Ça fait 184F, **en tout.** Merci bien, Madame. Et **bonne journée.** (in all / have a good day)
— Au revoir, Monsieur Garant.

Note Culturelle

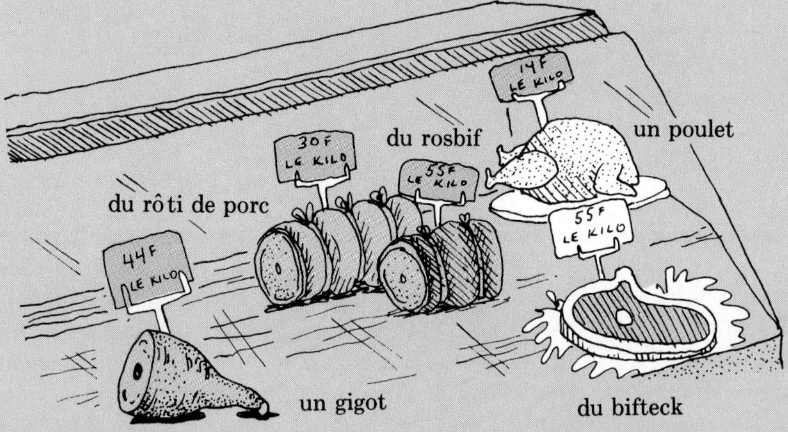

The French **boucherie** sells pork roasts and chops **(du porc)** as well as beef **(du bœuf)**, lamb **(du mouton)**, and chicken. The **boucher (bouchère)** is very helpful in determining how much meat you might need for a particular number of people. Prices of meat are usually stated by the kilogram (2.2 American pounds).

un canard: a duck

À vous!

Vocabulary activities

A. **Qu'est-ce qu'ils ont acheté à la boucherie?** Use the drawings of various meats to determine what each person bought.

MODÈLE: Simone
Simone a acheté un poulet.

1. Mme Ricard
2. Alain
3. M. Sylvain

Follow-up, Ex. A: Have students imagine what *they* bought. This allows them to name their favorite meats.

B. **Où est-ce qu'on va pour acheter. . . ?** Say where you go to buy each item.

MODÈLE: du pâté
Pour acheter du pâté, on va à la charcuterie.

1. du poulet
2. une tarte aux fraises
3. des saucisses
4. du pain
5. du jambon
6. des pâtisseries
7. du pâté
8. un rôti de porc
9. du saucisson
10. du bœuf

REPRISE

Recycling activities

Ex. C: ⇄

Suggestion, Ex. C: Do one item with the whole class before dividing students into pairs. You may also wish to follow up on the paired work by having some students say what they found out about their classmates.

C. **Une célébrité.** *(A celebrity.)* When reporters interview famous people, they want to know every detail of their lives. In this case, you are being interviewed by a nosy person who is particularly interested in your eating habits. Answer the questions according to the cues provided.

1. Où est-ce que vous allez d'habitude pour le petit déjeuner? (café)
2. Qu'est-ce que vous commandez d'habitude? (café au lait / croissants)
3. Est-ce que vous aimez les croissants? (adorer)
4. Qu'est-ce que vous mangez pour le déjeuner? (salade de tomates)
5. Est-ce que vous aimez le jambon? (non / ne pas aimer)
6. Et pour le dîner, qu'est-ce que vous mangez? (bifteck ou rosbif)
7. Vous mangez du porc aussi? (non / détester)
8. Et comme dessert? Qu'est-ce que vous préférez? (éclairs ou gâteau au chocolat)

Ex. D: ⇄

Reminder, Ex. D: Note that the breakfast items listed are American ones. This is so that the students can answer the question. Explain to them that these are not French breakfast items.

D. **Mon petit déjeuner.** Ask one of your classmates what he/she eats for breakfast. Follow the model.

MODÈLE: — *Est-ce que tu prends du café?*
— *Non, je ne prends pas de café. Je préfère le thé.* ou:
— *Oui, je prends du café.*

Le petit déjeuner		
le pain	le café	les œufs *(eggs)*
le pain au chocolat	le thé	le bacon
les croissants	le lait	le jambon
la confiture *(jam)*	le jus d'orange	les saucisses
le beurre *(butter)*		
le toast (le pain grillé)		
les céréales		

Follow-up, Ex. D: Have a few students tell the class what they found out about their classmates.

STRUCTURE

Demonstrative adjectives

Je vais prendre **ce** rôti de porc. — I'll take *this* pork roast.
Et aussi **cette** baguette et **ces** croissants. — And also *this* bread and *these* croissants.

The demonstrative adjective is used to point out specific things. It has three singular forms that are equivalent to the English words *this* or *that:*

ce	masculine singular before a pronounced consonant **(ce livre)**
cet	masculine singular before a vowel or vowel sound **(cet hôtel)**
cette	feminine singular **(cette maison)**

The demonstrative adjective has only one plural form that is equivalent to the English words *these* or *those:*

ces plural **(ces bananes, ces fruits)**

The **s** of **ces** is silent, except before a vowel or a vowel sound **(ces‿amis, ces‿hôtels).**

Suggestion, Demonstrative adjectives: Since this is usually an easy grammar point for students, you may wish to present it deductively: i.e., simply tell them the meaning and the agreement rules, then move on to examples and exercises.

Application

E. Replace the definite article with the demonstrative adjective.

MODÈLE: la pharmacie
cette pharmacie

1. le pain
2. les tomates
3. l'hôtel
4. la bouteille
5. les fruits
6. la banque
7. l'étudiante
8. le garçon
9. l'étudiant
10. les saucisses
11. le vélo
12. l'appareil-photo
13. l'église
14. les éclairs
15. le pain de campagne

F. **C'est combien?** Find out the price of each item. Use the demonstrative adjective in your question.

MODÈLE: poulet
C'est combien, ce poulet?

à la boucherie

1. rôti de bœuf
2. biftecks
3. gigot
4. rosbif
5. canard

à la charcuterie

6. pâté
7. salade
8. saucisses
9. jambon
10. saucisson

à la boulangerie

11. éclairs
12. tarte aux pommes
13. pain de campagne
14. gâteau au chocolat
15. tartelette au citron

Suggestion, Note grammaticale: Use the objects students have with them to ask about their preferences: **Est-ce que vous préférez ce livre-ci ou ce livre-là? (stylo, cahier, sac, sac à dos, notes,** etc.). Give explanation and then move on to the exercise.

NOTE GRAMMATICALE

Sometimes it may be important to distinguish between *this* and *that* or between *these* and *those.* When you're faced with a lot of choices and you want to be precise about the object or people you're referring to, use the demonstrative adjective with the noun and add **-ci** *(this, these)* or **-là** *(that, those)* to the noun:

Donnez-moi **ces** biftecks**-ci.**	Give me *these* steaks (over here).
Et je prends **ce** rôti**-là.**	And I'll take *that* roast (over there).

Remember to use **-ci** and **-là** only if the distinction is necessary to make the meaning clear for someone else.

G. **Lequel?** *(Which One?)* You're doing some shopping with a friend. Because there are so many things to choose from, you always have to explain which objects you're referring to. Use **-ci** or **-là** in your answer according to the cue in parentheses.

MODÈLE: Quels livres est-ce que tu vas acheter? (those)
Ces livres-là.

1. Quelle calculatrice est-ce que tu préfères? (this one)
2. Quel portefeuille est-ce que tu vas acheter? (that one)
3. Quels fruits est-ce que tu préfères? (those)
4. Quelles pâtisseries est-ce que tu aimes mieux? (these)
5. Quel pâté est-ce que tu vas acheter? (this one)
6. Quelle confiture est-ce que tu préfères? (that one)

1100, rue St-Jean
Québec, Québec
694-1141

DÉBROUILLONS-NOUS!

H. **Où est-ce que tu l'as acheté?** *(Where did you buy it?)* When your mother/father returns from shopping, you want to know where he/she bought each of the items on the kitchen counter. Ask each question using a demonstrative adjective. Your classmate will answer by naming the appropriate store.

Review of the **étape**

Ex. H: ⇄

Suggestion, Ex. H: Do one item with the entire class before dividing students into pairs.

MODÈLE:
— *Où est-ce que tu as acheté ces religieuses?*
— *À la pâtisserie Vert Galant.*

1.

2.

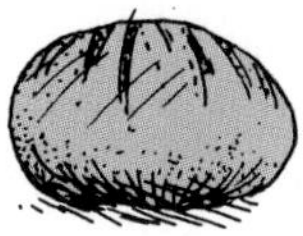

3.

4.

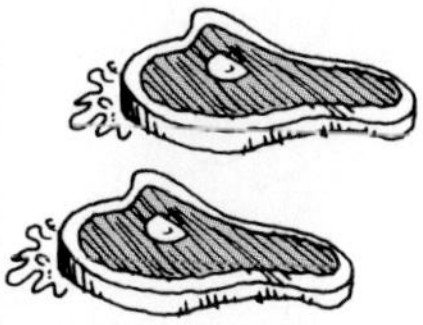

5.

6.

7.

8.

la charcuterie la pâtisserie la boucherie la boulangerie

Written Work: See Workbook.

Lexique

Pour se débrouiller

Pour indiquer ce qu'on veut acheter

Je vais prendre. . .
Je prends. . .
Je voudrais. . .
J'ai besoin de. . .
Est-ce que vous avez. . . ?
Donnez-moi. . . ?

Pour demander le prix de quelque chose

C'est combien?
Combien coûte. . . ?
Combien est-ce que je vous dois? *(How much do I owe you?)*

Pour indiquer la quantité

un demi-kilo de
une gramme de
un kilo (kilogramme) de
un litre de
une livre de
une tranche de
assez pour . . . personnes

Thèmes et contextes

La boulangerie-pâtisserie

une baguette
un croissant
un éclair
un gâteau au chocolat
un mille-feuille
le pain
un pain au chocolat
un pain de campagne
une pâtisserie
un petit pain
une religieuse
une tarte (aux pommes, aux fraises)
une tartelette (au citron)

La charcuterie

le jambon
le pâté
un rôti de porc cuit
une saucisse
un saucisson
une salade (de tomates, de concombres, de thon)

La boucherie

un bifteck
le bœuf
le canard
le gigot
le mouton
le porc
le poulet
un rôti
la viande

Le petit déjeuner

le bacon
le beurre
les céréales *(f.pl.)*
la confiture
le jus d'orange
le lait
les œufs *(m.pl.)*
le toast

Vocabulaire général

Noms

un anniversaire
une banane
un(e) boucher(-ère)
un(e) boulanger(-ère)
un(e) charcutier(-ère)
un four à micro-ondes
un fruit
une journée
une orange

Verbes

donner
faire les courses

Adjectifs

beau (belle, beaux, belles)
bon (bonne)
fin(e)

Autres expressions

assez pour
bonne journée
en tout
Et avec ça?
il vaut mieux + *infinitive*
Quoi d'autre?

Chapitre dix-sept

Achetons des fruits et des légumes!

— *Qu'est-ce qu'on achète?*
— *Achetons des fruits et des légumes!*

Première étape

Point de départ:

Au marché

Transparency, Point de départ: fruits and vegetables

Suggestion, Point de départ: Use the transparency of fruits and vegetables to teach the new vocabulary. Ask students about their likes and dislikes. Then continue on to the dialogue, using any of the techniques described in previous **étapes.**

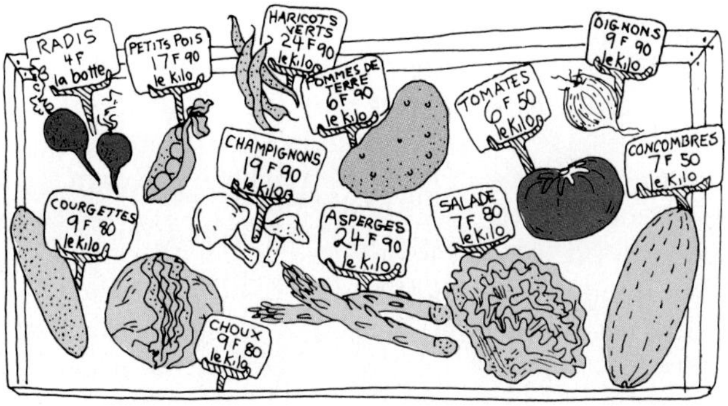

Enfin, Mme Thibaudet est allée au **marché en plein air** pour acheter des fruits et des légumes. — open-air market

— Mesdames, Messieurs... Achetez nos légumes... **frais** du jardin... — fresh
— Madame...
— Oui, Madame. À votre service.
— **Il me faut** des courgettes, un chou, des oignons, des pommes de terre et des haricots verts. C'est pour une soupe aux légumes pour 10 personnes. — I need
— **J'ai ce qu'il vous faut,** Madame. — I have what you need
— Pas **beaucoup d'**oignons, mais donnez-moi **une douzaine de** courgettes. — a lot of (many) / a dozen
— Voilà, Madame. **Ça suffit?** — Is this (that) enough?
— Oui, ça va. Merci bien.

Suggestion, Note culturelle: To get students into the context, ask them (in English) where their family shops. Is there an open-air market in the town; are there small general stores? Who does the shopping? Do they like vegetables and fruit? As you ask these questions, provide them with the information contained in the **Note culturelle.**

Note Culturelle

In France, one can buy fruits, vegetables, and staple food products in a variety of places. There is, of course, the supermarket **(le supermarché),** which is becoming more and more popular as the pace of life increases and as more and more women are at jobs away from home. In addition, there are the open-air markets **(le marché en plein air),** which are usually held only on certain days of the week but where one can buy the freshest produce brought directly from the farms. Finally, there is the general store **(une épicerie)** found in every neighborhood. The **épicerie** sells fruits and vegetables from displays on the sidewalk. Inside the store, you can buy dry goods, cheese, cleaning products, and the like.

Most families shop in all three of these places. The neighborhood **épicerie** is very convenient and caters to both the customers who have ample time to shop and those who shop on their way home from work. Supermarket shopping tends to be done less frequently but for larger quantities. Frozen foods are becoming more and more important as people stock up to avoid frequent shopping trips. The **marché en plein air** is still very popular because the prices are often better and the produce is particularly fresh. Besides the family shoppers, the **marché en plein air** also caters to the chefs of exclusive restaurants, who buy only the freshest produce.

Vocabulary activities

À vous!

A. **Qu'est-ce que c'est?** Identify the following fruits and vegetables.

MODÈLES: *C'est une banane. Ce sont des fraises.*

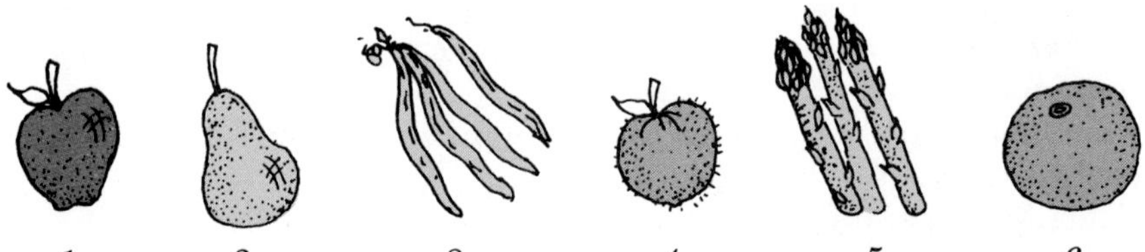

1. *2.* *3.* *4.* *5.* *6.*

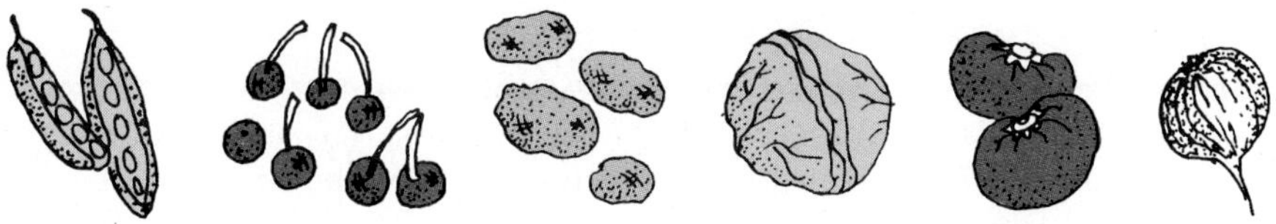

7. 8. 9. 10. 11. 12.

B. **Dans le filet de Mme Thibaudet.** Calculate the cost of the items in Mme Thibaudet's shopping bag.

MODÈLE: 2 kilos de tomates / 6F50 le kilo
Deux kilos de tomates à six francs cinquante le kilo, ça fait treize francs.

1. 2 kilos de pommes / 10F50 le kilo
2. 3 bottes *(bunches)* de radis / 4F la botte
3. 1 kilo d'abricots / 16F90 le kilo
4. une livre de petits pois / 19F90 le kilo
5. un kilo et demi de poires / 21F10 le kilo
6. une livre de champignons / 19F90 le kilo
7. 2 kilos d'oranges / 8F90 le kilo
8. une livre d'asperges / 24F90 le kilo

C. Engage in short conversations imitating the model. As long as you get across the same ideas expressed in the model, you need not necessarily use the same words. The important thing is to make yourself understood. One of you plays the shopkeeper, the other plays the customer.

MODÈLE: fruits / cerises, 12F le kilo / pêches, 25F10 le kilo
— *Vous avez besoin de fruits?*
— *Oui, donnez-moi une livre de cerises.*
— *Et avec ça?*
— *Je voudrais aussi un kilo de pêches.*
— *Bon. Une livre de cerises, ça fait six francs. Et un kilo de pêches, ça fait douze francs cinquante-cinq. C'est tout?*
— *Oui, c'est tout.*
— *Bon, ça fait dix-huit francs cinquante-cinq.*

1. fruits / poires, 21F10 le kilo / abricots, 16F90 le kilo
2. légumes / haricots verts, 24F90 le kilo / pommes de terre, 6F90 le kilo
3. fruits / oranges, 8F90 le kilo / fraises, 10F le carton
4. légumes / salade, 7F80 le kilo / courgettes, 9F80 le kilo

Le savez-vous?

A *kiosque* sells
a) magazines and newspapers
b) candy and snack foods
c) clothes
d) vegetables

réponse

Ex. C: ⇄

Suggestion, Ex. C: Go over the model with the whole class before dividing students into pairs. Be sure to stress that they don't need to use the exact words of the model, as long as they get the idea across. You also need to indicate that it is up to the customer to determine the quantities of each item bought.

REPRISE

Recycling activity

Implementation, Ex. D: Make sure that students are using a demonstrative adjective in the question.

D. **À la boucherie-charcuterie.** Ask the shopkeeper how much each of the following items cost.

MODÈLE:
— *Combien coûtent ces saucisses?*
— *Elles coûtent quarante-neuf francs le kilo.*

1.

2.

3.

4.

5.

6.

7.

8.

a

Suggestion, Expressions of general quantity: You can begin the presentation with a series of personalized statements and questions using the expressions of general quantity. (**Moi, j'ai beaucoup de disques. Et vous? J'ai très peu de vidéos. Et vous? Je n'ai pas beaucoup de cassettes. Et vous? J'ai beaucoup de livres. Et vous?** Etc.) If you prefer, you can use abstract nouns for this presentation (**tact, courage, imagination, patience**).

STRUCTURE

Expressions of general quantity

Combien de disques est-ce que tu as?	*How many* records do you have?
J'ai **beaucoup de** disques mais j'ai **très peu de** cassettes.	I have *a lot of* records but I have *very few* cassettes.
Ah, tu **n'**as **pas beaucoup de** cassettes?	Ah, you *don't* have *a lot of (many)* casettes?

When you want to find out *how much* or *how many* someone has of something, ask the question with **combien de. . . .** The answer to this question can be either specific or general. When the answer is a general quantity, use one of the four expressions provided below. Note that all of these expressions are followed by **de** regardless of the gender and number of the noun they modify:

General quantity

beaucoup de	a lot, a great deal, many, much
pas beaucoup de	not many, not much
un peu de[1]	a little, a little bit
très peu de	very little, very few
quelques	

Application

E. Add the expressions in parentheses to each of the sentences.

MODÈLE: Georges a de la limonade. (beaucoup)
Georges a beaucoup de limonade.

1. Nous avons des amis. (pas beaucoup / très peu de / beaucoup)
2. Elles ont des disques. (beaucoup / très peu / pas beaucoup)
3. Mon oncle a des sœurs. (pas beaucoup / beaucoup / très peu)

F. Describe each person's financial situation using the expressions **beaucoup, pas beaucoup, un peu,** and **très peu.** The word for *money* is **argent** *(m.)*.

Monique: 60F Sylvie: 7 000F Edgar: 2F Jean-Paul: 25F

MODÈLE: Est-ce que Monique a de l'argent?
Oui, mais elle n'a pas beaucoup d'argent.

1. Est-ce qu'Edgar a de l'argent?
2. Et Sylvie?
3. Et Monique?
4. Et Jean-Paul?

[1]The expression **un peu** can be used only with non-count nouns (nouns that are always singular.) To indicate the idea of *a few* with a plural noun, French uses **quelques: un peu de thé,** but **quelques pommes.**

Suggestion, Note grammaticale: Begin by asking personalized questions that require a number as an answer (**frères, sœurs, ordinateurs, sacs à dos, magnétoscopes, télévisions, radios,** etc.). Then move to specific quantities that students learned in Ch. 16 (**kilo, demi-kilo, tranche**). Introduce the rest of the expressions by indicating the quantity of food that would be required for different numbers of people (**Pour six personnes, il me faut deux litres d'eau minérale.** Etc.). As you use the new expressions, you can give a quick illustration and/or explanation.

NOTE GRAMMATICALE

Expressions of specific quantity

Je suis allé à la charcuterie.
À la charcuterie, j'ai acheté **un morceau de** pâté et dix **tranches de** jambon. — At the delicatessen, I bought *a piece of* pâté and ten *slices of* ham.

Sometimes, expressing general quantities is not enough when you're trying to communicate effectively. You also need to express yourself using specific quantities. You already know how to do this with numbers **(Combien de frères et de sœurs est-ce que tu as? J'ai deux frères et trois sœurs.)**. Now you'll learn another set of expressions that allow you to be precise about quantity. Notice that each of these expressions is again followed by **de** regardless of the gender and number of the noun it modifies.

Specific quantities

un kilo de	a kilogram of
un demi-kilo de	a half a kilogram of
une livre de	a pound (French) of
50 grammes de	50 grams of
un litre de	a liter of
une bouteille de	a bottle of
une douzaine de	a dozen
un morceau de	a piece of
un bout de	a piece of
une tranche de	a slice of

G. Use the cues to answer the salesperson.

MODÈLE: Qu'est-ce que je peux faire pour vous? (2 kilos / pommes de terre; une livre / salade de tomates)
Il me faut deux kilos de pommes de terre, et une livre de salade de tomates.

1. Qu'est-ce que je peux faire pour vous? (1 litre / lait; 8 tranches / saucisson)
2. Qu'est-ce qu'il vous faut? (1 bouteille / Perrier; 2 kilos / pêches)
3. À votre service. (50 grammes / pâté; 1 morceau / saucisson)
4. Qu'est-ce que vous désirez? (une douzaine / œufs; 1 livre / bacon)

H. **Qu'est-ce qu'ils ont acheté?** Based on the drawings, indicate how much of something the various people bought.

MODÈLE:
Combien de pâté est-ce que Paul a acheté?
Il a acheté cinquante grammes de pâté.

1.
Et Marie, qu'est-ce qu'elle a acheté?

2.
Combien de pommes est-ce que Mme Thibaudet a achetées?

3.
Et vous, combien de pâté est-ce que vous avez acheté?

4.
Qu'est-ce qu'elles ont acheté?

5.
Et qu'est-ce que tu as acheté?

DÉBROUILLONS-NOUS!

I. Several friends of yours are about to spend the weekend at your house. Since they are your guests, your family expects you to do the food shopping for everyone. Your friends are vegetarians, so you buy only fruit and vegetables at the **épicerie.**

Review of the **étape**

Ex. I: ⇄

1. Greet the salesperson.
2. Explain that you need some fruit: bananas, apples, pears, or peaches.
3. Tell him/her that you want a pound of mushrooms, 2 kilos of green beans, a dozen onions, and a half-kilo of asparagus.
4. Tell him/her that you need 3 bottles of mineral water.
5. Ask how much your purchases cost.
6. Pay the person and say good-bye.

Written Work: See Workbook.

Deuxième étape

Transparency, Point de départ: canned goods, dairy products and frozen foods

Suggestion, Point de départ: First have students look at the photo and say where they are (**au supermarché**) and what they see (have them read the signs in the aisles, etc.). This **Point de départ** shows the family Pharand going from one section of the supermarket to another. In the drinks section, ask students personalized questions to review the names of the drinks they learned in Unit. 1. Then use the transparency of canned goods, dairy products and frozen foods to introduce vocabulary. Finally, give them the names for different packaged goods and condiments.

The vocabulary in this **Point de départ** is not intended to be exhaustive. You will undoubtedly wish to add other items, and students are likely to ask about words they would like to know.

Point de départ:

Au supermarché

shel (section of supermarket)
what they need

Samedi, les Pharand vont au supermarché. Ils passent d'un **rayon** à l'autre pour acheter **ce qu'il leur faut.**

D'abord, ils passent au rayon des boissons.

— Qu'est-ce que vous voulez?
— Moi, je veux du Coca.
— Et moi, je voudrais de l'eau minérale.

Ensuite, ils passent au rayon des **conserves.**

canned goods

Puis, il leur faut des **produits laitiers.**

dairy products

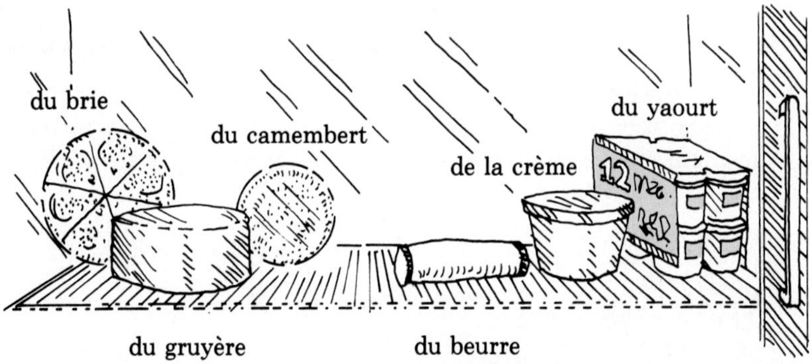

Ensuite, ils passent au rayon des produits **surgelés** où ils achètent du poulet, du **poisson,** de la pizza, des **pommes frites** et une **glace** au chocolat.

frozen
fish / french fries / ice cream

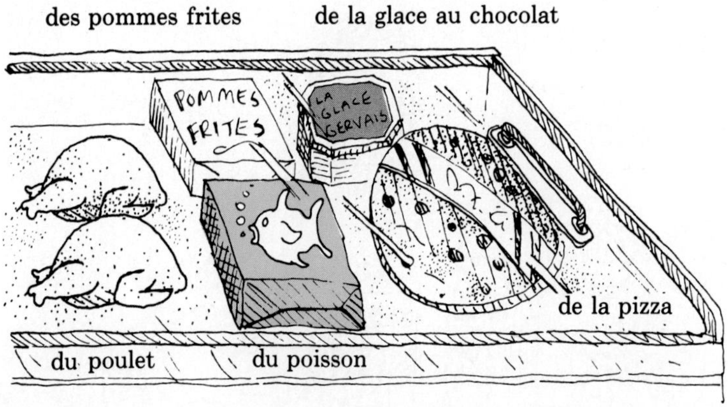

Et pour **terminer,** ils achètent du **riz,** des **pâtes,** de la **farine,** du **sucre,** du **sel,** du **poivre,** de la mayonnaise, de la **moutarde** et du ketchup. Leur **chariot** est maintenant **plein** de bonnes choses.

finish / rice / pasta (noodles, etc.) / flour / sugar
salt / pepper / mustard
shopping cart / full

Note Culturelle

The supermarket has become the most convenient way to shop for many French people. Although thirty years ago they would not have believed it, they are relying more and more on frozen and canned foods. The supermarket provides wide varieties of everything, including bakery counters, extensive delicatessen sections, and sometimes seafood counters.

Vocabulary activities

À vous!

A. **Dans le chariot de Jean-Jacques il y a. . .** Jean-Jacques' mother sent him to the supermarket. Since he forgot the shopping list, he buys things from memory. Look at the drawings and indicate what he's buying.

MODÈLE:
Il y a une pizza.

B. **Qu'est-ce que Jean-Jacques a oublié?** When Jean-Jacques gets home, his mother looks at the shopping list and tells him what he forgot to buy. Look at the drawings and name the things he forgot.

MODÈLE:
Il a oublié la mayonnaise.

1.

2.

3.

4.

5.

6.

7.

8.

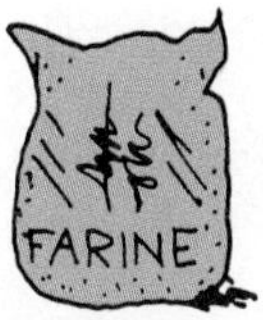

9.

Prononciation: *The vowels* **è** *and* **ê**

The letters **è (mère)** and **ê (fête)** are pronounced like the **e** in the English words *bed* and *belt.*

Le savez-vous?

France did not have supermarkets until
a) the fifties
b) the sixties
c) the seventies
d) the eighties

réponse

Pratique

C. Read each word aloud, being careful to pronounce **è** and **ê** in the same manner.

1. mère
2. frère
3. père
4. crème
5. achète
6. scène
7. bibliothèque
8. tête
9. êtes
10. fête

REPRISE

Recycling activity

Ex. D. ⇄

Suggestion, Ex. D: Act out one of the items with the entire class before dividing students into pairs.

D. **Des achats.** *(Purchases.)* Use the cues to role play scenes in a store.

MODÈLE: 5 kg / pommes de terre / beaucoup / 7F le kilo
— *Je voudrais cinq kilos de pommes de terre.*
— *Oui, nous avons beaucoup de pommes de terre.*
— *C'est combien?*
— *À sept francs le kilo, ça fait trente-cinq francs.*

1. 2 kg / abricots / beaucoup / 17F le kilo
2. 1 livre / cerises / beaucoup / 18F le kilo
3. 3 bottes / radis / beaucoup / 4F la botte
4. 2 kg / concombres / beaucoup / 7F50 le kilo
5. 3 bouteilles / Vittel / beaucoup / 5F50 la bouteille
6. 2 kg / poires / beaucoup / 21F le kilo

→ b

Suggestion, Expressions of comparison: Give students different numbers of objects (pencils, pens, etc.) to illustrate the comparative (**Jane a plus de crayons que Phillip. Phillip a moins de crayons que Jane. Veronica a autant de crayons que Jane.**). To make the meaning clear, first count the number of objects each student has. Then ask personalized questions: **Frank, est-ce que vous avez beaucoup de patience? Et Emily, est-ce que vous avez beaucoup de patience aussi? Emily, est-ce que vous avez plus de patience que Frank?** Continue with other abstract nouns **(imagination, tact, courage, intelligence).** Have each student take out a small amount of money and make comparisons using **argent.**

STRUCTURE

Expressions of comparison

Marie a **plus de** frères **que** moi.	Mary has *more* brothers *than* I do.
Mais j'ai **autant de** cousins **que** Marie.	But I have *as many* cousins *as* Mary.
Et Marie a **moins d'**oncles que moi.	And Mary has *fewer* uncles *than* I.

You often use quantities to compare what you have to what others have. In order to do so, you need expressions of comparison. In French, there are three basic expressions that can be used:

Comparison

plus de (+ noun) **que**	more . . . than
autant de (+ noun) **que**	as much/as many . . . as
moins de (+ noun) **que**	less/fewer . . . than

Application

E. Replace the words in italics with the words in parentheses.

1. Nous avons *plus de* livres que vous. (moins de / autant de)
2. Il a *moins d'argent* que Jean. (autant de / plus de)
3. J'ai acheté *autant de* fruits que ma mère. (moins de / plus de)

F. Make comparisons, using the expressions **plus de, moins de,** and **autant de.**

Nelly: 3 cousins	Bénédicte: 6 cousins	Georgette: 5 cousins
Étienne: 12 cousins	Liliane: 6 cousins	Hervé: 9 cousins

MODÈLE: Comparez Étienne et Liliane.
Étienne a plus de cousins que Liliane.

1. Comparez Nelly et Bénédicte.
2. Comparez Georgette et Nelly.
3. Comparez Liliane et Bénédicte.
4. Comparez Bénédicte et Étienne.
5. Comparez Hervé et Georgette.
6. Comparez Hervé et Étienne.

G. **Mes amis et moi.** Use the nouns provided to compare yourself to your friends. Use the expressions **plus de, moins de,** and **autant de.**

MODÈLE: cassettes
J'ai plus de cassettes que mon amie Becky.

1. frères
2. disques
3. livres
4. amis
5. sœurs
6. cassettes
7. argent
8. vêtements *(clothes)*

NOTE GRAMMATICALE

Expressions of sufficiency

Elle a **assez d'**argent pour acheter une cassette.	She has *enough* money to buy a cassette
Moi, je **n'**ai **pas assez d'**argent pour acheter un vélo.	I *don't* have *enough* money to buy a bike.

There are three basic expressions of quantity that allow you to indicate whether you have enough, too much, or not enough of something. Like most expressions of quantity, these expressions of sufficiency are followed by **de** regardless of the gender and number of the nouns they modify. Note that the preposition **pour** followed by an infinitive is used to indicate what one has (or does not have) enough for.

trop de	too much, too many
assez de	enough
pas assez de	not enough

Suggestion, Note grammaticale: To introduce expressions of sufficiency, give each student a slip of paper with an amount of money written on it. Next put the prices of various objects on the board. Then illustrate the structure by saying whether students have too much, enough, or not enough money to buy the various things. *Reminder:* Since students have not had numbers above 69, don't ask them to say how much money they have.

H. Replace the words in italics with the expressions in parentheses.

1. J'ai *trop de* patience. (assez de / trop de / pas assez de)
2. Il a *trop d'*argent. (assez de / pas assez de / trop de)
3. Elles ont *assez de* vêtements. (trop de / pas assez de / assez de)
4. Nous avons *trop de* légumes. (pas assez de / assez de / trop de)

I. Evaluate the amounts, using the expressions **trop de, assez de,** and **pas assez de.**

MODÈLES: Une calculatrice coûte 60 francs. Yves a 65 francs.
Yves a assez d'argent pour acheter une calculatrice.

Mme Leroux a fait trois gâteaux. Elle a invité deux personnes à dîner.
Mme Leroux a fait trop de gâteaux.

1. Un transistor coûte 60 dollars. Jean-Jacques a 50 dollars.
2. Mme Barron a acheté quatre canards. Il y a deux personnes pour le dîner.
3. Anne a acheté trois tartelettes. Il y a trois personnes pour le déjeuner.
4. Un ordinateur coûte 12 000 francs. Nathalie a 9 500 francs.
5. M. Riboux a acheté huit biftecks. Il a invité cinq amis à dîner.

J. **Ils peuvent acheter. . .** Answer the questions based on the amounts people have in the bank and the prices of the objects.

À la banque		**Les prix**	
Monique	3 000F	un vélo	1 200F
Raymond	25F	un transistor	150F
Albert	200F	une calculatrice	225F
Pascale	1 000F	une chaîne stéréo	2 800F
Yves	500F	un disque	25F

MODÈLE: Comparez l'argent de Monique et l'argent d'Albert.
Monique a plus d'argent qu'Albert.

Est-ce que Monique a assez d'argent pour acheter un vélo?
Oui elle a assez d'argent pour acheter un vélo.

1. Comparez l'argent de Raymond et l'argent d'Yves.
2. Est-ce que Raymond a assez d'argent pour acheter un transistor?
3. Est-ce que Raymond a assez d'argent pour acheter un disque?
4. Comparez l'argent de Pascale et l'argent d'Albert.
5. Est-ce que Pascale a assez d'argent pour acheter un transistor et une calculatrice?

6. Comparez l'argent de Monique et l'argent d'Yves.
7. Est-ce que Monique a assez d'argent pour acheter une chaîne stéréo?
8. Comparez l'argent d'Albert et l'argent de Raymond.
9. Est-ce qu'Albert a assez d'argent pour acheter un transistor?
10. Est-ce qu'Albert a assez d'argent pour acheter un vélo?

DÉBROUILLONS-NOUS!

K. **Un dîner spécial.** You and your friend are inviting some special people for dinner. You've written out the menu. Now you have to tell your friend what to buy.

Review of the **étape**

Ex. K: ⇄

Salade de concombres

boeuf bourguignon

petits pois

tarte aux pommes

1. Tell him/her that you need cucumbers for the salad.
2. You also need beef and potatoes for the stew.
3. Tell him/her to buy peas.
4. Explain that you need flour and eggs for the pie.
5. Explain that you have enough apples and sugar.

l'Épicerie

51, RUE SAINT LOUIS-EN-L'ILE TEL: 43.25.20.14

Written Work: See Workbook.

Lexique

Pour se débrouiller

Pour indiquer une quantité

beaucoup de
pas beaucoup de
un peu de
quelques
très peu de
un kilo de
un demi-kilo de
une livre de
50 grammes de
un litre de
une bouteille de
une douzaine de
un morceau de
un bout de
une tranche de
trop de
assez de
pas assez de

Pour faire une comparaison

plus de . . . que
autant de . . . que
moins de . . . que

Thèmes et contextes

Les légumes

une asperge
une carotte
un champignon
un chou
un concombre
une courgette
un haricot vert
un oignon
un petit pois
une pomme de terre
un radis
une salade
une tomate

Les fruits

un abricot
une banane
une cerise
un citron
une fraise
une framboise
un melon
une orange
une pêche
une poire
une pomme

Les produits laitiers

le beurre
la crème
le fromage (le brie,
le camembert, le gruyère)
le yaourt

Les produits surgelés

la glace
la pizza
le poisson
les pommes frites

Autres choses à manger

la farine
le ketchup
la mayonnaise
la moutarde
le pâté
les pâtes *(f.pl.)*
le poivre
le poulet
le riz
le sel
le sucre

Vocabulaire général

Noms

un achat
l'argent *(m.)*
une botte
un carton
un chariot
une boîte de conserves
une épicerie
un filet
l'imagination *(f.)*
un marché en plein air
la patience
un produit
un rayon
un supermarché
un vêtement

Verbe

terminer

Adjectifs

frais (fraîche)
laitier(-ère)
surgelé(e)

Autres expressions

ça suffit
il faut
il me faut
il leur faut
il vous faut

Chapitre dix-huit

Moi, j'ai des courses à faire

—On va au centre commercial?
—Oui. Moi, j'ai des courses à faire.

Première étape

Point de départ:

À la Fnac

Suggestion, Point de départ: Before beginning the dialogue, you can deal with the two realia pieces (Hit-Parade, Vidéos) as readings. Have students read quickly and answer some questions about them. Sample questions: How many French songs do you find on the Hit-Parade? What are some American singers or groups you recognize? What is number 16 on the Hit-Parade? What number on the chart is Tina Turner's song? Have you ever heard of "Level 42?" Which of the music videos are you familiar with? What do you notice about all of these videos (they all have English titles)? Which video is in black and white? Etc.

HIT-PARADE

Salut ! vous propose son hit-parade qui est la synthèse du Top 50 d'Europe 1, des hits des radios RTL, NRJ, RMC et de celui de notre rédaction.

1 The final countdown Europe	11 A question of time Depeche Mode
2 Flash Stéphanie	12 Typical male Tina Turner
3 Eve lève-toi Julie Pietri	13 Belle Ile-en-Mer Laurent Voulzy
4 L'enfant Jeanne Mas	14 Adelaïde Arnold Turboust
5 La vie par procuration Jean-Jacques Goldman	15 Venus Bananarama
6 True blue Madonna	16 Libertine Mylène Farmer
7 Holiday rap Mc Miker "G" and Deejay Sven	17 Boule de flipper Corynne Charby
8 Epaule tattoo Etienne Daho	18 Andy Rita Mitsouko
9 Rien que pour toi François Feldman	19 Les brunes comptent pas pour des prunes Lio
10 Toi mon toit Elli Medeiros	20 Lessons in love Level 42

U GOT THE LOOK: PRINCE

Si ce clip est une indication des choses à venir lors de la prochaine tournée de Prince, alors là, il vaut mieux se tenir! Quelle sensualité! Et Prince qui trône en gourou au-dessus de tout ça! Il s'entoure d'une pléiade de danseurs et de musiciens, tous vêtus de façon à provoquer les fantasmes les plus osés chez l'auditeur. Et il ne faut surtout pas oublier la présence de Sheena Easton qui nous fait perdre la mémoire quand il s'agit de se souvenir de son premier hit, le mielleux Morning Train. Et puis, c'est un clip rempli de tellement de choses, qu'une fois ne suffit pas pour le regarder. ★★★★

CAN'T WE TRY: DAN HILL

Encore du noir et blanc! Quoiqu'ici, ça passe un peu mieux, même si ce clip n'a absolument rien d'exceptionnel. Lui est en noir, elle (Vonda Sheppard) est en blanc. Vraimen, rien à dire sur ce clip on ne peut plus commun. ★★

TOO GOOD TO BE ENOUGH: COREY HART

Un 45 tours, sorti juste comme ça, histoire de surprendre les fans. Et quelle surprise! Corey prend un nouveau virage musical, s'attardant, l'espace de quelques minutes, sur un style plus funky, plus rythmé. Et le vidéo, tourné dans les bayous de la Louisiane, est une petite merveille ensoleillée. Avec la présence des chanteuses Ruby Turner et Hellen Terry déguisées en sorcières vaudou, il y a de quoi se régaler! ★★★★

François et son ami Julien se trouvent à la Fnac. Ils adorent la musique et la **lecture,** et ils regardent donc les disques, les vidéos, les cassettes, les disques compacts, et les livres. **De quoi** parlent-ils? Des **derniers** vidéo-clips, bien sûr!

reading
what / latest

— Est-ce que tu as entendu la dernière **chanson** de Prince? — song
— Bien sûr! Et j'**ai** aussi **vu** son vidéo-clip. C'est **extra!** — saw / short for **extraordinaire**
— **Je pense que** je vais acheter son disque. Et je vais aussi **louer** une vidéo. — I think that / rent
— Moi, j'ai besoin de vidéos et de cassettes **vierges.** — blank
— Après, on va chez moi regarder la vidéo.
— D'accord.

Suggestion, Note culturelle: Have students name stores in their town that are comparable to the Fnac. Then have them tell you which of the items on the vocabulary list they already own. They can also state what they would like to own. Note that many vocabulary items were learned earlier. Many of the new words are cognates.

Note Culturelle

The chain of French stores called **Fnac** specializes in audio, video, and reading materials. The **Fnac** is a discount store that caters to all age groups and all tastes in music, videos and books. It's particularly popular among teenagers who spend entire afternoons browsing through the huge selections. The **Fnac** is located in Paris, Mulhouse, Marseille, Strasbourg, Grenoble, Toulouse, Bordeaux, and Nice.

Important terminology

une chaîne stéréo	stereo system
un magnétoscope	video cassette recorder
un magnétophone	tape recorder
une radio-cassette	cassette recorder with radio
un enregistreur à cassette	cassette recorder
un walk-man	personal stereo
un disque	record
une bande magnétique	audiotape
une cassette	audio cassette
une cassette vierge	blank cassette
un disque compact	compact disc
un vidéo-clip	music video
une vidéo	videotape
une vidéo vierge	blank video
la musique classique	classical music
le rock	rock music
le jazz	jazz

À vous!

Vocabulary activities

A. **Pour mon anniversaire...** Complete the following sentences, which will constitute your "wish list" for your next birthday. You can only use items that can be bought at the **Fnac.**

1. Je voudrais deux...
2. J'ai besoin d'un(e)...
3. Il me faut...
4. Je voudrais six...
5. Tu veux m'acheter...
6. Tu as assez d'argent pour m'acheter...

B. **Des cadeaux.** You're at the **Fnac** buying presents for your family and friends. Name what you'll buy for each of your family members and three of your friends.

MODÈLE: *Pour mon frère, je vais acheter un disque de Prince. Pour Cindy, je vais acheter une radio-cassette. Etc.*

Prononciation: *La voyelle e*

The letter **e** without a written accent can represent three different sounds in French:

1. the sound also represented by **é** (acute accent)
2. the sound also represented by **è** (grave accent)
3. the sound in single-syllable words such as **le**

At the end of a word, the letter **e** is pronounced [e] when it is followed by a silent consonant **(chanter, les).** The letter **e** is pronounced [ɛ] when it is followed by a consonant in the same syllable **(elle, personne).**[1] The letter **e** is pronounced [ə] at the end of a syllable in the middle of a word **(petit, cerise).** It is also pronounced [ə] in certain two-letter words **(le, ne, me).** Remember that **e** without an accent is usually silent at the end of a word.

Le savez-vous?

Young people in France save most of their money to buy
a) books
b) presents
c) a car
d) clothes

réponse

Pratique

C. Read each word aloud, being careful to distinguish among the three sounds of **e.**

[e] : des, mes, aller, il est, poulet, assez
[ɛ] : cassette, verre, appelle, hôtel, asperges, express
[ə] : de, le, petit, demain, pamplemousse, retour

[1]As a rule, French syllables end in a vowel **(vé lo, bou che rie).** However, two consonants next to each other in the middle of a word usually split into different syllables **(char cu te rie).**

D. Read the following words aloud. Each contains at least two different pronunciations of the letter **e.**

1. regarder
2. mercredi
3. chercher
4. elle est
5. se dresser
6. traverser
7. Perrier
8. église

REPRISE

Recycling activity

Suggestion, Ex. E: The chart contains more information than is dealt with in the exercise. You may wish to continue the exercise by drawing more comparisons.

E. **Des comparaisons.** Use the statistical information provided in the following chart to make comparisons. Remember the comparison expressions **plus de . . . que** *(more . . . than),* **autant de . . . que** *(as much . . . as, as many . . . as),* and **moins de . . . que** *(less . . . than, fewer . . . than).*

	habitants	**cinémas**	**théâtres**	**musées**
Paris	2 176 243	515	61	85
Lyon	413 095	128	33	21
Marseille	874 436	185	37	24
Lille	168 424	120	9	7
Bordeaux	208 159	163	14	9
Toulouse	347 995	163	17	13

d

MODÈLE: cinémas / Paris / Marseille
Paris a plus de cinémas que Marseille.

1. habitants / Bordeaux / Toulouse
2. cinémas / Toulouse / Bordeaux
3. musées / Paris / Marseille
4. théâtres / Lille / Paris
5. habitants / Marseille / Lyon
6. musées / Toulouse / Lille
7. cinémas / Lyon / Paris
8. théâtres / Lyon / Bordeaux

STRUCTURE

Numbers from 70 to 100

70	**soixante-dix**	80	**quatre-vingts**
71	**soixante et onze**	81	**quatre-vingt-un**
72	**soixante-douze**	82	**quatre-vingt-deux**
73	**soixante-treize**	83	**quatre-vingt-trois**
74	**soixante-quatorze**	84	**quatre-vingt-quatre**
75	**soixante-quinze**	85	**quatre-vingt-cinq**
76	**soixante-seize**	86	**quatre-vingt-six**
77	**soixante-dix-sept**	87	**quatre-vingt-sept**
78	**soixante-dix-huit**	88	**quatre-vingt-huit**
79	**soixante-dix-neuf**	89	**quatre-vingt-neuf**

90	**quatre-vingt-dix**
91	**quatre-vingt-onze**
92	**quatre-vingt-douze**
93	**quatre-vingt-treize**
94	**quatre-vingt-quatorze**
95	**quatre-vingt-quinze**
96	**quatre-vingt-seize**
97	**quatre-vingt-dix-sept**
98	**quatre-vingt-dix-huit**
99	**quatre-vingt-dix-neuf**
100	**cent**

The **t** of **vingt** in **quatre-vingts, quatre-vingt-un,** etc., and the **t** of **cent** are not pronounced. **Quatre-vingts** is written with an **s** only when it is *not* followed by another number: **quatre-vingts francs.**

Suggestion, Numbers 70-100: You may not want to emphasize spelling changes in numbers since it is rare that students will ever be asked to write them out. They would only be called upon to write out numbers if they were making out checks, an activity that is also unlikely to occur since students rarely have checking accounts in French-speaking countries.

Application

F. Do the following number exercises.

1. Count from 60 to 100.
2. Give the odd numbers from 1 to 99.
3. Give the even numbers from 0 **(zéro)** to 100.
4. Count from 0 to 100 by tens.
5. Read the following phone numbers: 46 23 39 57, 57 83 92 42, 98 66 54 32, 34 52 76 92.

NOTE GRAMMATICALE

Numbers from 101 to 1 000 000

100	**cent**	200	**deux cents**
101	**cent un**	201	**deux cent un**
102	**cent deux**	202	**deux cent deux**
1 000	**mille**	2 000	**deux mille**
1 001	**mille un**	2 500	**deux mille cinq cents**
1 002	**mille deux**	2 550	**deux mille cinq cent cinquante**
1 000 000	**un million**[2]	2 000 000	**deux millions**

Deux cents, trois cents, etc., are written with an **s** only when they are *not* followed by another number. **Mille** is invariable; it never takes an **s.** The commas used in English to write numbers in the thousands and millions are either omitted or replaced by a period: 3,560 = **3 560** or **3.560.** To express percentages, the French use a comma: 3.3 = **3,3 (trois virgule trois).**

G. Go back to Exercise E and read the numbers given in the chart for the various cities.

MODÈLE: *Paris a 2 176 243 habitants, 515 cinémas, 61 théâtres et 85 musées.*

H. **Faisons des calculs!** *(Let's do some math!)* Do the following math problems.

MODÈLES: 200 + 300 =
Deux cents et trois cents font cinq cents.

200 ÷ 50 =
Deux cents divisé par cinquante font quatre.

25 × 3 =
Vingt-cinq multiplié par trois font soixante-quinze.

30 − 15 =
Trente moins quinze font quinze.

1. 5 000 − 3 000 =
2. 225 × 4 =
3. 90 + 60 =
4. 600 ÷ 3 =
5. 608 − 16 =
6. 155 × 6 =
7. 450 ÷ 5 =
8. 950 + 250 =
9. 1000 ÷ 20 =

[2]When followed by a noun, **un million** is treated as an expression of quantity and therefore requires **de: un million de téléspectateurs, six millions de francs.**

I. **Le Mali.** Mali is a French-speaking country in northwestern Africa. Its capital city is Bamako. Read aloud the following facts about Mali.

1. La superficie *(area)* du Mali est 1 240 km.
2. La population du Mali est 6 300 000 habitants.
3. La distance entre la capitale Bamako et les villes suivantes est:

Bamako	⟶	Alger	2 878 km
Bamako	⟶	Rome	3 793 km
Bamako	⟶	Genève	3 971 km
Bamako	⟶	Paris	4 169 km
Bamako	⟶	Londres	4 378 km
Bamako	⟶	Francfort	4 430 km
Bamako	⟶	Stockholm	5 653 km
Bamako	⟶	New York	7 065 km

DÉBROUILLONS-NOUS!

J. **Rêvons!** *(Let's dream!)* Using the vocabulary you have learned in this chapter as well as previously learned words, talk to one of your classmates about the things you would like to own. As you mention each item, state what it probably costs (use **dollars**).

Review of the **étape**

Ex. J: ⇄

MODÈLE: *Moi, je voudrais avoir un ordinateur. Les ordinateurs coûtent probablement deux mille dollars.*

fnac

FORUM DES HALLES
1 à 7, rue Pierre Lescot
75001 Paris - 40.26.81.18
MONTPARNASSE
136, rue de Rennes
75006 Paris - 45.44.39.12
ETOILE
26, avenue de Wagram
75008 Paris - 47.66.52.50

Written Work: See Workbook.

Deuxième étape

Point de départ:

Au centre commercial

François et Julien se trouvent enfin au centre commercial. C'est samedi et il y a beaucoup de **monde.**

people

Suggestion, Point de Départ: Use the drawings on the transparencies to introduce the vocabulary from the **Note culturelle.** You may wish to do this one drawing (store) at a time, then go to the short conversation before moving on to the next store. You can also intersperse your presentation with personalized questions about what students own or prefer.

— Ah, tiens. Salut les **amis!**
— Salut, François. Salut, Julien. Qu'est-ce que vous faites ici?
— Nous avons **pas mal de** courses à faire. Et vous?
— Nous sommes là pour retrouver des amis et pour faire du lèche-vitrine.

quite a bit

— Tiens. Tu **vois** ce bracelet? Je vais **l'**acheter pour Janine.
— Tu ne penses pas qu'elle **préférerait** cette chaîne ou ces **boucles d'oreille?**
— Oui, peut-être. Qu'est-ce que tu penses de ce **pendentif?**
— Il est très **joli** aussi.

see / it
would prefer / earrings
pendant
pretty

— Je **dois** acheter des enveloppes et du papier pour ma mère.	have to
— Et moi, j'ai besoin d'une carte d'anniversaire et d'un carnet.	
— Je vais peut-être acheter un **conférencier** pour mon frère. Il vient de trouver un job.	leather case for paper and pen

— Regarde tous ces **jouets!** Tu vas acheter quelque chose pour ta petite sœur?	toys
— Je ne sais pas. Elle est **tellement gâtée. . . .**	so spoiled
— Oui, mais c'est bientôt son anniversaire.	
— D'accord. Je vais lui acheter un **jeu vidéo.**	video game

— Je voudrais bien acheter une raquette de tennis ou un ballon de foot. Mais c'est trop **cher.**	expensive
— Tu peux toujours acheter un sac pour la raquette et ensuite demander à tes parents de **t'**acheter la raquette!	for you

Note culturelle: Much of the vocabulary in this list was presented earlier in the book. It is included here so that it can be reviewed easily by students and so that it can be grouped under the particular stores.

Note Culturelle

In France and Canada, a shopping mall is organized more or less like malls in the United States. In addition to one or two department stores **(grands magasins),** one can find a large number of small specialty stores and boutiques, hair salons **(coiffeurs),** and fast-food places. Young people tend to use the malls for browsing, meeting friends, and, of course, shopping.

Specialty shops

Une bijouterie *(jewelry store)*

une chaîne	*neck chain*
un bracelet	*bracelet*
des boucles d'oreille *(f. pl.)*	*earrings*
un pendentif	*pendant*
une bague	*ring*
une montre	*watch*

Une papeterie *(stationery store)*

une enveloppe	*envelope*
du papier à écrire	*stationery*
des crayons *(m. pl.)*	*pencils*
des stylos *(m. pl.)*	*pens*
des gommes *(f. pl.)*	*erasers*
des carnets *(m. pl.)*	*notebooks*
des calendriers *(m. pl.)*	*calendars*
des cartes *(f. pl.)*	*cards*
de Noël	*Christmas*
d'anniversaire	*birthday*
pour le Nouvel An	*New Year's*
un conférencier	*leather case for paper and pen*

Un magasin de jouets *(toy store)*

une poupée	*doll*
un train électrique	*electric train*
un ballon	*ball*
un jeu vidéo	*video game*
un camion	*truck*
un robot	*robot*

Un magasin de sport *(sporting goods store)*

une raquette (une balle) de tennis	*tennis racket (ball)*
un ballon (de foot)	*(soccer) ball*
des skis *(m. pl.)*	*skis*
un vélo	*bike*
un appareil de gymnastique	*exercise machine*

À vous!

Vocabulary activities

A. **Des cadeaux d'anniversaire.** *(Birthday gifts.)* Say what you'll buy for each member of your family and for three of your best friends.

MODÈLE: *Pour mon père, je vais acheter un ballon de foot.*

B. **Achetons quelque chose.** Engage in a short conversation with a salesperson in each of the stores named. Say what you would like (need), ask the price, pay, and thank the salesperson.

Ex. B: ⇄

MODÈLE: bijouterie
—Bonjour, Madame (Monsieur). Je voudrais un bracelet.
—Voilà, Madame (Monsieur), nos bracelets.
—Combien coûte ce bracelet-ci?
—Il coûte 600F.
—Bon. Voilà 600 francs. Merci bien.

1. papeterie
2. magasin de sport
3. Fnac
4. magasin de jouets
5. bijouterie

Le savez-vous?

***Mammouth* is a**
a) fast-food chain specializing in meats
b) wholesale food outlet
c) department store
d) stationery store

réponse

REPRISE

C. State the population of the following cities.

Recycling activity

MODÈLE: Lyon: 413 095
À Lyon, il y a quatre cent treize mille quatre-vingt-quinze habitants.

1. Nancy: 96 317
2. Rouen: 101 945
3. Tours: 132 204
4. Reims: 177 234
5. Le Mans: 147 297
6. Pau: 83 790
7. Montpellier: 197 231
8. Calais: 76 527
9. Nîmes: 124 220

Structure, Devoir: We have limited the presentation of **devoir** to the present tense *(to owe, to have to)*, leaving the more complex aspects of the **passé composé** until later in the program. The two meanings presented here are the ones students are most likely to use in conversation.

Suggestion, Devoir: Introduce the verb through a short narrative about what you have to do after school. You can make the meaning clear by simply telling the class that **je dois** means **il est nécessaire.** Alternatively, you can present the verb through the meaning "to owe." Give a student a dollar, then point at him/her and say: **Frank doit un dollar à son professeur.**

STRUCTURE

The irregular verb ***devoir***

Tu dois 20 francs à ta sœur. — *You owe* your sister 20 francs.
Nous devons rentrer ce soir. — *We have to* go home tonight.

The verb **devoir** is irregular in the present tense:

devoir	
je **dois**	nous **devons**
tu **dois**	vous **devez**
il, elle, on **doit**	ils, elles **doivent**

The verb **devoir** in the present tense can have two meanings:

1. **devoir** = to owe (money or objects)
2. **devoir** = to have to, to be supposed to do something

Application

D. Replace the words in italics with the words in parentheses.

→ c

1. *Elle* doit beaucoup d'argent. (tu / Jacques / je / nous / vous / ils)
2. *Nous* devons rentrer demain. (elles / ma sœur / Jules / je / tu)
3. *Ils* doivent aller à la librairie. (je / nous / elle / vous / ils / tu)

E. **D'abord. . .** Each time someone is going to do something, you indicate that something else has to be done first. Use the present tense of **devoir** and the cues in parentheses.

MODÈLE: Je vais aller au cinéma. (faire tes devoirs)
D'abord tu dois faire tes devoirs.

1. Ils vont regarder la télévision. (aller à la papeterie)
2. Simone va aller au centre commercial. (manger quelque chose)
3. Je vais aller au café. (aller à la charcuterie)
4. Nous allons faire une promenade. (faire vos devoirs)
5. Jacques va faire du ski. (parler à son père)
6. Je vais écouter mes disques. (aller chercher ton frère)

Ex. F: ⇄

F. **Mes obligations.** Explain to one of your classmates what you have to do next week. Use the present tense of the verb **devoir.** Suggestions: **faire les devoirs, travailler, téléphoner à, aller, parler à, acheter, apprendre, faire les courses.**

DÉBROUILLONS-NOUS!

G. **Au centre commercial.** You and some friends are going to the mall. Once you're there, you can't agree on what to do. When one of you makes a suggestion, someone else says that he/she has to do some other things first.

Review of the **étape**

Ex. G: ⇄

MODÈLE: —*Allons au magasin de sport.*
—*Non. D'abord je dois aller à la papeterie.*

Lexique

Thèmes et contextes

La musique

une bande magnétique
une chaîne stéréo
une chanson
une cassette
une cassette vierge
un disque
un disque compact
un enregistreur à cassette
le jazz
un magnétophone
un magnétoscope
la musique classique
une radio-cassette
le rock
une vidéo
un vidéo-clip
une vidéo vierge
un walk-man

Une bijouterie

une bague
des boucles d'oreille *(f. pl.)*
un bracelet
une chaîne
une montre
un pendentif

Une papeterie

un calendrier
un carnet
une carte (de Noël, d'anniversaire, pour le Nouvel An)
un conférencier
un crayon
une enveloppe
une gomme
le papier à écrire
un stylo

Un magasin de jouets

un ballon
un camion
un jeu vidéo
un jouet
une poupée
un robot
un train électrique

Un magasin de sport

un appareil de gymnastique
un ballon (de foot)
une raquette (une balle) de tennis
des skis *(m. pl.)*
un vélo

Vocabulaire général

Noms

un cadeau
une capitale
un centre commercial
un coiffeur (une coiffeuse)
la distance
un dollar
un grand magasin
un(e) habitant(e)
la lecture
la population
la superficie

Verbes

chanter
devoir
louer
penser
rêver

Adjectifs

cher (-ère)
dernier (-ère)
extra (extraordinaire)
gâté(e)
joli(e)

Adverbes

probablement
tellement

Autres expressions

beaucoup de monde
de quoi
pas mal de

Mise au point

Lecture: *Les grands noms du rock—The Who*

Prereading: Ask students about their favorite rock groups and singers. This activity can be done in English and is simply intended to set the context of the reading. As students talk about their favorite groups, you can insert some vocabulary words that appear in the reading.

The following text is taken from *Fan Club* magazine, published in Quebec, Canada. *Fan Club* is widely read by teenagers both in Canada and in France. Every issue of the magazine contains portraits of the greats in rock and roll history. The group chosen for this article is The Who. As you read the article, pay particular attention to the many cognates that help you understand not only the gist of the text but also much of the detail. No words have been glossed, so you'll be reading this article just like anyone else who would pick up this magazine.

Lorsque Pete Townshend a déclaré: «Le rock n'a rien à voir avec la perfection. C'est une musique spontanée, souvent mauvaise, rauque, dure; c'est un immense bûcher funéraire,» il venait de définir non seulement le rock, mais aussi les idées véhiculées par **The Who,** l'archétype du groupe «mod» et pop-art contestataire. **Townshend, Roger Daltrey, John Entwistle** et **Keith Moon** se connaissent depuis leur enfance, à Londres. Les trois premiers forment d'abord les **Detours** de '61 à '63, puis les **High Numbers** en '64. Ils enregistrent un 45 tours, **I'm the Face/Zoot Suite. Keith Moon** est engagé comme batteur le soir où il monte sur scène et remplace violemment **Doug Sanden** en le traitant d'imbécile! Le nouveau groupe, alors nommé **The Who,** deviendra le porte-parole d'une nouvelle jeunesse exaltée et élégante. Violente et sauvage, leur musique s'inspire de la soul de Tamla Motown et James Brown. Fin '64, les **Who** sont engagés par le célèbre Marquee Club, et **I Can't Explain** est lancé le 15 janvier '65. C'est un triomphe, car le titre, copié sur une chanson des **Kinks,** se vend à plus de 100 000 exemplaires en un mois! **Townshend** tire de sa guitare, qu'il détruit après chaque concert, des sons inimaginables, et sa musique se veut de plus en plus expérimentale: **My Generation, Happy Jack, I'm a Boy, I Can See for Miles.** Mais c'est 1969 qui sera l'année des **Who** avec la publication de **Pinball Wizard** tirée de l'opéra rock **Tommy,** leur chef-d'oeuvre. En '70, c'est au tour de **Live at Leeds,** et en '71, de **Who's Next,** qui sera leur meilleure vente grâce à **Won't Get Fooled Again.** En '72, ils réalisent une nouvelle rock, **Quadrophenia,** double album où apparaît pour la première fois le mot punk **(The Punk and the Godfather).** Après 10 ans de carrière, le groupe participe au tournage du film de **Ken Russell** tiré de **Tommy,** qui met en vedette **Tina Turner, Jack Nicholson, Eric Clapton, Elton John** et **Roger Daltrey.** La mort subite de **Moon** en '78 précipite le constat d'usure du groupe qui annonce sa fin sur scène en 1982.

FAN CLUB, Vol. 2, No. 10, 31 Oct. 1987.

Compréhension

A. **Compréhension générale.** Answer the questions about the basic ideas that the text conveys.

1. According to Pete Townshend, rock has nothing to do with perfection. How does he define "rock"?
2. What was the importance of the year 1969?
3. What word appeared for the first time on the 1972 album *Quadrophenia*?
4. What current rock group is comparable in popularity to The Who?

B. Find as many cognates (French words that resemble English words) as you can in the text. Decide which ones are key words for the understanding of the article.

REPRISE

Recycling activities

C. **Combien est-ce que je vous dois?** Use the prices given to find out how much each person has to pay.

MODÈLE: Jacques / cassette / 22F
—Jacques va prendre cette cassette. Combien est-ce qu'il doit?
—Une cassette? Il doit vingt-deux francs.

1. ma mère / disque / 83F
2. je / magazine / 6F50
3. nous / vidéo / 225F
4. Simone et Jean / magnétoscope / 3.800F
5. Philippe / radio-cassette / 915F
6. je / livre / 198F

Ex. D: ⇄

D. **Échange.** Ask the following questions of a classmate, who will answer them.

1. Qu'est-ce que tu dois faire ce soir?
2. Est-ce que tu dois aider tes parents à la maison? Qu'est-ce que tu dois faire?
3. Est-ce que tu dois étudier beaucoup pour cette classe?
4. Est-ce que tu dois de l'argent à quelqu'un? Combien? À qui?

RÉVISION

In this **Révision,** you will review:

- the interrogative adjective **quel;**
- the partitive article;
- the demonstrative adjectives;
- expressions of quantity;
- the irregular verb **devoir.**

E. **Les magasins français.** Friends of your family are about to leave for France. Since they plan to do a lot of shopping, explain to them what they can buy in each of the following stores: **boulangerie–pâtisserie, charcuterie, boucherie, épicerie, Fnac, papeterie, bijouterie, magasin de sport, magasin de jouets.**

MODÈLE: *À la boulangerie-patisserie, vous pouvez acheter du pain, des éclairs, des mille-feuilles, etc.*

The interrogative adjective *quel*

Quel has four forms **(quel, quelle, quels, quelles)** and means *what* or *which* in English. It must agree in gender and number with the noun it modifies. Use a form of **quel** when you want to ask someone to identify something.

Quel can be used in two ways: **quel** + noun
quel + **être** + noun

Quels desserts est-ce que tu préfères?
Quelle est ta voiture préférée?

F. **À la Fnac.** Find out what your friends bought at the **Fnac.** Use the forms of **quel** in your questions.

MODÈLE: disque / Prince
— *Qu'est-ce que tu as acheté?*
— *J'ai acheté un disque.*
— *Quel disque?*
— *Le dernier disque de Prince.*

1. vidéo / Madonna
2. cassette / U2
3. disque / Europe
4. disque compact / Téléphone
5. cassette / Prince
6. vidéo / Bruce Springsteen

The partitive

Je voudrais **de la** salade de tomates, **du** jambon et **des** saucisses.

The partitive article is used when you want to indicate *part of* something. To form it, simply add **de** to the definite articles:

de + le = **du (du** jambon, **du** saucisson, **du** pâté, **du** courage)
de + la = **de la (de la** salade, **de la** soupe, **de la** patience)
de + l' = **de l' (de l'**imagination, **de l'**eau minérale)
de + des = **des (des** tomates, **des** pâtisseries, **des** saucissons)

After a negative expression, the partitive articles become **de** regardless of the gender and number of the noun:

Je **n'**ai **pas de** disques.
Nous **n'**avons **pas de** jambon.
Ils **n'**ont **pas de** salade.

G. **Une fête.** You planned a big party and have bought a great deal to eat and drink. Now you tell your friend about your purchases. Add the partitive article to the items you bought.

1. pâté
2. fruits
3. pain
4. eau minérale
5. Coca
6. salade de concombres
7. jambon
8. saucisson
9. salade de tomates
10. petits pains
11. croissants
12. rôti de porc cuit
13. salade de thon
14. ketchup
15. mayonnaise
16. moutarde
17. pâtisseries
18. limonade
19. fraises
20. pommes
21. bananes
22. cerises
23. poulet

The definite, indefinite, and partitive articles

Unlike English, French usually requires an article with each noun. You have now learned three types of articles.

Use:	**to describe:**	
the definite articles: **le, la, l', les**	a noun used in the general sense	**J'aime le pain.** *I like bread (in general).* 
	a specific thing	**Voici le pain que j'ai acheté.** *Here is the (specific loaf of) bread that I bought.* 
the indefinite articles: **un, une, des**	one (or several) whole items	**J'ai acheté un pain.** *I bought (a loaf of) bread.* 
the partitive articles: **du, de la, de l', des**	a part of something	**Je mange du pain.** *I'm eating some bread.* 

H. **Allons au centre commercial!** Complete the following dialogue by adding the appropriate articles—definite, indefinite, and partitive.

— Par où est-ce qu'on commence?
— Moi, je voudrais acheter _____ cartes pour le Nouvel An. Et il me faut aussi _____ stylo. Je n'ai plus _____ stylo.
— Tu veux donc aller à _____ papeterie? Ce n'est pas très intéressant. Moi, je préfère aller à _____ bijouterie. Ils ont _____ pendentif que j'aime beaucoup.
— Ah oui. Ils ont aussi _____ boucles d'oreille formidables.
— Eh ben. . . Moi, je dois acheter _____ jouet pour mon frère. Il adore _____ jeux vidéo.
— Il préfère peut-être _____ ballon de foot. _____ petits garçons aiment jouer au football.
— Non. Il n'aime pas _____ football. Il préfère la musique. Je vais peut-être acheter _____ disques ou _____ cassette.
— Bon. Écoutez. Rendez-vous dans trois heures devant _____ magasin de sport.

Demonstrative adjectives

Demonstrative adjectives are used to designate or point to a specific object or person. In English, they are translated as *this* or *these*. Demonstrative adjectives agree in gender and number with the nouns they modify.

ce → masculine singular before a consonant **(ce livre)**
cet → masculine singular before a vowel or vowel sound **(cet étudiant)**
cette → feminine singular **(cette voiture)**
ces → feminine and masculine plural **(ces disques, ces maisons)**

When you want to make a distinction between *this* and *that* or *these* and *those*, use the demonstrative adjective and add **-ci** *(this, these)* or **-là** *(that, those)* to the noun:

— Je préfère **ce** disque-**ci.**
— Moi, j'aime mieux **ce** disque-**là**.

I. **Combien est. . . ?** While you're at the mall, you want to find out the prices of different items. As you go from store to store, use demonstrative adjectives to inquire about the prices.

MODÈLE: chaîne
Combien est cette chaîne?

boucles d'oreille
Combien sont ces boucles d'oreille?

1. enveloppes
2. stylo
3. portefeuille
4. bague
5. train électrique
6. skis
7. cartes de Noël
8. calendriers
9. montre
10. bracelets
11. vélo
12. radio-cassette
13. disque
14. raquette de tennis
15. camion
16. vidéo
17. papier à écrire
18. jouets
19. appareil de gymnastique
20. poupée

Expressions of quantity

General quantity

beaucoup de	*a lot, a great deal, many, much*
pas beaucoup de	*not many, not much*
un peu de	*a little, a little bit*
quelques	*some*
très peu de	*very little*

Specific quantity

un kilo de	*a kilogram of*
un demi-kilo de	*a half-kilogram of*
une livre de	*a pound (French) of*
50 grammes de	*50 grams of*
un litre de	*a liter of*
une bouteille de	*a bottle of*
une douzaine de	*a dozen of*
un morceau de	*a piece of*
un bout de	*an end (piece) of*
une tranche de	*a slice of*

Comparison

plus de (+ noun) **que**	*more... than*
autant de (+ noun) **que**	*as much/as many... as*
moins de (+ noun) **que**	*less/fewer... than*

Sufficiency

trop de	*too much, too many*
assez de	*enough*
pas assez de	*not enough*

Remember that in expressions of quantity, the form of **de** remains the same, regardless of the gender and number of the noun.

J. **Soyons précis!** *(Let's be precise!)* Whenever you make a general statement, someone asks you to be specific. In your first statement, use an expression of general quantity; in the second, use an expression of specific quantity.

MODÈLE: pommes
— *J'ai acheté beaucoup de pommes.*
— *Combien de pommes est-ce que tu as achetées?*
— *J'ai acheté trois kilos de pommes.*

1. saucisses
2. pâté
3. Vittel
4. concombres
5. pommes de terre
6. salade de tomates
7. jambon
8. haricots verts
9. saucisson
10. poulet
11. Coca
12. oranges

K. **Comparons.** Compare the people in the chart based on their possessions.

	disques	**vidéos**	**cassettes**	**livres**
Simone	50	3	15	112
François	26	16	27	112
Roland	80	16	44	75
Chantal	50	23	27	68

MODÈLE: disques / Simone et Roland
Simone a moins de disques que Roland.

1. vidéos / François et Roland
2. livres / Roland et Chantal
3. cassettes / Chantal et Simone
4. disques / François et Roland
5. livres / Simone et François
6. vidéos / Roland et Chantal
7. cassettes / François et Chantal
8. disques / Chantal et François

L. **Combien d'argent est-ce que tu as?** Four friends are at the mall. According to the amounts of money indicated, decide if they have enough money to buy the various items.

			Prix
Marie-France	234F	disque	112F
Robert	123F	enveloppes	29F
Sylvie	549F	vidéo	258F
Marc	25F	carte d'anniversaire	15F
		livre	113F
		stylo	8F
		poupée	98F
		skis	467F
		cassette vierge	12F

MODÈLES: Marie-France / livre
Marie-France a assez d'argent pour acheter le livre.

Marc / enveloppes
Marc n'a pas assez d'argent pour acheter les enveloppes.

1. Marie-France / disque
2. Sylvie / skis
3. Robert / vidéo
4. Marc / carte d'anniversaire
5. Marie-France / vidéo
6. Robert / poupée
7. Sylvie / skis et disque
8. Marc / cassette vierge

Numbers from 70 to 1 000 000

70 **soixante-dix**	80 **quatre-vingts**	90 **quatre-vingt-dix**
71 **soixante et onze**	81 **quatre-vingt-un**	91 **quatre-vingt-onze**
72 **soixante-douze**	82 **quatre-vingt-deux**	92 **quatre-vingt-douze**
73 **soixante-treize**	83 **quatre-vingt-trois**	93 **quatre-vingt-treize**
74 **soixante-quatorze**	84 **quatre-vingt-quatre**	94 **quatre-vingt-quatorze**
75 **soixante-quinze**	85 **quatre-vingt-cinq**	95 **quatre-vingt-quinze**
76 **soixante-seize**	86 **quatre-vingt-six**	96 **quatre-vingt-seize**
77 **soixante-dix-sept**	87 **quatre-vingt-sept**	97 **quatre-vingt-dix-sept**
78 **soixante-dix-huit**	88 **quatre-vingt-huit**	98 **quatre-vingt-dix-huit**
79 **soixante-dix-neuf**	89 **quatre-vingt-neuf**	99 **quatre-vingt-dix-neuf**

100 **cent**	200 **deux cents**
101 **cent un**	201 **deux cent un**
102 **cent deux**	202 **deux cent deux**
1 000 **mille**	2 000 **deux mille**
1 001 **mille un**	2 500 **deux mille cinq cents**
1 002 **mille deux**	2 550 **deux mille cinq cent cinquante**
1 000 000 **un million**	2 000 000 **deux millions**

M. Do the following number exercises.

1. Count from 100 to 300 by tens.
2. Count from 500 to 100 by fifties.
3. Count from 69 to 99.
4. Give the even numbers from 70 to 100.
5. Read the following numbers: 19, 29, 39, 59, 79, 89, 90, 99, 109, 1 076, 1 176, 1 276, 1 376, 1 476, 1 576, 7 500 000, 7 600 000, 7 700 000, 7 800 000, 7 900 000, 8 000 000.

N. Read the following addresses.

1. 178, avenue de la Libération
2. 879, boulevard Raspail
3. 216, boulevard Montparnasse
4. 3486, avenue des Champs-Élysées
5. 98, avenue de la République
6. 284, boulevard Kennedy

O. Read the year of each event.

1. 1776 la Révolution américaine
2. 1789 la Révolution française
3. 1492 Christophe Colomb en Amérique
4. 1945 la fin de la Seconde Guerre mondiale
5. 1815 la fin de l'empire de Napoléon
6. 1963 l'assassinat du président Kennedy
7. 1988 les élections présidentielles en France
8. 1889 la construction de la Tour Eiffel

The irregular verb devoir

je **dois**	nous **devons**
tu **dois**	vous **devez**
il, elle, on **doit**	ils, elles **doivent**

The irregular verb **devoir** means *to owe* (money or objects) and expresses obligation or what one is supposed to do.

P. **Nous leur devons beaucoup d'argent!** *(We owe them a lot of money!)* Based on the cues, tell how much money each person owes to whom.

MODÈLE: Christophe / $125 / père
Christophe doit 125 dollars à son père.

1. je / $36 / sœur
2. nous / $1389 / parents
3. Simone / $88 / amie Francine
4. ils / $159 / Richard
5. tu / $99 / frère
6. Marc et Monique / $775 / tante

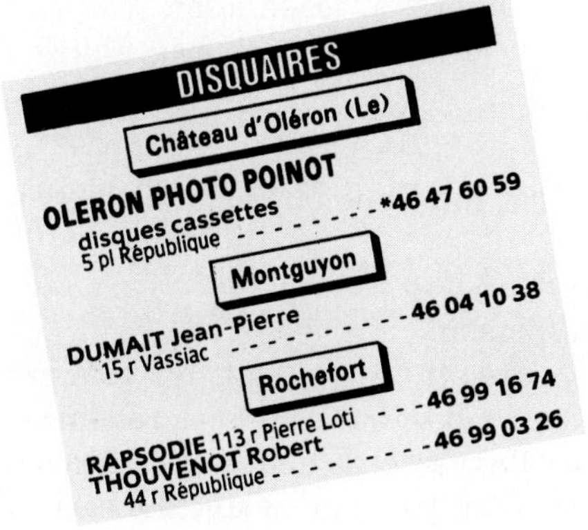

Point d'arrivée

Ex. Q: ⇄

Q. **Faisons un pique-nique.** You are going on a picnic and one of your friends is going to do the shopping. Explain to him or her where to go and what to buy.

MODÈLE: *D'abord tu vas aller à la boulangerie. Tu vas acheter une baguette ou un pain de campagne. Ensuite tu vas aller...*

Ex. R: ⇄

Suggestion, Exs. R and S: Have students act out a skit based on the directions given. In exercise R, one student plays the shopkeeper and another plays the shopper. In exercise S, one student plays the old woman and another plays the person who did the shopping.

R. **Faisons les courses.** You're shopping for an elderly woman. Using the list below, go to the appropriate stores and make your purchases. She has given you 200 francs. Is it enough?

rôti de bœuf (pour 4 personnes)
pommes de terre (1 kilo)
salade de concombres (1)
tomates (1 livre)
baguettes (2)
tarte (ou gâteau)
Vittel (2 bouteilles)
poulet
2 éclairs
brie (250 grammes)
saucisson (16 tranches)
jambon (4 tranches)

Ex. S: ⇄

S. **Est-ce que tu as oublié... ?** When you come back from your shopping trip in Exercise R, the woman questions you about what you bought and what you forgot. You may have to explain that you didn't have enough money for everything.

Ex. T: ⇄

T. **À l'épicerie.** You're in an **épicerie** buying food for a dinner you're making for your friends.

1. Greet the shopkeeper.
2. Explain what you want and specify quantities.
3. Ask how much you owe for each item.
4. Explain that you have a shopping bag, thank the person, and say good-bye.

U. **À la Fnac.** You're at the **Fnac** buying a birthday present for your best friend.

1. Greet the salesperson.
2. Explain that you want to buy a gift for your friend.
3. Your friend loves music but also likes reading.
4. Ask about the latest records and music videos.
5. Make your selection, pay, and thank the salesperson.

Written Work: See Workbook.

Jean Hébert

J'ai seize ans et j'habite avec ma famille dans un grand appartement. Je m'intéresse à beaucoup de choses, mais surtout, j'adore la musique. Je joue de la guitare et je chante assez bien. J'ai un chien qui s'appelle "Jim." Je passe beaucoup de temps avec mes amis. Nous écoutons des disques, nous regardons des vidéos et nous allons souvent au centre commercial. Je n'ai pas beaucoup d'argent, mais quelquefois je peux acheter un disque ou des cassettes. Un jour je voudrais être compositeur.

Dernière étape

DÉBROUILLONS-NOUS !

Now that you have finished the first part of your introduction to the French language, you are ready to test your skills. As you work your way through the following activities, you will realize how much you have learned during the past year and how well you are able to cope with some situations that might occur in a French-speaking context.

Première partie

The activities in this section bring together contexts, structures, and vocabulary that you have worked with in **On y va! (Niveau premier).** As you role play these situations with other students or with your teacher, concentrate on communicating by using all the strategies that you have learned. If you can't remember a particular word or structure, make yourself understood by substituting other words and structures that you do remember.

A. Ask a classmate for the following information. Then go to a second pair of students, make introductions, and tell them what you have found out. Find out from your classmate:

1. his/her age
2. where he/she was born
3. how many brothers and sisters he/she has
4. his/her favorite leisure activities
5. whether or not he/she is planning to travel in the near future

B. Ask a classmate about one of his/her friends or teenage relatives (brother, sister, cousin). Find out:

1. this person's name
2. who he/she is (friend? relative?)
3. where he/she lives
4. what he/she looks like (size? hair? eyes?)
5. what sports and other activities he/she likes and dislikes
6. whether or not he/she plays a musical instrument

C. Ask a classmate about one of his/her parents or grandparents. Find out:

1. how old this person is
2. where he/she comes from originally
3. what kind of work he/she does
4. whether or not he/she owns a car (If yes, what kind?)
5. whether or not he/she uses the car or another means of transportation to get to work or to go downtown
6. what he/she likes to do in his/her spare time

D. Imagine that you're working at an information center located at a place of your choice (somewhere in the center of your town or city). Your classmates will play the roles of the tourists listed below and will ask you for help.

1. someone looking for a (the) post office
2. someone who wants to find the (or a particular) school
3. someone who needs to find a drugstore
4. someone looking for the (a) police station
5. someone looking for a toy store

E. You would like to invite a classmate to come to your house to listen to records (to watch TV, to play monopoly, etc.).

1. Ask if he/she likes to do the particular activity you have chosen.
2. Tell him/her that you're planning to do this particular activity on a certain day.
3. Invite him/her to join you.
4. Find out where your classmate lives.
5. Give him/her directions on how to get from his/her house to where you live.

F. You need to go downtown and would like two of your classmates to accompany you.

1. Indicate why you need to go downtown.
2. Find out if your classmate would like to go with you.
3. Suggest that you get something to eat while you're downtown.
4. Ask what they would prefer to do—go to a café, eat at a fast-food restaurant, or buy something at a **briocherie.** (They will each give a different answer.)
5. Find out the reason for each one's preference.
6. Choose one of the possibilities and try to convince the third person to agree to it.

G. You've just returned from a trip to Paris. Tell a friend what you did and saw during your month-long vacation. Your friend will ask you questions for clarification and additional information.

H. You've just returned from a vacation in a U.S. city (pick any city you know well). Tell your classmate about the trip. Who was with you? What did you do? How much time did you spend in the city? Where did you stay? Where did you eat?

I. At a class reunion, you meet the person who used to be your best friend. Explain what you did for the last few years, describe your family, and talk about your activities. Ask your friend some questions about his/her activities.

J. You're at the jewelry counter of a department store.

1. Tell the salesperson that you'd like to buy a bracelet for your mother.
2. It's your mother's birthday and you want to get her something special.
3. You have only $35 to spend.
4. Choose the gift and ask about the price.
5. Thank the salesperson.

K. You and your friend are planning a surprise party for one of your classmates. Tell your friend where the party will be held and what food you need. Then decide who will buy the various food items.

L. You and your friend are planning a shopping day. Decide where you'll go, how you will get there, and what you'll buy. Plan to go to a variety of stores.

M. You just bought the latest rock video and want to show it to your friend.

1. Invite your friend to your house.
2. Explain that you have the latest rock video (give the song and singer).
3. Tell your friend to come over this evening.
4. Find out if he/she can bring some other videos.

Deuxième partie

When you travel in a foreign country, you're surrounded by informational signs. Very often you may not know all the words in the signs, so you have to do your best to guess their meanings. Here are some signs that you are likely to encounter in a French-speaking context. Use the strategies you've learned to understand the message that each transmits.

CAMPING St GABRIE
tarif Journalier
Douche Chaude Comprise
Par Personne 9F75
Par Voiture 3F25
Par Caravane 7F25
Par Tente 7F25
ELECTRICITÉ 9,5
CHIEN 2F
44 EMPLACEMENTS — 154 CAM
A.C.S.I. CAMPING

PISCINE DELIGNY
BASSIN INDÉPENDANT DE LA SEINE
ALIMENTÉ en EAU POTABLE
Filtrée - Purifiée - Contrôlée
Jeux Ping-Pong
551.72.15
Leçons de Natation
SOLARIUM
RESTAURANT
BAR

Place des VOSGES
Maison de VICTOR HUGO (Musée)
6 bis, Pce des Vosges
Quartier du MARAIS

FRANPRIX Sd
OUVERT
sans interruption
DU MARDI AU SAMEDI
de 8H30 à 19H30
LE LUNDI
de 12H à 19H30
LE DIMANCHE
de 9H à 13H

nos sandwichs variés
HOT DOG 17
SAUCISSES CHAUDES 15
PATÉ 13
JAMBON CUIT 13
FROMAGE 13
CROQUE MONSIEUR 13

Décollez en anglais allemand italien espagnol.
APPELEZ-NOUS (1) 43.25.81.40
EUROCENTRES
FONDATION SANS BUT LUCRATIF
13 N. PASSAGE DAUPHINE 75006 PARIS

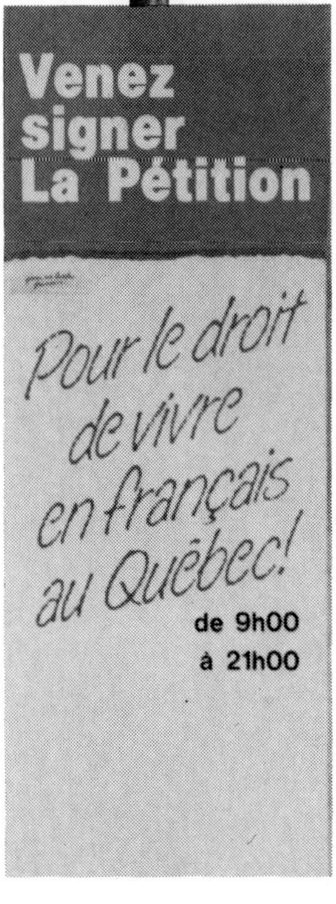
Venez signer La Pétition
Pour le droit de vivre en français au Québec!
de 9h00
à 21h00

Quick
LES MENUS ÉCONOMIQUES
MENU RUSÉ
2 HAMBURGERS
1 GRANDE FRITE
1 COCA-COLA 37 CL · 1 CAFÉ
30F

Glossary of functions

The numbers in parentheses refer to the chapter in which the word or phrase may be found.

Ordering something to eat or drink at a café
Je voudrais . . . (1)
Je vais prendre . . . (1)

Greeting and taking leave of someone
Bonjour. (1)
Ça va (bien)? (1)
Oui, ça va bien. (2)
Comment allez-vous? (2)
Je vais très (bien). (2)
Comment ça va? (1)
Salut. (1)
A bientôt. (1)
À tout à l'heure. (1)
Allez, au revoir. (1)
Au revoir. (1)

Being polite
S'il vous plaît. (1)
Merci (bien). (1)
Je vous en prie. (1)

Introducing
Enchanté(e). (2)
Je te présente . . . (1)
Je vous présente . . . (2)

Identifying personal possessions
Pour aller en classe, j'ai . . . (4)
Dans ma chambre, j'ai . . . (4)
Chez nous, nous avons . . . (4)
Pour aller en ville, j'ai . . . (4)

Talking about my preferences
J'adore . . . (5)
J'aime assez . . . (5)
bien . . . (5)
beaucoup . . . (5)
mieux . . . (5)
Je déteste . . . (5)
Je n'aime pas . . . (5)
Je préfère . . . (5)

Talking about my family
Je suis . . . (6)
Je m'appelle . . . (6)
J'ai . . . (6)

Getting information about other people
Combien de . . . ? (6)
Comment s'appelle . . . ? (6)
Où . . . ? (6)
Pourquoi . . . ? (6)
Quel âge avez-vous? (7)
J'ai . . . ans. (7)
Qu'est-ce que . . . ? (6)

Asking for directions
Est-ce qu'il y a un(e) . . . près d'ici? (7)
Où est . . . ? (7)
Où se trouve . . . ? (8)
Pardon . . . (7)
. . . s'il vous plaît? (8)

Giving directions
Il (elle) est à côté de . . . (8)
au bout de . . . (8)
au coin de . . . (8)
continuer tout droit jusqu'à . . . (6)
dans l'avenue . . . (8)
dans la rue . . . (8)
derrière . . . (8)
devant . . . (8)
en face de . . . (8)
entre . . . (8)
loin de . . . (8)
près de . . . (8)
sur (dans) le boulevard . . . (8)
sur la place . . . (8)

tourner à droite (à gauche) (8)
traverser (8)

Talking about leisure time activities
Allons . . . (9)
J'ai envie de . . .
Bonne idée. (9)
D'accord. (9)
Faison . . . (9)
Je voudrais voir . . . (9)
Oui. Pourquoi pas? (9)
Qu'est-ce que tu voudrais faire? (9)
vous voudriez voir? (9)

Making plans to meet
À quelle heure est-ce qu'on se retrouve? (9)
On se retrouve à. . . (9)
Où est-ce qu'on se retrouve? (9)
Rendez-vous à. . . (9)

Telling time
Quelle heure est-il? (9)
Il est une heure. (9)
une heure et quart. (9)
une heure et demie. (9)
deux heures moins le quart. (9)
midi. (9)
minute. (9)

Making plans to go into town
Avec plaisir. (11)
Bien sûr. (11)
C'est impossible. (11)
C'est une bonne idée. (11)
Il faut combien de temps pour y aller? (12)
Je ne peux pas. (11)
Mais oui. (11)
Pourquoi pas? (11)
Tu veux (tu voudrais) . . . ? (11)
Voulez vous (vous voudriez) . . . ?
Quand est-ce qu'on y va? (10)
Quand est-ce que tu voudrais y aller? (10)
aujourd'hui (10)
ce matin (10)
cet après-midi (10)
ce soir (10)
demain (matin, après-midi, soir) (10)
On prend . . .
On y va . . .
en autobus (12)
en métro (12)
à pied (10, 12)
en taxi (12)
en voiture (12)
à vélo (12)

Talking about what to do in town
J'ai rendez-vous avec . . . (10)
J'ai une course à faire. (10)
Je dois faire des achats. (10)
Je vais faire une course. (10)
Je n'ai rien à faire. (10)
Je vais retrouver quelqu'un. (10)
Je dois. . . (10)

Talking about the Paris subway
une bouche de métro (11)
changer (11)
une correspondance (11)
descendre (11)
prendre (11)
Quelle direction? (11)
une station de métro (11)

Taking a taxi
C'est combien? (12)
Il faut combien de temps pour y aller? (12)
Je vous dois combien? (12)
Voilà pour vous. (12)

Expressing wishes and desires
J'ai envie de . . . (12)
J'ai l'intention de . . . (12)
J'espère . . . (12)
Je voudrais. . . (9)
Nous voudrions. . . (9)

Talking about events in the past
l'année dernière (13)
d'abord (14)
enfin (14)
ensuite (14)

hier (13)
hier matin (13)
hier après-midi (13)
hier soir (13)
il y a une heure (deux mois, cinq ans) (13)
lundi (mardi, etc.) dernier (13)
le mois dernier (13)
premièrement (14)
puis (14)
la semaine dernière (13)
la semaine suivante (14)
le week-end dernier (13)
la veille (14)

Talking about actions in the future

Je vais . . . (15)
J'ai l'intention de . . . (15)
J'espère . . . (15)
Je voudrais . . . (15)
Je veux . . . (15)

Making purchases/choices

Est-ce que vous avez . . . ? (16)
J'ai besoin de . . . (16)
Je prends . . . (16)
Je vais prendre . . . (16)
Je voudrais . . . (16)
Donnez mois un bout de . . . (17)
une bouteille de . . . (17)
une douzaine de . . . (17)
un demi-kilo de . . . (16)
une gramme de . . . (16)
un kilo (kilogramme) de . . . (16)
un litre de . . . (16)
une livre de . . . (16)
un morceau de . . . (17)
un peu de . . . (17)
quelques . . . (17)
une tranche de . . . (16)
très peu de . . . (17)
assez pour . . . personnes. (17)
C'est combien? (16)
Combien coute . . . ? (16)
Combien est-ce que je vous dois? (16)

Expressing obligation

Je dois . . .

Making comparisons

autant de. . . que. . . (17)
moins de. . . que. . . (17)
plus de . . . que. . . (17)

Glossary

French–English

The numbers in parentheses refer to the chapter in which the word or phrase may be found.

A

à bientôt See you soon (1)
à côté de next to (8)
à part besides (14)
à pied on (by) foot (10), (12)
à tout à l'heure See you in a while (1)
à vélo by bicycle (12)
à vol d'oiseau a bird's-eye view (13)
abricot *m.* apricot (17)
abriter to house (13)
achat *m.* purchase (17)
acheter to buy (10)
acier *m.* steel (14)
acteur(-trice) *m. (f.)* actor (actress) (3)
adorer to love (5)
aéroport *m.* airport (7)
affaires *f. pl.* business (13)
âge age
agriculteur(-trice) *m. (f.)* farmer (3)
aimer to like (5)
aimer le mieux to like the best (5)
aimer mieux to prefer (5)
allée *f.* country lane (15)
allemand(e) German (3)
aller to go (7)
aller en ville to go into town (4)
alors then (9)
amandes almonds (2)
amener to take, to lead (13)
américain(e) American (3)
ami(e) *m. (f.)* friend (2)
ancien(ne) former (13)
anglais(e) English (3)
année *f.* year (9)
anniversaire *m.* birthday (16)
antiquités *f. pl.* relics (13)
appareil de gymnastique *m.* exercise machine (18)
appareil-photo *m.* camera (4)
appartement *m.* apartment (4)
apprendre to learn (10)
après-midi *m.* afternoon (10)
arc-boutants *m. pl.* flying buttresses (14)
argent *m.* money (17)
arrondissements *m. pl.* administrative divisions of Paris (13)
art *m.* art (5)
asperge *f.* asparagus (17)
assez enough (1), (16)
astronaute *m. or f.* astronaut (3)
attirer to attract (13)
au bord de on the banks of (9)
au bout de at the end of (8)
au coin de at the corner of (8)
au milieu de in the middle of (13)
au revoir goodbye (1)
au-dessus de above (14)
aujourd'hui today (10)
aussi also (1), (13)
aussi bien que as well as (15)
autant as much (17)
auto *f.* car (4)
autobus *m.* bus (10)
auto-école *f.* driving school (12)
avant before (13)
avec with (11)

avec plaisir with pleasure (11)
avenue *f.* avenue (7)
avocat(e) *m. (f.)* lawyer (3)
avoir to have (4)
avoir besoin de to need (4)
avoir envie de to feel like (10), (12)
avoir faim to be hungry (4)
avoir lieu to take place (13)
avoir l'intention de to intend to (12)
avoir raison to be right (4)
avoir rendez-vous avec to have a date to meet with (10)
avoir soif to be thirsty (4)
avoir tort to be wrong (4)

B

bacon *m.* bacon (16)
bague *f.* ring (18)
baguette *f.* long loaf of bread (16)
bal *m.* dance (9)
balle de tennis *f.* tennis ball (18)
ballon *m.* ball (18)
ballon de foot *m.* soccer ball (18)
banane *f.* banana (16)
bande magnétique *f.* audio tape (18)
banlieue *f.* suburb (14)
banque *f.* bank (7)
baseball *m.* baseball (7)
basket *m.* basketball (7)
bâtiment *m.* building (13)
batterie *f.* drums (8)
battu(e) beaten (14)
beau (belle) beautiful (14)
beaucoup very much (5)
beaucoup de a lot of (17)
belge Belgian (3)
berceau *m.* cradle (13)
beurre *m.* butter (17)
bibliothèque *f.* library (7)
bien well (1)
bien sûr of course (11)
bifteck *m.* steak (16)
bijouterie *f.* jewelry store (18)
billet *m.* ticket (11); paper money (12)
billet de seconde *m.* second-class ticket (11)
billet de tourisme *m.* tourist pass for subway (11)
blessé(e) wounded (14)
boeuf beef (16)
boisson *m.* drink (1)
boîte *f.* can (17)
bon(ne) good (9)
bonjour hello (1)
bord *m.* bank (of a river) (13)
botte *f.* bunch (17)
bouche *f.* mouth
bouche de métro *f.* metro entrance (11)
boucher(-ère) *m. (f.)* butcher (16)
boucherie *f.* butcher shop (7), (16)
boucles d'oreilles *f. pl.* earrings (18)
boulanger(-ère) *m. (f.)* baker (16)
boulangerie *f.* bakery that sells bread and rolls (7), (16)
boules *f. pl.* game played with metal and wooden balls (7)
boulevard *m.* boulevard (8)
boulon *m.* bolt (14)
bout *m.* piece (17)
bouteille *f.* bottle (17)
bracelet *m.* bracelet (18)
brie *m.* Brie cheese (17)
brioche *f.* light sweet bun raised with yeast and eggs (2)
briocherie *f.* bakery that sells brioche and other hot snacks (2)
brun(e) brown (6)
bureau *m.* desk (4)
bureau de poste *m.* post office (7)
bureau de tabac *m.* tobacco store that also sells stamps and newspapers (7)
butte *f.* hill (13)

C

ça suffit? is that enough? (17)
cachot *m.* prison cell (14)
cadeau *m.* gift (13), (18)
café *m.* coffee (1); café (1)

café au lait coffee with milk (1)
café crème coffee with cream (1)
cahier *m.* notebook (4)
calculatrice *f.* calculator (4)
calendrier *m.* calendar (18)
camion *m.* truck (18)
camembert *m.* Camembert cheese (17)
camping *m.* camping (5)
canadien(ne) Canadian (3)
canard *m.* duck (16)
capitale *f.* capital (18)
car because (14)
carnet *m.* small notebook (4), (18); book of metro tickets (11)
carotte *f.* carrot (17)
carte *f.* card (18)
carte d'anniversaire *f.* birthday card (18)
carte de Noël *f.* Christmas card (18)
carte orange *f.* monthly subway pass (11)
carte pour le Nouvel An *f.* New Year's card (18)
carton *m.* cardboard box (17)
cassette *f.* audio cassette (4), (18)
cassette vierge *f.* blank cassette (18)
cathédrale *f.* cathedral (7)
ce (cette) this (8)
célèbre famous (13)
cent one hundred (18)
centimes *m. pl.* coin divisions of the French franc (12)
centre commercial *m.* shopping mall (18)
céréales *f. pl.* cereal (16)
cerise *f.* cherry (17)
c'est décidé it's settled (9)
ceux *m. pl.* those (15)
chacun(e) each one (14)
chaîne *f.* neck chain (18)
chaîne stéréo *f.* stereo system (4), (18)
chambre *f.* bedroom (4)
champignon *m.* mushroom (17)
changer to change (11)
chanson *f.* song (17)
chanter to sing (1), (18)
charcuterie *f.* delicatessen (16)
charcutier(-ère) *m. (f.)* deli owner (16)
chariot *m.* shopping cart (17)
chat(te) *m. (f.)* cat (5)
chaud(e) hot (1)
chausson aux pommes *m.* a puff pastry filled with cooked apple slices (2)
cher(-ère) expensive (11), (18)
chercher to look for (6)
cheveux *m. pl.* hair (6)
chez moi at my house (4)
chien(ne) *m. f.* dog (5)
chinois(e) Chinese (3)
chocolat *m.* hot chocolate (1)
chose *f.* thing (2)
chou *m.* cabbage (17)
cinéma *m.* movies (5); movie theater (7)
cinq five (4)
cinquante fifty (12)
citron *m.* lemon (1), (17)
citron pressé *m.* lemonade (1)
clarinette *f.* clarinet (8)
classique classical (5)
clé *f.* key (4)
Coca *m.* Coca-Cola (1)
coiffeur *m.* hair salon; male hair stylist (18)
coiffeuse *f.* woman hair stylist (18)
combien (de) how many (6)
combien de temps how long (12)
Comment allez-vous? How are you? (2)
Comment ça va? How are you doing? (1)
commissariat de police *m.* police station (7)
comprendre to understand (10); to include (13)
comptable *m. or f.* accountant (3)
concert *m.* concert (9)
concert de rock *m.* rock concert (9)
concert d'orgue *m.* organ concert (9)
concombre *m.* cucumber (16)
concours *m.* contest (14)
conduire to drive (11)
conférencier *m.* leather case for paper and pen (18)
confiture *f.* jelly (16)

connaître to know (13)
conserves *f. pl.* canned goods (17)
correspondance *f.* change of train lines (11)
côté *m.* side (14)
couler to flow (14)
courage *m.* courage (17)
courgette *f.* squash (17)
course *f.* errand (10); race (13)
cousin(e) *m. (f.)* cousin (6)
crayon *m.* pencil (18)
crème *f.* cream (17)
croissant *m.* croissant (2), (16)
croque-madame *m.* open-faced grilled ham and cheese with egg (1)
croque-monsieur *m.* open-faced grilled ham and cheese (1)

D

d'abord first (7)
d'accord OK (3), (9)
dans in (4), (8)
danser to dance (1)
danses folkloriques *f. pl.* folk dancing (9)
d'autres *m. pl.* others (14)
de of, from (3)
de temps en temps from time to time (7)
défilé *m.* parade (9)
dégustation *f.* food tasting (9)
déjeuner *m.* lunch (1)
demain tomorrow (10)
demi-kilo *m.* half a kilogram (16)
dentiste *m. or f.* dentist (3)
depuis since (13)
dernier(-ère) last (14); latest (18)
derrière behind (8)
descendre to get off (11)
désirer to want (1)
dessin *m.* drawing (14)
deux two (3), (4)
devant in front of (8)
devoir to have to (18)
diabolo citron *m.* soft drink with lemon-flavored syrup (1)
diabolo fraise *m.* soft drink with strawberry-flavored syrup (1)
diabolo menthe *m.* soft drink with mint-flavored syrup (1)
dimanche Sunday (10)
discothèque *f.* disco (7)
disque *m.* record (4), (18)
disque compact *m.* compact disc (18)
distance *f.* distance (18)
dix ten (4)
dix-huit eighteen (7)
dix-neuf nineteen (7)
dix-sept seventeen (7)
dollar *m.* dollar (18)
donner to give (16)
douzaine *f.* dozen (17)
douze twelve (7)
droite right (8)

E

échecs *m. pl.* chess (7)
échouer to fail (12)
éclair *m.* eclair (16)
école *f.* school (general or elementary) (7)
écouter to listen to (5), (6)
écrivain(e) *m. (f.)* writer (14)
église *f.* church (7)
égyptien(ne) Egyptian (3)
élève *m. or f.* pupil (3)
l'embarras du choix *m.* the difficulty of choosing (15)
en autobus by bus (12)
en face de across from (8)
en métro by subway (12)
en taxi by taxi (12)
en tout in all (16)
en ville to town, downtown (10)
en voiture by car (12)
enchanté(e) delighted (2)
enfant *m. or f.* child (6)
enfin finally (14)
enrégistreur à cassette *m.* cassette recorder (18)
ensuite then; next (7)

entre between (8)
entrer (dans) to go into; to enter (10), (14)
enveloppe *f.* envelope (18)
épicerie *f.* neighborhood grocery store (7), (17)
escalier *m.* stairs (13); escalator (14)
espagnol(e) Spanish (3)
espérer to hope (12)
être to be (3)
étudiant(e) *m.(f.)* student (3)
étudier to study (1)
événement *m.* event (13)
examen *m.* test (12)
express *m.* espresso (1)
extra (extraordinaire) extraordinary (18)

F

facile easy (11)
façon *f.* way, manner (13)
faire to do; to make (6)
faire des achats to go shopping (10)
faire du lèche-vitrine to go window shopping (10)
faire du ski to go skiing (6)
faire du sport to participate in sports (6)
faire du tennis to play tennis (6)
faire la toilette to clean up (14)
faire peur to frighten (15)
faire une course to do an errand (10); to go shopping (16)
faire une promenade to take a walk (6)
faire un tour to go for a ride (6)
faire un voyage to take a trip (6)
famille *f.* family (6)
farine *f.* flour (17)
femme *f.* woman; wife (6)
femme d'affaires *f.* business woman (3)
festival *m.* festival (9)
feutre *m.* felt-tip pen (4)
feux d'artifice *m. pl.* fireworks (9)
filet *m.* net bag for shopping (17)
fille *f.* daughter (6); girl
fils *m.* son (6)
fin *f.* end (13)
fin(e) thin (16)
fleur *f.* flower (8), (13)
fleuve *m.* river (13)
flipper *m.* pinball (7)
flûte *f.* flute (8)
football *m.* soccer (7)
football américain *m.* football (7)
four à micro-ondes *m.* microwave oven (16)
frais (fraiche) fresh (17)
fraise *f.* strawberry (1), (17)
framboise *f.* raspberry (17)
franc *m.* French monetary unit (11)
français(e) French (3)
francophone *m. or f.* French-speaking person (8)
francophonie *f.* designates French-speaking countries (8)
frère *m.* brother (6)
frites *f. pl.* French fries (3)
froid(e) cold (1)
fruit *m.* fruit (16)
funiculaire *m.* rail cars (13)

G

gagner to earn (money) (2); to win (14)
garçon *m.* waiter (1)
garder to keep (12)
gare *f.* train station (7)
gargouille *f.* gargoyle (14)
gâté(e) spoiled (18)
gâteau *m.* cake (16)
gauche left (8)
gigot *m.* leg of lamb (16)
glace *f.* ice cream (13), (17)
gomme *f.* eraser (4), (18)
goût *m.* taste (5)
gramme *m.* gram (16)
grand(e) big, tall (6)
grand magasin *m.* department store (18)
grand-mère *f.* grandmother (6)
grand-père *m.* grandfather (6)
gruyère *m.* Gruyère cheese *(17)*
guerre *f.* war (14)
guichet *m.* ticket window (11)

guitare *f.* guitar (8)

H

habitant(e) *m. (f.)* inhabitant (13), (18)
habiter to live (1)
haïtien(ne) Haitian (3)
haricot vert *m.* green bean (17)
haut(e) high, tall (13)
hauteur *f.* height (13)
heures de pointe *f. pl.* rush hour (11)
homme d'affaires *m.* business man (3)
hôpital *m.* hospital (7)
hôtel *m.* hotel (7)
hôtel de ville *m.* town hall (7)
huit eight (4)

I

idée *f.* idea (9)
il faut it is necessary (11)
il me faut I need (17)
il vaut mieux it is better (16)
il y a there is; there are (4)
île *f.* island (13)
imagination *f.* imagination (17)
immeuble *m.* office or apartment building (13)
inconnu(e) unknown (13)
ingénieur *m.* engineer (3)
italien(ne) Italian (3)

J

jambe *f.* leg (14)
japonais(e) Japanese (3)
jardinier(-ère) *m. (f.)* gardener (13)
jazz *m.* jazz (18)
jeu vidéo *m.* video game (18)
jeudi Thursday (10)
joli(e) pretty (18)
jouet *m.* toy (18)
jour *m.* day (12)
journaliste *m. or f.* journalist (3)
journée *f.* day (16)
jus d'orange *m.* orange juice (16)
jusqu'à to, until (8)
justement as a matter of fact (10)

K

ketchup *m.* catsup (17)
kilo *m.* kilogram (16)

L

là-bas over there (7)
lait *m.* milk (1), (16)
lait fraise *m.* milk with strawberry syrup (1)
laitier(-ère) dairy (17)
langues *f. pl.* languages (5)
large de with a width of (13)
lecture *f.* reading (18)
lendemain *m.* the next day (14)
lever to raise (14)
librairie *f.* bookstore (7)
limonade *f.* a sweet carbonated soft drink (1)
lit *m.* bed (4)
litre *m.* liter (16)
littérature *f.* literature (5)
livre *m.* book (4)
livre *f.* (French) pound (16)
loin de far from (8)
louer to rent (18)
lumière *f.* light (9)
lundi Monday (10)
lunettes *f. pl.* glasses (6)
lycée *m.* high school (3), (7)

M

ma my (4)
machine à écrire *f.* typewriter (4)
magasin *m.* store (13)
magasin d'antiquités *m.* antique store (13)
magasin de jouets *m.* toy store (18)

magasin de sport *m.* sporting goods store (18)
magnétophone *m.* tape recorder (18)
magnétoscope *m.* video player (4), (18)
maintenant now (11)
mais but (3)
mais non no (emphatic) (3)
mais oui yes (emphatic) (11)
maison *f.* house (4)
mal poorly (1)
mammifères *m. pl.* mammals (15)
manger to eat (1)
marche *f.* step (14)
marché en plein air *m.* open-air market (17)
mardi Tuesday (10)
mari *m.* husband (6)
marié(e) married (6)
marque *f.* make, brand (12)
mathématiques *f. pl.* mathematics (5)
matin *m.* morning (10)
mayonnaise *m.* mayonnaise (17)
mécanicien(ne) *m. (f.)* mechanic (3)
médecin *m.* doctor (3)
melon *m.* melon (17)
mener to lead (14)
menthe à l'eau *f.* water with mint-flavored syrup (1)
merci thank you (1)
mercredi Wednesday (10)
mère *f.* mother (6)
métro subway (10)
mexicain(e) Mexican (3)
midi noon (9)
mille one thousand (18)
mille-feuille *m.* napoleon (pastry) (16)
millions *m. pl.* millions (14)
minuit midnight (9)
moi me (1)
moins less (11)
mois *m.* month (8)
mon my (2)
monde *m.* world (13); people (18)
monnaie *f.* change (12)
monopoly *m.* Monopoly (board game) (7)
monter to climb; to go up (14)
monter dans to get in (11)
montre *f.* watch (18)
morceau *m.* piece (17)
mot *m.* word (13)
moto *f.* motorcycle (4)
motocyclette *f.* motorcycle (4)
moutarde *f.* mustard (17)
mouton *m.* lamb (16)
moyen âge *m.* Middle Ages (13)
musée *m.* museum (7)
musique *f.* music (5)
musique classique *f.* classical music (18)

N

naissance *f.* birth (13)
nature *f.* nature (5)
ne ... jamais never (7)
n'est-ce pas isn't that so? (1)
neuf nine (4)
nom *m.* name
nom de famille *m.* last name (6)
nombreux(-euse) numerous, big (6)
non plus either (2) (5)
nous we; us (14)
nuit *f.* night (13)

O

oeuf *m.* egg (16)
oeuvre *f.* work (13)
oignon *m.* onion (17)
oiseau *m.* bird (15)
omelette *f.* omelet (1)
oncle *m.* uncle (6)
onze eleven (7)
orange *f.* orange (16)
orange pressée *f.* orangeade (1)
Orangina *m.* orange-flavored soft drink (1)
ordinateur *m.* computer (4)
orgue *m.* organ (9)
os *m. pl.* bones (15)
ossuaire *m.* gravesite (15)
où where (6)
où est where is (7)

où se trouve where is (8)
oublier to forget (15)
ouest west (13)

P

pain *m.* bread (16)
pain au chocolat *m.* roll with a piece of chocolate in the middle (2)
pain aux raisins *m.* roll with raisins (2)
pain de campagne *m.* round loaf of bread (16)
papeterie *f.* stationery store (18)
papier à écrire *m.* stationery (18)
par mois per month (8)
parc *m.* park (7)
parce que because (6)
pardon excuse me (7)
parler to speak (1)
part *f.* a slice (2)
pas mal de quite a bit of (18)
passer un examen to take a test (12)
pâté *m.* meat spread (16)
pâtes *f. pl.* pasta (17)
patience *f.* patience (17)
pâtisserie *f.* bakery that sells pastry (16)
patrie *f.* homeland (nation) (14)
pêche *f.* peach (17)
peinture *f.* painting (5); paint (14)
pendentif *m.* pendant (18)
penser to think (18)
père *m.* father (6)
permis de conduire *m.* driver's license (12)
peser to weigh (14)
pétanque *f.* game played with metal and wooden balls (7)
petit(e) small, short (6)
petit(e) ami(e) *m. (f.)* boy (girl) friend (5)
petit déjeuner *m.* breakfast (1)
petit pain *m.* small breakfast roll (16)
petit pois *m.* pea (17)
peu little (1)
pharmacie *f.* drugstore (7)
pharmacien(ne) *m. (f.)* pharmacist (3)
piano *m.* piano (8)
pièce de théatre *f.* play (5)
pièces de monnaie *f. pl.* coins (12)
piéton *m.* pedestrian (14)
piscine *f.* swimming pool (7)
pizza *f.* pizza (2), (17)
place *f.* square (8)
plaisir *m.* pleasure (11)
plan *m.* map (8)
plan de métro metro map (11)
plante verte *f.* green plant (4)
plein(e) full (17)
plusieurs several (15)
poisson *m.* fish (17)
poire *f.* pear (17)
poivre *m.* pepper (17)
politique *f.* politics (5)
pomme *f.* apple (17)
pomme de terre *f.* potato (17)
pommes frites *f. pl.* French fries (17)
pont *m.* bridge (13)
populaire popular (5)
population *f.* population (18)
porc *m.* pork (16)
portefeuille *m.* wallet (4)
porter to wear (6)
portugais(e) Portuguese (3)
poster *m.* poster (4)
poteaux *m. pl.* pillars (14)
poulet *m.* chicken (16)
poupée *f.* doll (18)
pour in order to (4)
pour quoi faire in order to do what (10)
pourboire *m.* tip (1)
pourquoi why (6)
pourquoi pas why not (3), (11)
pourtant however (5)
préférence *f.* preference (5)
préférer to prefer (18)
premièrement first (14)
prendre to take (10)
prendre une correspondance to change trains (11)
prénom *m.* first name (5)

près de near (8)
probablement probably (18)
prochain(e) next (11)
produit *m.* product (17)
produits laitiers *m.* dairy products (17)
professeur *m.* teacher (3)
puis then; next (14)

Q

quarante forty (12)
quartier *m.* neighborhood or city section (13)
quatorze fourteen (7)
quatre four (4)
quatre-vingt-dix ninety (18)
quatre-vingts eighty (18)
quatre-vingt-un eighty-one (18)
quelque chose something (2)
quelquefois sometimes (7)
quelques some (17)
qu'est-ce que what (6)
qui that, who (6)
quiche *f.* an open-faced pie filled with an egg and cheese mixture (2)
quinze fifteen (7)
quitter to leave (10)
quoi d'autre what else (16)

R

radio-cassette *f.* cassette recorder with radio (4), (18)
radio-réveil *m.* radio alarm clock (4)
radis *m.* radish (17)
rangé(e) arranged (15)
raquette *f.* racket (18)
rarement rarely (1); (7)
rayon *m.* shelf, section of a supermarket (17)
reconnaissant(e) grateful (14)
regarder to look at; to watch (5)
région *f.* region, area (9)
reine *f.* queen (14)
relié(e) connected (13)
religieuse *f.* pastry filled with chocolate or coffee filling (16)
rempli(e) filled (14)
rendu(e) made (13)
rentrer to go back (14)
restaurant *m.* restaurant (7)
rester to stay; to remain (10), (14)
retourner to go back, to return (14)
retrouver to meet (arranged in advance) (10)
réunir to bring together, to unite (13)
rêver to dream (18)
rien nothing (10)
rive droite *f.* right bank of the Seine (13)
rive gauche *f.* left bank of the Seine (13)
riz *m.* rice (17)
robot *m.* robot (18)
rock *m.* rock music (18)
roi *m.* king (13)
rôti *m.* roast (16)
rôti de porc *m.* roast pork (16)
rue *f.* street (7)
russe Russian (3)

S

sac *m.* bag (4)
sac à dos *m.* backpack (4)
sac à main *m.* pocketbook (4)
salade *f.* salad, lettuce (16)
salé(e) salty (2)
salon d'automobile *m.* automobile showroom (13)
salut hi! (1)
samedi Saturday (9), (10)
sandwich *m.* sandwich (1)
s'appeler to be named (6)
s'asseoir to sit down (14)
sauce béchamel *f.* white cream sauce (1)
saucisse *f.* sausage (16)
saucisson *m.* salami (16)
sauvage wild (15)
saxophone *m.* saxophone (8)
sciences *f. pl.* science (5)
sculpture *f.* sculpture (5)

se détendre to relax (15)
se renseigner to get information (15)
se retrouver to meet (9)
se réunir to meet (13)
secrétaire *m. or f.* secretary (3)
seize sixteen (7)
sel *m.* salt (17)
semaine *f.* week (11)
sénégalais(e) Senegalese (3)
sept seven (4)
serveuse *f.* waitress (1)
s'étendre to stretch out (13)
siècle *m.* century (13)
s'il vous plaît please (1), (8)
s'installer to move in (14)
six six (4)
skis *m. pl.* skis (18)
société *f.* company (14)
soeur *f.* sister (6)
soir *m.* evening (10)
soixante sixty (12)
soixante-dix seventy (18)
son *m.* sound (8)
souterrain(e) underground (15)
souvent often (1); (7)
spécialité *f.* specialty (9)
spectacle *m.* show (9)
sports *m. pl.* sports (5)
stade *m.* stadium (sports complex) (7)
station de métro *f.* subway stop (11)
stylo *m.* ballpoint pen (4), (18)
sucre *m.* sugar (17)
sucré(e) sweet (2)
sud south (9)
suisse Swiss (3)
suivant(e) following (14)
superficie *f.* area (18)
supermarché *m.* supermarket (17)
sur on (8)
surgelé(e) frozen (17)
synagogue *f.* synagogue (7)

T

taille-crayon *m.* pencil sharpener (4)
tante *f.* aunt (6)
tarte *f.* pie (16)
tarte à l'oignon a kind of quiche made with onions (2)
tarte aux pommes apple pie (16)
tarte aux fraises strawberry pie (16)
tartelette *f.* a small open-faced pie in various flavors (2), (16)
taxi *m.* taxi (10)
télévision *f.* television (4)
tellement so (18)
tennis *m.* tennis (5); (7)
terminer to finish (17)
terrasse *f.* sidewalk in front of a café (1)
têtes de morts *f. pl.* skulls (15)
thé *m.* tea (1)
thé au lait *m.* tea with milk (1)
thé citron *m.* tea with lemon (1)
thé nature *m.* regular tea (1)
théâtre *m.* theater (5); (7)
thon *m.* tuna (16)
tiens! see! (18)
toast *m.* toast (16)
toi you (1)
tomate *f.* tomato (16)
tomber to fall (14)
toujours always (7)
tourner to turn (8)
tous les ans every year (9)
tout very (13); all
tout droit straight ahead (8)
tout un mois a whole month (11)
train électrique *m.* electric train (18)
tranche *f.* slice (16)
travailler to work (2)
traverser to cross (8)
treize thirteen (7)
trente thirty (12)
très very (1)
trois three (3), (4)
trombone *m.* trombone (8)
trompette *f.* trumpet (8)
trop too much (17)
tuyaux *m. pl.* pipes (14)

U

un(e) one (4)
université *f.* university (7)
usine *f.* factory (14)

V

valable valid, good (12)
vanille *f.* vanilla (3)
veille *f.* eve (14)
vélo *m.* bicycle (4), (10), (18)
vélomoteur *m.* moped (4)
vendredi Friday (10)
verre *m.* glass (14)
vers toward (13)
vertige *m.* dizziness (14)
vêtement *m.* article of clothing (17)
viande *f.* meat (16)
vidéo *f.* videotape (18)
vidéo vierge *f.* blank video (18)
vidéo-clip *m.* music video (18)
vie *f.* life (12)
vietnamien(ne) Vietnamese (3)
vieux (vieille) old (13)
ville *f.* city (7)
vingt twenty (7)
violon *m.* violin (8)
voici here is (5)
voilà there is; there are (4)
voie *f.* way, route (13)
voir to see (9), (14)
voiture *f.* car (4), (10); subway cars (11)
voiture de première *f.* first class train or subway car (11)
voiture de seconde *f.* second class train or subway car (11)
volley *m.* volleyball (7)
vouloir to wish; to want (12)
voyager to travel (1)

W

walkman *m.* personal stereo (18)

Y

y there (13)
yaourt *m.* yogurt (17)
yeux *m. pl.* eyes (6)

Z

zéro zero (4)

Glossary

English–French

The numbers in parentheses refer to the chapter in which the word or phrase may be found.

A

above au-dessus de (14)
accountant comptable *m. or f.* (3)
across from en face de (8)
actor (actress) acteur(-trice) *m. (f.)* (3)
afternoon après-midi *m.* (10)
age âge
airport aéroport *m.* (7)
all tout
almonds amandes *f. pl.* (2)
also aussi (1), (13)
always toujours (7)
American américain(e) (3)
antique store magasin d'antiquités *m.* (13)
apartment appartement *m.* (4)
apple pomme *f.* (17)
apple pie tarte aux pommes (16)
apricot abricot *m.* (17)
area superficie *f.* (18)
arranged rangé(e) (15)
art art *m.* (5)
as a matter of fact justement (10)
as much autant (17)
as well as aussi bien que (15)
asparagus asperge *f.* (17)
astronaut astronaute *m. or f.* (3)
at my house chez moi (4)
at our house chez nous (4)
at the corner of au coin de (8)
at the end of au bout de (8)
(to) attract attirer (13)
audio cassette cassette *f.* (4), (18)
audio tape bande magnétique *f.* (18)
aunt tante *f.* (6)
automobile showroom salon d'automobile *m.* (13)
avenue avenue *f.* (7)

B

backpack sac à dos *m.* (4)
bacon bacon *m.* (16)
bag sac *m.* (4)
baker boulanger(-ère) *m. (f.)* (16)
bakery that sells bread and rolls boulangerie *f.* (7), (16)
bakery that sells brioche and other hot snacks briocherie *f.* (2)
bakery that sells pastry pâtisserie *f.* (16)
ball ballon *m.* (18)
ballpoint pen stylo *m.* (4), (18)
banana banane *f.* (16)
bank banque *f.* (7)
bank (of a river) bord *m.* (13)
baseball baseball *m.* (7)
basketball basket *m.* (7)
(to) be être (3)
(to) be named s'appeler (6)
(to) be right avoir raison (4)
beaten battu(e) (14)
beautiful beau (belle) (14)
because car (14)
because parce que (6)
bed lit *m.* (4)
bedroom chambre *f.* (4)
beef boeuf (16)
before avant (13)
behind derrière (8)
Belgian belge (3)

besides à part (14)
between entre (8)
bicycle vélo *m.* (4), (10), (18)
big, tall grand(e) (6)
bird oiseau *m.* (15)
bird's-eye view à vol d'oiseau (13)
birth naissance *f.* (13)
birthday anniversaire *m.* (16)
birthday card carte d'anniversaire *f.* (18)
blank cassette cassette vierge *f.* (18)
blank video vidéo vierge *f.* (18)
bolt boulon *m.* (14)
bones os *m. pl.* (15)
book livre *m.* (4)
book of metro tickets carnet *m.* (11)
bookstore librairie *f.* (7)
bottle bouteille *f.* (17)
boulevard boulevard *m.* (8)
boy (girl) friend petit(e) ami(e) *m. (f.)* (5)
bracelet bracelet *m.* (18)
brand marque *f.* (12)
bread pain *m.* (16)
breakfast petit déjeuner *m.* (1)
bridge pont *m.* (13)
Brie cheese brie *m.* (17)
(to) bring together réunir (13)
brother frère *m.* (6)
brown brun(e) (6)
building bâtiment *m.* (13)
(office or appartment) building immeuble *m.* (13)
bunch botte *f.* (17)
bus autobus *m.* (10)
business affaires *f. pl.* (13)
business man homme d'affaires *m.* (3)
business woman femme d'affaires *f.* (3)
but mais (3)
butcher boucher(-ère) *m. (f.)* (16)
butcher shop boucherie *f.* (7), (16)
butter beurre *m.* (17)
(to) buy acheter (10)
by bicycle à vélo (12)
by bus en autobus (12)
by car en voiture (12)
by subway en métro (12)
by taxi en taxi (12)

C

cabbage chou *m.* (17)
café café *m.* (1)
cake gâteau *m.* (16)
calculator calculatrice *f.* (4)
calendar calendrier *m.* (18)
Camembert cheese camembert *m.* (17)
camera appareil-photo *m.* (4)
camping camping *m.* (5)
can boîte *f.* (17)
Canadian canadien(ne) (3)
canned goods conserves *f. pl.* (17)
capital capitale *f.* (18)
car auto *f.* (4); voiture *f.* (4), (10)
card carte *f.* (18)
cardboard box carton *m.* (17)
carrot carotte *f.* (17)
cassette recorder enrégistreur à cassette *m.* (18)
cassette recorder with radio radio-cassette *f.* (4), (18)
cat chat(te) *m. (f.)* (5)
cathedral cathédrale *f.* (7)
catsup ketchup *m.* (17)
century siècle *m.* (13)
cereal céréales *f. pl.* (16)
(neck) chain chaîne *f.* (18)
change monnaie *f.* (12)
(to) change changer (11)
changes of train lines correspondances *f.* (11)
(to) change trains prendre une correspondance (11)
cheese fromage *m.* (1), (17)
cherry cerise *f.* (17)
chess échecs *m. pl.* (7)
chicken poulet *m.* (16)
child enfant *m. or f.* (6)
Chinese chinois(e) (3)
(hot) chocolate chocolat *m.* (1)
Christmas card carte de Noël *f.* (18)
church église *f.* (7)

city ville *f.* (7)
clarinet clarinette *f.* (8)
classical classique (5)
classical music musique classique *f.* (18)
(to) clean up faire la toilette (14)
(to) climb; (to) go up monter (14)
clothing vêtements *m. pl.* (17)
Coca-Cola Coca *m.* (1)
coffee café *m.* (1)
coffee with cream café crème (1)
coffee with milk café au lait (1)
coins pièces de monnaie *f. pl.* (12)
cold froid(e) (1)
compact disc disque compact *m.* (18)
company société *f.* (14)
computer ordinateur *m.* (4)
concert concert *m.* (9)
connected relié(e) (13)
contest concours *m.* (14)
country lane allée *f.* (15)
courage courage *m.* (17)
cousin cousin(e) *m. (f.)* (6)
cradle berceau *m.* (13)
cream crème *f.* (17)
croissant croissant *m.* (2), (16)
(to) cross traverser (8)
cucumber concombre *m.* (16)

D

dairy laitier(-ère) (17)
dairy products produits laitiers *m.* (17)
dance bal *m.* (9)
(to) dance danser (1)
daughter fille *f.* (6)
day jour *m.* (12); journée *f.* (16)
deli owner charcutier(-ère) *m. (f.)* (16)
delicatessen charcuterie *f.* (16)
delighted enchanté(e) (2)
dentist dentiste *m. or f.* (3)
department store grand magasin *m.* (18)
desk bureau *m.* (4)
disco discothèque *f.* (7)
distance distance *f.* (18)
dizziness vertige *m.* (14)
(to) do; (to) make faire (6)
doctor médecin *m.* (3)
dog chien(ne) *m. f.* (5)
doll poupée *f.* (18)
dollar dollar *m.* (18)
dozen douzaine *f.* (17)
drawing dessin *m.* (14)
(to) dream rêver (18)
drink boisson *m.* (1)
(to) drive conduire (11)
driver's license permis de conduire *m.* (12)
driving school auto-école *f.* (12)
drugstore pharmacie *f.* (7)
drums batterie *f.* (8)
duck canard *m.* (16)

E

each one chacun(e) (14)
(to) earn (money) gagner (2)
earrings boucles d'oreilles *f. pl.* (18)
easy facile (11)
(to) eat manger (1)
eclair éclair *m.* (16)
egg oeuf *m.* (16)
Egyptian égyptien(ne) (3)
eight huit (4)
eighteen dix-huit (7)
eighty quatre-vingts (18)
eighty-one quatre-vingt-un (18)
electric train train électrique *m.* (18)
eleven onze (7)
end fin *f.* (13)
engineer ingénieur *m.* (3)
English anglais(e) (3)
enough assez (1), (16)
(to) enter entrer (dans) (10), (14)
envelope enveloppe *f.* (18)
eraser gomme *f.* (4), (18)
errand course *f.* (10)
escalator escalier *m.* (14)
espresso express *m.* (1)
eve veille *f.* (14)
evening soir *m.* (10)

event événement *m.* (13)
every year tous les ans (9)
excuse me pardon (7)
exercise machine appareil de gymnastique *m.* (18)
expensive cher(-ère) (11), (18)
extraordinary extra (extraordinaire) (18)
eyes yeux *m. pl.* (6)

F

factory usine *f.* (14)
(to) fail échouer (12)
(to) fall tomber (14)
family famille *f.* (6)
famous célèbre (13)
far from loin de (8)
farmer agriculteur(-trice) *m. (f.)* (3)
father père *m.* (6)
(to) feel like avoir envie de (10), (12)
felt-tip pen feutre *m.* (4)
festival festival *m.* (9)
fifteen quinze (7)
fifty cinquante (12)
filled rempli(e) (14)
finally enfin (14)
(to) finish terminer (17)
fireworks feux d'artifice *m. pl.* (9)
first d'abord (7); premièrement (14)
first class train or subway car voiture de première *f.* (11)
first name prénom *m.* (5)
fish poisson *m.* (17)
five cinq (4)
flour farine *f.* (17)
(to) flow couler (14)
flower fleur *f.* (8), (13)
flute flûte *f.* (8)
flying buttresses arc-boutants *m. pl.* (14)
folk dancing danses folkloriques *f. pl.* (9)
following suivant(e) (14)
food tasting dégustation *f.* (9)
football football américain *m.* (7)
(to) forget oublier (15)
former ancien(ne) (13)
forty quarante (12)
four quatre (4)
fourteen quatorze (7)
French **français(e)** **(3)**
French fries (pommes) frites *f. pl.* (3), (17)
French monetary unit franc *m.* (11)
French-speaking person francophone *m. or f.* (8)
fresh frais (fraiche) (17)
Friday vendredi (10)
friend ami(e) *m. (f.)* (2)
(to) frighten faire peur (15)
from de (3)
from time to time de temps en temps (7)
frozen surgelé(e) (17)
fruit fruit *m.* (16)
full plein(e) (17)

G

gardener jardinier(-ère) *m. (f.)* (13)
gargoyle gargouille *f.* (14)
German allemand(e) (3)
(to) get in monter dans (11)
(to) get information se renseigner (15)
(to) get off descendre (11)
gift cadeau *m.* (13), (18)
girl fille *f.*
(to) give donner (16)
glass verre *m.* (14)
glasses lunettes *f. pl.* (6)
(to) go aller (7)
(to) go back rentrer; retourner (14)
(to) go for a ride faire un tour (6)
(to) go into town aller en ville (4)
(to) go shopping faire des achats (10)
(to) go skiing faire du ski (6)
(to) go window shopping faire du lèche-vitrine (10)
good bon(ne) (9)
goodbye au revoir (1)
gram gramme *m.* (16)
grandfather grand-père *m.* (6)

grandmother grand-mère *f.* (6)
grateful reconnaissant(e) (14)
gravesite ossuaire *m.* (15)
green bean haricot vert *m.* (17)
(open-faced) grilled ham and cheese croque-monsieur *m.* (1)
(open-faced) grilled ham and cheese with egg croque-madame *m.* (1)
grocery store épicerie *f.* (7), (17)
Gruyère cheese gruyère *m.* (17)
guitar guitare *f.* (8)

H

hair cheveux *m. pl.* (6)
hair salon coiffeur *m.* (18)
hair stylist coiffeur(-euse) *m. (f.)* (18)
Haitian haïtien(ne) (3)
half a kilogram demi-kilo *m.* (16)
ham jambon *m.* (1), (16)
(to) have avoir (4)
(to) have a date to meet with avoir rendez-vous avec (10)
(to) have nothing to do n'avoir rien à faire (10)
(to) have to devoir (18)
height hauteur *f.* (13)
hello bonjour (1)
here is voici (5)
hi! salut (1)
high school lycée *m.* (3), (7)
high haut(e) (13)
hill butte *f.* (13)
homeland (nation) patrie *f.* (14)
(to) hope espérer (12)
hospital hôpital *m.* (7)
hot chaud(e) (1)
hotel hôtel *m.* (7)
house maison *f.* (4)
(to) house abriter (13)
How are you doing? Comment ça va? (1)
How are you? Comment allez-vous? (2)
how long combien de temps (12)
how many combien (de) (6)
however pourtant (5)
husband mari *m.* (6)
(to be) hungry avoir faim (4)

I

ice cream glace *f.* (13), (17)
idea idée *f.* (9)
imagination imagination *f.* (17)
in dans (4), (8)
in all en tout (16)
in front of devant (8)
in order to pour (4)
in the middle of au milieu de (13)
(to) include comprendre (13)
inhabitant habitant(e) *m. (f.)* (13), (18)
(to) intend to avoir l'intention de (12)
(to go) into entrer (dans) (10), (14)
island île *f.* (13)
it is necessary il faut (11)
it's settled c'est décidé (9)
Italian italien(ne) (3)

J

Japanese japonais(e) (3)
jazz jazz *m.* (18)
jelly confiture *f.* (16)
jewelry store bijouterie *f.* (18)
journalist journaliste *m. or f.* (3)

K

(to) keep garder (12)
key clé *f.* (4)
kilogram kilo *m.* (16)
king roi *m.* (13)
(to) know connaître (13)

L

lamb mouton *m.* (16)
languages langues *f. pl.* (5)
last dernier(-ère) (14)
last name nom de famille *m.* (6)

latest dernier(-ère) (18)
lawyer avocat(e) *m. (f.)* (3)
(to) lead mener (14)
(to) learn apprendre (10)
(to) leave quitter (10)
left gauche (8)
leg jambe *f.* (14)
leg of lamb gigot *m.* (16)
lemon citron *m.* (1), (17)
lemonade citron pressé *m.* (1)
less moins (11)
lettuce salade *f.* (16)
library bibliothèque *f.* (7)
life vie *f.* (12)
light lumière *f.* (9)
(to) like aimer (5)
(to) like the best aimer le mieux (5)
(to) listen to écouter (5), (6)
liter litre *m.* (16)
literature littérature *f.* (5)
little peu (1)
(to) live habiter (1)
(long) loaf of bread baguette *f.* (16)
(to) look at regarder (5)
(to) look for chercher (6)
(a) lot of beaucoup de (17)
(to) love adorer (5)
lunch déjeuner *m.* (1)

M

made rendu(e) (13)
mammals mammifères *m. pl.* (15)
map plan *m.* (8)
married marié(e) (6)
mathematics mathématiques *f. pl.* (5)
mayonnaise mayonnaise *m.* (17)
me moi (1)
meat viande *f.* (16)
meat spread pâté *m.* (16)
mechanic mécanicien(ne) *m. (f.)* (3)
(to) meet se retrouver (9); se réunir (13)
(to) meet (arranged in advance) retrouver (10)
melon melon *m.* (17)
metro entrance bouche de métro *f.* (11)
metro map plan de métro (11)
Mexican mexicain(e) (3)
microwave oven four à micro-ondes *m.* (16)
Middle Ages moyen âge *m.* (13)
midnight minuit (9)
milk lait *m.* (1), (16)
milk with strawberry syrup lait fraise *m.* (1)
millions millions *m. pl.* (14)
mixed herbs fines herbes (1)
Monday lundi (10)
money argent *m.* (17)
Monopoly (board game) monopoly *m.* (7)
month mois *m.* (8)
moped vélomoteur *m.* (4)
morning matin *m.* (10)
mother mère *f.* (6)
motorcycle moto, motocyclette *f.* (4)
mouth bouche *f.*
(to) move in s'installer (14)
movie theater cinéma *m.* (7)
movies cinéma *m.* (5)
museum musée *m.* (7)
mushroom champignon *m.* (17)
music musique *f.* (5)
music video vidéo-clip *m.* (18)
mustard moutarde *f.* (17)
my mon (2); ma (4)

N

name nom *m.*
napoleon (pastry) mille-feuille *m.* (16)
nature nature *f.* (5)
near près de (8)
(to) need avoir besoin de (4)
neighborhood or city section quartier *m.* (13)
neither non plus (2), (5)
never ne ... jamais (7)
New Year's card carte pour le Nouvel An *f.* (18)

next prochain(e) (11); ensuite (7); puis (14)
(the) next day lendemain *m.* (14)
next to à côté de (8)
night nuit *f.* (13)
nine neuf (4)
nineteen dix-neuf (7)
ninety quatre-vingt-dix (18)
noon midi (9)
notebook cahier *m.* (4)
(small) notebook carnet *m.* (4), (18)
now maintenant (4)
numerous, big nombreux(-euse) (6)

O

of course bien sûr (11)
of de (3)
often souvent (1), (7)
OK d'accord (3), (9)
old vieux (vieille) (13)
omelet omelette *f.* (1)
on sur (8)
on (by) foot à pied (10), (12)
on the banks of au bord de (9)
one un(e) (4)
one hundred cent (18)
one thousand mille (18)
onion oignon *m.* (17)
open-air market marché en plein air *m.* (17)
orange orange *f.* (16)
orange juice jus d'orange *m.* (16)
orange-flavored soft drink Orangina *m.* (1)
orangeade orange pressée *f.* (1)
organ orgue *m.* (9)
organ concert concert d'orgue *m.* (9)
others d'autres *m. pl.* (14)
over there là-bas (7)

P

paint peinture *f.* (14)
painting peinture *f.* (5)
paper money billet *m.* (12)
parade défilé *m.* (9)
park parc *m.* (7)
pasta pâtes *f. pl.* (17)
pastry filled with chocolate or coffee filling religieuse *f.* (16)
patience patience *f.* (17)
pea petit pois *m.* (17)
peach pêche *f.* (17)
pear poire *f.* (17)
pedestrian piéton *m.* (14)
pencil crayon *m.* (18)
pencil sharpener taille-crayon *m.* (4)
pendant pendentif *m.* (18)
pepper poivre *m.* (17)
per month par mois (8)
personal stereo walkman *m.* (18)
pharmacist pharmacien(ne) *m. (f.)* (3)
piano piano *m.* (8)
pie tarte *f.* (16)
piece bout, morceau *m.* (17)
pillars poteaux *m. pl.* (14)
pinball flipper *m.* (7)
pipes tuyaux *m. pl.* (14)
pizza pizza *f.* (2), (17)
plant plante verte *f.* (4)
play pièce de théatre *f.* (5)
(to) play tennis faire du tennis (6)
please s'il vous plaît (1), (8)
pleasure plaisir *m.* (11)
pocketbook sac à main *m.* (4)
police station commissariat de police *m.* (7)
politics politique *f.* (5)
poorly mal (1)
popular populaire (5)
population population *f.* (18)
pork porc *m.* (16)
Portuguese portugais(e) (3)
post office bureau de poste *m.* (7)
poster poster *m.* (4)
potato pomme de terre *f.* (17)
(French) pound livre *f.* (16)
(to) prefer aimer mieux (5); préférer (18)
preference préférence *f.* (5)

pretty joli(e) (18)
prison cell cachot *m.* (14)
probably probablement (18)
product produit *m.* (17)
pupil élève *m. or f.* (3)
purchase achat *m.* (17)
pâté (meat spread) pâté (1)

Q

queen reine *f.* (14)
quite a bit of pas mal de (18)

R

race course *f.* (13)
racket raquette *f.* (18)
radio alarm clock radio-réveil *m.* (4)
radish radis *m.* (17)
rail cars funiculaire *m.* (13)
(to) raise lever (14)
rarely rarement (1), (7)
raspberry framboise *f.* (17)
reading lecture *f.* (18)
record disque *m.* (4), (18)
region, area région *f.* (9)
(to) relax se détendre (15)
relics antiquités *f. pl.* (13)
(to) remain rester (14)
(to) rent louer (18)
restaurant restaurant *m.* (7)
(to) return retourner (14)
rice riz *m.* (17)
right droite (8)
ring bague *f.* (18)
river fleuve *m.* (13)
roast rôti *m.* (16)
roast pork rôti de porc *m.* (16)
robot robot *m.* (18)
rock concert concert de rock *m.* (9)
rock music rock *m.* (18)
rush hour heures de pointe *f. pl.* (11)
Russian russe (3)

S

salad salade *f.* (16)
salami saucisson *m.* (16)
salt sel *m.* (17)
salty salé(e) (2)
sandwich sandwich *m.* (1)
Saturday samedi (9), (10)
sausage saucisse *f.* (16)
saxophone saxophone *m.* (8)
school (general or elementary) école *f.* (7)
sciences sciences *f. pl.* (5)
sculpture sculpture *f.* (5)
second class train or subway car voiture de seconde *f.* (11)
second-class ticket billet de seconde *m.* (11)
secretary secrétaire *m. or f.* (3)
See you in a while à tout à l'heure (1)
See you soon à bientôt (1)
see! tiens! (18)
(to) see voir (9), (14)
Senegalese sénégalais(e) (3)
seven sept (4)
seventeen dix-sept (7)
seventy soixante-dix (18)
several plusieurs (15)
shelf, section of a supermarket rayon *m.* (17)
(to go) shopping faire des achats (10); faire une course (16)
shopping cart chariot *m.* (17)
shopping mall centre commercial *m.* (18)
short petit(e) (6)
show spectacle *m.* (9)
side côté *m.* (14)
since depuis (13)
(to) sing chanter (1), (18)
sister soeur *f.* (6)
(to) sit down s'asseoir (14)
six six (4)
sixteen seize (7)
sixty soixante (12)

skis skis *m. pl.* (18)
skulls têtes de morts *f. pl.* (15)
slice tranche *f.* (16); part *f.* (2)
small petit(e) (6)
so tellement (18)
soccer football *m.* (7)
soccer ball ballon de foot *m.* (18)
soft drink with lemon-flavored syrup diabolo citron *m.* (1)
soft drink with mint-flavored syrup diabolo menthe *m.* (1)
soft drink with strawberry-flavored syrup diabolo fraise *m.* (1)
some quelques (17)
something quelque chose (2)
sometimes quelquefois (7)
son fils *m.* (6)
song chanson *f.* (17)
sound son *m.* (8)
south sud (9)
Spanish espagnol(e) (3)
specialty spécialité *f.* (9)
(to) speak parler (1)
spoiled gâté(e) (18)
sporting goods store magasin de sport *m.* (18)
sports sports *m. pl.* (5)
square place *f.* (8)
squash courgette *f.* (17)
stadium (sports complex) stade *m.* (7)
stairs escalier *m.* (13)
stationery papier à écrire *m.* (18)
stationery store papeterie *f.* (18)
(to) stay rester (10)
steak bifteck *m.* (16)
steel acier *m.* (14)
step marche *f.* (14)
stereo system chaîne stéréo *f.* (4), (18)
store magasin *m.* (13)
straight ahead tout droit (8)
strawberry fraise *f.* (1), (17)
strawberry pie tarte aux fraises (16)
street rue *f.* (7)
(to) stretch out s'étendre (13)
student étudiant(e) *m.(f.)* (3)
(to) study étudier (1)
suburb banlieue *f.* (14)
subway métro (10)
subway cars voitures *f. pl.* (11)
(monthly) subway pass carte orange *f.* (11)
subway stop station de métro *f.* (11)
sugar sucre *m.* (17)
Sunday dimanche (10)
supermarket supermarché *m.* (17)
sweet sucré(e) (2)
swimming pool piscine *f.* (7)
Swiss suisse (3)
synagogue synagogue *f.* (7)

T

(to) take prendre (10)
(to) take a test passer un examen (12)
(to) take a trip faire un voyage (6)
(to) take a walk faire une promenade (6)
(to) take place avoir lieu (13)
(to) take, (to) lead amener (13)
tall haut(e) (13)
tape recorder magnétophone *m.* (18)
taste goût *m.* (5)
taxi taxi *m.* (10)
tea thé *m.* (1)
(regular) tea thé nature *m.* (1)
tea with lemon thé citron *m.* (1)
tea with milk thé au lait *m.* (1)
teacher professeur *m.* (3)
television télévision *f.* (4)
ten dix (4)
tennis tennis *m.* (5), (7)
tennis ball balle de tennis *f.* (18)
test examen *m.* (12)
thank you merci (1)
That's neat c'est chouette (3)
that, who qui (6)
theater théâtre *m.* (5), (7)
then alors (9)
then ensuite (7); puis (14)

there y (13)
there is; there are il y a; voilà (4)
thin fin(e) (16)
thing chose *f.* (2)
(to) think penser (18)
(to be) thirsty avoir soif (4)
thirteen treize (7)
thirty trente (12)
this ce (cette) (8)
those ceux *m. pl.* (15)
three trois (3), (4)
Thursday jeudi (10)
ticket billet *m.* (11)
ticket window guichet *m.* (11)
tip pourboire *m.* (1)
to jusqu'à (8)
toast toast *m.* (16)
tobacco store bureau de tabac *m.* (7)
today aujourd'hui (10)
tomato tomate *f.* (16)
tomorrow demain (10)
too much trop (17)
toward vers (13)
town ville *f.* (10)
town hall hôtel de ville *m.* (7)
toy jouet *m.* (18)
toy store magasin de jouets *m.* (18)
train station gare *f.* (7)
(to) travel voyager (1)
trombone trombone *m.* (8)
truck camion *m.* (18)
trumpet trompette *f.* (8)
Tuesday mardi (10)
tuna thon *m.* (16)
(to) turn tourner (8)
twelve douze (7)
twenty vingt (7)
two deux (3), (4)
typewriter machine à écrire *f.* (4)

U

uncle oncle *m.* (6)
underground souterrain(e) (15)
(to) understand comprendre (10)
(to) unite réunir (13)
university université *f.* (7)
unknown inconnu(e) (13)
until jusqu'à (8)
us nous (14)

V

valid, good valable (12)
vanilla vanille *f.* (3)
very très (1); tout (13)
very much beaucoup (5)
video game jeu vidéo *m.* (18)
video player magnétoscope *m.* (4), (18)
videotape vidéo *f.* (18)
Vietnamese vietnamien(ne) (3)
violin violon *m.* (8)
volleyball volley *m.* (7)

W

waiter garçon *m.* (1)
waitress serveuse *f.* (1)
wallet portefeuille *m.* (4)
(to) want désirer (1); vouloir (12)
war guerre *f.* (14)
watch montre *f.* (18)
(to) watch regarder (5)
water with mint-flavored syrup menthe à l'eau *f.* (1)
way, manner façon *f.* (13)
way, route voie *f.* (13)
we nous (14)
(to) wear porter (6)
Wednesday mercredi (10)
week semaine *f.* (11)
(to) weigh peser (14)
well bien (1)
west ouest (13)
what qu'est-ce que (6)
what else quoi d'autre (16)
where où (6)
why pourquoi (6)
why not pourquoi pas (3), (11)
wild sauvage (15)

(to) win gagner (14)
wiring fils *m. pl.* (14)
(to) wish vouloir (12)
with avec (11)
with pleasure avec plaisir (11)
woman femme *f.* (6)
word mot *m.* (13)
work oeuvre *f.* (13)
(to) work travailler (2)
world monde *m.* (13)
wounded blessé(e) (14)
writer écrivain *m.* (14)
(to be) wrong avoir tort (4)

Y

year année *f.* (9)
yogurt yaourt *m.* (17)
you toi (1)

Z

zero zéro (11)

Index

TEXT PERMISSIONS

We wish to thank the authors, publishers and holders of copyright for their permission to reprint the following:

p. 220 Paris mètro map, reproduced courtesy of the RATP; p. 246 "Histoire de billet" adapted from SNCF brochure *The Ticket Story;* p. 292 map of Paris, reproduced courtesy of the Office de tourisme, Paris; p. 293 "la tour Eiffel", p. 295 "Beaubourg", p. 308 "le jardin des plantes", p. 309 "le zoo de Vincennes", "le bois de Boulogne", p. 310 "les bateaux mouches", "les catacombes" text adapted from *Paris (les petits bleus),* Hachette, 1984; p. 294 la Villette brochure reproduced courtesy of the Cité des sciences et de l'industrie; p. 296 la Dèfense map, p. 308 le jardin des plantes map, p. 309 le zoo de Vincennes map, *Paris,* Pneu Michelin, 1986; p. 303 Parisiennes, Parisiens ad, p. 304 Paris Cable *Ville de paris,* Association pour l'information municipale; p. 304 concert list adapted from *Phosphore,* No. 77, juin 1987; p. 318 monument map, Quènelle, *La France j'aime,* Hatier, 1985; p. 319 "Le tout Paris acclame Prince", *OK!,* Éditions Filipacchi, 1986; p. 397 "Hit-Parade", *Salut!,* Éditions Filipacchi, No. 291, Nov-Déc 1986; p. 367 "Vidéos", p. 381 "Les grands noms du rock — The Who", *Fan Club,* Vol. 2, No. 10, 31 Oct 1987.

PHOTO CREDITS

All photos were taken by **Stuart Cohen** except the following: page T 16 **J. Michael Miller;** 7 **Alain Mingam** (left, top and bottom); 79 **Jacques Delière;** 231 **Alain Mingam;** 275 **Andrew Brilliant;** 285 **Alain Mingam;** 324 © **Stuart Cohen/Comstock;** 432 **Caroline Jalbert**

Cover photos: **Marsha Cohen** (top front); © **Stuart Cohen** (bottom front, back)

Maps provided by **Herb Heidt/Mapworks**

TERMINUS
80
49